Doing Ethnography

Doing Ethnography

Giampietro Gobo

Translated by Adrian Belton

Los Angeles • London • New Delhi • Singapore

First published 2008

The translation of this work has been funded by SEPS
Segretariato Europeo per le Pubblicazioni Scientifiche

Via Val d'Aposa 7 - 40123 Bologna - Italy
seps@alma.unibo.it - www.seps.it

SAGE Publications Ltd
1 Oliver's Yard
55 City Road
London EC1Y 1SP

SAGE Publications Inc.
2455 Teller Road
Thousand Oaks, California 91320

SAGE Publications India Pvt Ltd
B 1/I 1 Mohan Cooperative Industrial Area
Mathura Road, Post Bag 7
New Delhi 110 044

SAGE Publications Asia-Pacific Pte Ltd
33 Pekin Street #02-01
Far East Square
Singapore 048763

Library of Congress Control Number 2007931482

British Library Cataloguing in Publication data
A catalogue record for this book is available from the British Library

ISBN 978-1-4129-1920-3
ISBN 978-1-4129-1921-0 (pbk)

Typeset by C&M Digitals (P) Ltd, Chennai, India
Printed in Great Britain by The Cromwell Press Ltd, Trowbridge, Wiltshire
Printed on paper from sustainable resources

To Mattia,
twice-born

Contents

Companion Website

Visit the Companion website at www.sagepub.co.uk/gobo to find additional case studies and exercises.

Preface

Dear Student,

This is a book of recipes. It teaches you how to cook . . . an ethnography. Methodologists are not accustomed to giving recipes; they do not go into the basic details of how research should be done. They believe it more important to transmit an attitude, a reasoning procedure, a way to deal with problems. They leave it to the researcher to draw upon his or her creativity and experience to resolve contingent problems, applying general guidelines to particular research contexts. They are quite right to do so: ethnomethodologists said as much in the 1960s, and I agree. But the concept of 'recipe' is misleading. Some years ago the American ethnomethodologist, Hugh Mehan, devised an instruction-following procedure which advised thus:

> take a recipe from a cookbook and do only what the instructions say. Do not improvise or make allowances.
> [You will] discover that the activities cannot be done. In following a recipe, for example, instructions are given for preparing the food, and for preheating the oven. There are seldom explicit instructions to put the food in the oven. Sometimes the instructions indicate that eggs still in their shells are to be placed in mixing bowls, or beaten with a stick, or whipped with a belt. Cookies sometimes must be dropped on the floor, not on cookie sheets. [You] search in vain for behavioral representations of 'cook until tender', 'sauté', 'blanch', 'fold' (Mehan and Wood, 1975: 234).

It is therefore clear that following a recipe, just like following a rule (as the Austrian philosopher Ludwig Wittgenstein said many years ago), does not automatically ensure the production of a good dish. There is a large amount of tacit knowledge acquired from experience, and essential for success, which is not to be found in a recipe. However, if you want to cook a dish, a book of recipes is preferable to an essay on culinary science. Why? Because recipes, though limited and reductive, are practical. In this they are quite unlike the majority of textbooks on methodology, which are still too principle-oriented and too little practice-based. They do too little, that is, to reduce the gap between 'knowing' and 'knowing how.'

So why not get started with ethnography straight away? Why waste time reading a book (which is stuffed with theory) rather than begin practical action immediately? I shall explain with another story.

My grandmother died some years ago at the venerable age of 101. She started working in a mill when she was 13 and therefore only had elementary schooling. She was a good cook who knew how to prepare marvellous dishes but she was a bad teacher. She knew what to do, but she did not know how to teach it. When you asked her 'how much salt should I add?' she would reply, 'a bit'; if you asked 'how long should I cook it for?' she would say, 'until you see that it's cooked.' These were decidedly vague and unhelpful instructions. Because she was poorly educated she was unable to make her tacit knowledge explicit. She therefore 'knew how' but she did not 'know,' which is just the reverse of what we find in textbooks. The only way to acquire my grandmother's knowledge, and therefore learn how to cook, was to observe her. Moreover, because of her poor education, she was unable to follow a recipe. In the end she had a repertoire of dishes which she cooked to perfection, but they were always the same. She was certainly able to improve, but only within her tradition: she was unable to change 'paradigm.' I once talked to her about macrobiotic food and showed her how to prepare it. But in vain: she had a mental resistance to change.

What lessons can we draw from these two examples? First, that a methodology which does not strive to produce recipes, advice and suggestions is sterile; second, that recipes without the guidance of a theory (both common sense and scientific) are impracticable. In other words, we need a theory founded on practice and a practice founded on theory.

This is what I have tried to accomplish with this book.

Kind regards,

Giampietro Gobo

Dear Colleague,

What a hard life we lead! We must research, publish articles, take part in our department's intellectual life, compile dozens of assessment forms and constantly evade the obstacles of academic bureaucracy. And then we have to teach! What a grind it is preparing lessons that interest our students and make them fall in love with our subject. Examples, so many examples, are needed to make an abstract discipline like methodology comprehensible and appealing. But where can we find them?

   This book has been conceived not only for students (although they are its principal audience) but also their teachers, so that they need devote less effort to preparing their lessons and thus have more energy to teach them well. The book abounds with questions with which to enliven lessons and prompt discussion; with examples to make even the most difficult concepts clear; with exercises (often for groups) which can be done either during class (by you or by tutors) or outside class. I will be particularly happy if I have been able to alleviate (at least to some extent) the burden of our demanding but extraordinary profession.

Warmest wishes,

Giampietro Gobo

Acknowledgements

I wish to thank Anna Maria Ajello, Barbara Czarniawska, Jay Gubrium and Anna Lisa Tota for the help they have given me, and for their valuable suggestions and comments as my work has proceeded. My thanks go also to Chiara Segafredo and Raffaella Colombo of SEPS for support in publication of the book and to Adrian Belton for his inestimable work.

I am especially grateful to David Silverman and Patrick Brindle for their encouragement, support and suggestions that they generously gave throughout their reading of the draft, and for their patience with me. Last but not least, I am indebted to the Italian Senior Editor, Gianluca Mori, who has believed in the project from the outset, and to Carocci Editore.

Introduction

Although more than a century has passed since the ethnographic method was invented, on considering the panorama of empirical research in the social sciences, we realize that (with the exception of a few sectors) ethnography is decidedly a marginal method, and that basic ethnographic research amounts to very little. Nevertheless, were we to ask sociologists what type of research they find most seductive, many would probably answer 'participant observation' – and among the finest research studies in the history of sociology they would probably cite William Foote White's *Street Corner Society*, Robert and Helen Lynd's *Middletown*, Erving Goffman's *Asylums* and the researchers of the Chicago School.

The reasons for this contradiction are many and they will be thoroughly discussed in this book.

It is the desire of many sociologists to conduct ethnographic research. Yet, because of idleness, or for fear of beginning an endeavor with unpredictable results or one which seems not to furnish sufficient guarantees, this desire is rarely put into practice. The fall-back solution is methodologies and methods already known or which require less time and effort.

Yet the situation is changing. The signals of change are evident in handbooks and textbooks, in a growing body of ethnographic studies, and in the increasing space allocated to them by an ever larger number of journals. Obviously, the re-emergence of ethnography after the epic years of the 1960s is part of a more general tendency which has led to revaluation of, and demand for, 'qualitative' research.

The aim of this handbook is to introduce the co-ordinates and the bases of a research practice which has been unjustly considered anti-methodological, as bereft of standard procedures and encoded usages. In reality, the 1980s and 1990s saw the publication of numerous textbooks and the production of softwares that converted the experiences of ethnographic practice accumulated during the 1900s into a body of technical expertise. Obviously, *one* ethnographic approach, unique and universal, does not exist; but neither does haphazardness prevail. Instead, there is a circumscribed set of research strategies to be adopted according to the theoretical perspective taken. Accordingly, this textbook is not (or at least is not intended to be) aridly technical, but rather a text which constantly shows how theory and technique on the one hand, and technique and practice on the other, can be connected.

This textbook consists of four parts devoted respectively to the:

(1) definition and history of ethnographic methodology and research design issues;
(2) theoretical, ethical and technical issues concerning information collection and the organization of a database;

(3) analysis of materials and the accountability of findings;
(4) the communication of findings to diverse audiences.

The book is full of examples and case studies (some of them, also on the internet), and exercises designed to introduce students to the methodology and to make it readily comprehensible to them. As regards the exercises, these are *really* practicable: they are conceived to actually be done; they are not just space-fillers paying lip-service to the current fashion in textbook writing. And they are exercises designed to convey the flavor of research, although the research itself will be quite a different matter!

Finally, I have tried to make the book more international than other textbooks: examples are drawn from countries like the UK and the USA, obviously, but also from Australia, Austria, Brazil, Canada, Cuba, Ethiopia, France, Germany, Hungary, India, Italy, Japan, Mexico, New Guinea, Nigeria, New Zealand, Norway, Morocco, Pakistan, the Philippines, Poland, Russia, Rwanda, Samoa, Sudan, Sweden, Switzerland, Thailand and Uzbekistan. This does not mean that I have succeeded, but at least it is in the direction that I wanted to go. However, despite my best efforts, the book is still culturally restricted: it has been written by a European for Westerners, and it suffers from ignorance about many cultures, such as African, Asian and Latin-American cultures.

Part One
The Methodology

What is Ethnography?

> When Hermes took the post of messenger of the goods, he promised Zeus not to lie. He did not promise to tell the whole truth. Zeus understood. The ethnographer has not.
>
> Vincent Crapanzano, 1986: 53

LEARNING OBJECTIVES

- To gain an overview of what constitutes ethnography.

- To understand the difference between attitude and behavior.

- To grasp the main characteristics of ethnographic methodology.

- To understand the advantages and drawbacks of ethnographic methodology.

- To get a general idea of its historical development.

- To identify the main methodological differences between doing an ethnography in sociology and in classical anthropology.

1.1 Introduction

Most forms of knowledge are situated. They arise from *certain* people, for *certain* purposes, in a *certain* historical period whose features they reflect, including its stereotypes and prejudices. Ethnography is therefore not immune to this tendency.

Ethnography is a methodology with more than 100 years of history. It arose in the Western world as a form of knowledge about distant cultures (typically non-Western ones) which were impenetrable to analysis consisting only of fleeting contact or brief conversations. Despite its good intentions (to gain deeper understanding), ethnography is still a colonial method that must be . . . de-colonialized. And you, students in every part of the world, can make a crucial contribution to that end.

Ethnography is gaining increasing currency in social research and applied research, and it may become a mass phenomenon in the years to come. Why? Because we now live in the 'observation society' (see Chapter 17).

The purpose of this first chapter is to define the concept of ethnography, to outline its advantages and drawbacks and to outline the tasks of ethnographic research in contemporary societies.

1.2 An overview of ethnography

Read the following two passages carefully.

'SECONDARY ADJUSTMENTS'

The first thing to note is the prevalence of make-do's. In every social establishment par-
ticipants use available artifacts in a manner and for an end not officially intended thereby
modifying the conditions of life programmed for these individuals. A physical reworking
of the artifact may be involved, or merely an illegitimate context of use (. . .) In Central
Hospital many simple make-do's were tacitly tolerated. For example, inmates widely
used freestanding radiators to dry personal clothing that they had washed, on their own,
in the bathroom sink, thus performing a private laundry cycle that was officially only the
institution's concern. On hard-bench wards, patients sometimes carried around rolled-
up newspapers to place between their necks and the wooden benches when lying down.
Rolled-up coats and towels were used in the same way . . . Older patients who were dis-
inclined or unable to move around sometimes employed strategies to avoid the task of
going to the toilet: on the ward, the hot steam radiator could be urinated on without leav-
ing too many long-lasting signs; during twice-weekly shaving visits to the basement
barber shop, the bin reserved for used towels was used as a urinal when the attendants
were not looking . . . In Central Hospital, toilet paper was sometimes 'organized'; neatly
torn, folded, and carried on one's person, it was apologetically used as Kleenex by some
fastidious patients (Goffman, 1961: 207–9).

'SOCIAL DEATH'

When, in the course of a patient's illness his condition is considered such that he is dying
or terminally ill, his name is posted on the critical patients list . . . Posting also serves as
an internally relevant message, notifying certain key hospital personnel that a death may
be forthcoming and that appropriate preparations for that possibility are tentatively
warranted. In the hospital morgue, scheduling is an important requirement. Rough first
drafts of the week's expected work load are made, with the number of possible autopsies
being a matter which, if possible, is to be anticipated and planned for. In making such
estimates the morgue attendant consults posted lists from which he makes a guess as to
the work load of the coming week. The posted list is also consulted by various medical
personnel who have some special interest in various anatomical regions. County's morgue
attendant made it a practice to alert the ward physician that Doctor S. wanted to get all
the eyes he could (Doctor S. was a research ophthalmologist). To provide Doctor S. with
the needed eyes, the morgue attendant habitually checked the posted list and tried, in
informal talk with the nurses about the patient's family, to assess his chances of getting
the family's permission to relinquish the eyes of the patient for research. Apparently,
when he felt he had located a likely candidate, a patient whose family could be expected

to give permission at the time of death, he thus informed the pathologist, who made an effort, via the resident physician, to have special attention given to the request for an eye donation. (At several places in the hospital: on the admission nurse's desk, in the morgue, in doctors' lounges, and elsewhere, there were periodically placed signs that read 'Doctor S. needs eyes,' 'Doctor Y. needs kidneys,' etc.) (Sudnow, 1967: 72–3).

For some of you this may have been your first encounter with an 'ethnographic account,' a distinctive literary genre which in certain respects resembles a novel.

EXERCISE 1.1

Discuss with your instructor or classmates:
• Your reactions to the two passages.
• The emotions that they aroused in you.
• Did you ever think that such things could happen in a hospital?

1.3 Defining ethnography

The two passages above were written on the basis of *observations*. The authors (Erving Goffman and David Sudnow) were present when these things happened and saw them with their own eyes. A second striking feature is the precision of the observations, the large number of details described and the vividness of the account. The two authors document the normal routines of an organization with great acumen and insight.

But, one might ask, couldn't these details have been collected in a different way, for instance by interviewing some of the patients? Perhaps, but this would have required the interviewee to possess a high degree of awareness and a great power of recall. Very few interviewees have these abilities. Could the details have been gathered by administering a questionnaire to the personnel? Certainly not. No questionnaire, however well made, could garner all these details. And besides, doing so is not the aim of the survey method, which was invented for other purposes.

So what is an ethnography and how does it differ from an interview or a survey?

1.4 A definition of ethnography

To know things we use our five senses: sight, hearing, smell, taste and touch. But these senses do not acquire knowledge separately, each on its own account. Rather, during the knowledge-gathering process, they constantly interact with each other. In this interaction, however, it may happen that one sense acts as the pivot for the others (see 2.4), rather like the playmaker in a basketball team. Indeed, we can imagine the five senses as five basketball players who alternate in the role of pivot but always need the co-operation of all the others when they occupy that role.

In ethnographic methodology the pivotal cognitive mode is 'observation.' Of course, it is also essential to listen to the conversations of the actors 'on stage,' read the documents produced by the organization under study, ask people questions and so on. Yet what most distinguishes ethnography from other methodologies is the role of 'protagonist' assigned to observation. Bearing this well in mind, we can now move on to other issues.

Ethnographic methodology comprises two research strategies: *non-participant* observation and *participant* observation. In the former case the researcher observes the subjects 'from a distance' without interacting with them. Those who use this strategy are uninterested in investigating the symbolic sphere, and they make sure they do not interfere with the subjects' actions so as not to influence their behavior. There are several intermediate situations between the two extremes of participant and non-participant observation (see 6.3).

On the contrary participant observation has the following attributes:

(1) the researcher establishes a direct relationship with the social actors;
(2) staying in their natural environment;
(3) with the purpose of observing and describing their behavior;
(4) by interacting with them and participating in their everyday ceremonials and rituals, and;
(5) learning their code (or at least parts of it) in order to understand the meaning of their actions.

As mentioned, ethnographic methodology gives priority to observation as its primary source of information. This purpose is also served, in a secondary and ancillary manner, by other sources of information used by the ethnographer in the field: informal conversations, individual or group interviews and documentary materials (diaries, letters, class essays, organizational documents, newspapers, photographs and audiovisual aids). However, the over-riding concern is always to observe actions as they are performed in concrete settings. From this point of view, community studies should not to be considered ethnographies as, although the researchers stayed for a relatively long period of time in the environment of the group studied, their analyses were based mainly on interviews and documents gathered on the spot. As Heritage stresses, if one is interested in action, the statements made by social actors during interviews cannot be treated 'as an appropriate substitute for the observation of actual behavior' (1984: 236). In fact, there is an oft-documented gap between attitudes and behaviors (La Piere, 1934), between what people say and what they do (Gilbert and Mulkay, 1983).

1.5 The gap between attitudes and behavior

Many years previously, the American sociologist Edward C. Lindeman (1885–1953), had argued in this way against surveys in his book *Social Discovery*:

> if, say the behaviorists, you wish to know what a person is doing, by all means refrain from asking *him*. His answer is sure to be wrong, not merely because he does not know what he is doing but precisely because he is answering a

question and he will make the reply in terms of you and not in terms of the objective thing he is doing (1924, quoted by Converse, 1987: 54).

Numerous studies have shown the extent of the gap between what we say and what we do, between what people think and feel and what they do, between behavior and attitude, between sentiments and acts. Some of the best-known have been collected in the fine book edited by Deutscher (1973). One of them is the pioneering study by La Piere (1934), which focused on the existence or otherwise of consistency between people's attitudes and their behavior (a topic subsequently much debated in the 1940s and 1950s). La Piere concluded that there was no relation between them: social actors are often inconsistent, unconscious and irrational. A Chinese couple used by La Piere for his experiment traveled around the United States for two years, and on no occasion were they refused service by the proprietors of cafes and restaurants or hotels. La Piere then sent a postal questionnaire to the same proprietors that had served or accommodated the Chinese couple and obtained a surprising result: 92% of the proprietors of the cafes and restaurants and 91% of the hoteliers replied that they would refuse to accept Chinese clientele, thus contradicting their previous behavior.

CASE STUDY
Rewriting actions

In 1954 the American sociologist, Harold Garfinkel, was conducting (together with Saul Mendlovitz) research on the work of a jury during a trial. By interviewing the jurors and recording their dialogues, the aim of the research was to reconstruct and describe how the jurors acted, and in particular how they came to the decision that the accused was guilty or innocent.

Garfinkel (1967: 104–15) noted that there was an informal set of rules that the jurors had to follow to reach the 'correct' decision. Nevertheless, on observing the concrete work of the jurors, he found that these rules were rarely applied. Rather, they were used *retrospectively* to justify a decision taken. This was a way to impose order on a decision-making process that was anything but straightforward. The jurors started from the result of the action and then backtracked to reconstruct the process leading up to it. They therefore used the rules to perform an *ex-post* rationalization whereby their accounts would show the good sense of *any* outcome, rather than reproduce what people thought at the time of the deliberative process.

1.6 The apparent paradox of participant observation

The ethnographic methodology requires the researcher to participate in the social life of the actors observed, while at the same time maintaining sufficient cognitive distance so that he or she can perform his or her scientific work satisfactorily. The researcher must therefore strike a difficult balance between two opposing situations which, to paraphrase the title of a well-known book by the German sociologist and historian Norbert Elias, we may call '*involvement and detachment.*'

From the philosophical point of view, this balance is impossible to achieve because 'society and people are so organized that the goals of scientific and empathic understanding (access of meanings) are competitive in principle. It may not be possible to be a participant *and* a scientist simultaneously' (Schwartz and Jacobs, 1979: 49). As the Austrian philosopher Alfred Schutz has pointed out, this cognitive impossibility does not concern the scientist alone; it also affects the social actors that the researcher wishes to study:

> the actor who lives in his ongoing process of acting has merely the in-order-to motive of his ongoing action in view, that is, the projected state of affairs to be brought about. Only by turning back to his accomplished act . . . the actor can grasp retrospectively the because-motive that determined him to do what he did or what he projected to do. But then the actor is not acting any more; he is an observer of himself (1953: 22).

The actor who acts/participates is therefore temporally and cognitively different from the actor who observes. Participation and observation are consequently not two contradictory attitudes; rather, they are two distinct aspects of social life (like research). They do not contradict each other because they never overlap.

Participant observation involves another paradox, which has been well described by the Italian anthropologist and linguist Alessandro Duranti:

> the more [the ethnographer] immerses himself in social reality and acquires a way of behaving and interpreting reality similar to those of the subjects he is studying, the more their behavior and relative vision of the world seem natural to him and therefore difficult for him to grasp (1992: 20).

From the practical point of view, however,

> total empathy is professionally and practically impossible. It is precisely the constant reflecting, taking notes, asking questions, completing questionnaires, taking photographs, recording and then transcribing, translating and interpreting imposed upon us by our profession that prevent us from getting completely 'inside' the culture which we want to study (1992: 20).

In light of these considerations the paradox attenuate from the practical point of view, although they still preserve their peculiarity of making research self-reflexive. Being simultaneously, or intermittently, 'inside' and 'outside' the cultural code is therefore a normal component of the researcher's role.

1.7 The birth of ethnographic methodology

The birth of ethnographic methodology is commonly dated to the period between the late nineteenth and early twentieth centuries. It developed internally to ethnology, a discipline which in the first half of the 1800s split away from traditional anthropology, which was then dominated by the physical and biological paradigm. Ethnology was more concerned with studying people (through comparison of their material artifacts) and their cultures and classifying their salient features. Before the advent of ethnographic methodology, ethnologists did not collect information by means of direct observation; instead, they examined statistics, the archives of government offices and missions, documentation centers, accounts of journeys, archeological finds, native manufactures or objects furnished by collectors of exotic art, or they conversed with travelers, missionaries and explorers. These anthropologists considered the members of native peoples to be 'primitives': they were savages to be educated, and they could not be used as direct informants because they could not be trusted to furnish objective information. This prejudice was also held towards the poor in the United Kingdom at the end of 1800s.

Ethnographic methodology did not suddenly erupt in anthropology; rather it arose gradually through the work of various authors, among them the English anthropologist of Polish origin, Bronislaw K. Malinowski (1884–1942), and the English anthropologist Alfred R. Radcliffe-Brown (1881–1955). British social anthropology of ethnographic stamp assimilated the positivist intellectual climate of its time and put itself forward, according to Radcliffe-Brown (1948), as a 'natural science of society'[1] which was better able to furnish an objective description of a culture than the other methods used by anthropologists at the time. Radcliffe-Brown's polemic was directed against the dominant speculative or 'desk' anthropology, which preferred to rely on secondary sources rather than undertake direct observation of social facts (customs, rituals and ceremonies) in order to uncover the 'laws' that govern a society.

Malinowski is commonly regarded as being the first to systematize ethnographic methodology. In his famous Introduction to *Argonauts of the Western Pacific* – the book which sets out his research conducted in the Trobriand Islands of the Melanesian archipelago off eastern New Guinea – Malinowski described the methodological principles underpinning the main goal of ethnography, which is 'to grasp the native's point of view, his relation to life, to realise *his* vision of *his* world' (Malinowski, 1922: 25). To this end, Malinowski lived for two years (between 1914 and 1918) among the Kula of the Trobriand Islands. He learnt their language (Kiriwinian), used natives as informants, and directly observed the social life of a village, participating in its everyday activities. Malinowski inaugurated a view 'from within' that American anthropologists of the 1950s would call the 'emic' perspective – as opposed to the 'etic' or comparative perspective, which instead sought to establish categories useful for the analyst but not necessarily important for the members of the culture studied (for details on the difference between emic and etic, go to www.sagepub.co.uk/gobo).

From the 1920s onwards, ethnographic methodology was incorporated into sociology – where it was adopted by researchers who mostly belonged to the Department of Sociology of the University of Chicago (see 3.2) – and then into psychology. Although it was imported from anthropology, however, fully 70 years previously the French mining engineer and later sociologist Pierre Le Play (1806–92) had used primitive forms of participant observation, when he had stayed with the working-class families that he was studying. The English philanthropist Seebohm B. Rowntree (1871–1954) also used primordial forms of participant observation (after 1886) for his inquiries into poverty and living conditions in the London slums. Nevertheless, still today, many anthropologists identify sociology with the survey, deeming themselves the sole (jealous) custodians of the ethnographic method (Atkinson, Coffey, Delamont, Lofland and Lofland, 2001: 2).

1.8 Anthropology and sociology: Methodological differences

When ethnographic methodology was adopted by social research – a disciplinary area different from anthropology – problems of adaptation required its partial revision – a revision which then affected the anthropology of the post-war period. In fact, at the beginnings of ethnographic methodology, according to Benedict's (1934: 7) authoritative opinion, anthropology differed from the other social sciences in that it subjected societies different from our own to study. But from the late 1940s onwards various anthropologists studied work communities in American and British factories. This gave rise to the 'Human Relations' movement and inaugurated applied anthropology, as well as industrial or organizational anthropology. This event marked the demise of the commonplace which social scientists study the industrial societies of the West while anthropologists study exotic societies.

Conducting ethnographic research in a society of which the researcher is part raises epistemological and practical problems which differ from those encountered by the classical anthropologist. Applying ethnographic methodology in the study of cultures alien to that of the researcher is a very different matter from conducting ethnography in an organization (a school, a social service or a business) which is part of the researcher's own culture. This was well understood by the American anthropologist Clark Wissler. On writing the foreword to *Middletown in Transition*, the celebrated study by Robert and Helen Lynd, which he described as 'a pioneer attempt to deal with a sample American community after the manner of social anthropology [by conducting] social anthropology of contemporary life' (1937: vi). Clark declared:

> and whatever may be the deficiencies of anthropology, it achieves a large measure of objectivity, because anthropologists are by the nature of the case 'outsiders'. To study ourselves as through the eye of an outsider is the basic difficulty in social science, and may be insurmountable (1937: vi).

1.8.1 Three main differences: Natural attitude, language and being a native

Anthropologists who study societies other than their own find it relatively easy to grasp their salient characteristics. As soon as these anthropologists arrive at their foreign destinations, a wide range of phenomena impact upon them cognitively (because they are extremely new) and need 'only' be recorded and interpreted. As Schutz wrote (1944), they are able to exploit the cognitive privilege of the immigrant, which consists in the ability to see the intersubjective nature of behaviors and beliefs which for the natives are natural, obvious, taken-for-granted and normal. Schutz (1889–1959) left Austria in 1939 under the threat of the Nazi occupation and settled in New York: he had thus experienced this cognitive status first hand. However, as Schwartz and Jacobs stress (1979: 251), in this case 'the attitude created by being a stranger – the sense of being on the edge of one's cognitive seat – can decay extremely rapidly.' Instead, anthropologists can 'maintain their natural attitude' even while they acquire knowledge about the alien culture. The estrangement technique (see 9.2) may be a way to maintain the immigrant's attitude as long as possible, so that the ethnographer continues to be surprised, and strangeness and newness are acquired by social scenes that seem normal to him or her.

Language

Language is another aspect which methodologically differentiates between the work of ethnographers studying organizations in their own society and that of anthropologists who analyze societies alien to them. Whereas the latter must learn a new language, the former have, at most, to learn a *communicative* code. Yet, paradoxically, knowing the subjects' language makes observation much more complicated. If the researcher has the same knowledge (or 'structures of everyday life,' to use an expression dear to phenomenologists) as the social actors, given that it is from this knowledge that he or she recognizes, codifies and investigates social structures, the researcher will use the same resources (common-sense social categories embodied in everyday language) as those employed by the social actors that he or she is studying (Zimmerman and Pollner, 1970). Unless this circular cognitive process is supported by a reflexive research practice at the level of the resources/constraints used for knowing (see 5.5), it may reproduce knowledge riddled with platitudes (hence the epithet 'folk sciences' dismissively applied by ethnomethodologists to the social sciences). By contrast, study of societies linguistically alien to the anthropologist involves methodological problems which concern the relationship between the inform-ant/interpreter and the anthropologist. When the Italian anthropologist, Cristina Giordano, was conducting research in Baluchistan, a district of northern Pakistan, she realized after a while that her informant (a *pashtu* social worker who also acted as interpreter) was altering the questions which the anthropologist was asking her women subjects. The manipulation was not deliberate but resulted from the interpreter's desire to present the anthropologist in a manner consistent with the social development programs then on-going in the area.

Who is a native?

Finally, the well-known study by Zimmerman and Pollner (1970) introduces a third consideration, this one relative to the distinction between natives and the ethnographer *qua* scholar of organizations and institutions in his or her society. Given that the ethnographer is in many respects a member of the society which he or she is studying, it seems inappropriate to persist with use of the term 'natives' for the subjects of his or her study. The term 'native' means 'a person inhabiting their place of birth.' However, it not infrequently happens that, say Mr Brown, who works for a services company, or Mr White, who teaches in a suburban secondary school, live in the same city as the ethnographer and perhaps frequent the same places in their free time. For the ethnographer working in his or her own country – even when he or she travels to areas or regions other than the one where he or she lives – the language (contrary to case of the anthropologist) continues to be an element shared with his or her subjects, and so are the food, attire, music, television and radio programs and press. Even cultures more alien to the country-based ethnographer – like the Chinese, Pakistani and Filipino communities of the United Kingdom – are communities not of natives, but of immigrants who devote part of their daily activities to integrating with the ethnographer's culture. The uncertain nature of the boundary between ethnographer and native is evident when doing research in our own societies. This is the same situation of, for example, an Indian ethnographer doing research in India.

The ethnographer who studies his or her own society is in the same situation as the classical anthropologist only on those rare occasions when he or she is researching largely closed societies to which access is particularly difficult: certain ethnic groups, cults or groups engaged in unlawful activities. In all other cases, even if the communities studied may be called Shetland Islanders, Orkneyans or Manxmen – exotic-sounding names resembling those of other, more alien peoples – the modes of dressing, driving and asking for food or drink are not radically different from those of the ethnographer's own community, in contrast to the experience of an anthropologist working in a foreign land. For these reasons, in what follows I shall avoid the term 'native,' preferring the more appropriate terms 'social actors' or 'participants.'

1.9 Concluding remarks

Ethnography is a particular form of knowledge that develops through specific techniques. Defining 'ethnography' is always difficult because, as we shall see in the next chapter, it is increasingly polysemous in meaning. There are at least three terms that merge with 'ethnography': 'participant observation,' 'fieldwork' and 'case study.' I suggest the following interpretation: the expression 'case study' denotes research on a system bounded in space and time and embedded in a particular physical and socio-cultural context. Research is conducted using diverse methodologies, methods and data sources like participant observation, interviews, audiovisual materials, documents and so on (Creswell, 1998: 61). The term 'fieldwork' stresses the continuous presence of the researcher in the field, as opposed to 'grab-it-and-run' methodologies like the survey, in-depth interview or analysis of documents and recordings. In this case, too, diverse methodologies and methods may be used. Finally, 'participant observation' is a distinctive research strategy. Probably, participant observation and fieldwork treat observation as a mere technique, while the term 'ethnography' underlines the theoretical basis of such work stemming from a particular history and tradition. Thus, if on the one hand the terms are in some senses equivalent, on the other they connote different practices.

However, if you want to gain a more precise idea, you can consult four comprehensive collected works: Bryman (2001) for ethnography, Pole (2004) for fieldwork, Matthew (2005) for the case study and Hughes and Sharrock (2008) for participation observation.

KEY POINTS

- The pivotal cognitive mode of ethnography is *observation.*
- Ethnographic methodology comprises two research strategies: *non-participant* observation and *participant* observation.
- The birth of ethnographic methodology is usually dated to the period between the late nineteenth and early twentieth centuries.
- The two authors who contributed most to the early development of ethnographic methodology were the anthropologists Bronislaw Kaspar Malinowski (1884–1942) and Alfred Reginald Radcliffe-Brown (1881–1955).
- Conducting ethnographic research in cultures and societies to which the researcher belongs is particularly difficult because he or she is likely not to see (precisely because of their familiarity) the fundamental social structures on which that culture or society rests.
- Ethnography should therefore be used with particular methodological caution in these cases.
- The ethnographer's main cognitive aim is to abandon the natural attitude that takes social conventions and everyday behavior for granted as normal or obvious.
- This natural attitude prevents the ethnographer from seeing conventions, behaviors or social structures as activities which are constantly, socially and situationally constructed.
- The natural attitude can be partly eliminated by using estrangement techniques. These help the ethnographer maintain the attitude of the stranger as long as possible, so that he or she continues to be surprised and sees social scenes to which he or she is accustomed as strange and new.

KEY TERMS

Case study (see p. 11)	Expression denoting research on a system bounded in space and time. The research is conducted using diverse methodologies, methods and data sources, like participant observation, interviews, audiovisual materials, documents, etc.
Ethnography (see p. 4)	A methodology which privileges (the cognitive mode of) observation as its primary source of information. This purpose is also served, in a secondary and ancillary manner, by other sources of information used by ethnographers in the field: informal conversations, individual or group interviews and documentary materials (diaries, letters, essays, organizational documents, newspapers, photographs and audiovisual aids). Ethnography comprises two research strategies: *non-participant* observation and *participant* observation.

Fieldwork (see p. 11)	Generic term for the researcher's continuing presence in the field, as opposed to 'grab-it-and-run' methodologies. Fieldwork can be conducted using diverse methodologies and methods, among them ethnography.
Non-participant observation (see p. 5)	A strategy where the researcher observes the subjects 'from a distance' without interacting with them. Those who use this strategy are not interested in investigating the symbolic sphere and take care not to interfere with the subjects' actions so as not to influence their behavior.
Participant observation (see p. 5)	A strategy with the following features: • the researcher establishes a direct relationship with the social actors, • staying for a period • in their natural environment • with the purpose of observing and describing their behavior • by interacting with them and participating in their everyday ceremonials and rituals, • learning their code (or at least parts of it) in order to understand the meaning of their actions.

RECOMMENDED READING

For undergraduates:
Silverman, David (2006a)

For graduates:
Atkinson, Paul and Hammersley, Martyn (1994)

For advanced researchers:
Delamont, Sara (2004)

EXERCISE 1.2

Take a monograph based on an ethnographic research.
Answer the following questions:
• Was participant or non-participant observation used?
• In what setting was it used?
• How long did the researcher stay in that setting?
• What was the purpose of the observation?
• What forms of behavior (routines, rituals, ceremonies) were observed?

EXERCISE 1.3

Now assess the study you have just read:
- Does it give precise and detailed descriptions of the social actors' routines?
- What have you learnt (from this study) that you did not know before?
- Did you find reading the study enjoyable or boring?
- Was it a study based exclusively on observation or did the researcher use other sources of information (interviews, documents, conversations among social actors or videos)?

SELF-EVALUATION TEST

Are you ready for the next chapter? Check your knowledge by answering the following open-ended questions:
1. What is ethnography?
2. What are the main characteristics of participant observation?
3. What is meant by a 'secondary source'?
4. What are the 'secondary sources' of ethnography?
5. What are the main differences between the use of the ethnographic method in anthropology and in sociology?

Note

1 This expression reflects the education received by this new generation of social anthropologists, who were scientists by training. Malinowski, for example, was a graduate in physics and chemistry from the University of London; Elliot Smith was a biologist; and William H. R. Rivers (1864–1922) was a doctor and a psychologist.

2

Method or Methodology? Locating Ethnography in the Methodological Landscape

LEARNING OBJECTIVES

- To understand that ethnography is a methodology (a style of thinking and doing), not a mere technique.

- To learn an alternative classification of the array of social research methodologies, avoiding the qualitative/quantitative opposition.

- To locate ethnography in the social research landscape.

2.1 Introduction

Defining a term is always difficult because there are as many definitions as there are different points of view. Atkinson and Hammersley observe that the:

> definition of the term *ethnography* has been subject to controversy. For some it refers to a philosophical paradigm to which one makes a total commitment, for others it designates a method that one uses as and when appropriate (1994: 248).

But the controversy extends further. More recently it has also involved the research practices that may or may not be included under the heading 'ethnography.' Since the 1980s (see 4.1) the meaning of ethnography has been expanded to such an extent that it encompasses forms of research extremely diverse from a methodological point of view. Everything is now ethnography: from life stories to the analysis of letters and questionnaires, from autobiography to narrative analysis, from action research to performance, from field research lasting a few days to that lasting several years. Some years ago, James Lull pointed out that 'what is passing as ethnography in cultural studies fails to achieve the fundamental requirements for data collection and reporting typical of most anthropological and sociological ethnographic research. ' "Ethnography" has become an abused buzz-word in our field' (1988: 242). The same opinion has been expressed by David Morley (1992: 186).

Contrarily, Beverly Skeggs argues that 'feminist ethnography is about understanding process' (2001: 427). However, even the American sociologist James S. Coleman (1926–95), a pioneer in the construction of mathematical models in sociology, with his *Foundations of Social Theory* (1990) would agree that the task of network analysis (a statistical technique) is to describe processes. Hence the definition of a methodology (in this case ethnographic) cannot be derived from the topic of the study (processes). The methodology has to be defined according to the concrete research practices that it comprises, not according to its knowledge objectives.

This is the only way to get out of this chaotic situation, as the term 'ethnography' has been diluted into a multitude of sometimes contrasting and contradictory meanings and become synonymous with qualitative studies. This is therefore a stretch of the term 'ethnography,' depriving it of its original meaning. But why do so many authors still persist in calling research conducted with interviews 'ethnographic'? Is the term 'interview' really so distasteful to them? One suspects that the term 'ethnography' has just become highly fashionable; it is still a term little known to a large part of the community of policy-makers and practitioners, but also to many members of the academic community; and it is a relatively new and esoteric methodology (compared to the discursive interview and survey). It is also a term that evokes the exotic, epic and heroic, so that the ethnographer is perceived as some kind of Indiana Jones figure (see Bryman, 1988: 8–9).

We shall now see how ethnography can be located in the panorama of contemporary social research in such a way that its differences and distinctions, with respect to the other methodologies, emerge. To do this means . . . classifying.

2.2 On classification

Barth's Distinction

There are two types of people: those who divide people into two types, and those who don't.

The Twin Towers

The date September 11, 2001 is tragically notorious. Two hijacked airplanes crashed into the Twin Towers that soared above the New York skyline. Following the fires caused by the impact, the two towers collapsed. A few days later, debate began in the upper echelons of politics and in the media: was the attack an 'act of terrorism' or was it an 'act of war'? To all appearances this was a purely *nominalist* issue, i.e. that words function like labels. Yet the problem of what name (term) to give to the event (referent) and the meaning (concept) to attribute to it was anything but banal. *Definition* of the event was not a simple intellectual exercise but had hugely significant concrete implications. If the attack was defined an 'act of war,' because the United States is a member of NATO (Article 5 of whose treaty states that an armed attack against one of the signatories must be considered an attack against them all), the other member-countries, among them England, France, Germany and Italy, would also have gone to war (as they did).

If, instead, the attack was defined an 'act of terrorism,' the United States alone would have responded. A huge difference, therefore, with serious consequences ensuing from a simple decision on what *name* to give to an event. But even more was riding on the outcome. The Twin Towers were insured and, as we know, compensation for damage depends on the type of contract stipulated, with its relative norms and clauses. In this case the towers were insured 'only' against terrorist acts, not against acts of war. So how the attack was defined had other practical consequences as well. Names are not simple labels; indeed, they themselves are things.

This tragic example helps us understand the importance of classifications, in social research as well. The latter concerns itself with a broad and complex panorama of practices, usages and customs. Those who seek to set order on this highly diverse array of research practices must bear in mind that any attempt to do so necessarily involves a classification.

Systemic theories have shown that reality (and therefore also the reality of research methods) is chaotic and turbulent. It is consequently nebulous, opaque and without clearly-defined boundaries. Any sort of classification is nothing more than an attempt to impose order and sense on a reality with no meaning apart from that given to it by the observer.

Hence, any classification (and therefore also the classification of social research into methods and practices) is the outcome of a subjective activity (Marradi, 1990), of a practical attempt at order-making. As such it is an imposition, a distortion of a reality always more complex than its classification. In other words, we may say that the classification constructs the reality.

This, however, is not to imply that we are free to construct reality as we wish. For our descriptions to become reality, they must acquire consensus in our linguistic community, and we must conduct long and constant work to persuade our interlocutors that our classifications are valid. Classifications and concepts are not *true* or *false*. They are not objective and they do not stand in a *direct* relationship with reality. Rather they are heuristic tools invented for practical purposes (*for all practical purposes*, ethnomethdologists would say), and which at most can hope to gain general consensus and become dominant in the public discourse.

2.3 Contemporary classifications of research methods

Diverse classifications of research methods (some of them alternative to each other) have been propounded in the past.

The earliest – and still today most widely-used – classification distinguishes between qualitative and quantitative methods. The former base their descriptions and explanations on accounts and detailed analyses of specific cases; the latter on figures and statistics. Historically, the distinction first arose from the contrast between positivism and hermeneutics, between explanation and understanding, between *idiographic* research (conducted to understand a single case) and *nomothetic* research (conducted to discover social laws), between positive methods and interpretative methods. This antithesis has today been attenuated into a less emphatic distinction between *qualitative research* and *quantitative research* which emphasizes practical aspects (research) more than strictly theoretical ones (methods).

More recently, the traditional qualitative versus quantitative opposition has been criticized as tenuous and artificial by several authors. It is argued that there is constant co-penetration between the two kinds of research, that a rigid distinction between them is not possible and that they converge and overlap at numerous points. It is consequently urged that the antithesis between them be resolved. However, it should be noted that the distinction in the literature between qualitative and quantitative research is by now also institutionally recognized: there exist, in fact, numerous university courses which teach either qualitative or quantitative methods.

There is nothing inherently wrong with any classification, given that it is merely a *heuristic* tool with which to investigate social phenomena. In other words, classifications are used to shed light on social phenomena and to bring out those of their aspects of interest to the researcher.

Nonetheless, every classification has two inevitable shortcomings:

(1) it simplifies reality ('it reduces complexity,' systemic theorists would say); and
(2) it emphasizes some aspects of a phenomenon to the detriment of others.

Bearing this caveat in mind, we now examine yet another classification of research methods: the one proposed by the author of this textbook. The reader might ask at this point whether yet another classification is really necessary. I believe that the answer is yes, and this is because the classifications currently available are highly abstract and only poorly depict the actual practices of social research. They do not aid understanding of the empirical decisions which researchers must take, the tacit knowledge on which they base their reasoning, or the local knowledge which they utilize in their research practices. The classification proposed here has precisely the purpose of giving sharper focus to the practical reasoning and behavior of researchers as situated actions.

Before I set out the classification, however, I must define two terms of central importance to my treatment: 'methodology' and 'method' (or 'technique').

2.4 What is a methodology?

There are some methodologies and numerous methods in the social sciences. A *methodology* can be defined as a global style of thinking, 'a general approach to studying research topics' (Silverman, 2000: 77, 88 and 300), or an 'overall research strategy' (Mason, 1996: 19).

A methodology comprises at least the following four components:

(1) a **pivotal cognitive mode** among the many available to us for knowledge-acquisition (for example listening, watching, observing, reading, questioning, conversing);

(2) a **theory of scientific knowledge**, or a set of pre-assumptions about the nature of reality, the tasks of science, the role of the researcher, and the concepts of action and social actor;

(3) a **range of solutions**, devices and stratagems used in tackling a research problem;

(4) a (more or less) systematic sequence of **procedural steps** to be followed once the cognitive mode has been selected.

CASE STUDY
The four components of a methodology

Each of these components is now examined in detail.

1. Cognitive modes. Every knowledge-gathering act is guided by at least one cognitive mode: we learn by *listening* (to the radio for example), *watching* (television for example), *reading* (a newspaper, magazine or a book), *questioning* someone (for example a person under arrest or a suspect), *talking* with someone, or with ourselves through *introspection*. The cognitive sciences have documented that our senses interact with each other in such a way that our learning is driven by multisensory processes. The examples abound and they pertain to our everyday experience. Our ears 'look' when we are convinced at the cinema that the voice of the actor is emanating from the screen, when instead the loudspeakers are positioned along the sides of the cinema hall. We 'understand' with our hands (like a doctor when he palpates a patient's body). Or we 'listen' with them: to decide whether wood has been planed to sufficient smoothness, a carpenter wipes the planed surface with a thin sheet of paper, so that he can better perceive any roughness through the scraping noise. We also 'see' with our hands, as in the case of a sightless painter able to draw by touch: recent studies have shown, in fact, that his visual cortex is activated on touching an object. The eyes are able to 'smell,' as exemplified by the oenologist who judges the density of a wine not only from its aroma but also from its color. Indeed, some researchers have been able to deceive sommeliers' taste buds by dyeing white wine red (Pascual-Leone, et al., 2005). Every methodology is guided predominantly (though not exclusively) by a particular cognitive mode.

2. Theories of scientific knowledge. A methodology is also the product of the particular conception of science adopted by the inventor of that particular methodology. This conception consists of assumptions concerning at least five aspects, viz.:

(a) **The nature of reality**. To simplify, we may say that there are some researchers who embrace the *neopositivist* paradigm; others who adopt the *realist* one (*a là* Popper); others who assume the *social constructivist* perspective (*a là* Glasersfeld) or the *costructionist* perspective (*a là* Latour); yet others who describe themselves as *relativists* (*a là* Bloor).

(b) The tasks of science. Again simplifying, some researchers believe that science should stop at the *description* and *explanation* of phenomena (positivism) but only find natural and solid laws; others argue that science should also *intervene* to change the phenomena investigated; others (like the Frankfurt School, psychoanalysis and Jurgen Habermas) maintain that the principal task of science is to *emancipate* humankind.

(c) The role of the researcher. Some contend that researchers should do no more than objectively *survey* and *record* the phenomena which they observe, and that they are *external observers* (neopositivism and positivism); others claim that researchers actively participate (albeit unwittingly) in construction of the reality observed: they are therefore 'co-constructors' and subjects internal (not external) to the phenomenon studied.

(d) Concepts of action. At least three different perspectives are taken on action:

    (i) *methodological collectivism* (holism);

    (ii) *methodological individualism;*

    (iii) *methodological situationism.*

Methodological collectivism pertains to theories which conduct structural analyses of society on the basis of an objectivist view of social phenomena (for example, *Marxism,* the *structural-functionalism* of Talcott Parsons, the *functionalism* of Robert K. Merton, the *structuralism* of Émile Durkheim in sociology and of Claude Levi Strauss in anthropology).

Methodological individualism instead takes a subjectivist view (Max Weber, Raymond Boudon, John Elster and the symbolic interactionism of Herbert Blumer), or sometimes even a solipsistic one (Alfred Schutz). Contemporary versions of methodological individualism are *utilitarianism,* which is based on a voluntarist theory of action whose parameters are the concepts of 'interest,' 'intention,' 'value-orientation,' 'rationality,' 'motivation'; and *phenomenology*, with its concepts of 'consciousness,' 'mental states' and so on.

Finally, *methodological situationism* (ethnomethodology, cognitive sociology, etc.) seeks to synthesize the above two approaches by transforming the mental processes of phenomenology into contextually-situated scenic activities which it investigates using ethnographic research methods. According to Randall Collins (1981), methodological situationism is a new practical empiricism which adopts a more radically empirical stance than does any previous sociological approach.

(e) Concepts of social actor. Some disciplines and approaches (for example, cognitivism, microeconomics, neo-utilitarianism, etc.) consider the social actor to be a rational subject; others as an irrational subject driven by the emotions and corporeality (postmodern theories); yet others as a situational subject conditioned by the context of action (ethnomethodology).

3. The range of solutions. The third component of a methodology consists of the 'tricks of the trade' (Becker, 1998a), the set of *ad hoc* procedures (Schutz, 1962), remedies and stratagems not usually found in textbooks but which are part of the researcher's experience and are exchanged informally among colleagues, sometimes being made public in papers or journal articles.

4. Procedural steps. Finally, a methodology is also a (more or less) systematic sequence of procedural steps (research design, research questions, sampling, grids for data collection, data organization, data analysis and so on) implemented once the methodology has been selected. This fourth aspect is the meaning usually attributed to the term 'methodology.' However, it should by now be clear that this is only one of the many components that make up a methodology.

A methodology can therefore be defined as a pathway which differs according to the cognitive mode adopted. Obviously, not everything is codified in a methodology. It sometimes happens that the solutions, devices, 'tricks of the trade' and procedures available to the researcher do not suffice to solve a particular problem – or a new problem arising in the course of research. The researcher must therefore invent a remedy. The one that he or she comes up with – if it is subsequently accepted by the scientific community (or at least a part of it) – increases the conceptual and material assets of the methodology in question.

2.4.1 What about ethnography?

It should be clear from the discussion thus far that it is reductive to define survey or ethnography as (simple) methods, tools selected by a competent researcher according to the occasion or according to the research problem at hand. The stereotype that research questions should dictate the method is without any empirical ground. In fact, if this were the case, we would expect to find a large degree of interchangeability among the methods employed by social researchers. But it is not the case. In fact survey, ethnography, discursive interview and so on, are not methods. Rather, they relate to the concept of 'paradigm' first formulated by Thomas Kuhn (1962). That is to say, they are sets of ways to *see* (cognitive) and sets of ways to *do* (social) things.

According to Kuhn, a scientist will embrace *at most* two paradigms during his or her career: the paradigm in which he or she has been trained; and should he or she decides to change, the one to which he or she subsequently converts. The majority of scientists, however, work within one particular paradigm throughout their careers (they also do so in order to save on cognitive and practical effort: it is costly to abandon habitual theories, and data collection and analysis techniques, and to learn new ones). Scientific paradigms are rather like religions: a believer usually embraces two religions *at most* in his or her lifetime.

The choice of methodology (survey rather than ethnography) is likewise not just a technical question; it also depends on the researcher's theoretical stance – this being made up of the various components previously described. When we reason from a particular theoretical standpoint, it never occurs to us to ask certain questions. For all these cognitive and practical reasons, therefore, a researcher normally embraces only one methodology in the course of his or her career. For these reasons I maintain that ethnography is a methodology and not a method.

2.5 What is a method?

A method can be a tool, a technique or a specific, codified and widely used operational procedure which comprises solutions devised over time in cumulated and reified form. There are techniques for collecting information or for constructing data; and there are techniques for analyzing that information and data.

Techniques for either data collection or analysis can be used in diverse methodologies, although each of them will employ the techniques for different purposes (Silverman, 2000: 89). An extreme case is what is commonly called the 'Delphi method' whereby information is collected first by in-depth interviews, and then by a questionnaire (Dalkey and Helmer, 1963).

We can gain clearer understanding of the relationship between methodology and technique by drawing an analogy with the treatment of anorexia (but also bulimia, alcoholism or addictions in general).

There are three main methodologies (or base philosophies) for the treatment of anorexia:

(1) the first considers it to be a **problem of the individual**, who suffers from a constant lack of appetite, sometimes accompanied by a disgust with food. Because anorexia is due to an 'interior' malaise, the methodology consists in acting upon the anorexic individual;
(2) the second methodology regards anorexia as a **relational problem**, one which is therefore internal to the patient's interactional context (typically the family). The methodology consequently consists in treating the unhealthy relationship, acting upon the distorted communication between the anorexic and his or her family members (parents or partner);
(3) finally, anorexia can be viewed as a **social problem** afflicting only the affluent societies (are there many anorexics in the so-called 'developing countries'?) or as a generational problem, in the sense that it spreads socially in a particular period (for example, in the Western world since the 1990s).

Table 2.1 shows that corresponding to each methodology is a particular technique (in this case a *therapy*): the **individual interview** for those who believe it essential to treat the individual (psychoanalysis, psychotherapy, psychiatry); the **family interview** for those who think it crucial to work on relations among the members of the family (family psychotherapy, relational psychotherapy, systemic approach, etc.); finally, the **group interview**, for those who consider anorexia to be a generational problem (sociotherapy).

Table 2.1   Methodologies and methods for the treatment of anorexia

Methodology (Base philosophy)	Therapy/Method
Problem of the individual (Treat the individual)	Individual interview
Relational problem (Treat the family)	Family interview
Social problem (Treat the group)	Group interviews

2.6 The main methodologies of the social sciences: An alternative classification

On the basis of the above terminological and conceptual premises, we can identify at least six methodologies with their relative cognitive modes.

The six main cognitive modes for the study of a social phenomenon are the following:

(1) listening;
(2) questioning;
(3) observing;
(4) reading;
(5) operating: i.e. seeking to change actors (putting them to the test, having them interact with each other or stimulating them in order to control their reactions); and
(6) introspecting/reflecting.

These cognitive modes constitute the family of methodologies. This is a rather small set, but it is connected with a wide range of research techniques (see Table 2.2).

The main purpose of the **discursive interview** methodology is to enable the researcher to hear what social actors have to say. Its distinctive feature is that the interviewee is given ample space to use his or her own words and to structure his or her discourse in accordance with personal schemas, metaphors and metonyms. It correspondingly restricts the space available to the interviewer, whose task is to adapt his or her cognitive aims (research objectives) and the interview outline to the situational context and to the subject's discursive needs. The interviewer may therefore reverse the order (if there is one) of the questions, change their form, or decide not to ask some of them. The discursive structure of the interview also determines the type of interaction that takes place.

The **survey and poll methodology** consists of questioning a person by means of a questionnaire. The interviewer reads the interviewee a series of questions (stimuli) in a fixed order and with standardized texts. The subject chooses a reply from a number of fixed response alternatives provided by the questionnaire itself. The respondent therefore expresses his or her thoughts through categories proposed by the researcher. These thoughts the interviewer merely records without comment, given that he or she follows a standardized procedure. In some (though rare) cases, the interviewee is able to reply in his or her own words. The conversation structure created by the questionnaire determines a particular type of interactive synchronism usually consisting in short verbal exchanges (turns).

Table 2.2 Main methodologies and techniques of social research

Methodologies	Pivotal cognitive modes	Research types	Gathering structure	Data collection techniques	Data management techniques	Data analysis techniques
DISCURSIVE (OR IN-DEPTH) INTERVIEW	Listening	Biographic Hermeneutic	Little or partly structured	**Individual interview** (in-depth, narrative, open-ended, semi-structured, topical, problem-centered, with the double, realistic, interview control question, ecocultural family interview, ethnographic interview) **Collective interview** (group, *focus* and *delphi*)	Transcription and coding	Narrative analysis Discourse analysis Thematic analysis Grounded Theory
SURVEY	Questioning	Market motivational survey and poll	Structured	Questionnaire + Random probe technique	Matrix	Covariance
ETHNOGRAPHY	Observing	Hermeneutic Ergonomic	Non structured Structured	Participant (e.g. cool-hunting, mystery shopping, shadowing) Non-participant	Fieldnote Grid Matrix	Fieldnote analysis Grounded Theory Factor analysis

DOCUMENTARY	Reading	Textual	Little or partly structured	Letters, diaries, documents, images (photo, video) class projects, transcripts	Coding	Thematic analysis, narrative analysis, discourse analysis,
				Large textual dataset (newspapers, magazines)	Matrix	Foucauldian discourse analysis, Grounded Theory,
						conversation analysis
		Archive	Structured	*Ecological files* census and registry office database		Content analysis
					Matrix	Covariance
		Action-research intervention res. *participatory res.* co-operative res. socioanalysis		Individual interview collective interview sociodrama candid camera breaching studies	Transcription/ coding fieldnote matrix	Thematic analysis Fieldnote analysis Covariance Sociograph
TRANSFORMATIVE	Operating	Psychoanalysis systemic	Little or partly structured	Individual interview couple interview family interview	Grid	Causal analysis of symptoms
		Experimental computational Evaluation	Structured	Experiment simulation Test	Vector	Causal analysis
					Matrix	Covariance sociograph
SPECULATIVE	Introspecting	Phenomenological	Non structured	Individual experience (thought experiments, breaching studies, inverted lenses)	Personal notes	Category analysis autoethnography Causal analysis (formal logic)
	Reflecting	Comparative	Structured	Database	Truth tables (dichotomous variables)	rating

The in-depth and survey methodologies jointly account for almost all the practices of social research. They also represent the mainstreams in respectively qualitative and quantitative research[1] (for details on the methodological and philosophical common roots of survey and discursive interview, go to www.sagepub.co.uk/gobo).

The cognitive mode of 'reading' guides the *documentary* methodology. Unlike the other methodologies, this one is based on the process-based collection of information created during the ordinary activities of people, or of private and public organizations, rather than in the course of surveys with more strictly scientific ends. Examples of documentary sources are registry office files or other public records, newspapers, television programs, ordinary conversations, the statistics gathered by corporations for their business plans, census data, the photographs collected in family albums, the official programs of political parties and so on. The researcher does no more than select the information, and adapt it to the purposes of his or her analysis.

Social researchers use the *transformative* methodology to study subjects by controlling and manipulating certain states (for example, with experiments and simulations) or by inducing changes in those states. This methodology thus combines knowledge-gathering with an operational intent. In the former case, the setting in which the study takes place is deliberately manipulated in order to produce (or help produce) behaviors which can then be collected and analyzed. In the latter case, the research starts from the assumption that knowledge and intervention are parts of the process itself of the researcher's cognitive structuring: hence, every analysis is already an intervention and every intervention is also an analysis. This approach shares several data-collection and data-analysis techniques with other methodologies. But it also uses 'active' ones designed to make social actors aware of their situation so that they are induced to modify it. Examples are the experimental approach or the psycho-social ones (as 'co-operative research,' 'participatory action research,' 'action science,' 'process consultation,' 'empowerment,' 'intervention research' among others) which might fit under the general heading of 'action-research.' The pivotal cognitive mode in transformative research is 'operation,' in the sense that the researchers work to change the properties under investigation. For example, the aim of evaluation research is to pass judgment, to improve social programs, and to help decision-makers take considered decisions, unlike basic research which only aims to acquire knowledge.

Speculative methodology is based on *introspection* (in the case of phenomenological inquiry) or on *reflection* (relative to the logical-formal connections among dichotomous variables). Phenomenological inquiry has its roots in Husserl's *Cartesian Meditations* (1950), Merleau-Ponty's armchair experiments (1945), Schutz's thought experiments (1962: 104–9). Although these studies are abstract, they have inspired various social and practical research studies such as Garfinkel's breaching studies (1967: 42–8), which are attempts to discover the foundations of experience and subjectivity: how we perceive and recognize (through the senses) the objects that surround us; the common-sense knowledge that guides us in our judgments; and the implicit presuppositions upon which our reasoning is based. Schutz describes this type of inquiry as follows:

> The phenomenologist does not deny the existence of the outer world, but for
> his analytical purpose he makes up his mind to suspend belief in its existence

– that is, to refrain intentionally and systematically from all judgments related directly or indirectly to the existence of the outer world. Borrowing terms from mathematical technique, Husserl called this procedure 'putting the world in brackets' . . . the technical device of phenomenology for radicalizing the Cartesian method of philosophical doubt, in order to go beyond the natural attitude of man living within the world he accepts, be it reality or mere appearance . . . the purpose of such technique is only to reach a level of indubitable certainty which lies beyond the real of mere belief – in other words, to disclose the pure field of consciousness (1962: 104).

These speculative practices do not rely on interviews, ethnographic or otherwise; instead, they consist exclusively of inquiry into the self and into personal knowledge.

Formally different, but substantially akin, is the *reflection* provided by Ragin's 'qualitative comparative analysis' (1987), which is based on the analysis of cases (Ragin and Becker, 1992), the characteristics of which are inserted into truth tables and analyzed according to formal causal logic. This is a formalized methodology which uses the structures of enunciative and predicative calculus as its syntax. The starting-point is, on the one hand, the algebra of George Boole (1815–64), who formalized logic by means of special connectors (accordingly called 'Boolean'), and on the other, the methods of John Stuart Mill (1872), who applied his 'five canons' to test causal propositions. The main concepts used by this methodology are 'cause/effect,' 'triggering cause,' 'structural cause,' 'simple, compound and multiple causes,' 'sufficient condition' and 'necessary condition.' Other approaches in this category are *comparative narrative analysis*, *sequence analysis* and *event structure analysis*, which has been applied, though only for exemplification purposes, also to ethnographic data (Corsaro and Heise, 1990). As well as in the social sciences, this methodology is widely used in political science, usually for the comparison of forms of government (for example, democracy) across hundreds of countries.

2.7 On methodological pluralism

As said at the beginning of this chapter, every classification highlights some aspects of reality and neglects others. Moreover, it is never possible to systematize an empirical reality in its entirety, with all its complexity and innumerable facets, into a classification. Definitions serve to specify categories; they are conceptual containers. Definitions are not accounting tools, and are not required to grasp all and everything; all they have to do is identify and characterize.

Hence the classification just proposed also has its shortcomings, one in particular: it does not take account of the research practices which fall under the headings of 'triangulation' (Webb et al., 1966; Denzin, 1970; Jick, 1979; Miles and Huberman, 1984), 'methodological pluralism' (Bell and Newby, 1977) or 'mixed methods' (Brannen, 1992).

According to Hammersley's interpretation (1996) of the ways in which researchers employ different types of data, these research practices compare different kinds of data (for example, qualitative and quantitative) and different methodologies (for example, ethnography and survey). They seek to:

(1) corroborate data sources reciprocally (triangulation) in order to determine the 'true state of affairs' and to reveal 'the whole picture' of a phenomenon;
(2) gain preliminary understanding about a topic in order to assist with the design of a survey (auxiliary function or facilitation); and
(3) fulfill diverse research objectives (for example, understanding a social process and its statistical distribution in the population (complementarity).

However, doubts have been expressed as to the plausibility of these research practices (Hammersley and Atkinson, 1983: 199; Silverman, 1993: 156–8; 2000: 99; Fielding and Fielding, 1986; Mason, 1996: 27). These authors argue that different types of data cannot be unproblematically added together; and they are doubtful whether it is methodologically sound to compare data collected with such diverse instruments and cognitive purposes.

As we have seen in the previous chapter, various studies have shown that there is a significant difference between what is said by interviewees and their observed behavior. In this case, should the researcher rely on the material collected from the interviews or should he or she rely on ethnography?

2.7.1 Measuring versus counting

I, personally, do not deny the existence or the feasibility of these practices, although I believe that a plurality of methods (techniques) is more plausible than mixed methodologies. I would point out, however, that there is a certain confusion as to what actually constitutes a quantitative method. It is not necessarily the case that researchers who use official statistics or the frequency distributions of a variable in qualitative inquiry are mixing methods. Just because research involves numbers does not mean that it is quantitative. More is required, especially a different way of thinking with numbers. The main difference between qualitative and quantitative methods, in fact, is that the latter adhere to the 'measurement paradigm' (formalized by psychometric Stevens in 1946) which affirms that it is possible to *measure* meanings, while the latter does not set out to measure things, but at most seeks to *count* them.

Consider for a moment why the verb 'measure' is used for height, but not for age. Have you ever heard talk of 'measuring' age or the number of children?

One should therefore not confuse measurement with counting; nor, therefore, *units of measurement* with *units of count*. **Measurement** concerns itself with the *continuous* properties of an object: properties, that is, for which there is no outright 'jump' between one state and another, so that the differences between them are difficult to discern. Income, for instance, belongs to this category: if one person earns \$1,264 and another \$1,265, there is no obvious 'jump' between the two states. But having one or two children is a different matter. Although one is the difference in both cases, we feel that there is a substantive difference between the two cases. It is likewise difficult to establish with precision the *height* of a person or the *distance* between two objects. We need an instrument (a tape-measure) to perform the operation accurately. By 'unit of measurement,' therefore, a standard quantity of the property that we want to measure is meant. A unit of measurement may also be a mathematical combination of other units of measurement (kilometers per hour, for example).

Counting instead concerns the *discrete* properties of an object; properties among which it is relatively easy (without the use of specific instruments) to discern differences: a person's number of children; the number of patients in the waiting room of a doctor's surgery; the number of times a person goes to the cinema in a month. Calculations of this kind are quite frequently made in ethnographic research in particular (see 12.5), and in qualitative research in general. It is therefore entirely inappropriate to consider discrete properties to be measurable. In this regard, Cicourel (1964: 18–22) stressed many decades ago that it is very difficult to talk of measurements in the social sciences because, unlike the general concepts of the physical sciences, those of the social sciences do not have corresponding definitions (lexical and operational) on which there is general consensus in the scientific community. Whilst a tape-measure, a pair of scales and a chronometer are (consensually considered) necessary for the operational definition of 'quantity of motion,' there are no equally (consensually accepted) instruments with which to obtain operational definitions of concepts like 'democracy,' 'rationalization,' 'authority' or 'political participation.'

2.8 Concluding remarks

It is consequently important to avoid a confusion frequently to be found in the methodology handbooks. First, it is incorrect to say that one of the main differences between quantitative and qualitative research is that, when they describe or explain phenomena, the former uses figures and the latter only words. Second, the fact that qualitative research also uses numbers and cross-tabulations does not mean that there is not a clear distinction between quantitative and qualitative research: in fact, *counting* is not the same as *measuring*.

Finally, I believe that the use of different methodologies in a single research project does not signify that all of them are of the same importance. For example, in recent years, several social researchers (as we shall see in 6.4, 8.5 and 9.5) have conducted visual ethnography, thus combining traditional ethnography with new tools for audio-visual documentation, and in some cases also multimedia systems for the transcription of speech and other components of interaction. In this case we have the integration of two methodologies: the ethnographic and the documentary. However, it is my impression that when a phenomenon is interpreted and studied, one methodology always prevails over the others: there is a dominant methodology which the researcher uses more extensively or intensively, and an ancillary methodology which backs up the dominant one. It is the methodology used to test or document the main research hypotheses that, I maintain, should be considered the more important.

For all these reasons, I believe that the classification which I have proposed, despite its shortcoming of not taking adequate account of methodological pluralism, is more satisfactory than those that are conventionally used.

KEY POINTS

- A *methodology* is a global style of thinking used to investigate a research topic.
- The concept of methodology can be likened to that of a 'paradigm': a set of ways to *see* (cognitive) and to *do* (social).
- A *method* is a tool, a technique or a specific, codified and widely used operational procedure which comprises solutions devised over time in cumulated and reified form.
- There are methods with which to collect information (to construct data) and methods with which to analyze data.
- The main methodologies in social research are the following: discursive interview, survey, ethnography, documentary, transformative and speculative.
- Therefore ethnography is not a (simple) method, but a general approach.

KEY TERMS

Classification (see p. 17)	Grouping of acts, objects and referents into classes. From a cultural point of view, a classification is an arbitrary tentative practice which imposes order and gives sense to a reality with no intrinsic meaning independently of the observer.
Concept (see pp. 70–1)	Idea, mental representation. A concept is a meaning. Moreover, a concept is *not* a snippet of reality, but a snippet of belief and experience.
Count (see p. 29)	The progressive numeration of objects (referents) to determine their quantity. Counting is a procedure which assigns values to discrete properties of an object; properties among which it is relatively easy (without the use of specific instruments) to discern differences. Counting is based on a *unit of count*. Counting is not the same as *measuring*.
Measurement (see p. 28)	*Measurement* takes place when the property quantified is continuous and there is a unit of measurement relative to it. From a practical point of view, a property is *continuous* when no 'jump' occurs from one of its states to the next. A *unit of measurement* is a standard quantity of the property being measured.
Methodology (see pp. 18–22)	A global style of thinking, a general approach to studying research topics or an overall research strategy. A methodology has at least four components:

(1) a *pivotal* cognitive mode;

(2) a theory of scientific knowledge;

(3) a range of solutions, remedies and 'tricks of the trade'; and

(4) a systematic sequence of procedural steps.

Method (see pp. 22–3)   A tool, a technique or a specific, codified and widely used operational procedure which comprises solutions devised over time in cumulated and reified form. There are techniques to collect information (to construct data) and techniques to analyze it/them.

Techniques of information and data collection can be used within diverse methodologies, although each of these will use them for different purposes and in different ways.

Term (see p. 70)   Word, linguistic expression.

RECOMMENDED READING

For undergraduates:
Silverman, David (2006b)

For graduates:
Silverman, David (2005)

For advanced researchers:
Gobo, Giampietro (forthcoming)

EXERCISE 2.1

Look at your bookshelves or go to the library. Choose a monograph (i.e. a book which sets out the results of empirical research) pertaining to any sector of the social sciences.

Answer the following questions:

• What methodology was used to conduct the research?

• Was one methodology used, or more than one?

• If more than one methodology was used, were the main arguments that the author put forward tested and documented through those methodologies?

• What method was used to collect (information to construct) the data?

• What method was used to analyze the data?

SELF-EVALUATION TEST

Are you ready for the next chapter? Check your knowledge by answering the following open-ended questions:

1. A method has four components. What are they?
2. What are the main methods used in the social sciences and political science? What are their main cognitive modes?
3. What is the documentary method?
4. What is the transformative method?
5. What is the discursive interview method?
6. What is the speculative method?
7. What is the survey method?
8. What is the main difference between a qualitative and quantitative method?

Note

1 The other four methodologies (described below) are still marginal, although they are becoming increasingly common, especially in ethnography.

3

Ethnographic Methodology: Approaches, Scholars and Modes

LEARNING OBJECTIVES

- To understand the usefulness of a historical reconstruction of research methodologies.

- To date and reconstruct the advent of the ethnographic methodology.

- To gain knowledge of the main ethnographic approaches and their main differences.

- To be aware of their main strengths and weaknesses.

- To recognize ethnographic styles.

3.1 Introduction

Felson's law

To steal ideas from one person is plagiarism; to steal from many is research.

Why a chapter on the history of ethnography? Is one really necessary? We have grown accustomed to viewing history as a sort of musty portrait gallery. When history is described thus, those who dismiss it as boring – as a discipline smelling of mothballs – are certainly right. However, history can be looked at from another point of view: it can be construed as an attempt to 'denaturalize' our categories of thought.

3.1.1 The usefulness of a historical gaze

Let me explain. We take numerous things for granted: we are convinced that we have a 'self,' an 'identity' and an 'individuality'; that human action is driven by 'intentions' and 'motivations' or that it results from 'causes'; and that there exists a past, present and future. Although these things seem natural and obvious, in actual fact they are not. The Ancient Greeks and Romans, and many other non-Western societies, did not possess these concepts, not even that of a 'future.' In fact, the future tense of verbs appeared much later than did those of the past and present. Ancient Greek culture between the twelfth and eighth centuries BC – the culture described by Homer – did not even have a unified concept of 'body.' The ancient Greeks did not perceive the body as a whole object; they saw only arms, necks, legs, feet and chests, describing them as separate objects. Ancient Greek had a term for the body (*cros*) which denoted it as 'skin, bodily surface and pigmentation'; the word *soma* instead denoted the body as a 'corpse, dead, lifeless, abandoned by the psyche (the breath of life),' and in Homer *soma* is never used to refer to living beings (Snell, 1953: 7). I could continue at length, and those interested will find innumerable examples in studies on ancient cultures or in anthropology. What I wish to stress, however, is that a historical overview helps us see that apparently natural concepts and categories are in fact products of a particular culture. History immunizes us against the ingenuousness (increasingly commonplace among contemporary social scientists) of proposing as novel things which have already been said 70 or 80 years ago. Knowledge of history saves us from having to constantly re-invent the wheel, to use the well-known expression.

Reviewing the birth of the ethnographic methodology is useful for various reasons. It furnishes understanding of the spirit of the times when the methodology was invented, the problems that it addressed and solved, and the directions in which it moved. But it also serves to put into perspective numerous current approaches which are propounded as innovative theories and methodologies yet already have been known for some time. Finally, it serves to highlight the link between social theory and ethnography. It is with this aim in mind that I shall now review the intellectual traditions that have fashioned ethnography into a resource for the discovery of things which other methodologies have failed to grasp. There, accordingly, follows a survey of the main theoretical contributions made by these traditions.

3.1.2 The making of the ethnographic methodology

Contrary to what one might think, ethnographic methodology (as we know it today) arose rather belatedly in sociology – doing so in the first years of the 1940s. Notwithstanding a first and inchoate appearance at the end of the 1910s, one can only speak of a proper 'ethnographic methodology' from the early 1940s onwards. In anthropology, though, the methodology was already in use at the end of the nineteenth century.

Ethnographic methodology has been used – in different forms and for different purposes – by numerous theoretical approaches. In the next two chapters, I shall provide brief outlines of the most important of them: the Chicago School, interactionism, grounded theory, structuralism, realism and ethnomethodology in this chapter; reception ethnography, feminist studies and postmodernism in the next. This is obviously not the only possible classification of the ethnographic tradition in sociology, but it follows (more or less) a chronological story.

3.2 The period of 'nosing around' and the ex-post facto construction of a myth: The 'First' Chicago School

As I have said, the ethnographic methodolgy was first introduced at the end of the 1910s by teachers and researchers at the Department of Sociology of the

University of Chicago. Empirical research in the department began under the guidance of the sociologists William Isaac Thomas (1863–1947) and Robert Ezra Park (1864–1944). The latter had begun his career in journalism, but in 1914 he left the profession to take up an appointment as director of the Chicago Department of Sociology. Because Park and Thomas were scholars of a strong practical bent, they were attentive to the changes taking place in their city. By that time Chicago was already a metropolis, and consequently had numerous social and urban problems. This was the period of prohibition, of rampant crime and subsequently of the Great Depression.[1] Chicago had expanded enormously following its already rapid development in the second half of the nineteenth century. One factor in this explosive growth was a huge influx of immigrants from Germany, Russia, Ireland, Poland, Italy and Sweden. Naturally, therefore, Park and Thomas's research interests centered on their great modern city and on the integration of its immigrants. Park, in particular, believed that social scientists should concern themselves with problems of urban malaise: such matters, he maintained, should not be left to socially engaged novelists like Émile Zola alone.

The Chicago Sociology Department was thoroughly dissatisfied with the statistical data furnished by the surveys commissioned by government agencies. First, the data only superficially described phenomena, failing to grasp their complexity; second, it did not cover certain aspects essential for the full understanding of a city's life. Consequently, under Park's leadership, a far-reaching research program began with the stated purpose of studying urban phenomena 'live,' in their concrete and everyday settings. Park urged his students thus:

> You have been told to go grubbing in the library, thereby accumulating a mass of notes and a liberal coating of grime. You have been told to choose problems wherever you can find musty stacks of routine records based on trivial schedules prepared by tired bureaucrats and filled out by reluctant applicants for aid or fussy do-gooders or indifferent clerks. This is called 'getting your hands dirty in real research.' Those who counsel you are wise and honorable; the reasons they offer are of great value. But one more thing is needful: first-hand observation. Go and sit in the lounges of the luxury hotels and on the doorsteps of the flophouses; sit on the Gold Coast settees and on the slum shakedowns; sit in the Orchestra Hall and in the Star and Garter Burlesk. In short, gentlemen, go get the seat of your pants dirty in real research (personal note by one of Park's students reported in Bulmer, 1984: 97).

If we cleanse Park's recommendation from its sexist spirit and the lack of reference to female students, his advice still holds today.

3.2.1 Findings

The Chicago researchers and students thus set about constructing sociological maps of their city. They did so by going into its neighborhoods and collecting first-hand information about their ethnic groups and social classes. Their approach was called 'ecological' in the sense that it sought out connections between the environment (its geographical and spatial aspects) and the social structure. This was a sort of human ethnology that contended that the morphology of the urban territory (rivers, main roads, bridges and railways) divides a city into relatively isolated zones, each with its particular economic and social structure (called 'natural areas'). Today this seems obvious, but at the time it was an absolute revelation. Park's approach enabled his researchers to show that apparently chaotic phenomena displayed regular patterns when they were examined carefully: suicide rates were high in areas of Chicago where people lived in furnished rooms; crimes occurred in particular zones of the city (called 'delinquency areas' by Frederic M. Thrasher); so too did prostitution and mental illness. Juvenile delinquency and gang activity characterized certain neighborhoods, while ethnic minorities were localized in particular zones of the city. The descriptions and the maps were (albeit with some excesses) extremely detailed, and the research for them took several years of fieldwork.

Park and his colleagues sought to reconstruct the sociological profiles and quantitative dimension (by the counting) of people who lived in hotels, furnished rooms, rented apartments, their own dwellings or on the street. They also collected information (almost entirely non-existent at the time) on their professions: in particular on people who worked as shopgirls, policemen, peddlers, cabmen, night watchmen and vaudeville performers, and on what they did in their everyday work (Madge, 1962: 90). Thus was born the sociology of the professions. These studies described the changes then traversing the city of Chicago (and American society in general) and the social disintegration that they caused: an example of which was the progressive replacement of guest houses – which still reproduced, albeit weakly, the rituals of family life – with furnished lodgings and hotel rooms. These transformations exacerbated the breakdown of family ties and cultural codes, generating anomie and the depersonalization and commercialization of social relations: themes developed 30 years earlier by the German sociologist George Simmel, whose student Park had been in Germany.

3.2.2 Criticism

Except for some particularly scrupulous and systematic researchers like Frederic M. Thrasher and Clifford Shaw, the research methods used by most of the Chicago School's members were rather primitive. As Madge recalls, 'a concern with method was left very much to the initiative of each investigator' (1962: 117) because 'the abiding fact . . . is that it is unified by its field of interest rather than by its methods' (p. 125), which were always of secondary concern. Participant observation was given no particular importance, being just one of the many methods that the Chicago School used. Indeed, strictly speaking, the Chicago School's methods cannot be termed 'ethnography'; and its members themselves only expressly used the terms *ethnography* and *participant observation* after the 1940s.[2] What authors since the 1960s have retrospectively called 'ethnography' (thus creating a myth – see Platt, 1983; Hammersley, 1989) was nothing but a general form of qualitative research. If anything, the Chicago researchers produced case studies[3] (Platt, 1983, 1992; Hammersley, 1989); monographs produced using a melange of methodologies and methods such as:

- use of informants (social workers, police officers, politicians, hotel porters and landlords);

- direct observation (participant observation and home visits);
- analysis of *primary* documents (letters, messages and school essays); and
- analysis of *secondary* documents (newspaper articles, official archives, census data, archives of charitable and voluntary organizations, social worker reports, federal documents on crime, court registers and clinical records).

But the marked methodological pluralism of the Chicago School was not the result of a deliberate choice – and it thus differed, for example, from the recent 'mixed methods' approach (see 2.7). Observation was one of the methods that the criminologist Sheldon Messinger (1925–2002) called 'nosing around' (see Lofland, 1980: 4) and which were unconcerned with the methodological problems – access to the field, the ethics of research, the relativity of informants' points of view – which only much later became important. Finally, although the Chicago School's monographs were empirically grounded, they suffered from two serious methodological shortcomings (Sacks, 1992: 254): (i) the data was presented in a such a way that the reader could not repeat the analysis; and (ii) they were excessively based on (and did not sufficiently contextualize) the informants' accounts and categories, so that it was impossible to develop more independent analysis (for details on Cressey's methodology, an important member of the 'First' Chicago School, go to www.sagepub.co.uk/gobo).

3.3 The institutionalization of ethnography: The 'Second' Chicago School

During the 1930s the Chicago Faculty of Sociology was joined by new members of staff, among them Louis Wirth (1897–1952), Herbert Blumer, Lloyd W. Warner (1898–1970) and Everett C. Hughes. These scholars were distinguished, amongst other things, by a greater methodological awareness which had a strong impact on their pupils and followers (most notably William F. Whyte, Howard Becker, Blanche Geer, Anselm Strauss, Melville Dalton, Erving Goffman, Fred Davis and Rosalie Wax), who after World War II produced a series of studies that revolutionized the current theories of deviance, education and work. And it was in this period, too, that ethnographic research became institutionalized by being taught, described in articles, subjected to methodological reflection, and eventually (in the 1960s) codified in textbooks.

Ethnographic methodology, as we know it today, came into being largely through the work of Hughes (1897–1983). After gaining his Ph.D. as a pupil of Park, Hughes worked in Canada. In 1938 he returned to Chicago to take up an appointment specifically to teach fieldwork at the university. As Herbert Gans, a doctoral student at the time, recalls,

> just after World War II, no one talked much about participant-observation; we just did it. Like many of my fellow sociology students, I enrolled in Everett Hughes's course 'Introduction to Field Work' and like them, I found it a traumatic introduction; we were sent to a census tract in nearby Hide Park[4] and asked to do a small participant-observation study. Everett Hughes gave us some words of introduction and of instruction, but good father that he was, he quickly pushed us out of the nest and told us to fly on our own (1968: 301).

Hughes was convinced that participant observation was a method to collect data which enabled objectivation of the activities and experiences of certain actors. Participation was in this sense ancillary to observation, although it was its complement for the correct production of theoretical material.

The methodological approach used by Hughes and his assistants gave great importance to comparison, synchronic as well as diachronic, so that research did not become merely self-referential. The information gathered was more than simply descriptive: it was constantly related to general theoretical issues, and its collection was guided by curiosity in other disciplines, especially anthropology and history. Hughes' pupils conducted participant observation on the activities of small groups in firms and institutions, or in specific situations, and their papers were often characterized by irreverence towards the self-definitions furnished by their interviewees. Under Hughes' guidance, they selected a research topic and then pursued it across a large number of professions. This method – essentially based on comparisons – enabled the Chicago researchers to grasp counter-intuitive aspects which they wittily pointed out: Hughes remarked that the sociologist of work can learn about doctors by studying plumbers, and about prostitutes by studying psychiatrists (Hughes, 1971: 88).

However, besides being a theoretical undertaking, Hughes' approach displayed a taste for debunking society, creating a deliberate confusion between the higher and lower levels of the social scale, harbouring a malicious irreverence towards the loftier professions and rejecting the traditional ranking of social prestige.

Although Hughes was scrupulous when analyzing his data, he was suspicious of the systematization of information collecting methods. He maintained that the situations and circumstances of fieldwork are so diversified that any textbook which attempts to lay down detailed rules is useless. Ethnographic research is marked by a high level of unpredictability which very often frustrates research designs conceived in the abstract. However, his approach was genuinely innovative – especially if viewed in relation to the methodological negligence predominant at the time, when no one thought it necessary to codify and teach research practices. Statistical techniques were regarded as abstruse, and they therefore required special training; but fieldwork, so it was believed, could only be learnt through doing it. Thus, until the second half of the 1980s, American departments of anthropology did not teach field research methods, their belief being that all they had to do was send their students into the field, where they would learn methodology by trial and error.

EXERCISE 3.1

When discussing the research studies by the 'first' Chicago School, I pointed out that some of them highlighted a particular fact: that the progressive demise of guest houses – which still reproduced, albeit weakly, the rituals of family life – and their replacement by furnished lodgings and hotel rooms, had increased anomie and depersonalized social relations.

Now think about your self-catering accommodation at university:
- If it didn't have a communal kitchen where you mix with other students at breakfast, when you take a study break, make yourself a cup of tea or prepare supper, what would your social relations be like?
- How many friendships have you made, how many confidences have you exchanged and how many laughs have you had in the kitchen?
- Would these have happened if you lived in a hotel or in a bedsit?

Discuss these questions among yourselves or with your professor. Think about the contingency of social relations and the role of spaces (in this case the kitchen) in friendship formation.

3.4 Interactionism

The participant observation method was given a privileged role and specific theoretical importance by interactionism, an approach developed between the 1930s and 1950s by Herbert Blumer (1900–87). Although the Chicago School (which developed within the Department of Sociology) and interactionism (this developed within the Department of Philosophy around the philosopher George H. Mead) were two distinct realities, there were numerous contacts and influences between them. Mead's work was a constant referent for Thomas, Park and their pupils; while the research methods of the latter provided the empirical bases and the methodological premises for the theories of Blumer, who never seriously involved himself in field research.

Blumer believed that social research must adopt a 'naturalistic' approach and rely on fieldwork in order to grasp the perspective of social actors and see reality from their point of view. In this Blumer contradicted his mentor, Mead, who instead recommended the experimental method already being used by psychologists. Blumer thus furnished the theoretical-methodological basis for a research practice which the first Chicago School had commendably introduced but had used in a confused manner. The methodological principles of interactionism have been well summarized by Denzin (1970: 7–19) and Silverman (1993: 48, Table 3.2). Stated extremely briefly, they are:

(1) relating symbols and interaction, showing how meanings arise in the context of behavior;
(2) taking the actors' point of view;
(3) studying the 'situated' character of interaction;
(4) analyzing processes instead of structures, avoiding the determinism of predicting behavior from class, gender, race, and so on; and
(5) generalizing from descriptions to theories.

Points of view

These principles together with Hughes' teachings inspired a new generation of researchers. Known as the 'neo-Chicagoans,' they distinguished themselves (as said) in the sociology of deviance and of the professions by conducting methodical and systematic research, of which the most outstanding example is Becker, et al. (1961), a three-year ethnographic study of students in a medical school. However, although the interactionists paid closer attention to methodological questions than their predecessors had done, their interest lay more in constructing theories on an empirical basis than in developing a rigorous method of inquiry. Consequently, while rejecting the positivist methodology of empirical research, they were not always able to avoid the accusation that their use of participant observation made the results unreliable: for they never made clear the extent of the researcher's involvement in the situation being observed. Moreover, the fact that the interactionists almost always chose to observe groups with little bargaining power aroused two suspicions among their critics: (i) that the information collected could be easily manipulated; and (ii) that the interactionists identified to a biased extent with the 'underdogs' – drug addicts, the mentally ill, homosexuals – that they most frequently opted to study.

3.5 Grounded Theory (GT)

The task of introducing methodological rules and procedural rigor into interactionism fell to two sociologists of medicine: Barney G. Glaser and Anselm Strauss (1916–96). The former had trained in the department of sociology of Columbia University, headed by Paul Lazarsfeld and Robert Merton; the latter at the University of Chicago. Glaser's logical-quantitative background, with a marked partiality *à la* Merton for the construction of 'theories of the middle range,' and Strauss' qualitative approach merged creatively in their book *The Discovery of Grounded Theory: Strategies for Qualitative Research* (1967), which rapidly became the standard methodological reference work – not least because it was the first structured study on qualitative methodology. Glaser and Strauss' aim was to bridge the gap between theory and empirical research that previous approaches had failed to close. To this end they set about constructing a logical procedure which led to discovery of a theory inductively – that is, by using solely empirical (grounded) observations. Grounded Theory (GT) was therefore an approach, a mode of reasoning, a way to analyze data that could be applied to both qualitative and quantitative research.

Glaser and Strauss' book was also the first study to organize ethnographic methodology into its various phases: the gathering of information, its classification and then its analysis. This was also by virtue of Strauss' wide experience as an ethnographer. Why did it take so long for a systematic work to be written? Probably because qualitative researchers did not feel threatened or challenged by their quantitative colleagues. In fact, according to Barry A. Turner (1988: 112), the main reason that induced Glaser and Strauss to write their book was, above all, political: supplying a methodological text which students and researchers could quote every once in a while when they presented a research project to institutional organizations usually prejudiced against qualitative research, which they deemed unscientific. Their book came out in a particularly contentious atmosphere (which no longer exists because qualitative methods are considered legitimate) where qualitative sociologists had to defend themselves against quantitative ones. Moreover, Glaser and Strauss had grown weary of seeing so many of their pupils' projects rejected because they were not based on surveys, tests or experiments; hence, their intention was to provide their students with adequate and reasonable answers. Unfortunately, however, Glaser and Strauss' book was used by their followers more to assert the scientific legitimacy of the qualitative method (and to oppose quantitative ones) than to conduct scrupulous research.

Later on the positivistic stance of 'emerging concepts' in GT, as described by Glaser (1978: 2002), is thus given up in favor of a social constructionist perspective that urges the researcher to constantly reflect on the choices made within the research process.[5]

GT has recently regained popularity through the work of Tom and Lyn Richards, two Australian sociologists who have transposed Glaser and Strauss' theoretical principles and instructions into a software program, originally termed QSR NUD*IST – now NVIVO, which assists researchers in the classification and analysis of data.

EXERCISE 3.2

Go to the website http://www.groundedtheory.com/vidseries1.html and listen to the interview with Barney G. Glaser, the inventor (with Anselm Strauss) of Grounded Theory. Then answer the following questions:

• What is GT?
• How can we do GT?
• Is it a quantitative or qualitative method?

3.6 Structuralist ethnography

Another fruitful approach that has contributed to the prestige of ethnography is 'structural' analysis. The term denotes an approach less interested in the subjective aspects of action (contrary to interactionism) than in its social context. To use a celebrated phrase from Goffman (a representative of this approach), it is an approach concerned with: 'Not, then, men and their moments. Rather moments and their men' (1967: 3).

3.6.1 William Foote Whyte

Whyte (1914–2000) was a protagonist of structuralist ethnography. While studying for a masters degree in economics at Harvard between 1936 and 1940, he conducted ethnography in North End, a poor district of Boston (which he renamed Cornerville) inhabited by a large number of Italian immigrants. His aim was to study the relationship between everyday life in Boston's juvenile gangs, the formation of their leaderships and politics in the slums. His monograph, published with the striking title *Street Corner Society* (1943a), was the first urban ethnography ever produced. Focusing on the bottom-up growth of political activities and their relationships with the politics of the city in general, Whyte observed Cornerville in light of its dependent relationship with the broader urban context. In this respect his approach differed from that of the urban studies conducted by the Chicago School, which described the slums as autonomous and isolated spaces.

Whyte's approach differed from the Chicago School in another respect. For Thomas and Znaniecki suicides, crime, divorces, political corruption, violence and mental illness demonstrated that the anonymous and chaotic nature of the city generated 'social disorganization.' These phenomena, they maintained, were symptomatic of a decline in collective values and social rules which were being superseded by individualism. This was a vision of the city that Park and his colleagues had learnt from Simmel. Whyte, by contrast – presumably because of his ignorance of the Chicago tradition – propounded the opposing view, that he had probably gained from his direct observation of interactions within and among the district gangs. According to Whyte the gangs produced 'social organization,' not disorganization. The poverty of Cornerville, and its inhabitants' myriad activities (including illegal ones like racketeering), were sources of an order whose existence only a strongly deductive (and therefore prejudiced) view like that embraced by Park and his colleagues would deny:

> For too long sociologists have concentrated their attention upon individuals and families that have been unable to make a successful adjustment to the demands of their society. We now need studies of the way which individuals and groups have managed to reorganize their social relations and adjust conflicts (1943b: 37).

Whyte's ethnography is not only important on the substantive and structural level; it also has methodological implications. After its publication, *Street Corner Society* had very little impact. However, in 1955, when the publisher was deciding whether to bring out a second edition of the book, the idea came to Whyte of giving it greater interest by adding a methodological appendix. For the first time in research the appendix recounted how the ethnographic research had been conducted. Whyte thus introduced what is now termed *reflexivity*: the self-aware analysis of the dynamics between researcher and participants, the critical capacity to make explicit the position assumed by the observer in the field, and the way in which the researcher's positioning impacts on the research process. Whyte also emphasized his 'subjectivity' in regard to both the less edifying aspects of his behavior in the field (as when he took part in an electoral fraud) and the problems that usually arise in fieldwork. The appendix introduced innovations which are today treated as obvious, or almost banal, but this is largely because since 1955 it has been studied and emulated by ethnographic researchers.

3.6.2 Erving Goffman

Another leading representative of structural ethnography was the Canadian Goffman (1922–82). His intellectual development was influenced by four theoretical traditions which I have already outlined: the Chicago School, Simmel's theory, Everett C. Hughes' work and Durkheim's analysis. As regards the first tradition, although Goffman never specifically concerned himself with urban sociology, he was very much aware of the ecological dimension of social behavior: as witnesses his concept of 'personal territory,' his division of interactional space into 'front and back regions,' and his definition of institutions in specifically spatial terms. It was Simmel's theory that aroused Goffman's interest in the structure of face-to-face interaction (Simmelian dyads and triads), and in those aspects of everyday life apparently ephemeral and marginal but which instead underpin the social order and co-existing. Superficially, Goffman argued, good manners, courtesy rules, small sanctions, greetings, blushing from embarrassment, etc., seem irrelevant elements of social life, but in actual fact they are the foundations of social action. Thus, in Goffman's theory, banalities became the prime subject matter of sociological study; they lost their triviality and acquired rich significance.

Also profoundly influential on Goffman were a group of sociologists and ethnographers of work at the University of Chicago who researched under the brilliant guidance of Hughes – whose student Goffman had been. Finally, the fourth tradition that shaped Goffman's intellectual development consisted of the theories of Durkheim. Goffman's work therefore, represents the continuation of this structuralist tradition. His interest in the sacral and ceremonial nature of the self, in the rituals of everyday life and their importance to the constitution of identity, derived from radical application of Durkheim's theories (Collins, 1986). Goffman, however, recast those theories and eventually distanced himself from them.

Goffman's method of empirical research was almost exclusively ethnographic observation. However, he was not a systematic researcher, and his works do not refer to specific settings.[6] Some authors have sought in vain to reconstruct Goffman's method by examining his writings. Yet those who saw Goffman's ethnographic notes remember them as simple jottings made according to his impressions of the actual moment. His research strategy reflected Hughes' approach, with its unusual comparisons among apparently antithetical categories, behaviors and professions: all mixed together by an unsystematic procedure and an impressionistic style, which on Goffman's own admission (see the 'Preface' of 1959), deliberately emulated Simmel's. To conclude, therefore, methodology was not Goffman's principal concern; as evidenced by the following passage:

> Obviously, many of these data are of doubtful worth, and my interpretations – especially of some of them – may certainly be questionable, but I assume that a loose speculative approach to a fundamental area of conduct is better than a rigorous blindness of it . . . my own experience has been mainly with middle-class conduct in a few regions of America, and it is to this that most of my comments apply (Goffman, 1963: 4–5).

3.7 Ethnomethodology

During the 1950s, alongside interactionism and the works of Goffman, there arose a new approach developed by Harold Garfinkel (1917–), which he subsequently termed *ethnomethodology*. By this term he meant the study of the means (*methods*) that people (*ethno*) use in their everyday lives to recognize, interpret and classify their own and others' actions. As a young student of Talcott Parsons (under whose supervision he obtained a Ph.D. in philosophy at Harvard in 1952), Garfinkel developed his ideas at the end of the 1940s while attending seminars held by Schutz. His theories gave rise to the revelatory exercises or 'breaching studies' which Garfinkel devised for his students. The aim of these exercises was to violate a social convention, a rule or a norm. In some cases the students were invited to behave (from 15 minutes to an hour) as if they were boarders in their own homes; in others their task was to enter a shop and talk to a customer as if he were a member of the sales staff; or to enter a supermarket with fixed prices and try to negotiate a discount. Garfinkel's breaching studies were not a complete novelty; they resembled the stunts of the film/TV producer Allen Funt (1914–99), the inventor of the television program *Candid Camera* (1947), where he filmed the reactions of unwitting victims of surreal hoaxes. Garfinkel's breaching studies also resembled the laboratory experiments conducted at the end of the 1940s by social psychologists interested in how subjects resolved incongruities, and the psychological reaction mechanisms of compliance with, or rebellion against, group pressure. However, Garfinkel was not interested in individual psychological mechanisms, but rather in the strength of common-sense assumptions and the resistance of the moral and social order. Indeed, by means of his breaching studies, Garfinkel sought to show that the essence of the social order consists not in socially shared values, but in common-sense conventions, trust and reciprocal expectations. His breaching studies, which 'are not properly speaking experimental' (Garfinkel, 1967: 38), became so famous that they created the stereotype of the ethnomethodologist: a peculiar fellow who, impertinently and sometimes annoyingly, enjoys putting his interlocutors in awkward situations, the purpose being to bring out the tacit conventions that underpin social relations and to disrupt the social order.

The theoretical core of ethnomethodology drew on the work of various authors: it continued the study of the conditions (trust, normative expectations, etc.)

which sustain the *social order* (Parsons); it examined the properties of the *natural attitude* (Schutz) represented by common-sense reasoning in the everyday world or *Lebenswelt* (Husserl); and it criticized the concept of *rule* as a cognitive resource able to determine human actions (Wittgenstein). Ethnomethodology mixed these and other ingredients together in an original synthesis whose strength consisted in the radicalism with which theories were applied to the analysis of concrete, everyday activities. In particular, besides his emphasis on 'tacit knowledge,' Garfinkel empirically demonstrated the presence of two essential and (in his opinion) intrinsic characteristics of social practices: indexicality and reflexivity (see 5.6.3).

In the second half of the 1950s Garfinkel also conducted a series of ethnographic observations in institutional settings: he studied, for example, a courtroom jury (with Saul Mendlovitz) and the psychiatric staff of the U.C.L.A. School of Medicine (with Egon Bittner). These ethnographies were not conducted methodically and systematically probably because they were intended as *demonstrations* of the inescapability of indexicality and reflexivity rather than as empirical *findings*. But they nevertheless opened the way for a new type of process-based ethnography which sought to grasp phenomena as they unfolded. This approach inspired a series of ethnographic studies conducted by Garfinkel's colleagues, assistants and pupils during the 1960s and 1970s in a variety of institutional settings: police departments, newspaper editorial offices, law courts, therapy sessions, hospitals, halfway house and so on.

From the second half of the 1960s onwards, Garfinkel's theories attracted an increasing number of adherents: indeed, in the state universities of Southern California – principally Los Angeles (where Garfinkel taught from 1954 until his retirement), Santa Barbara and San Diego – there developed a veritable ethnomethodological movement. Besides Garfinkel, its main exponents were Aaron Cicourel (1928–) and Harvey Sacks (1934–75). Cicourel represents the methodological side of ethnomethodology, or its less radical component that is more amenable to dialogue with the traditional social sciences. His research in education, on the relationship between the police, prosecutors and juveniles under arrest, and doctor/patient relations contributed to creating an ethnographic method of ethnomethodological stamp. Although not based on ethnography, the work of Sacks inaugurated a new sector of inquiry within ethnomethodology which gained great currency from the late 1960s onwards: conversation analysis.

3.8 Realist ethnography: Ergonomics and human ethology

It is usually believed that ethnographic methodology belongs naturally to the category of 'interpretative methods' – or, at least, this is how it is described by the contemporary methodological literature. In reality, however, ethnography has also been widely used as part of a positivist approach. The French philosopher August Comte (1798–1857), considered the founder of sociology, stated that 'pure observation' (together with experiments and the comparative method) was one of the three tools of positive sociology. In more recent times, however, ethnography was conducted within ergonomics.

The purpose of ergonomics, which has a long tradition of applied research, is to adapt environments to human needs, reasonings and behaviors by modifying the technologies already in use or by introducing new ones. Most well-known is 'physical' ergonomics, mainly based on anthropometrics and physiology, which seeks to adapt objects (like chairs, tables, glasses, handles and so on) to the human body. Ergonomic ethnography arose after World War II as an attempt to overcome the limitations of laboratory experimental methods. Even today, the main shortcoming of laboratories is that they are artificial environments and therefore differ greatly from the natural settings of everyday life. Consequently, the subjects of laboratory experiments are required to perform tasks and to solve problems very different from those which they encounter in their everyday lives. For this reason, at the end of the 1940s 'ergonomic ethnography' was developed as a method to observe real behaviors. An idea of this style of research can be gained from the film *Kitchen Stories* made by the Norwegian director Bent Hamer in 2003. The film narrates the friendship that slowly developed between a researcher (the observer) and a Norwegian farmer (the observed). The basis of the story is a study in ergonomic ethnography conducted by the Swedish Home Research Institute, an organization which designed appliances to streamline the work of housewives as they did their daily chores. The new appliances were then tested in laboratories by the housewives themselves, as illustrated by the following still taken from the film (Photograph 3.1).

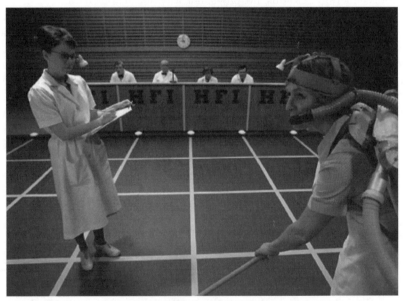

Photograph 3.1   Test on the physical effort produced when using a vacuum cleaner

However, the ethnographies yielded some surprising results: experts on house and home found out that simply by organizing the kitchen's workstations properly, using the assembly-line layout of factories as their model, the financial benefits for a household could be enormous. Or, as a Swedish advertisement for the new ideal kitchen put it: instead of a housewife having to walk the equivalent of

Sweden to the Congo during a year of cooking, she now only needed to walk to Northern Italy in order to get food on the table.

After thoroughly mapping the Swedish housewife's behavior in the kitchen, scientists at the Home Research Institute felt ready to venture beyond their own geographic and gender-based limitations. This is the social philosophy that underlies IKEA, the household furnishings multinational. The film narrates how in the early 1950s the Institute sent 18 observers to the rural district of Landstad, Norway, with its surplus of bachelors, to study the kitchen routines of single men. In order to be on 24-hour call, the observers lived life in egg-shaped campers outside each subject's house. From high, custom-made observation chairs strategically placed in each kitchen (see Photograph 3.2), few activities would escape this new science.

Photograph 3.2   The researcher observes the participant in his everyday kitchen activities

These details encapsulate the positivist conception of research and its ethics: the observers adopted a neutral, objective stance; they were allowed to come and go as they pleased, and under no circumstances could they be spoken to or included in kitchen activities. Ergonomic ethnography is an extremely apt metaphor for social engineering, the blind faith in progress, positivism and behaviorism, the golden age of social democracy.

Over the years, ergonomics has not only furnished applications but also made a major contribution to theory and knowledge about human behavior.

3.9 Concluding remarks

The different traditions described in this chapter are often grouped in the literature under the heading 'qualitative studies.' This drastic simplification has produced confusion among theories which, on careful consideration, reveal irreducible differences with important consequences for research practice.

The best way to grasp these differences is to read the original texts. However, today this is rather difficult as the proliferation of handbooks, textbooks, critical summaries and re-interpretation books has dramatically increased the reading of third-hand texts, rather than the original ones. This tendency facilitates the simplification that ends up by concealing the theoretical and methodological differences among the various schools of thought.

EXERCISE 3.3

Recognizing ethnographic styles

The three texts in this exercise exemplify three different ways of 'doing' ethnography. Ethnographic methodology is not a neutral tool that automatically produces results. These stem from a research project's cognitive objectives, which are determined both by common-sense theories and by the scientific theories to which the researcher refers.

Your task is therefore to read the texts (available at www.sagepub.co.uk/gobo), and as you do so identify the main methodological differences among the ethnographic styles of the three authors. You can then compare your conclusions with my observations that follow the texts. The first extract is taken from the well-known study by Howard Becker (1951), 'The Professional Dance Musician and his Audience,' first published in the *American Journal of Sociology* and then included in Becker's book, *Outsiders: Studies in the Sociology of Deviance* (1963: 85–91). Becker carried out his research in 1948–49 when, still a university student, he worked as a musician in a number of Chicago clubs.

The second text, taken from *Behavior in Public Places: Notes on the Social Organization of Gatherings* (1963: 181–5), is a typical example of Erving Goffman's style.

Finally, the piece by the ethnomethodologist David Sudnow is an extract from his best-known study, begun in the summer of 1963 at two hospitals, entitled *Passing on: The Social Organization of Dying* (1967: 77–83).

KEY POINTS

- Historical overview helps us see that apparently natural concepts and categories are in fact products of a particular culture.
- The history of research methodologies and techniques immunizes us against the ingenuousness of proposing as novel things that have already been said 70 or 80 years ago.
- In sociology, ethnographic methodology (as we know it today) arose rather belatedly, in the first years of the 1940s.

- However a first and inchoate appearance of ethnographic methodology dates back to the end of the 1910s and the work of the 'first' Chicago School.
- The main schools and ethnographic styles are: Chicago School, interactionism, Grounded Theory, structuralism, realism, ethnomethodology, reception, feminist and postmodernism.
- The first phase of ethnographic research (1910–40) has been termed 'nosing around.' By this expression is meant a haphazard use of ethnography jointly with many other methods.
- The institutionalization of ethnographic research as a methodology distinct from others began in the 1940s with the 'second' Chicago School.
- In this period the sociologist Everett C. Hughes (1897–1983) was one of the first to teach ethnography as a methodology, into which he introduced the comparative method.
- Subsequently, in the 1950s, interactionism adopted the actors' point of view to uncover the meanings of action that arose in the context of behavior.
- Instead, in the 1960s, the Grounded Theory developed by Barney G. Glaser and Anselm Strauss gave greater systematicity to ethnographic research (which was divided into various phases) and a more rigorous way to reason on hypotheses and theories.
- Structuralist ethnography (William F. Whyte, Erving Goffman and others) once again paid close attention to the social context of action, the structural conditionings on people's behavior, but without neglecting the creative ability of individuals to alter situations in their favor.
- With ethnomethodology, these two – only apparently opposing – tendencies (structure and action) were explored further by focusing on the social order and the strategies (*methods*) routinely used by actors (*ethno*) to recognize, make sense of, and classify the actions of others and themselves.
- Finally, we should not forget that since the 1950s ethnographic methodology has been used (within a realist and positivist framework) for applied research, in particular, to conduct ergonomic studies.

KEY TERMS

Actors' point of view (see p. 39)	Taking the actors' point of view means learning their everyday conceptions of reality, their way to see the world.
Comparative method (see p. 38)	Comparing and contrasting are ordinary intellectual activities which seek to uncover a basic process which assumes many forms in many situations. Hughes was one of the first to demonstrate the importance of

comparison, the purpose of which is to discern conceptual similarities, to refine the discriminatory power of categories, and to discover patterns. Glaser and Strauss (1967) then outlined a systematic way to perform this intellectual process which they called the *constant comparative method.*

Ecological approach
(see pp. 35–6)

This approach is a theoretical and methodological proposal first put forward by Ernest W. Burgess (1925), an authoritative member of the first Chicago School. It is 'ecological' in the sense that it seeks out connections between the environment (its geographical and spatial aspects) and the social structure. It recognizes that urban expansion is not haphazard but quite strongly controlled by community-level forces such as land values, zoning ordinances, landscape features, circulation corridors and historical contingencies. External factors are neither random nor intended, but rather arise from natural forces in the environment which limit the adaptive spatial and temporal relationships among individuals.

Ethnomethods
(see pp. 44–5)

These are the means (*methods*) that people (*ethno*) use in their everyday lives to recognize, interpret and classify their own and others' actions. They are routinized strategies, procedures and techniques with which to manage everyday affairs.

Meanings and context
(see p. 39)

Meaning is a social product: it arises from the context and is created through interactions among individuals. It is not intrinsic to things and it cannot be taken as given.

Reflexivity
(see p. 43)

The self-aware analysis of the dynamics between resear-cher and participants, the critical capacity to make explicit the position assumed by the observer in the field, and the way in which the researcher's positioning impacts on the research process.

RECOMMENDED READING

For undergraduates:
Silverman, David (2006c)

For graduates:
Gubrium, Jaber (1988a)

For advanced researchers:
Pollner, Melvin and Emerson, Robert (2001)

SELF-EVALUATION TEST

Are you ready for the next chapter? Check your knowledge by answering the following open-ended questions:

1. What did Erving Goffman mean when he said that one should observe 'not, then, men and their moments. Rather moments and their men' (1967: 3)?
2. List some of the main methodological differences among Howard Becker (interactionism), Erving Goffman and David Sudnow (ethnomethodology).
3. What criticisms, from the methodological point of view, have been made of the Chicago School?
4. On what theoretical principle is Grounded Theory based?
5. What is the main novelty of Goffman's approach?

Notes

1 To gain an idea of the period and the social climate in which the Chicago School worked, watch the following absorbing films: *Chimere* by Michael Curtiz (1950), *The Sting* by George Roy Hill (1973), *The Untouchables* by Brian De Palma (1987), *Bix* by Pupi Avati (1991) and *Chicago* by Rob Marshall (2002).

2 Although the expression 'participant observation' had been used as early as 1924 (by Edward C. Lindeman), it became methodologically important only in 1937 (in Joseph Dean Lohman's book), to be then used systematically and in codified manner only after the end of the 1940s (Hammersley, 1989: 81–3; Platt, 1996: 47). As Jennifer Platt writes, 'the term *participant observation* did not become current and institutionalized in its modern sense until the late 1940s and early 1950s. It was then rationalized and advocated in terms of access to meanings' (Platt, 1996: 40).

Indeed, when Lindeman (1924) used the expression *participant observer* he was referring to the researcher's assistant who recruited subjects for study and helped the researcher gain a view 'from within': in many respects he or she corresponded to the social actor later termed the 'informant.'

3 A case study consisted essentially of an interview written by the person being studied. The interview was very similar to a life history and it was designed to bring out the subjective meaning attributed by the inteviewee to his or her biography. Consequently, the term 'case study' was used interchangeably with 'life history' or 'personal documents' (Platt, 1996: 46).
4 The neighborhood in which the University of Chicago was situated.
5 For a constructivist reformulation of GT, and a discussion of the difference within GT in Glaser' and Strauss' views – see Charmaz, 2000.
6 With the exception of three books: his Ph.D. dissertation (1953) partly based on two years of observation conducted on a community of 300 people living in the Shetland Islands; *Asylum* (1961), the result of one year's observation at St. Elizabeth's Hospital, a horrific mental hospital in Washington D.C.; *Where the Action is* (1967), based on observation at Las Vegas gambling casinos.

New Ethnographic Styles

LEARNING OBJECTIVES

- To gain knowledge of the ethnographic styles developed from the 1980s.

- To comprehend how they differ from traditional ethnographic styles.

- To understand how the concept of ethnography has changed over time.

- To learn how to recognize the new ethnographic styles.

4.1 Introduction

The approaches described in the previous chapter were current, with alternating fortunes, until the end of the 1970s. Thereafter new approaches arose (reception ethnography, postmodernist ethnography feminist ethnography, and so on) which critically distanced themselves from the previous ethnographic traditions, although the latter obviously did not disappear and continued to operate in parallel with the new approaches. The ethnographic panorama, consequently, grew highly diversified.

As we have already seen in 2.1, the new ethnographic styles stretched the term 'ethnography,' with a consequent dilution of its meaning into a multitude of sometimes contrasting and contradictory senses so that it grew synonymous with qualitative studies. Previously, the term essentially denoted participant observation, and therefore a situation in which the researcher was *present* at the scene where the actions took place and *observed* them at first hand. From the 1980s onwards, the term 'ethnography' came to refer to highly diverse practices, including the conversational interview and analysis of textual and visual documents. As Shaun Moores, a leading representative of 'reception ethnography,' confessed:

> a comparison between recent qualitative studies of media reception and the tradition of anthropological and sociological research . . . might lead us to wonder whether there is anything very ethnographic about 'the new audience ethnography' (see Nightingale, 1989). With few exceptions, the studies [of media reception] have relied mainly on audio-taped conversations with viewers, listeners and readers which may not last much more than an hour each. The inquiries can sometimes incorporate short periods in the company of

media consumers, with academics attempting to share in the routine cultural experiences of those being investigated – but these are clearly not the same as the lengthy spells of participant observation carried out by pioneers in the field research (1993: 4).

4.2 Reception ethnography

At the end of the 1970s research on media consumption went through what has been called the 'ethnographic turn' (Moores, 1993: 1) in the broad British intellectual tradition of 'cultural studies' founded by the Briton Richard Hoggart (1918–), the English socialist historian Edward P. Thompson (1924–93), and the Welsh Marxist novelist and critic Raymond Williams (1921–88) in the late 1950s. This 'turn' gave rise to a new approach within media studies that was variously called 'reception ethnography,' 'new audience ethnography' or 'critical ethnography.'

4.2.1 From television programs to audiences

Of what did this new approach consist? Prior to the 'ethnographic turn,' media analysts had attributed enormous power to television in conditioning people's tastes and opinions. This theoretical view derived from a Marxist doctrine (developed in France by the philosopher Louis Althusser, and in Germany by Theodor Adorno and Max Horkheimer of the Frankfurt School) which asserted that communication media were instruments used by the state to propagate the dominant ideology. The scholars working in the area of cultural studies were not entirely opposed to this view, in so far as they acknowledged that television was a powerful means of persuasion, but they criticized the doctrine's 'textual determinism' and its claim that a television program was able *per se* (automatically and immediately, as if indeed by simple transfusion) to influence or predetermine its audience's opinions. Instead, according to Stuart Hall, another leading representative of cultural studies, consumers were not at all the passive recipients of meanings: they actively produced their own meanings, and they could even reject those proposed by the televisual text. Of course the text sought to transmit messages, but if these were not actively accepted by the audience, they would have no impact. The media theoreticians, therefore, had improperly separated the text (the television program) from the context (its reception), forgetting that interpretation of a text was profoundly influenced by the conditions in which it was viewed. Watching television was not the isolated activity performed in perfect silence, alone in a darkened room, that the academics imagined it to be (Hobson, 1982: 110). Rather, it was an activity undertaken in a broader domestic context which conditioned the reception: television programs are, for example, watched during dinner while those at the table discuss, intervene in, and thus interrupt the media flow. There is consequently a space between the producer (of the program) and the final consumer (the viewer) where domestic activities condition the program's reception, with outcomes not easily predictable.

'Critical ethnography' therefore conducted a twofold critique against first the media theories dominant hitherto, and second the methodologies which were (and still are) much employed to study media consumption. For example, Ien Ang (1991) incisively criticized the television industry's research methodology, and in particular the 'audience measurement' methods (the set meter, the diary, the 'people meter' and so on) used to compile ratings figures. Although these research techniques served the commercial interests of the advertising industry, they were unable to grasp media audiencehood as lived experience. Ethnography, by contrast, could describe consumption practices 'from the virtual standpoint of actual audiences' (Ang, 1991: 165) by delineating the meanings that media consumers attribute to the texts and technologies that they encounter in their everyday lives.

4.2.2 Centers and researchers

There were three principal institutions engaged in reception ethnography: the Centre for Contemporary Cultural Studies (CCCS) at the University of Birmingham; the Centre for Research into Innovation, Culture and Technology at Brunel University; and the German Ludwig-Uhland-Institut für Empirische Kulturwissenschaft (EKW) at the University of Tübingen. However, the first study to make extensive use of ethnographic methodology was an American three-year project conducted by James Lull (1980) on the 'social uses' of television by families.

CASE STUDY
The social uses of television

This study was a large-scale research project which confuted the prejudice that qualitative studies can only be performed on small samples. It was carried out in Wisconsin and in California, where observations and interviews were conducted on a sample of more than 300 families for periods of between three and seven days. Ninety observers were simultaneously placed with families unknown to them. The families were approached through schools, clubs and community organizations. The observers then spent entire afternoons and evenings in the company of household members and thereby gained access to their everyday routines. They 'ate with the families, performed chores with them, played with the children, and took part in group entertainment, particularly television watching' (Lull, 1980: 201). On the basis of data from his study, Lull identified two principal social uses of television in the home: structural and relational. In the former case, the television was used as an 'environmental resource' – 'a companion for accomplishing household chores and routines . . . a flow of constant background noise which moves to the foreground when individuals or groups desire' (pp. 201–2) – and as a 'behavioral regulator' which served to structure domestic time around chores and everyday activities. The relational use of television, which Lull examined in much more detail, consisted in 'ways in which audience members use television to create practical social arrangements' (p. 202). Lull furnishes various examples of active negotiations around the television drawn from his ethnographic observations: the married couple for whom television offered an opportunity to sit together on the sofa and exchange physical affections (p. 203); a young blue-collar family which was able to enjoy some privacy because the television kept the in-laws living next door entertained in the evenings (p. 204); a television program which encouraged parents and children to discuss particular issues (contrary to the prejudice that television has put an end to communication in families). To conclude: television consumption not only consists of interaction between texts and viewers, it is also interaction among the members of the family.

Towards the end of the 1980s, James Lull, Dorothy Hobson, David Morley, Roger Silverston, Shaun Moores, Ien Ang, Janice Radway and many other reception ethnographers began to reflect on their research methodologies and to critically examine the validity of their findings. For they had never seriously considered the extent to which the researcher's presence in so private a sphere as the family might influence the behavior of the subjects observed. Moreover, on the wave of post-colonial anthropology (see Marcus and Fischer, 1986), they began to ask themselves about the power relations between researchers and participants, and how this asymmetry might distort the behavior of the latter and constrain their responses. These topics subsequently became the main items on the agendas of feminist and postmodern ethnographers.

4.3 Feminist ethnography

Most of the knowledge that we possess today has been produced by men. Why is this so? Are women unable to make discoveries, invent new concepts, or conduct research? The answer is quite simple: until only recently, women were excluded from many sectors of scientific, social or political life. And then, why, until the end of the nineteenth century, were almost all philosophers, scientists, writers, politicians or managers men? Because few women were autonomous individuals acting independently from men and endowed with decision-making capacity outside the home. A woman could hope, at most, to become the inspiring muse of a male artist or the assistant of a successful man, or his wife (for a very interesting case study about a super talented woman obliged to act as a wife only, go to www.sagepub.co.uk/gobo).

Until recently it was customary for men to thank their wives in the acknowledgement section of their books: to give just one example among the many thousands that could be cited, Goffman (1959, x) writes 'without the collaboration of my wife, Angelica S. Goffman, this report would not have been written.'

4.3.1 Epistemological consequences on methods

These observations have an epistemological consequence in that they entail reflection on the foundations of scientific knowledge. If such knowledge has been produced mostly by men, it follows that it is not neutral or universal. Instead, it is biased knowledge reproducing the (prejudices and stereotypes of) the particular mentality of the male (Haraway, 1991). The male (or 'masculist' some might say) perspective is so pervasive that it has conditioned even methods, techniques, data collection and technologies – as scholars of science and technology studies well know. For example, most of traditional medical practices have,

> been developed around a male model and applied also on women without taking into consideration social and bio-psychological differences between the two sexes . . . the surgical instruments for *coronary revascularization* (by-pass, coronary angioplasty) are the same as those used for men and little attention has been paid to the fact that women have smaller coronary arteries and blood vessels (Reale, 2004: 103).

Given this premise, the next step is to ask ourselves the following question: if science, like politics or the economy, were dominated by women (or by another social group suffering discrimination like blacks or the disabled, or even for the sake of argument, children), would science be different? Would we have a different kind of scientific knowledge? In this case the answer is less simple. It does, however, enable us to address the issue of whether or not there exists a feminist methodology in general, and a feminist ethnography in particular.

Various feminist authors have stressed that ethnography (and for that matter all social research methods) is a methodology invented by men: there were, for example, very few female members of the First Chicago School (Ruth S. Canvan, Frances Donovan, Vivine M. Palmer and a handful of others). Moreover, some feminist scholars argue that, when women do research, they make different use of traditional (and therefore male) research methods and recast them. This prompts two questions: how does ethnography change when it is women that carry it out? And of what does a feminist methodology consist?

4.3.2 Feminist versus traditional (male) ethnographies

On reading feminist ethnographic reports and comparing them against ones written by men, two main differences are apparent: the first concerns the research topic selected; the second is more strictly methodology in nature. Apropos the former difference, feminist ethnographies are studies conducted 'on, by and for women' (Stanley and Wise, 1983: 17): their purpose is to reveal the social relations producing and maintaining the inequalities from which women suffer. These ethnographies consequently deal *inter alia* with: sexual violence (rape and harassment), discrimination against women in the workplace, their subjugation in civil society and the family, their difficulties in balancing family responsibilities with work, their relations with welfare services and hospitals, domestic violence and women's sexual lives as heterosexuals or lesbians. These are ethnographies primarily concerned with the condition of women in contemporary society: 'very simply, to do feminist research is to put the social construction of gender at the center of one's inquiry' (Lather, 1988: 571). By contrast, male ethnographies very infrequently treat women as warranting study in and of themselves; instead, they depict them as members of some or other social category (patients, the poor, deviants, etc.) or of a professional group (doctors, psychotherapists, blue-collar workers, etc.), but not as individuals.

From the methodological point of view, feminist ethnographies follow (or should follow) a set of guiding principles which distinguish them from traditional (male) ethnographies:

- pay closer attention to the process of action, its 'doing' in time and space, rather than adopting a structuralist view of social activities;
- listen to participants and let them talk using active listening techniques;
- give emancipatory intent to research, which should aim at the 'conscientization' of women so that they become aware of their inequality, and empower them to free themselves from oppressive social constraints: as Mary Maynard writes, 'to challenge the subordination, passivity and silencing of women by encouraging them to speak out about their own condition and in so doing to confront the experts and dominant males with the limitations of their own knowledge' (1994: 93);
- hence, research must have a political impact and not be merely descriptive (like most male ethnographies), in the sense that it must aid understanding of how and why women are oppressed and the solutions that are possible;
- produce research that will alleviate oppression, promote equal opportunities in corporations, 'correct both the *invisibility* and *distortion* of female experience in ways relevant to ending women's unequal social position' (Lather, 1988: 571), adopting an advocacy perspective;
- access the experience of participants, grasping the more subjective, emotional and irrational aspects of their lives;
- 'give voice' to marginalized groups (women who have suffered violence, women who have been exploited, women who are defenceless or abandoned by their husbands, lesbians, etc.), adopting a multi-voice approach which lets those who are usually silent speak out;
- pay closer attention to reflexivity, to the ways in which researchers construct their data by unconsciously imbuing them with their prejudices and stereotypes;
- adopt different research ethics based on 'reciprocity, honesty, accountability, responsibility, equality, etc., in order to treat participants of ethnography with respect . . . [and to] establish the intention of non-exploitation' (Skeggs, 2001: 433);
- be more caring (than men) towards the research participants and acknowledge 'that the emotional content of women's lives is an integral part of the research agenda' (Kasper, 1994: 268), because the aim is to engage in dialogue with the participants, instead of treating them simply or structurally as the sources of data;
- put the observed and the observer on the same footing so that the power relation usually exploited by the latter is reduced or even eliminated: to do this, the researcher may, for example, devote time to sharing her experiences and opinions with the participants;
- relinquish control over the research, in the sense that the observed should have some control over the data, be able to express themselves, and if need be, contest the descriptions and explanations offered by the ethnographer;
- pay closer attention to the narratives of the ethnographic text, to the politics of representation, and to how ethnographic texts construct reality.

4.3.3 What is specifically feminist about feminist methodology?

These are the main guiding principles of feminist ethnography. However, the majority of feminist scholars (Dickens, 1983; Harding, 1987; Wheatley, 1994) are not convinced that a specific feminist research methodology actually exists. What, we may ask, is specifically feminist about feminist methodology? Are the above methodology prescriptions exclusive to a feminist ethnography or are they to be found in other ethnographic styles, like ethnomethodology, interactionism, phenomenology and so on?

In the early 1990s, a debate on precisely this issue was conducted in the columns of *Sociology*, the journal of the British Sociological Association. Hammersley argued that 'many of the ideas on which feminist methodologists draw are also to be found in the non-feminist methodologies' (1992a: 202), and he therefore contested the claim that there was something specifically feminist in so-called feminist methodology. In reply to Hammersley, a number of feminist scholars stressed that feminist research was not homogeneous and that it comprised a variety of stances: from those which most radically embraced the idea of a feminist methodology (Patti Lather, Dorothy Smith), through more neutral ones (Beverley Skeggs), to sceptical positions (Judith Stacey, Elizabeth Wheatley). However, all of them pointed out that it was somewhat suspicious that the allegation that feminist methodology is nonsense had been made by a man.

The issue is evidently complex and difficult to resolve. Whilst it is indubitable that the *theory* (scientific or social) is profoundly modified when a gendered gaze intervenes, the *methodology* appears to be much less permeable.

Consequently, the distinction between traditional (male) ethnographic methodology and feminist ethnography is perhaps less a sharp antithesis than a difference of degree: when women do research, the majority of them pay closer attention (than do the majority of men) to certain methodological aspects. However, this greater sensitivity is not a feature intrinsic to women, for there are many male researchers (especially younger ones) now conducting research on the basis of less traditional (and masculist) models.

4.4 Postmodern ethnography

We live in what has been called the '*postmodern* age,' an expression that first gained currency at the end of the 1970s through the work of French philosophers, most notably Jean-François Lyotard (1924–88) and Jacques Derrida (1930–2004). The postmodern age is characterized by a series of features that contrast it with the modern age, which began (according to some) with the conquest of America (1492) and ended in 1989 with the fall of the Berlin Wall and the dissolution of the Soviet empire.

CASE STUDY
Main features of the modern age

Simplifying to the extreme, we may say that the modern age embraced a realist view which believed in the ostensive and objective nature of reality, and accordingly maintained that it is possible to distinguish between truth and falsehood. Moreover, according to the neopositivists and the critical rationalism of Popper, reality is orderly and can be investigated by means of logic and rationality. Science, the modernist argument ran, is an enterprise fundamentally different from any other human activity, and its truths are not contaminated by the beliefs of the moment because they are objective and impersonal verities arising from man's direct relationship with nature. As Steven Weinberg (Nobel Prize in Physics, 1979) put it, modern science was born by creating a ditch between the physical sciences and human culture: the difference between the rules of nature and those of culture (for example, the game of soccer) is that we do not create the former but merely discover them. According to Galileo Galilei (1564–1642), the inventor of the experimental method together with Francis Bacon, we create (socially) only the languages with which we describe the laws of nature; but those laws exist independently of any language.

CASE STUDY
Postmodern thought

Although a basic definition of postmodernism has yet to be established, one may say that postmodernism (also called *poststructuralism*) is a philosophy that attempts to undermine current ideologies and single truths. Drawing on the philosophical theories of Friedrich Nietzsche (1844–1900) and Martyn Heidegger (1889–1976), postmodern thought claims that all general theories explaining history, nature or the world – Marxism for instance – are nothing but 'metanarratives': they are, that is to say, constructs which endeavor to fit reality into specific paradigms but are constantly thwarted by the onset of pluralities and elements which resist such pigeon-holing. Consequently, new knowledge and new rationality must dispense with unitary and universal models and instead be compound, pluralist and regionalized, so that every sector of reality has its own logic.

Postmodern thought has also developed an interesting approach to text analysis, and in particular a school of literary criticism known as 'deconstructionism' (Derrida). Starting from relativist principles, or at least eschewing grand theory, this approach criticizes the overarching theoretical and anthropocentric constructs of Western culture. It propounds the *anti-systematicity* and *lightness* of thought, as opposed to the intellectualism of the Western tradition, and thus lays the basis for a critique (or a dissolving) of the notion of 'subject.'

Postmodern thought (which is sometimes lumped together with relativism or constructivism) also maintains that the distinction between nature and culture does not adequately explain the contemporary situation with its huge (and constantly increasing) number of 'hybrid' objects (Bruno Latour) or 'mixtures' (or 'cyborgs' as Donna Haraway terms them): frozen embryos, transgenic seeds, whales fitted with radio-transmitter collars, contact lenses, silicone-enhanced breasts (also lips and buttocks), subcutaneous microchips, transplants of artificial veins, livers and hearts (or ones of animal origin), facial plastic surgery, hair transplants, and the like – objects of this kind are the fruit of co-penetration between nature and culture (i.e. human inventions).

Finally, postmodern thought argues that reality is disordered and irrational, that the strength of scientific explanations is not based on evidence but on rhetoric, and that only relative and conventional truths exist.

Postmodern ethnography springs from methodological reflection within the cultural paradigm of postmodernism that transposed its principles into ethnographic practice. 'Postmodern ethnography' is an umbrella term used to denote several variants of the approach: *interpretative ethnography* (Denzin, 1997), *critical ethnography* (Kincheloe and McLaren, 1994) rooted in the sociology of Pierre Bourdieu, *ethnographic philosophy*, and *autoethnography* (Reed-Danahay, 2001). There is insufficient space here to itemize the differences between these styles. But it is important to have a mental map of a sector which is rapidly expanding and diversifying.

Postmodern ethnography is a strand within the post-colonial anthropology (see Marcus and Fischer, 1986; Clifford and Marcus, 1986) that conducts lucid and pitiless analysis of the ethnocentric prejudices of traditional anthropology, a science whose objective and factual prose concealed an attitude of superiority towards 'other' cultures. Such analysis has provoked what has been called the 'crisis of representation' by throwing into question the ways (rhetorical, stylistic and textual) in which cultures are described and objectified (see 15.4.2).

Postmodern ethnography disputes the authority of the objective participant observer and criticizes the classical ethnographies (those described in previous sections) for being realist, impersonal and falsely neutral (Denzin, 1997). These ethnographies found their authority from the principle 'I know because I was there,' which needs to be dismantled. Moreover, participant observation perpetuates, perhaps unwittingly, the repressive scientific purpose (Turner, 1989: 13) for which it was invented: that of observing and noting the behavior of prisoners, the mentally ill and the poor, thereby exerting control over them, the 'panoptic gaze' (Foucault, 1975) is a limitless intrusion into private life which, in the name of an extreme interpretation of the rights of science, tramples on the rights of people, treating them as objects.

The postmodern research movement has raised doubts over the privilege of any one method for obtaining authoritative knowledge about the social world. According to postmodern ethnographers, objectivity and impartiality are not features of the ethnographer's interpretative work, but fictions promoted through rhetorical strategies of textual type known as the 'poetics and politics of writing' (Clifford and Marcus, 1986). In other words, it is through writing (for example, the drafting of the ethnographic account or the research report) that the ethnographer's *interpretations* (subjectivity) are transformed into *data* (objectivity). The researcher thus constructs fictitious cultures through narrative. From whence derives the expression 'paper cultures,' which indicates that writing artificially constructs representations of cultures often distant from the lived experiences of the participants (see 15.4.1).

The effect of this style of cultural critique is demystification: it detects interests behind and within cultural meanings expressed in ethnographic texts; it reveals forms of domination and power; and it is consequently often put forward as a critique of ideology. Radical deconstructionists indeed believe that totalizing theories are highly restrictive, hegemonic, and even fascist. They therefore discern in 'semiotics, the study of contemporary life as systems of signs . . . a major tool of demystifying cultural critique' (Marcus and Fischer, 1986: 114).

Many postmodern ethnographers believe that instead of understanding *the other* more fully, what field workers should do is gain a fuller understanding of themselves, by uncovering their prejudices, ideology and tacit knowledge. As we saw in 3.6.1, this process of 'conscientization' has been called 'reflexivity': the writer must analyze every aspect relevant to the process, including his or herself and the style he or she employs in writing. More recently this style has taken the name of *autoethnography*.

CASE STUDY
Autoethnography

The term (and presumably also the concept) of autoethnography is of very recent origin and has developed in the field of television and the cinema. It is a variant on the old standard documentary film. As the term suggests, it differs from the latter in that its subject is the film-maker him/herself. An autoethnography typically communicates the life experiences and thoughts, views and beliefs of the film-maker, and as such it is often considered to be rife with bias and image manipulation. Unlike other documentaries, autoethnographies do not aim at objectivity. However, they are nowhere near as popular as traditional documentaries.

In anthropology and sociology, the activity denoted by this oxymoronic label is considered one of the emergent ethnographic writing practices. It is a genre of writing and research that connects the personal to the cultural, placing the self within a social context. It involves highly analytical personal accounts about the self/writer as part of a group or culture, in a dual endeavor to explain the self to others and to analyze the situation of being different or an outsider.

Autoethnographies are usually written in the first person, and they feature dialogue, emotion, and self-consciousness as relational and institutional stories affected by history, social structure and culture (Ellis and Bochner, 2000). By writing themselves into their own work as major characters, autoethnographers have challenged accepted views about silent authorship, where the researcher's voice is not included in the presentation of findings. This development may have liberated some researchers from the constraints of the dominant realist representations of empirical ethnography because, as Richardson (1995) argued, how are researchers expected to write influences what they can write about. In fact, writing is also a political and institutional act on which the professional careers of the authors themselves depend.

An autoethnography should not be a traditional personal narrative or a simple description or story, or the account of a single event, incident or experience. Even less should it be configured as a solipsistic activity written to the self as the major audience. However, the boundary is very indistinct and few authors manage to fulfill the requirements of an autoethnography; most of them instead lapse into some sort of intellectual masturbation.[1]

Postmodern ethnography has just as many detractors as proponents: indeed, it has been roundly criticized. Whilst the grounded theory tradition appears to ignore the postmodern movements (Travers, 2001b: 171), symbolic interactionists like Gans (1999) maintain that describing one's own experiences (autoethnography) has nothing to do with analyzing what people do, how institutions work, or what problems are of concern to communities. One suspects that turning into oneself and examining one's inner lucubrations is a convenient alternative to the demanding and time-consuming task of fieldwork. Moreover, if the researcher focuses on his or her own actions and thoughts, with no practical or methodological payoff, he or she may wind up in a self-reflexive dead end. Ethnomethodology is likewise distant from the subjectivism, phenomenologism, and relativism entailed by postmodern ethnography (Lynch, 2004) and which give the impression that someone has lost touch with reality.

4.5 Breaking news . . .

The last century has bequeathed to us a hotchpotch of new (or allegedly new) ethnographic approaches which, with perhaps excessive nominative zeal, have proliferated: *constitutive ethnography* (Mehan, 1979: 16–24), *institutional ethnography* (Smith, 1986), *performance ethnography* (McCall, 2000), *global ethnography* (Burawoy et al., 2000). Only time will tell how genuinely innovative these proposals are, or whether they are merely makeovers of already-existing approaches. For reasons of space I shall discuss only two of them.

4.5.1 Global Ethnography (GE)

At the end of the 1970s the American sociologist Aaron V. Cicourel and the German sociologist Karin Knorr-Cetina (1981) set about founding a sociology which would connect (micro) interactions with (macro) social structures. Their intention was to merge the microsociological and macrosociological traditions, which hitherto had moved in separate directions. Their proposal (called the 'micro-macro link') was subsequently revitalized, albeit for different purposes, by the American social theorist Jeffrey Alexander (1987) and the American sociologist Randall Collins (2004). Today it has received renewed impetus from the global ethnography (GE) proposed by the American sociologist of work, Michael Burawoy and nine young scholars, all part of a dissertation discussion group led by him.

They start from the assumption that globalization challenges current social scientific methods of inquiry and units of analysis because it destabilizes the embeddedness of social relations in particular communities and places. Ethnographic sites have been globalized by connections that traverse multiple spaces and permeable and contested boundaries. The fact that ethnographic settings extend across time and space raises practical and conceptual problems for ethnographers, and political problems as well. However, if ethnographers place themselves within the time and space of social actors 'living the global,' they can show how global processes are collectively and politically constructed, and demonstrate the variety of ways in which globalization is grounded in the local. GE envisages the local and global dimensions as mutually constitutive and examines how local struggles and global forces shape each other reciprocally. For example, Lynne Haney, one of these authors, has examined the welfare agencies of a country – Hungary – now reconstructing its welfare institutions after decades of socialist rule. She describes all too painfully the human consequences of the 'forces' – the IMF, the World Bank, UNESCO and the Western think tanks – that have advised, indeed coerced, the former socialist countries to base their welfare systems on the precepts and practices of the United States. In Hungary this new form of colonialism has led to the materialization of need, the reduction of 'welfare' to poor relief, and a system that is humiliating and stigmatizing.

According to Burawoy, globalization is not a hyper-level macro process. Rather, it can be studied 'from below' by participating in the lives of those who experience it. Burawoy and his pupils set out methodological principles for 'extended case study' and which should inform well-crafted ethnography. They bring globalization 'down to earth' and show how it impacts on people's everyday lives (they examine, amongst others, Kerala nurses, US homeless recyclers, Irish software programmers, Hungarian welfare recipients and Brazilian feminists) through the medicalizing of breast cancer, dumping of toxic waste, privatization of nursing homes, deskilling of work, denial of welfare rights and the assertion of body politics.

4.5.2 Institutional Ethnography (IE)

Similar purposes are pursued by institutional ethnography (IE), which can be defined as a method which enables people to explore the social relations that structure their everyday lives. It was first developed as a 'sociology for women' by the Canadian sociologist and feminist Dorothy E. Smith (1986), and it is now used by researchers in the social sciences, education, human services and policy research. Smith uses the metaphor of the cube, which appears in three dimensions when its points are connected, to illustrate how IE maps the translocal relations which co-ordinate people's activities in particular local sites.

Like GE, IE also empirically investigates the micro-macro connections amongst local settings of everyday life, organizations and translocal processes of administration. It examines how social systems and institutional relations shape individual experience; how macro-level political discourse and organizational knowledge translate into micro practices that impede educational access, govern employment opportunities and shape the quality of life.

CASE STUDY
Vocational training policies

Human capital theory pervades vocational training policy and continues to ascribe blame for being unemployed to a lack of education and skills of the 'unskilled.' However, in a study of employment training programs, Grahame and Grahame (2000) examined the notion of 'skill.' They showed how the skill deficit-model permeates employment training policy and program planning and is imposed on the disadvantaged (poor, racial/ethnic minorities women). On studying Asian immigrant women, Grahame and Grahame found that participants entered employment training with a variety of skills, and that there was a discrepancy between their perceptions of their skill needs and that of the employment training system. Although participants and the community agencies recognized that English language proficiency was the most pressing need of the Asian participants, enrollment on English language courses was prohibited because this was not permissible according to parameters fixed by the job training agencies. Programs continued to emphasize work habits, not English language skills.

IE considers social relations as systematic processes and practices that control people's lives through ruling relations, which can be defined as the textual venues (such as legislation, governing boards, program planners, management or administration) where power is generated and perpetuated in society across multiple sites. Power is centrally important to analysis as it illuminates practices that marginalize, and shows how ruling relations are conveyed through knowledge, experience, discourse and institutions.

IE also aims to merge research and practice. From a practical point of view, it contributes to adult education and human resource development by: (a) addressing both micro and macro contexts; (b) connecting issues across multiple sites; (c) revealing the ability of texts to shape and control lives in unrecognized ways; and (d) providing practical tools which foster change at the local level by assisting adult educators in finding ways to change our lives and the lives of others – individually, organizationally and socially. IE is a well-organized and growing network of scholars such as Marjorie DeVault, Peter Grahame and others (see http://faculty.maxwell.syr.edu/mdevault/Default.htm).

4.6 Concluding remarks

The methodological styles described in this chapter cohabit with the more traditional, but no less current and efficacious, styles outlined in the previous chapter. Consequently, a wide variety of theoretical-methodological approaches today rely on ethnography as their principal methodology. Which of them is selected depends on the researcher's theoretical position, inclinations and sensibility.

Having completed this necessary survey, the following chapters will concentrate on how ethnography is actually 'done,' describing in detail the main steps, problems and remedies of this fascinating research practice.

KEY POINTS

- The new ethnographic styles stretched the term 'ethnography' with a consequent dilution of its meaning into a multitude of sometimes contrasting and contradictory senses so that it grew synonymous with qualitative studies.
- 'Reception ethnography' studies audiences of media products (television, radios, books etc.). This approach threw back traditional mass media theories, stating that consumers were not at all the passive recipients of meanings: they actively produced their own meanings.
- Feminist ethnographies are different from male ethnographies in two aspects: on the one side they aim to reveal the social relations which reproduce and maintain social inequalities, particularly against women; on the other side they follow a set of guiding methodological principles: ethics, active listening, conscientization, 'giving voice' to marginalized groups, reflexivity and caring.
- Postmodern ethnography is a strand within the post-colonial anthropology that conducts lucid and pitiless analysis of the ethnocentric prejudices of traditional anthropology, a science whose objective and factual prose concealed an attitude of superiority towards 'other' cultures. Such analysis has provoked what has been called the 'crisis of representation.'

KEY TERMS

Autoethnography (see pp. 62–3)	It is a genre of writing and research that connects the personal to the cultural, placing the self within a social context. It involves highly analytical personal accounts about the self/writer as part of a group or culture, in a dual endeavor to explain the self to others and to analyze the situation of being different or an outsider.

Crisis of representation (see p. 61)	The throwing into question of the ways (rhetorical, stylistic, textual) in which cultures are described and objectified. According to the postmodern ethnographers, objectivity and impartiality are not features of the ethnographer's interpretative work, but fictions promoted through rhetorical strategies.
Global ethnography (see pp. 63–4)	An attempt, carried forward by Michael Burawoy, to study globalization 'from below' by participating in the lives of those who experience it; to grasp the micro-macro link through 'extended case study'; and to bring globalization 'down to earth,' showing how it impacts on people's everyday lives.
Institutional ethnography (see pp. 64–5)	A method of inquiry proposed by social relations that structure their everyday lives. It empirically investigates linkages among local settings of everyday life, organizations, and translocal processes of administration; how social systems and institutional relations shape individual experience.
Modernism (see pp. 59–60)	The modern age embraced a realist view which believed in the ostensive and objective nature of reality, and accordingly maintained that it is possible to distinguish between truth and falsehood.
Postmodernism (see pp. 60–1)	It is a philosophy that attempts to undermine current ideologies and single truths. It also maintains that the distinction between nature and culture does not adequately explain the contemporary situation with its huge (and constantly increasing) number of 'hybrid' objects. Finally, postmodern thought argues that reality is disordered and irrational, that the strength of scientific explanations is not based on evidence but on rhetoric, and that only relative and conventional truths exist.

RECOMMENDED READING

For undergraduates:

- Moores, Shaun (1993)
- Travers, Max (2001a)
- Travers, Max (2001b)

For graduates:

- Spenser, Jonathan (2001)
- Kitzinger, Celia (2004)

For advanced researchers:

- Hammersley, Martyn (1992a)
- Gelsthorpe, Loraine (1992)
- Ramazanoglu, Caroline (1992)

SELF-EVALUATION TEST

Are you ready for the next chapter? Check your knowledge by answering the following open-ended questions:

1. What are the main differences between the traditional ethnographies and the new styles?
2. What novelties were introduced by the 'ethnographic turn' in media studies?
3. What features are shared by feminist and postmodernist ethnographies?
4. Why is it problematic to talk of 'feminist methodology'?
5. What is autoethnography?
6. What criticisms have been made of postmodernist ethnography?

Note

1 This is not to say that I am against masturbation. It is an activity which gives pleasure and does not hurt anyone. Indeed, the assertion of the well-known film-maker Woody Allen's character is: 'Don't knock masturbation. It's sex with someone I love' (in *Annie Hall*, 1977). Nevertheless, masturbation is an action that gives pleasure only to oneself, not to anyone else. I prefer ethnographies whose reading gives pleasure to an audience larger than just the author him or herself.

5

Designing Research

Hlade's Law

If you have a difficult task, give it to a lazy man – he will find an easier way to do it.

LEARNING OBJECTIVES

- To understand what a research design is and the purpose that it serves.

- To learn how to identify, conceptualize and construct a research topic.

- To understand and control one's pre-assumptions.

- To gain confidence in the construction of operational definitions.

5.1 Introduction

Reality has many facets; not all of which can be studied by a single research study alone. For this reason the research problems that ethnographers set themselves should not, and cannot, cover every aspect.

When ethnographers design their research, they need to define the meaning of some phenomenon for the practical purposes of their study. They do so by:

- connecting different concepts together;
- observing and interacting with social actors;
- selecting information-gathering strategies; and
- deciding which aspects to explore and which to ignore, etc.

Research design is concerned with precisely these decisions. To put it in more technical – and at first sight somewhat daunting – language, as they proceed with their research, ethnographers must define the:

- attributes relative to the research topic;
- empirical indicators of these attributes;
- operational definitions with which to collect and record information;
- units of analysis; and
- research sample.

Not all these decisions are taken consciously. Quite the opposite, in fact, for a researcher is a human being not a robot. However, there is no doubt that these decisions are taken, and repeatedly so, during research.

The research design is therefore one of the crucial phases in any inquiry. On it depends a conceptual rigor which is not always present in ethnographic research, and which in fact prompts one of the criticisms most frequently made of ethnography: that it is imprecise and lacks rigor.

5.2 The interactional work of interpreting actions

Look at Photograph 5.1.

Photograph 5.1

What does it show: a human being? A man? A face? A white man? A person with dark hair? A young man? A son? A citizen? A customer or user? A resource for the country? A sexual object (why not?)? Something else besides? The answer is: all these things (or none of them) *simultaneously*. It all depends on the aspects that interests us or that we want to emphasize.

Likewise, when talking about his dog, the Viennese philosopher Alfred Schutz said:

> I look at him as my friend and companion Rover . . . without a special motive, not induced to look at Rover as a mammal, an animal, an object of the outer world, although I know that he is all this too (1953: 8).

What does this tell us? With this example Schutz recalled the 'conventionalist' thesis. Conventionalism argues that the relationship between an object and its name is not absolute but arbitrary. Consider the symbol below (Figure 5.1). It can assume at least four different meanings (and you will certainly be able to think of others).

If you remind yourself of the approaches discussed in previous chapters, ethnomethodology and postmodernism would have no hesitation in embracing Schutz's position. Consequently, when ethnographers observe and take notes on events, they are not recording a reality that exists 'out there' independently of themselves as observers, because:

> strictly speaking, there are no such things as facts, pure and simple. . . . They are, therefore, always interpreted facts. . . . This does not mean that, in daily

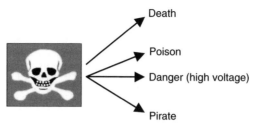

Figure 5.1   One sign for four meanings; therefore four different symbols

> life or in science, we are unable to grasp the reality of the world. It just means
> that we grasp merely certain aspects of it, namely those which are relevant to
> us either for carrying on our business of living or from the point of view of a
> body of accepted rules of procedure of thinking called the method of science
> (Schutz, 1953: 5).

If the bare facts do not exist, the ethnographer is obliged not only simply
to record the facts that he or she observes but also to interpret them. In other
words, the classifications that ethnographers draw up by observing the
actions of actors are therefore essentially *constructions* due in large part to
their mental schemes and practical needs. Do you not believe this? Read the
following example.

CASE STUDY
Science in action

Between October 1975 and August 1977 the French philosopher and sociologist
Bruno Latour, a leading figure in science studies, conducted ethnographic
research at the Salk Institute, a Californian university research center situated at La
Jolla, San Diego.

Latour entered the community of Salk scientists and stayed with them for 21
months, just as anthropologists used to live among African tribes or clans. He
adopted the same attitude of surprise as well. But above all he used a 'gaze' that
was ingenuous and naturalistic; the same gaze that in a classroom would perceive
(for example), not the mathematical formulas written on the board by the lecturer,
but only signs and, 'ultimately . . . chalk on the board. On adopting this radically
materialist stance, a laboratory seems an environment made up essentially of
signs, or better, *inscriptions*:[1] traces, spots, points, histograms, recorded numbers,
spectra, peaks, and so on' (1979: 88, note 2) are present everywhere. These
inscriptions are produced by 'inscription devices' (scientists, technicians,
machines and laboratory equipment constantly connected to a computer or a
printer, which produce outputs).

In Latour and Woolgar's theory, a laboratory is a system of statements (words, assertions, affirmations) and inscriptions. According to Latour and Woolgar, there are five types of statements. They lie at a higher level than inscriptions and are arrayed in a hierarchy according to the degree of arbitrariness attributed to them by the community of scientists (see Figure 5.2). In other words, the lower levels in the scale are occupied by (what scientists consider) to be facts, while the higher levels are occupied by opinions (pp. 76–80) (for details on this important case study, go to www.sagepub.co.uk/gobo).

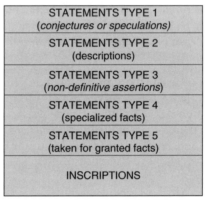

Figure 5.2   The stratification of statements

Latour and Woolgar would probably not find even a single scientist willing to admit that their findings correspond to the laboratory reality, or that their classifications are real – not because they are not – but because classifications are always the constructions of those who produce them; they are inventions.

Nor could it be otherwise, for, as cognitive psychologists have shown, the process of understanding, remembering and recalling information is a mix of recognition and construction. What we codify and store is our interpretation of an event (a representation), not the event itself. By drawing the inference, we add something of ourselves to the event. Hence, because we have performed this act of conglomeration, we are no longer able to distinguish what we have seen or heard from what we have inferred; or under the influence of 'scripts' which induce us to reconstruct events in stereotypical form, we invent/remember details non-existent in the event remembered. Consequently, what an ethnographer remembers is a mixture of the event that has really occurred and items drawn from the standard elements offered by the mental script.

**CASE STUDY
The pitfalls of memory**

The influence exerted by scripts on the perception, interpretation and memory of an event has been the subject of numerous studies, most of them conducted during the 1970s. By way of example, we may take the experiment conducted by Anderson and Pickert (1978). A group of students were told to read a description of a building, and while they did so, imagine themselves as its potential pur-chasers. A second group of students were instead told to read the description while imagining themselves as burglars. Each group was then asked to recall the description. Owing to the influence of the two different scripts (that of purchaser and that of burglar), the first group remembered features from the purchaser's point of view, while the second group remembered features from that of the bur-glar. It was if the two groups had read different descriptions (for another case study, go to www.sagepub.co.uk/gobo).

Given that the ethnographer in part creates the facts that he or she then records, it is advisable for him or her reflexively to monitor the construction activity (which is often unconscious). The research design is therefore an opportunity (more than an encumbrance) because it helps the researcher decide more con-sciously what to look at – or in other words, include within his or her observa-tional range. Just as Schutz decided to see his dog as a friend (rather than as a mammal), so the ethnographer in an organization may decide to look at infor-mal relations rather than hierarchies, conflicts rather than harmony and consen-sus, efficient departments rather than chaotic and disorganized ones, irrational aspects rather than rational ones and so on.

We may therefore say that the ethnographer's work, at bottom, consists in using concepts and inventing new ones (unfortunately less and less frequently).

5.3 Constructing the research topic

Patton's Law

A good plan today is better than a perfect plan tomorrow.

Except for cases where research ensues from specific intentions or hypotheses, the research topic is initially only non-specific and nebulous. It is so for numer-ous reasons. When research is commissioned, contrary to what one might expect the commissioners have often only a vague idea of what they want to know, and their cognitive interest only becomes clear (*is constructed*, one might say) during the colloquium and interaction with the researcher. In other cases, the commis-sioners (especially if they are private individuals) are more interested in solving a problem than in analytical reflection. Even in the most normal case of research projects presented to funding bodies, the project is unlikely to be an exact copy of the research actually done. Finally, in the case of self-commissioned research (theses, dissertations and post-doctoral research), the research topic only assumes precise form *in the course* of the research or results from negotiation with the heads of the organization that the researcher wants to study. I deliberately use the term research 'topic' (i.e. concepts) rather than the more frequent 'object,' because it should be clear by now that the world of the social sciences is populated more by concepts than by objects. In order to clarify this statement – which at first sight might seem provocative – I shall cite the following example.

CASE STUDY
Understanding the orient

The Palestinian writer Edward Said (1936–2003) has argued that the object that we in the West call 'the Orient' is actually a 'European invention' or a fiction, the product of an imaginative geography. Of course, there are real living cultures in the lands which Europe denotes with the term 'Orient.' However, Said observes, emphasizing the many differences rather than the many similarities between Europe and the so-called Orient, insisting that these conceptual categories are dichotomous and often the opposites of each other, pertains to an imagery which over time has been discursively *constituted* by Western explorers, art dealers, novelists, historians, anthropologists and archaeologists. But there is also a political dimension to the matter, stresses Said. This fictional construct serves to justify the West's position of superiority: 'The relationship between Occident and Orient is a relationship of power, of domination . . . Orientalism, therefore, is not an airy European fantasy, but a created body of theory and practice in which . . . there has been a considerable material investment' (1978: 5–6).

So what we call 'objects' are in fact concepts, topics shaped by theoretical assumptions which, in their turn, are based mainly on common-sense knowledge rather than on scientific knowledge, as the following case studies will show.

CASE STUDIES
Researching family and poverty

Consider two examples: research on the family, and studies on poverty. The family is a much less palpable object than is commonly believed. Discuss what it is that constitutes a family with your classmates or professor. Is a group of monks or students living under the same roof a family? Is a gay couple a family? Must there be a couple for a family to exist? If you answer 'yes,' then you exclude separated or divorced mothers (with children). In the past, 'family' meant the union of two people of opposite sex (i.e. a heterosexual couple) formalized by a marriage ceremony. Today the *concept* of family is very different and extends to include many other types of relationship, and social research has adjusted accordingly. Which is another example of how society influences science.

Take the second example, that of studies on poverty. Try to define a poor person: that is, someone who can be defined as poor by someone above the poverty line. You will see that poverty too is something impalpable – even if this statement may seem ridiculous. But if we set aside the starving children on television, and concentrate on the poor in Europe or America, we realize how difficult it is to define a poor person (i.e. specify the concept). Is poverty only an economic phenomenon? If so, how can we account for elderly people who live in conditions (commonly defined) as poverty, but it is then discovered when they die that they had a large sum of money in the bank or hidden under the mattress? Is not poverty, therefore, a cultural phenomenon as well? And if we cannot define poverty clearly, how can we begin to study it?

In conclusion, therefore, social phenomena are primarily concepts, ideas (Hayek, 1949; Jarvie, 1972).

5.4 Outlining the research topic

In light of the previous discussion it seems clear that – unless definitive hypotheses have already be formulated – a research topic is defined with greater precision *in the course* of the research: the focus narrows, new aspects (ethical, social or political) of the problem emerge, and resources are totted up (funding obtained, time available before deadlines or number of collaborators). This is a strength of qualitative research, not a weakness; an element of its flexibility and adaptive ability diametrically opposed to the rigidity of much quantitative research, which 'bends' the research topic to the requirements of the method (rather than the reverse).

The decision to restrict the cognitive field is usually taken after *problematizing* three levels which recur and interweave in ethnographic research:

(1) conceptualization of the phenomenon to investigate;
(2) operational definition; and
(3) choice of the type of sample to use.

Indeed, several authors (among them Spradley, 1980: 34; Hammersley and Atkinson, 1983: 175; Silverman, 1993: 46) have written that the 'funnel' is the best metaphor with which to describe the course of ethnographic research.

When selecting a research topic, it is preferable to avoid overly ambitious projects, because they carry high risks of dispersion or may produce only superficial results. A preoccupation with obtaining a complete picture of a phenomenon with just one research project is the best recipe for wrecking an inquiry (Silverman and Gubrium, 1994).

A research design should also be made flexible so that it can be adapted to the irregular flow of decisions required to deal with unexpected events in the field;

as exemplified, for instance, by the American organization scholar, Alvin W. Gouldner. While Gouldner was studying the bureaucracy of a small American mining company, a wildcat strike unexpectedly forced him to modify his initial design, and he therefore shifted to study – and then to development of a general theory about – group conflicts. It is therefore important for the research design to be 'cognitively open': that is to say, configured so that 'the unexpected is expected.' Well known in this regard is Blumer's (1969: 148) proposal that the concepts and categories of research should be treated as 'sensitizing concepts' (guiding concepts) rather than as 'definitive concepts.' The former do not enable

> the user to move directly to the instance and its relevant content [in that they] give the user a general sense of reference and guidance in approaching empirical instances. Whereas definitive concepts provide prescriptions of what to see, sensitizing concepts merely suggest directions along which to look.

Sensitizing concepts help researchers to approach the empirical reality by ensuring that they can always correct themselves.

5.5 Managing researchers' pre-assumptions, pre-judgments and prejudices: The role of reflexivity

Baruch's Observation

If all you have is a hammer, everything looks like a nail.

Before I describe the three main levels of a research design, I would stress a danger ever-present in the researcher's work of interpretation: that, like authors who unthinkingly use assumptions about the 'Orient' (Said), he or she may be *excessively* conditioned by his or her pre-assumptions and prejudices.

Prejudices may be either positive or negative. We may be favorably disposed towards the socially excluded (as were some members of the Chicago School) or hold a negative attitude towards them (as did the structural-functionalist theory of the American sociologist Talcott Parsons). Whether positive or negative, this is always a prejudice. All of us therefore have pre-assumptions, make pre-judgments and harbor prejudices: they are inescapable. However, our reasoning may be more or less influenced by them; we may be biased by them to a greater or lesser extent.

And here the reflexive attitude by the researcher comes into play. The social sciences are (unfortunately) replete with culture-bound theories.

CASE STUDY
Who is deprived?

The American anthropologist James P. Spradley recalls that in the 1960s the theory of 'cultural deprivation' came into fashion. This theory was an attempt to explain the educational failure of numerous children, the majority of whom belonged to particular social groups: native American, black, Hispanic. Although this was seemingly a progressive theory critical of the American social system, it overlooked the fact that these social groups had developed sophisticated and adaptive cultures that were simply different from the ones espoused by the traditional educational system. This is a typical example of the distortion produced by the prejudices present in researchers' culture. In other words, 'cultural deprivation is merely a way of saying that people are deprived of "my culture"' (Spradley, 1980: 14). (For another case study on European ethnographers' prejudices toward Eskimos, go to www.sagepub.co.uk/gobo.)

Widely acknowledged today, therefore, is the risk of attributing characteristics to the culture being studied which do not belong to that culture but stem instead from the researcher's prejudices (Cicourel, 1964; Garfinkel, 1967; McHugh, 1968; Zimmerman and Pollner, 1970; Mehan and Wood, 1975). Scientists are in danger of ingenuously constructing a sociological object into which they transfer the properties of the conceptual apparatus used for their research.

Is it possible to escape from this circularity? The broad debate on the question that developed in the past essentially answered 'no, from a theoretical point of view it is not.' From a more practical point of view, however, it should be borne in mind that the hermeneutic circle is remediable to various extents. As the American cultural anthropologist Clifford Geertz (1926–2006) wisely put it:

> I have never been impressed by the argument that, as complete objectivity is impossible in these matters (as, of course it is), one might as well let one's sentiments run loose. As Robert Solow has remarked, that is like saying that as a perfectly aseptic environment is impossible, one might as well conduct surgery in a sewer (1973: 30).

It is therefore possible to invent strategies that can help the researcher reflexively to avoid gross errors, at least, and partly to remedy the irremediability of the hermeneutic circle. One of these strategies is *conceptualization*.

5.6 Conceptualizing the topic

Stated in technical language, the main aim of research is to *determine the status of cases on an attribute relative to a concept* (or research topic). To the uninitiated this expression may seem incomprehensible. Nevertheless, examples will help clarify its meaning. I begin with a very simple one.

Anne is 5 feet 10 inches tall. Lucky her, one might say! But leaving aside (understandable) feelings of envy and concentrating on the apparently incomprehensible phrase above, we may state as follows: the *concept* (research topic) could be the population of London; one of that population's *attributes* is height; the *case* is Anne; and her *status* on the attribute 'height' is 5 feet 10 inches tall. Not convinced? Consider another example.

We want to study the quality of the relationship between telephony companies and their customers. Quality is made up of many attributes: the speed with which calls are answered; efficiency in handling requests for information; the attention paid to dealing with complaints; and so on. Let us take the last attribute: our research might conclude that the five companies in the sample are largely inattentive to customer complaints. Using technical language, what we have surveyed is the status (inattentive) of the five cases observed on the attribute 'ability to deal with customer complaints' relative to the research topic (concept) 'quality of the relationship with customers.'

Why have I called 'height' an *attribute* rather than a characteristic or property of the population of London? Likewise, why have I called the 'ability to deal with customer complaints' an *attribute* rather than a characteristic or aspect of a business organization?

Because *characteristic* or *aspect* imply that height or the ability to deal with customer complaints are *properties of the objects* 'person' (in the former case) or 'organization' (in the latter), that they are components of those objects, and that the researcher's task is only to observe them and measure them. The term *attribute* more clearly conveys the idea that these are concepts which the researcher *attributes* (constructively) to his or her research topic. What are improperly called the characteristics of an object are not 'things'; rather, they are 'cognitive instruments' which always result from a discretionary operation performed by the researcher.

5.6.1 Decomposing the topic

It is evident from these examples that it is important to reflect carefully on the topic of one's research before going into the field and making observations. Conceptualization helps clarify what information is necessary for the research and must be collected in the field.

The first step in conceptualization consists in reflecting on the relations between the research topic and its attributes. For this purpose the research topic is broken down into simpler elements or parts (see Figure 5.3).

This cognitive process suggests which aspects should be carefully observed and which can be omitted from observation as irrelevant or liable to make the research too extensive – bearing in mind that here 'omit' does not mean eliminate but 'leave in the background.' Given that observing everything is cognitively impossible, it is advisable to focus on a few aspects and study them with care. This is entirely natural, for the memory and inferential processes have already made this selection without our being aware of it.

5.6.2 Research questions

Reflection on the research topic (or concept) and breaking it down into its attributes helps the researcher define the units of analysis and, subsequently, the sample. If these operations are neglected, information will be collected on cases so disparate that comparative analysis will be difficult. As the researcher reflects on the relation between the attributes and the research topic, a number of questions arise. These are the so-called 'research questions.'

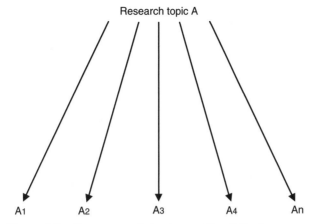

Figure 5.3   The research topic and its attributes

CASE STUDY
Research questions at work

To grasp the importance of this point fully, consider the following imaginary conversation between two colleague researchers:

A   I want to study the doctor/patient relationship . . .

B   Why precisely that relationship and not something else, like health policies, hospital bureaucracy, the lobbies of doctors and pharmaceutical companies?

A   Because I'm interested in interactions.

B   So you've got a specific theoretical approach in mind, have you?

A   Yes, I'm interested in interactional approaches.

B   What do you mean by interaction? What interactions do you want to observe? Those between the doctor and the patient or also those between the patient and the doctor's secretary, those between the doctor and his secretary, or the interactions among the patients in the waiting room?

A   Er . . . I don't know . . . I'll have to think about it . . .

B   But what aspect of the doctor/patient interaction do you want to observe? What particular details interest you? Welcome rituals, presentation rituals, the doctor's rhetorical strategies, misunderstandings between the doctor and the patient, the patient's difficulties in describing his symptoms, the power relation and asymmetry between them?

A   I don't know . . . I don't know . . . I've still got to think about all that . . .

Although B's insistent questioning might seem rude (and reminiscent of Garfinkel's breaching studies), these research questions are in fact extremely useful for A because they prompt him to reflect on his research topic and to specify and circumscribe it. Moreover, as you will have noted, this kind of exercise is much more fruitful if it is conducted with another person or in a group, rather than by one researcher engaged in solitary meditation. After all, four eyes are better than two, as the saying goes.

Obviously, it is not always necessary for the researcher to ask him or herself all these questions *before* entering the field. But it is certain that conceptualization is a necessary pre-requisite for accurate research because it breaks a research topic down into empirically observable aspects. In addition it helps to formulate 'clear and testable research questions' (Yin, 1984: 29–35).

5.6.3 The role of theory in conceptualization

You will certainly have noticed that the research questions asked in the above imaginary dialogue privilege a particular approach, one which concentrates on the participants' actions rather than their inner states. It dwells on what people do, as opposed to what they think, and it focuses on relations rather than individuals. As Sacks (1992) points out, this approach requires the researcher to deal with what is most directly observable (actions) while giving only secondary importance to motives, attitudes and mental schemes. The latter are not eliminated (as they were by behaviorism) but may eventually be reconsidered on the basis of what is seeable and hearable: namely actions and conversations:

> The question that ethnographers have traditionally asked – 'How do participants see things?' – has meant in practice the presumption that reality lies outside the words spoken in a particular time and space. The [alternative] question – 'How do participants do things?' – suggests that the microsocial order can be appreciated more fully by studying how speech and other face-to-face behaviors constitute reality within actual mundane situations (Maynard, 1989: 144, quoted in Silverman, 1993: 54).

An ethnographic account therefore does not have to coincide with the meanings expressed by people or with their thoughts, because 'the sociologists' rendering of trivia in everyday life cannot by definition correspond to the actors' experience of trivia' (Schwartz and Jacobs, 1979: 183). As Silverman critically remarks, 'if ethnography reduces social life to the definitions of the participants, it becomes a purely "subjectivist" sociology which loses sight of *social* phenomena' (1993: 54).

The same considerations apply to cognitive anthropology and to psycho-sociological research on the social representations that reveal mental models or cognitive schemas stable or recurrent within a social group or an organization. These maintain that culture is located in the minds and hearts of social actors and, according to the famous expression of the American cognitive anthropologist, Ward Goodenough (1957), consists of 'whatever it is one has to know or believe in order to operate in a manner acceptable to its members' in all requisite social situations. On this view, a culture can be described by reconstructing categories, taxonomies and systematic rules to produce something akin to an ethnographic algorithm whereby the person applying it is mistaken for a competent member of the group. Geertz draws an apt analogy with a Beethoven quartet: 'no one would, I think, identify it with its score, with the skills and knowledge needed to play it, with the understanding of it possessed by its performers or auditors' (1973: 11). Just as the music does not consist of the score, so a society does not consist in its rules.

5.7 Operationalizing concepts: Why do we need it?

The research work of the ethnographer consists mainly in making sense of events (that he or she observes) by classifying them.

EXERCISE 5.1

Consider the way that nursing staff at many rest homes keep the elderly residents in bed as long as possible. Why do you think they do so? Discuss this question among yourselves or with your professor and try to find an explanation.

This behavior may be a *sign* or a *clue* of:

(1) the nursing staff's concern for the well-being of the elderly residents;
(2) the existence of practices designed to achieve greater social control; or
(3) an organizational response to a shortage of staff.

The relation between the event and the three different concepts (explanations) proposed takes the form of a *relationship of indication*, where the event is *evidence* for the presence or otherwise of a particular concept. It is not a prerogative of scientific reasoning (and even less of quantitative methodology). It is a formal property of common-sense reasoning. In other words, when social actors (researchers included) interpret behavior, they constantly connect together concepts and attributes, indicators and variables. Interpretation is nothing but the rapid, tacit and recurrent activation of relationships of indication. Garfinkel, explicitly borrowing an expression from the Hungarian sociologist and philosopher Karl Mannheim (1893–1947), has called this process the 'documentary method of interpretation':

> The method consists of treating an actual appearance as 'the document of,' as 'pointing to,' as 'standing on behalf of' a presupposed underlying pattern. Not only is the underlying pattern derived from its individual documentary evidences, but the individual documentary evidences, in their turn are interpreted on the basis of 'what is known' about the underlying pattern. Each is used to elaborate the other (Garfinkel, 1962: 691).

5.7.1 Operational definitions
We now examine a topic which has often been considered (by qualitative researchers) to be a 'mere positivistic worry.' I refer to the operational definition.

Are you ready to learn something different from what the traditional textbooks on qualitative methods maintain?

CASE STUDY
What is difficult?

My dissertation consisted of a study of the 'response process' in standardized interviews, that is, interviews using a questionnaire. At that time, the end of the 1980s, there existed numerous (mainly behaviorist) studies on the behavior of the interviewer or on standardized questions (wording, question order, item order, response alternatives and so on). But there were relatively few studies on what happens *during* an interview and on response behavior, or the interactional process (between interviewer and respondent) which produces the response. This required study of the interview from the respondent's point of view, not from that of the researcher or interviewer, as had hitherto been the usual practice.

My dissertation was based on listening to, and discourse analysis of, around a 100 tape-recorded standardized interviews which four interviewers had kindly made for me. One of the things that I wanted to focus upon was whether respondents found it relatively easy to reply to closed-ended (or multiple choice) questions, or whether they had difficulties in selecting a response alternative. The first methodological problem that I encountered concerned the concept of 'difficulty.' By simply listening to the tapes (seeing that I had not been present during the interview), how could I decide when the respondents were finding it difficult to answer? What for me seemed to be difficulty might not seem so for another researcher who listened to the tape after me (the concept of reliability). I wanted my interpretations to be well-argued, in order to forestall the criticisms of carelessness or arbirtrariness certain to be made of my work by survey researchers annoyed by my findings and critical of the standardized interview (see Gobo, 2006). To solve my methodological problem, I first established the meaning (therefore the definition) of 'difficulty in selecting a response alternative' and then considered what might be good indicators of this concept. In short, I invented an operational definition of 'difficulty.' For the record, I operationalized the concept by means of three indicators:

1. the time taken by respondents in selecting a response alternative;
2. the perplexities/hesitations that they expressed; and
3. their comments disapproving or critical of the multiple-choice format.

Operational definition consists of the set of conventions that guide the researcher's interpretative activity. It is called *operational* (in order to distinguish it from the kind of *lexical* definition found in dictionaries) because it tells us what *do*: it has, that is to say, a practical intent. Hence, through these conventions the status of each case on the attribute X is determined, assigned to one of the categories established, and recorded so that it can be analyzed with the techniques that the researcher intends to use. Many of these conventions are customs which guide the knowledge-gathering process. Among these customs are the procedures used to gain access to the field, the devices (guarantees, informal contracts etc.) employed to overcome the actors' diffidence, the way in which the ethnographic notes are collected, and the procedures followed to check the truthfulness of the replies obtained.

The operational definition helps the ethnographer to discipline the observation, the information-gathering, and the attributes that he or she deems connected to the topic studied, within a relationship of indication. In other words, the operational definition gives rigor to the researcher's interpretative activity. Although Glaser and Strauss (1967) and Denzin (1971) recommend that the operational definition of the concept be developed only *after* the research has begun, when the researcher has got an initial understanding of the phenomenon and 'the situated meaning of concepts is discovered' (Denzin, 1971: 268), there is nothing to stop the researcher from developing it *before* the research starts if he or she already has specific hypotheses to control (see 5.8).

The operational definition is the cognitive activity unique to science that distinguishes it from other knowledge-gathering endeavors. All the other cognitive activities to be found in science (like formulating hypotheses, sampling, generalizing, drawing comparisons, making forecasts, checking the veracity of statements, etc.) are also present in common-sense reasoning. But operational definition is not. It enables us to 'problematize the observation' (Cicourel, 1964: 128), *de-naturalize* the social world that we are investigating, in contrast to the behavior of the member who observes it as natural, obvious, taken-for-granted, normal. If we consider the last case study expounded, a lay person would obviously be unlikely to operationalize the concept of 'difficulty' as I did. At most, he or she would stop at the level of the definition: that is, he or she would ask (would problematize) 'what is a difficulty?' A scientist, however, must go further than this.

5.7.2 Rescue the variable!

Osborne's Law

Variables won't. Constants aren't.

As in the case of indicators, qualitative researchers have been much criticized for their use of variables and their belief that qualitative research should not be curbed by such rigid restraints. This contention was put forward in a well-known article by Blumer (1956) where he argued against 'variable analysis.' However, Blumer was criticizing not the use of variables in itself – 'obviously the study of human groups calls for a wide range of variables' (1956: 683) – but their standardized use, meaning the automatic use of the same operational definition for any research: 'each of these variables, even though a class term, has substance only in a given historical context. The variables do not stand directly for items of abstract human group life' (1956: 684). However, for historical reasons, Blumer's article has been considered only in its more superficial aspects. The majority of qualitative researchers have 'thrown the baby out with the bath water,' forgetting that the use of variables and indicators is part of common-sense reasoning. We saw in 5.7 that indicator-based reasoning is intrinsic to the 'documentary method of interpretation'; we shall now see that variables, are constantly present in our discourses and thoughts too. Consider the following verbal exchange between student A and two of his friends who he sees eating slices of cake in the cafeteria:

A   How's the cake?
B   So so.
C   For me it's quite good.

What difference is there between this evaluation and the scale of five response alternatives (very good/fairly good/half and half/fairly bad/very bad) commonly used in questionnaires? None.

EXERCISE 5.2

Consider weather forecasts. Go to the web page of *The Times* newspaper entitled 'weather services' (http://www.timesonline.co.uk). Look at the range of (response alternative) weather concepts. Then answer the following: what are the response alternatives of 'rain'? And 'snow'? How many for 'hail'?

Are these not variables? Of course they are. Hence the polemic waged against variables by qualitative methodologists and researchers is groundless. Indeed, if we analyze the work of ethnographers without too many ideological prejudices, we find that they use indicators and variables to distinguish among the status of attributes.

CASE STUDY
Indicators and variables in Balinese cockfights

Clifford Geertz studied the clandestine bets wagered on cockfights in Bali. It seems odd that Geertz should have chosen such an esoteric topic for research; yet he wrote that it was 'a revelation of what being Balinese "is really like" as these more celebrated phenomena' (1972: 417) like art, forms of law, educational models, and so on. Geertz watched a total of 57 cockfights and constructed the meaning of the practice, the logic of betting and other details. He then classified the clandestine bets (using a dichotomous variable, I would say): 'deep' and 'shallow.' In the former case, usually:

> the amounts of money are great (as opposed to smaller amounts of money wagered in shallow games), much more is at stake than material gain: namely, esteem, honor, dignity, respect – in a word . . . status. It is at stake symbolically, for (a few cases of ruined addict gamblers aside) no one's status is actually altered by the outcome of a cockfight (p. 433).

But how could a deep game be distinguished from a shallow one? How could the observer know that one type of situation rather than the other was in progress? What was it that differentiated between the two types of game?

Geertz lists 17 'facts' (p. 473) – what we can straightforwardly call *indicators* – for the presence of a deep game. The first of these indicators was:

> A man virtually never bets against a cock owned by a member of his own kingroup. Usually he will feel obliged to bet for it, the more so the closer the kin tie and the deeper the fight. If he is certain in his mind that it will not win, he may just not bet at all, particularly if it is only a second cousin's bird or if the fight is a shallow one. But as a rule he will feel he must support it and, in deep games, nearly always does (1972: 437).

By the way, first cousin or second cousin and so on reflect status in the variable kingroup! Had he so wished, Geertz could also have constructed a grid showing the frequency of each of the 17 indicators. For example, he could have associated the indicator 'kin loyalty' with the variable 'betting against a kinsman's cock,' and then added the following alternative responses: 'never,' 'sometimes' and 'often.' The systematic observation might have shown that there was kin loyalty in 95% of cases, or in only 72%. The latter finding would have made a major difference to the assessment of the level of the community's compliance with the kin loyalty convention – which at first sight had seemed unwaivering.

EXERCISE 5.3

Read the whole of Geertz's essay and then answer the following question: what are the remaining 16 indicators for the presence of a deep game?

To summarize everything said thus far, and to do so in technical language, the operational definition transforms the indicators relative to the attributes of a concept into variables. A variable is therefore the outcome of the operational definition, its terminal, the device with which the researcher collects information or analyses him or her ethnographic notes. Indicator and variable are therefore two sides of the same coin: the indicator pertains to the conceptual plane; the variable pertains to the practical one. Variables serve to detect differences and to communicate them. The main difference from quantitative research is the *standardized use* of these devices (see Table 5.1). Unlike survey and experimental researchers, ethnographers do not reify, objectualize or standardize their devices, using them always in the same way in all their research. They instead construct their devices *situationally*, finding *ad hoc* remedies for every research problem.

Table 5.1 Some differences between quantitative and qualitative research

| Terms | Concepts (meanings) | |
	Quantitative research	Qualitative research
Operational definition	An activity that must be done before beginning research	Activity rarely done before beginning research. More frequently it is performed *during* research, when the researcher has gained understanding of the phenomenon

Table 5.1   Some differences between quantitative and qualitative research—cont'd

	Concepts (meanings)	
Terms	**Quantitative research**	**Qualitative research**
Indicator	*Standardized* conceptual device to design the understanding of a phenomenon	*Situational* conceptual device to better understand the relationship between evidence and the underlying pattern
Variable	*Standardized* operative device for *measuring* a phenomenon	The possibility of measurement is rejected. Variables are *situational* operative devices for improving the rigor of the researcher's interpretation
Hypotheses	Assertions to be *verified* or *tested*	Assertions to be *checked* or *documented* through rhetorical devices

5.7.3 Conceptualization and operationalization: a reflexive process

In ethnographic research the coding of an event is not the final act in the data-gathering process; rather, it is only an intermediate stage in the construction of the variables. Given the reflexive and spiraling nature of ethnographic research (see Figure 5.4), the operational definition is partly or wholly recast in successive phases of research: the concepts, hypotheses and indicators change. Hence conceptualization and operationalization interweave in a constant reflexive process

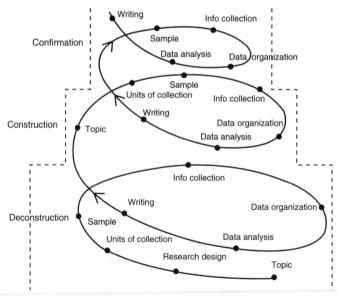

Figure 5.4   The (spiral-shaped) model of ethnographic research

of reciprocal adjustments by virtue of the possible re-specification of the original formulation of a concept, or the re-conceptualization of the datum: 'a series of empirical indicators relevant to each data base and hypothesis must be constructed, and, last, research must progress in a formative manner in which hypotheses and data continually interrelate' (Denzin, 1971: 269).

To conclude: the operational definition is of decisive importance in giving coherence to the researcher's interpretations and in reducing the disputability of his or her results; certainly not giving them certainty, but at least endowing them with greater intersubjectivity.

5.8 Inventing hypotheses

Another commonplace view of qualitative research is that it approaches its research topic devoid of hypotheses, its intent being merely to understand and describe phenomena (Agar, 1986: 12). Yet, I believe that having hypotheses does not conflict with this intent, for hypotheses (to repeat once again) are also forms of common-sense reasoning which we routinely use, often unconsciously.

CASE STUDY
Hypothesis as a form of common-sense reasoning

Consider the following two examples:

- You are on the way to catch the bus. From a distance you see a large crowd of people at the bus stop. What do you do? Walk faster because such a large number of people means that the bus is about to arrive? Or do you think that there is no point in hurrying because the bus must have had an accident or broken down? Each of the three options that you consider is a hypothesis.

- You are driving your car. At a certain point there is a queue of vehicles in front of you. What do you think? That the queue has formed: (a) because of an accident; (b) because of road works; (c) because of traffic lights ahead? In this case, too, you have unconsciously produced three different hypotheses which may have practical consequences according to which of them seems most plausible. If it is the first, you will make a U-turn (watch out for the police!) and look for another route to your destination. If you instead decide to wait until the traffic starts moving again, you may check your hypotheses and discover the cause of the tailback.

Hence *from the conceptual point of view*, a hypothesis is an assertion – conjectural in nature – about the relationships among certain attributes of a research topic. Instead, *from the operational point of view*, a hypothesis is an assertion about the relationships between two or more variables. Glaser and Strauss (1967), Schatzman and Strauss (1973), Strauss and Corbin (1990) argue that hypotheses are indispensable for research, but they should be formulated and verified only *after* the ethnographic notes have been collected (inductive hypotheses) so that the researcher goes into the field without preconceived ideas. The American anthropologist Hymes (1978), the British methodologist Silverman (1993: 44) and the well-known market researcher Yin (1984: 29–35) instead maintain that an ethnographer can conduct an hypothesis-oriented ethnography perfectly well if he or she already has a good level of knowledge about the culture that he or she is studying. As Silverman ironically points out, 'qualitative research would look a little odd, after a history of over 100 years, if it had no hypotheses to test!' (2000: 8).

Hypotheses may therefore be made either before the information is collected or afterwards. Moreover, whether hypotheses are generic or specific depends on the amount of knowledge about the topic that the researcher believes he or she possesses. In the former case (genericness) we may formulate *working hypotheses*, in the latter *guiding hypotheses*.

CASE STUDY
Guiding hypotheses

Guiding hypotheses have been used, for example, by the American psychologist David Rosenhan in his well-known study – a quasi-experimental ethnography – on the construction of mental illness by psychiatric institutions. Prompted by the doubt (widespread at the time in the scholarly community) that mental illness 'may not be quite as accurate as people believe they are' (1973: 250) or a 'myth,' Rosenhan formulated the hypothesis that insanity was a construction by psychiatric hospitals and psychiatrists. He therefore asked himself the following question: 'Do the salient characteristics that lead to diagnoses reside in the patients themselves or in the environments and contexts in which observers find them?' (Rosenhan, 1973: 250). The answer could be obtained:

> by getting normal people (that is, people who do not have and have never suffered symptoms of serious psychiatric disorders) admitted to psychiatric hospitals and then determining whether they were discovered to be sane and, if so, how. If the sanity of such pseudopatients were always detected, there would be prima facie evidence that a sane individual can be distinguished from the insane context in which he is found . . . and abnormality is carried within the person. If, on the other hand, the sanity of the pseudopatients were never discovered, serious difficulties would arise for those who support traditional modes of psychiatric diagnosis (p. 250).

In order to test the initial hypothesis, eight researchers gained admission to 12 different psychiatric hospitals in five states of the USA. Although they behaved entirely 'normal' from the outset, all the researchers were kept in hospital for several months and then discharged with a diagnosis of 'schizophrenia in "remission".' To see whether the tendency toward diagnosing the sane insane could be reversed (1973: 252), Rosenhan conducted a second ethnographic experiment, which represented a sort of counter-proof. He told the medical staff of a teaching and research hospital – who knew of Rosenhan's previous research but claimed that such gross errors could not happen at their hospital – 'that at some time during the following three months, one or more pseudopatients would attempt to be admitted' (p. 252). Out of the 193 patients admitted to the hospital in that period, 41 were identified as pseudopatients by the staff. But Rosenhan stated that 'no genuine pseudopatient (at least from my group) presented himself during this period!'

(For the risks run by those who work with hypotheses, go to www.sagepub.co. uk/gobo).

EXERCISE 5.4

We have seen that *from the operational point of view* a hypothesis is an assertion about the relationships between two or more variables. Look at the following assertions (which are three hypotheses) and find the variables. Then compare your answers with mine at www.sagepub.co.uk/gobo.

1. Students of political science are more politically left-wing than students of engineering.
2. Working students sit fewer examinations than full-time students.
3. AIDS (Acquired immune deficiency syndrome) is a disease that afflicts gay people.[2]

5.9 Drawing models

Models are graphical representations of hypotheses, which are the verbal equivalents of models. A hypothesis may be *descriptive*, in that it states the existence of a relationship between two attributes or variables, or it may be *explanatory* because it hypotheses a causal relation: the model A → B is the graphical equivalent of the sentence: 'it is hypothesized that there is a relationship between variable A and variable B, and that this relationship is unidirectional, in the sense that A influences B but is not influenced by it.' For example, Strauss, Buchner, Ehrlich, Schatzman and Sabshin (1964) conducted an empirical study on the rules and informal agreements present in various psychiatric hospitals. They then constructed a causal model in which the differences among the rules applied at the hospitals were explained by the existence of different patient care practices. But these practices were in their turn conditioned by the professional models learned (at different schools) by the hospital staff, models which reflected different psychiatric ideologies.

The relationship between variables may take various forms; a simple association, a symmetric relation or an asymmetric relation. In the first case, we know that there is a relation between variables A and B, but it is not clear which of the two influences the other. In the second case, both variables influence each other. In the third case, the asymmetry is due to the fact that a specific causation has been constructed through our research.

Finally, variables may be of three kinds: independent, dependent and intervening. The first are variables that exert influence on other variables; the second are those which undergo the influence; the third are variables which intervene in the relation between two variables, impinging on both and reducing the strength of a relation. What I have just said concerns the logic of causality and has nothing to do with statistics. Some examples will clarify the point.

EXERCISE 5.5

According to you:

1. does the *fashion industry* (A) condition the way in which a *society* (B) dresses itself; or
2. does the *society* (B) condition the *fashion industry* (A), or
3. do they reciprocally influence each other (symmetric relation)?

Discuss these issues among yourselves or with your professor. For my view, go to www.sagepub.co.uk/gobo.

Understanding the direction of causation is especially important if ethnography is to provide practical suggestions for administrators and managers. What, one may ask, is the point of social scientists if they are unable to furnish the advice that other professionals cannot?

CASE STUDY
Environmental degradation and civic sense

Consider the depressed state of certain areas of large cities. Is it a *lack of civic sense* (A) that contributes to *environmental degradation* (B), or does *environmental degradation* (B) create a *lack of civic sense* (A)? While the former hypothesis is rather obvious, the latter is more counter-intuitive: it means that if you happen to be in a place which is very dirty, you are not cognitively conditioned to refrain from dropping litter because 'it's already full of rubbish anyway,' whereas you might not drop litter if the place was clean. This second hypothesis belongs to the 'broken windows' theory by Wilson and Kelling (1982) and prompted the policy (renamed improperly as 'zero tolerance') enforced by the Republican Rudolph Giuliani, Mayor of New York from 1994 to 2001. This hypothesis can be summarized by the following example: if a window pane of a building (a school, an abandoned factory, etc.) is broken and not replaced, passers-by will not feel guilty about breaking another pane or panes in the future. If broken window panes are instead immediately replaced, children will be less tempted to break other windows. Hence, if an ethnography conducted in that city or that neighborhood concludes (amongst other things) that a *lack of civic sense* (A) → *environmental degradation* (B), then a policy targeted on education (schools, recreational facilities) is necessary. If instead the study concludes that *environmental degradation* (B) → *lack of civic sense* (A), then the administration should take action on the environment. These are two opposed public policies, and there is often insufficient money to implement both of them.

Spurious associations

Let us now consider the case of spurious association: when, that is to say, we believe that A → B, but this is an illusion because both A and B are influenced by C, an intervening variable which we have not considered. The trap of spurious association is often lying in wait, and it is not always easy to avoid.

As we have seen, if the reasoning is extended to include spurious associations, the research becomes more complex and difficult. But it makes our explanations much less ingenuous, our theories more refined, and social research more credible. Consider the following example, taken from the sociology of music.

CASE STUDY
Are females less talented than males?

In nineteenth-century Vienna, women pianists did not play the music of Beethoven (1770–1827). According to music critics of the time, the reason was that female pianists were not as accomplished as their male counterparts in executing pieces by the great composer. If talent (A) → accomplished execution (B) of Beethoven, then females were less talented than males. What do you think? Do you agree with this explanation? Neither do I. Yet this was the theory argued by the music critics of the time. Do you find it a spurious association? So do I; but can you think of an alternative explanation? The sociologist of music, Tia Denora, has suggested one in an article significantly entitled 'Gendering the Piano.' On reconstructing the social environment of the time, Denora notes that in the 50 years before the advent of Beethoven, both male and female pianists gave public performances. How come half a century later women had become so mediocre at the piano? Denora (1986) notes that Beethoven innovated not only the music of the time but also the manner of its execution: from whence derived the stereotype of the romantic musician flamboyantly emoting at the keyboard. But could a woman perform in the same way? No she could not, because the social conventions of the time would not permit it. Women had to appear restrained and genteel in their public piano performances. Even their clothing was designed to remind them how they should move on the stage: tight bodices with plunging necklines (to show off necklaces and jewelry) restricted their movements. Can you imagine a female pianist decorated like a Christmas tree pounding a piano? Denora also notes that wind instruments (except for the flute) had already been precluded to women because playing them required unfeminine postures and unseemly 'grimaces.' Hence the intervening variable that influenced (supposed) talent and musical performance was the etiquette of the time. It was not that Beethoven's music was unsuited to women; rather, the social conventions of the time that prevented women from playing as the fashion of the time demanded.

(For another interesting case study – taken from evaluation research – on closed-circuit television (CCTV) and crime, go to www.sagepub.co.uk/gobo.)

Spurious associations are very common in both common-sense reasoning and social theory, and in the hard and bio-medical sciences. It is therefore not easy to discover the *principal* cause of a phenomenon (among the *many* that contribute to it).

5.9.1 Simple is more beautiful

Those who argue that models are simplified representations, and that the reality is more complex, are undoubtedly correct. As the Polish semanticist Alfred H. S. Korzybski (1879–1950) in the 1930s concluded in a celebrated phrase: 'a map is not the territory' (1933: 58). However, to entrench oneself in this position is sterile, for those who do so forget the need to communicate and to make themselves clear to others. The simplest theories are usually the most successful ones. They are also the most esthetically attractive, elegant and parsimonious; they comply with the famous principle of *Occam's razor* to the effect that if there are two theories explaining the same thing, it is better to choose the more economical one (that is, the one using fewer concepts). Moreover, software is now available for textual data analysis (NVIVO, Atlas, etc.) which graphically represent hypotheses and theories (which are nothing other than sets of congruent hypotheses).

CASE STUDY
Social loss

Glaser and Strauss (1967) developed a grounded theory of 'social loss.' These two authors noticed that when some nurses discussed deceased patients they did not consider the deaths as equal losses: some deaths were considered grievous social losses (children, young people or mothers of small children); other deaths were treated as almost natural losses (elderly people and the chronically ill).

Glaser and Strauss concluded that a patient's age, education and occupation were key elements in the nurses' judgments of what constituted a social loss. They also noted that the 'composure' of the nurses often broke down when a grave social loss occurred. This theory was depicted by Seale (2000: 170) thus (see Figure 5.5):

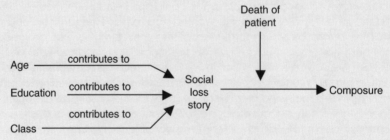

Figure 5.5   Graphical representation of Glaser and Strauss'
theory of social loss

This – *pace* the detractors of formalization – is an excellent example of how attributes/indicators/variables (age, education and class), operational definitions, hypotheses and models play a central role in ethnographic reasoning. Although the provision of models is still a relatively uncommon practice, it is very useful and has great communicative impact. A graphical representation is an extremely intuitive, though necessarily somewhat banalizing, narrative. Consider for instance, the difference between the verbal description of a kinship system and its graphical representation.

5.10 Concluding remarks

In communication studies when discussing the 'audience,' the English mass-media analyst John Hartley has stressed that 'in no case is the audience "real," or external to its discursive construction' (1987: 25), which is a natural or self-evident fact. The so-called 'object' of a research project is always a fiction which serves the needs of the institution or researchers that have conceived it and imagined it as naturally given so that they can monitor and measure it. For this reason research design is not simply a matter of understanding some pre-existing phenomenon.

KEY POINTS

- Strictly speaking, there are no such things as facts pure and simple. There are, therefore, always and only interpreted facts.
- In the majority of cases, the research topic is constructed *during* the research. It is the derivative of the contingent situation, of the constraints and resources present within that situation, of interactions with the commissioners of the research, and with the social actors investigated.
- The world of social sciences is populated more by concepts than by objects. The social phenomena that we study are primarily ideas.
- Conceptualizing a research topic is to break it down into more circumscribed and elementary attributes.
- Operationalizing serves to make the observation more accurate, and it enables researchers to document their findings more convincingly (for themselves and their audience).
- Our cultural pre-assumptions and prejudices tacitly condition (in part) our perception of events. They cannot be frozen or deactivated. However, with the help of conceptualization, we can reflexively learn to deal with them so that they do not excessively mislead us.
- Although objectivity can never be achieved, this is not to imply that 'anything goes.' There are numerous gradations between these two extremes, and it is on these that we should concentrate. As Robert Solow put it many years ago: just because a perfectly aseptic environment is impossible, this does not authorize us to conduct surgery in a sewer.

KEY TERMS

Association   A ↔ B
(see p. 89)

Asymmetric relationship (see pp. 89–90)	$A \rightarrow B$ or $A \leftarrow B$
Attribute (see p. 78)	Aspects, elements or components that the researcher discerns in the phenomenon studied. While the concept of 'characteristic' or 'property' pertains to an objectualist view, the concept of 'attribute' emphasizes the constructive aspect of research.
Conventionalism (see p. 70)	A philosophical theory according to which all principles are not natural but pure and simple conventions.
Dependent variable (see p. 90)	The variable that is influenced by another variable.
Hypothesis (see pp. 87–9)	*From the conceptual point of view*, a hypothesis is an assertion – conjectural in nature – about the relationships among certain attributes of a research topic. *From the operational point of view*, a hypothesis is an assertion about the relationships between two or more variables.
Independent variable (see p. 90)	The variable that influences or contributes to creating the state of another variable.
Indexicality (see pp. 70 and 83)	Term introduced by Y. Bar-Hillel (1954) and reprised by Garfinkel. It indicates that the meaning of an utterance always depends on the context in which it is said. In other words, there are no objective expressions, that is, ones which are context-free.
Indicator (see pp. 81–5)	This is the sign or clue of a concept. It is important to remember that indicators are always cognitive tools, not things as a certain kind of objectivist methodology believes.
Intervening variable (see p. 91)	A third variable impinging on two variables believed to be connected by a symmetric or asymmetric relation. This relation was instead a spurious association.
Model (see pp. 89–93)	Models are graphical representations of hypotheses.
Operational definition (see pp. 81–3)	The set of conventions that guide the researcher's interpretative work and with which the status of each case on the attribute X is determined, assigned to one of the categories established, and recorded so that it can be analyzed with the techniques that the researcher intends to use. The operational definition helps the ethnographer 'discipline' the observation.

Pre-assumptions (see pp. 76–7)	Introduced by the German hermeneutic philosopher Hans-Georg Gadamer (1960), the concept of 'pre-assumption' reminds us that our observations are never direct; rather, they are mediated by pre-formed schemas, common-sense and congealed knowledge which exist *before* experiences and are transmitted by socialization and study.
Research questions (see pp. 78–9)	These help the researcher specify and circumscribe the research topic. Asking research questions is much more effective if it is done with another person or in a group.
Script (see p. 72)	A model or schematized knowledge.
Symmetric relationship (see pp. 89–90)	$A \leftrightarrows B$
Variable (see pp. 83–6)	A variable is the outcome of the operational definition, its terminal, the device with which the researcher collects information. Variables serve to detect differences and communicate them. Indicator and variable are therefore two sides of the same coin: the indicator pertains to the conceptual plane, the variable to the practical one.

RECOMMENDED READING

For undergraduates:
Silverman, David (2006c)

For graduates:
Silverman, David (2005a)

For advanced researchers:
Hammersley, Martyn and Atkinson, Paul (1983a)

SELF-EVALUATION TEST

Are you ready for the next chapter? Check your knowledge by answering the following open-ended questions:

1. The American cognitive anthropologist Michael H. Agar has said that 'hypotheses . . ., samples, and instruments are the wrong guidelines' (1986: 12). The British qualitative methodologist David Silverman has instead said that 'qualitative research would look a little odd, after a history of over 100 years, if it had no hypotheses to test!' (2000: 8). What do you think?
2. Do facts exist?
3. What is the purpose of reflexivity?
4. Why are indicators and variables two sides of the same coin?
5. What is the only difference between common-sense reasoning and scientific reasoning?
6. What does the sentence mean: 'a map is not the territory'?

NOTES

1 Inscriptions originated as stylized signs or commemorative symbols (for example, sepulchral, honorary inscriptions) in the epoch before writing was invented.

2 Although this statement may seem absurd, it is what official medicine believed in 1979, when the first cases of AIDS appeared. Indeed, until 1982 the disease was called GRID (Gay Related Immune Deficiency). Then in 1982, a physician in Denver, Colorado reported a case of a non-gay patient who had contracted the disease from a blood transfusion. The initial hypothesis thus collapsed. This seems a perfect example of Popper's falsification principle at work.

Project Management

6.1 Introduction

The theoretical bases for research are laid down by the research design. However, theoretical goals must be combined with the contingencies of the situation. Project management concerns itself with defining and achieving targets while optimizing (or merely allocating) the use of resources such as time, money, people and materials.

CASE STUDY
The inconclusive debate on call centers

Some scholars have called call centers organizations 'new service factories' in order to emphasize their similarities with the work organizations of the Fordist period: repetitive and rigidly scheduled work, close surveillance, the parceling out of jobs, alienation and the concentration of numerous workers in a single physical place. They equate call center work with so-called 'bad jobs' in services, low-skilled and low-paid and with scant career prospects. Some commentators have even gone so far as to describe call centers as 'computerized Taylorism' based on 'body rental,' or as the 'new factories of the new economy.' Yet these analyses are marred by a reductionism which confuses the part with the whole: they are based on studies of commercial and private call centers, and they neglect public and non-profit ones, which have rather different organizational principles and work practices.

This example helps us to understand the importance of sampling.

6.2 Sampling

Coveyou's Claim

The generation of random numbers is too important to be left to chance.

As you are now able to argue, contrary to the traditional conception of qualitative research, it cannot be conducted without sampling. Indeed, though sampling is obviously a part of scientific endeavor, it is also an activity intrinsic to people's everyday lives: a seller shows a sample of cloth to the customer; in a paint shop the customer skims through the catalog of color shades in order to select a paint; the buyer tastes samples in order to choose a wine or a cheese; and the teacher asks a student questions to assess his or her knowledge about the syllabus. So from now on if you fail your end-of-course examination, you can always claim that the lecturer did his or her sampling badly!

Another commonplace view about ethnographic research is that it has no need of sampling because it is based on case studies, that is, analyses of single settings. This view too, however, is epistemologically groundless, for as Gomm, Hammersley and Foster acutely observe:

> the very meaning of the word 'case' implies that what it refers to is a *case* [setting or instance or example] of something. In other words, we necessarily identify cases in terms of general categories . . . the idea that somehow cases can be identified independently of our orientation to them is false. It is misleading to talk of the uniqueness of cases . . . we can only identify their distinctiveness on the basis of a notion of what is typical or representative of some categorial group or population (2000: 104).

Sampling, therefore, is unavoidable no matter what point of view one takes. The only question is whether one should deliberately govern the process or alternatively leave oneself at the mercy of events.

How is a sample selected? The process moves through two stages: conceptualization (discussed in the previous chapter), and selection of the units of observation. By means of conceptualization the researcher clarifies the attributes of the topic that he or she intends to study; then, for each attribute, he or she determines first the units of observation (i.e. the sampling frame), second the setting(s) to be visited and then the set of cases (the sample).

6.2.1 New observational units

Defining the *units of observation* is of extreme importance if the research is not to be botched and empirically inconsistent.

CASE STUDY
What is an artist?

On analyzing a series of Finnish studies on 'artists,' Mitchell and Karttunen (1991) found that the results differed according to the definition given to 'artist' by the researchers, a definition which then guided construction of the sample. In some studies, the category 'artist' included: (i) subjects who defined themselves as artists; in others (ii) those permanently engaged in the production of works of art; in others (iii) those recognized as artists by society at large; and in yet others (iv) those recognized as such by associations of artists. The obvious consequence was that it was subsequently impossible to compare the results of these studies.

The standard practice in sociology and political science is to choose clearly defined and easily detectable individual or collective units: persons, households, groups, associations, movements, parties, institutions, organizations, regions or states. However, choosing individuals implies an atomistic rather than organic conception of society, whose structural elements are taken for granted or reckoned to be mirrored in the individual, while the sociological tradition that gives priority to relations over individuals is neglected. As a consequence, the following more dynamic units are neglected as well:

- behaviors, social relations, meetings, interactions, ceremonies, rituals, networks;
- cultural products (such as pictures, paintings, movies, theater plays and television programs); and
- rules and social conventions.

Hence, 'a reliable sampling model that recognizes interaction must be adopted [so that sampling is conducted on] interactive units (such as social relationships, encounters, organizations)' (Denzin, 1971: 269).

The researcher should focus his or her investigation on these kinds of units, not only because social processes are more easily detectable and observable, but also because these units allow more direct and deeper analysis of the characteristics observed.

6.2.2 Sampling settings versus sampling individuals or incidents

Having chosen the observational unit, the next step is to select one or more settings on which to conduct the research. For example, Sudnow (1967) and Cicourel (1968) respectively visited two hospitals and two police districts. The third step is then to select the events, individuals or incidents to observe: Geertz (1972) watched 57 cockfights; the Italian anthropologist de Martino (1961) observed 21 victims of tarantism (see 13.5); Becker (1951) observed an unspecified number of professional dance musicians; Goffman (1963) analyzed numerous 'byplays.' This is a widespread practice in ethnographic research, although it is not always performed consciously.

Unfortunately, there is an unconscious confusion in the literature between (sampling) *settings* and (sampling) *individuals, events and incidents.*

These different referents are all denoted by the same term: cases. This creates much confusion, because it leads to sites being confounded with behaviors, settings with individuals and events. The ethnographer does not observe a setting (a hospital, a prison or a company) *per se*, but rather behaviors, rituals and actions (in a word 'incidents') which take place *in* it. Consequently, for the time being I shall avoid using the word 'case,' an ambiguous term which gives rise to several misunderstandings.

The widespread confusion between settings and incidents derives from the treatment of such matters by survey methodologists, who do not study settings but only individuals. In fact, they usually bypass settings and go from observational units (for example, racist attitudes or religious beliefs) directly to individuals (interviewees). For this reason, surveys have been accused for decades of not taking due account of settings.

But the ethnographer proceeds differently. He acts more cautiously because he or she must sample at two levels: that of the setting, and that of individuals or incidents. And for each level (as we shall shortly see) he or she must deal with the problem of representativeness.

Instead, qualitative methodology literature perpetuates this confusion. It is a sign that it has not yet engaged in fully autonomous and innovative reflection on the fundaments of research methodology and is still dependent on survey methodology's cultural frames.

6.2.3 Simple samples versus representative samples

Having chosen the setting(s), the next step is to select incidents or individuals to observe. Having established that ethnographers always conduct their research on samples, it is important to distinguish between a *representative* sample and a sample. Let us return to the initial examples of the shopper and the teacher. Both of them concentrate on a part in order to obtain information about the whole, in the belief that the part (the sample) is *representative* of the whole (sampling frame), which is in some sense its 'miniature.' But whilst a glass of wine is likely to be similar to the entire bottle from which it has been poured, it cannot be assumed that a student knows the entire syllabus because he or she has correctly answered a few questions about it. It is therefore crucial to distinguish between a representative sample (a sub-set which stands as a miniature of the sampling frame) and a sample (a sub-set of occurrences on which every researcher concentrates, whatever the type of inquiry). The glass of wine is a representative sample; the student's answers, instead, can only be a sample.

But is representativeness so important? I believe it is. Consider the two following examples.

CASE STUDY
Sampling school activities

A classic illustration is provided by Berlak et al.'s study of progressive primary school practice in Britain in the 1970s (Berlak and Berlak, 1981; Berlak et al., 1975). They argued that previous American accounts had been inaccurate because observation had been brief and had tended to take place in the middle of the week, not on Monday or Friday. On the basis of these observations, the inference had been drawn that in progressive classrooms children simply chose what they wanted to do and got on with it. As Berlak et al. document, however, what typically happened was that the teachers set out the week's work on Mondays, and on Fridays they checked that it had been completed satisfactorily. Thus, earlier studies were based on false temporal generalizations within cases they investigated (Gomm, Hammersley and Foster, 2000: 109–10).

CASE STUDY
Reductionism 1

Another example is provided by Gouldner (1970: 378–90). He pointed out that Goffman's extraordinary descriptions of the rituals and ceremonies that guide interactions did not reflect the behavior of Westerners as a whole, only the behavior of the American middle class, as Goffman himself (1963: 5) had been the first to state. Moreover, if we consider the recent controversies provoked almost everywhere in Europe by the wearing in public *situations* of particular kinds of veil – like the *burqa* (a tent-like outer garment), the *khimar* or *niqāb* (a veil which covers the entire face leaving only a slit for the eyes) – by Muslim women, we understand even better the extent to which Goffman's observations on facework were culturally situated.

Hence, as also Denzin (1971: 269) has argued, representative samples are extremely useful for ethnographic research, for 'it is necessary for researchers to demonstrate the representativeness of those units in the total population of similar events.' Also Becker (1998b: 67) has reaffirmed this necessary requirement.

As choosing sites and selecting events, individuals or occurrences are both sampling activities, in order to clearly distinguish them I will introduce two different expressions to denote such diverse sampling procedures: 'settings sampling' and 'incidents sampling.'

6.2.4 Sampling settings

Generally speaking, researchers have three main options available to them when choosing a setting: they can opt for either an *opportunistic* (convenience); a *reasoned* or a *random* sample. If we set the last option aside, because it is impracticable in ethnographic research (but only in surveys), two possible choices remain. The former means selecting the first setting that becomes available. The latter instead requires close scrutiny of existing settings and the choice of those best suited to the conceptualization produced during the research design.

Opportunistic setting sample is usually determined by practical considerations: insufficient time for calm selection of settings; a lack of resources, funding or facilities; the laziness of the researcher, etc. This strategy has invariably been regarded with disapproval: indeed, the methodology handbooks dismiss it as 'haphazard.' However, this is a criticism that stems from prejudice, given that an important part of sociological theory, written by authors of such stature as Alvin Gouldner, Melvin Dalton, Howard Becker, Erving Goffman, Harold Garfinkel and Aaron Cicourel, derives from research conducted in convenience settings. Hence, we must either reject these studies or conclude that the criticism of convenience sample is too severe and is not empirically justified.

But, one may ask, if we can get significant results by using an opportunistic setting, why should we bother with the laborious process of reasoned sampling? The answer is because only the latter can protect us against criticism that our research findings are non-generalizable (see 13.9). The examples abound, but here I shall cite only one.

CASE STUDY
Reductionism 2

Gouldner (1954) pointed out that Max Weber's *ideal type* of bureaucracy was based on studies of a particular category of bureaucracies: those which work for a government. Weber's reductionist error induced him to place excessive emphasis on the importance of (democratically defined) formal rules in obtaining consensus. But when Gouldner studied the observance of rules in the private sector, he found that it was obtained through other sources of consensus.

Researchers, who opt for reasoned (setting) sampling, have at least two main options: *purposive* settings sampling and *emblematic* settings sampling.

Purposive settings

Purposive settings sampling consists in identifying sites with an extreme status of particular attributes, or sites which comprise a range of the status available such that all of the possible status are present. For example, we can choose two elementary schools where, from press reports, previous studies, interviews or personal experience, we know we can find two extreme situations: in the first school there are severe difficulties of integration between natives and immigrants, while in the second there are virtually none. We can also pick three schools: the first with severe integration difficulties, the second with average difficulties and the third with rare ones. In the 1930s and 1940s, the American sociologist and anthropologist Lloyd W. Warner (1898–1970) and his team of colleagues and students carried out studies on various communities in the United States. When Warner set about choosing the samples, he decided to select communities whose social structures mirrored important features of American society. He chose four communities (given assumed names): a city in Massachusetts (Yankee City) ruled by traditions on which he wrote five books; an isolated county in

Mississippi (Deep South, 1941); a Chicago black district (Bronzetown, 1945) and a city in the Midwest (Jonesville, 1949).

The emblematic settings

The *emblematic settings* sampling may have up to three features: *average* (the typical provincial hospital, the organization of a typical mountain municipality), *excellence* (a well-known car manufacturing firm) and *emerging* (or avant-garde, like a recent juvenile fashion). *Middletown*, the two famous studies by Robert S. and Helen M. Lynd (1929; 1937), were pioneering attempts to study a typical American community (Muncie, Indiana) by applying social anthropology methods. The households chosen were 'typically' American and not statistically representative. Other examples are Dalton's research (1959) conducted as a covert observer at Milo and Fruhling, two companies in a highly industrialized area of the US; or Kanter (1977), who made a five-year observation of a company with high technological density. Because particular elements are more easily detectable through comparison, it is advisable to observe at least two sites during the course of a research study.

6.2.5 Sampling incidents and individuals

Observation real and proper only begins after the setting has been selected. It is at this point that the ethnographer turns his or her attention to the phenomena which he or she intends to observe (events, individuals, occurrences and so on) according to his or her theoretical perspective.

There are three types of incidents and individuals sampling: theoretical, quota and snowball.

Theoretical sampling

Researchers opt for theoretical sampling[1] when they possess incomplete information about the sampling frame, and consequently select incidents according to their status on one or more attributes identified as the subject matter for research. As Mason writes:

> theoretical sampling means selecting groups or categories to study on the basis of their relevance to your research questions, your theoretical position and analytical framework, your analytical practice, and most importantly the explanation or account which you are developing. Theoretical sampling is concerned with constructing a sample . . . which is meaningful theoretically, because it builds in certain characteristics or criteria which help to develop and test your theory and explanation (1996: 94).

Theoretical sampling performs best with incidents, episodes and occurrences like actions, behaviors and interactions. Less interesting and fruitful is its traditional use, that is, sampling individuals.

Theoretical sampling has three main characteristics:

- incidents are chosen in light of the theory to be developed or verified;
- also 'deviant' incidents are selected; and
- the sample may change in size during the course of the research (Silverman, 2000: 105).

Quota sampling

Quota sampling concerns individuals and groups, not incidents. It is employed for topics which contain a wide range of possible status. Moreover, unlike other types of sample, this one is constructed according to what we believe are the independent variables (see 5.9), those that help explain the phenomenon under study: gender, political preference, education level, etc. There is a theory behind these choices, therefore, and it should be made clear in the conceptualization (see 5.6).

The sampling frame is divided up into as many sub-sets as there are attributes we want to observe, and the proportion of each sub-set in the sample is the same as in the sampling frame. Ethnographic research with a sample of this kind obviously requires a conspicuous investment of time, and it may even last for several years. Consequently, there are few instances of quota sampling in the ethnographic literature. A good example of the application of this sampling method (with non-proportional quotas) in ethnographic research is Jankowski's (1991) study of criminal gangs. Jankowski spent ten years observing 37 different gangs, which he selected according to their ethnicity, size and members' age in Los Angeles, New York and Boston. Another example is Gouldner's (1954) research at a gypsum mine situated close to the university where he taught (a convenience setting, therefore) and which at that time employed approximately 225 people. In his methodological appendix, Gouldner reported that his team conducted 174 interviews – and therefore on almost all the sampling frame (precisely 77%). One hundred and thirty-two of these 174 interviews were carried out with a 'representative sample' of the blue-collar workers at the company, for which purpose Gouldner used quota sampling stratified by age, rank and tasks. He then constructed another representative sample of 92 blue-collar workers, to whom a questionnaire was administered.

Snowball sampling

Snowball sampling involves the picking of individuals only, who display the necessary attributes, and then, through their recommendations, finding other individuals with the same characteristics. If the researcher is lucky, after a few rounds he or she will have a sample made up of numerous participants. The research by Whyte (1943a) provides an example: through his informant 'Doc,' a young unemployed man who frequented the neighborhood social service center, Whyte gradually gained entry into the network of Doc's acquaintances, the people and groups belonging to the 'street corner society.' This type of sample is usually the one best suited to researching highly sensitive topics: socially stigmatized behavior, for example, or behavior of which the subjects are ashamed or which is illegal.

6.2.6 Incidents and individuals sampling as a progressive, interactive and iterative process

Given the spiral path followed by ethnographic inquiry, sampling is not necessarily performed on just one occasion. As the research proceeds, the ethnographer may make several incidents and individual samplings as concepts are refined 'funnel-wise' and hypotheses become more precise. In other words (and this is the distinctive feature of theoretical sampling) the sample changes in function of the concepts and attributes which the researcher wants to document, of the hypotheses that he or she wants to test, and also in reaction to unforeseen events.

Because the researcher cannot conduct observations for 24 hours a day – or in other words, because he or she cannot constantly observe the sampling frame of the practices going on within the sample organization – in order to give system-aticity to his or her observations and generalizability (or 'intra-representative-ness' within the organization) to his or her findings, he or she may decide at what times and in what places to conduct the observation (Schatzman and Strauss, 1973: 39–41; Corsaro, 1985: 28–32). This is not difficult to do, because after some time the researcher will find that social practices tend to repeat them-selves recursively in certain places and at certain times of the day.

Sampling is never an automatic procedure. Instead, it is a process which is:

- interactive, because it engages in dialogue with incidents as and when they arise;
- iterative, because it is repeated; and
- progressive, because the appropriateness of incidents is revealed as the research proceeds.

In summary, ethnographic observations tell us to what extent and how the incidents we have selected are representative.

EXERCISE 6.1

Form a group with two other students, then choose a setting to go and observe. In order not to waste too much time negotiating access to the site, choose a free-entry location like a park, a supermarket, a cafeteria, a railway station, a museum, a library, or a shopping mall.

Now draw up an observation schedule. One of you will be present in the place from 7 am to 11 am; the second from 11 am to 3 pm; the third from 3 pm to 7 pm. Take notes on the types of people you see frequenting the place at those times. Then compare your observations.

Finally answer the following questions:

- Was it really necessary to sample all three time periods?
- If you had made observations during only one of the time periods, would you have collected information representative of behavior in the setting throughout the day?

6.3 Types of participation and degrees of involvement

Ethnographers can become part of a group or an organization in various ways: they may participate from time to time in the organization's life, or they may do so assiduously. In other words, the extent to which they participate and are involved may vary considerably. Spradley (1980: 58) listed five types of partici-pation and involvement (see Table 6.1).

Table 6.1   Participation and involvement[2]

Type of participation	Degree of involvement
Complete	High
Active	Medium-high
Moderate	Medium-low
Passive	Low
Non-participation	No involvement

Source: adapted from Spradley (1980: 58).

There are a number of caveats to be borne in mind. Denzin (1970) warns against assuming two opposing roles, that of complete observer (who has no involvement) and that of complete participant (who feels a high involvement), which he identifies with the old-style ethnographer. The methodological literature requires the ethnographer to strike a balance between participation and observation, between involvement and detachment – or between, to use Davis' (1973) apt terms, the stance of the 'convert' and that of the 'Martian.' This is not always easy to achieve, however, because the actors being studied may demand that the researcher become involved. This is exemplified by the 'Jesus Freaks' studied by Robbins, Anthony and Curtis (1973).

CASE STUDY
Attempting to convert the ethnographer

The members of the cult were convinced that anyone who completely understood their beliefs would automatically be converted to them. They were consequently perplexed to find that the researcher was still not a convert even when he had fully understood their doctrines. They came up with various explanations for the conundrum:

(1) they were mistaken to believe that there is a relation between comprehension and conversion;

(2) the researcher had not fully understood their beliefs;

(3) he was less well disposed towards them than he seemed;

(4) they were not true Christians and the Holy Spirit had not been speaking through them to the researcher; or

(5) a person can be good without necessarily being a Christian.

The repeated attempts by the cult's members to convert the researcher damaged their relationship, which eventually turned into outright hostility: the members thought that the researcher was an impostor, while the latter lost his initial empathy with the cult's disciples.

This episode demonstrates that the interaction between observed and observer involves reciprocal influences which may throw belief (5) or conduct (4) into doubt. One should also remember the role of emotions in the researcher's psychology: Whyte recalls that he began his research as a 'non-participant observer,' but as his relationship with the actors grew more intimate (especially with Doc, his preferred informant), he often found himself in the role of 'non-observer participant.'

6.4 Types of observation

While participation and involvement concern the researcher's attitude, stance and emotional state, observation instead concerns the actors: more specifically, it concerns their perception and knowledge of the researcher, of how he or she presents him or herself to them, and in what guise. Three types of participant observation are usually distinguished in the literature: covert, semi-overt and overt.

6.4.1 Covert observation

In a situation termed 'covert observation' the actors are unaware of the researcher's identity and of the purposes of his or her research: the researcher acts 'incognito,' so to speak. Although this type of observation is relatively rare in ethnographic practice, certain covert studies have become celebrated. For example, Roy (1952) studied blue-collar culture by taking a job in a factory which manufactured railway wagon components, where he worked incognito for ten months. This study was exactly replicated 30 years later by Michael Burawoy. Dalton (1959), as a manager at Milo and at Fruhling – two fictitiously named companies located in a highly industrialized area of the United States – analyzed the discrepancies between the hierarchical structures depicted by the organization chart and the informal power wielded by 'cliques,' relational networks which exerted great influence. Mann (1969) studied a phenomenon unusual in the history of sociology: queues in public places. By carrying out research in diverse settings (theaters, stadiums, agencies, bars and bus stops) and in diverse countries (Australia, Nigeria, Cuba, United States, England, Japan, Mexico and Russia), Mann discovered that the organization of a queue was related to the values system of the culture concerned. Rosenhan and his colleagues (1973) mingled with the patients at psychiatric clinics; while Van Dijk (1987) studied racism by sending people from different ethnic groups to negotiate with car dealers.

Advantages and disadvantages

Covert observation has some advantages as well as numerous disadvantages. The technique is usually employed when it is believed that the presence of a researcher may *heavily* alter the usual behavior of actors (the concept of 'reactivity'). Although the researcher's presence is still bound to influence action, there are topics (for instance racism, unlawful behavior and socially unacceptable practices) which are likely to involve a high degree of reactivity. A second advantage of covert observation is that it does not require negotiation to gain entry to the field: intermediaries, guardians and gatekeepers are avoided at a stroke. However, as said, there are numerous disadvantages to covert observation. First, there is the risk of being discovered and taken to be a spy, with embarrassing – or sometimes dangerous – consequences. Second, it is difficult to comply with organizational rules that documents (sick notes, for example) must be produced to justify absence. Third the researcher is confined to the role assigned to him or her, which means that he or she has little opportunity (especially in routine roles) for cognitive movement to observe other places and other social relations – although the situation is different if, as in Dalton (1959), the researcher occupies a managerial post. Fourth, the researcher is unable to conduct formal interviews or to be excessively insistent in his or her questioning, because 'people will not put up with interviews and observations for which no purpose is explained' (Whyte, 1984: 31).

Ethics and exceptions

Finally, covert observation raises an unavoidable ethical issue. Actors are entitled to their privacy and they have the right to know who they are dealing with, so that they can decide whether or not to take part in the research. Researchers are not police officers, private detectives or investigative journalists. Their code of ethics, as well as recent data protection legislation, do not permit deceit or the betrayal of the interlocutor's good faith. However, there are two situations in which exceptions to these rules are possible. The first is when the researcher conducts his or her observation without interacting with the actors and therefore maintains a certain distance from them. Representative situations of this kind are settings like stadiums, beaches, political rallies, buses, dance halls, queues in public places and public squares. In this case, covert observation is similar to non-participant observation. The second exception concerns situations where the actors under observation perform a public function or provide a customer service (shopkeepers, police officers, front-office staff, shop assistants, bank tellers, etc.), and whose work is therefore impersonal and aimed at satisfying the patient or customer, whether or not this happens to be a researcher. The above-mentioned research by Rosenhan and Van Dijk can be justified on these grounds.

In other situations several authors consider it reprehensible to take advantage of people's good faith, however scientifically or morally valuable the aims of the research may be, and however lofty the researcher's ethical motives (the so-called '*utilitarian ethics of consequences*' model, which is based on the well-known aphorism by the Florentine political thinker Nicolò Macchiavelli [1469–1527] that 'the ends justify the means'). Imagine you are a hospital patient who talks to an ethnographer in the belief that he or she is a medical student (because he or she has been introduced as such) and confide your fears about your illness in him or her. How would you feel?

The decision to opt for covert observation should therefore take account of both the research topic and the profession or position of the actors involved. Covert research may also create moral problems for the researcher him or herself. In a case study on the police, Holdaway (1982) recalls finding himself in situations where the policemen he was observing used violence with suspects. He did not know how to react: defend the suspects (and thus reveal his true identity) or show indifference (which he found morally difficult to accept). Nor is this the only ethical dilemma that arises in fieldwork, as we shall see in Chapter 7.

6.4.2 Semi-covert observation

Standing midway between covert and overt observation is the technique termed either 'semi-covert' or 'semi-overt' according to the perspective from which it is viewed, or according to whether the majority or the minority of the subjects observed are aware that research is going on. In the case of semi-covert observation only some members of the group, organization or community know the identity of the ethnographer. For example, Becker reports 'Most of the people I observed did not know that I was making a study of musicians' (1951: 84). Whyte (1984: 30) recalls that only few of the many people with whom he interacted in the Little Italy neighborhood of Boston were aware of the purposes of his research. Likewise, the knowledge objectives of Soloway and Walters (1977), in their study on heroin users, and of Keiser (1969), who conducted participant observation of the Vice Lords, a neighborhood gang, were known only to their intermediaries and some other people.

6.4.3 Overt observation

Overt observation is indubitably the technique most widely employed by ethnographers and has been used to compile the majority of the ethnographic accounts in the literature. From the point of view of their advantages and disadvantages, the covert and overt forms of observation are the reverse of each other, in the sense that the disadvantages of covert observation are crucial resources for overt observation. In the same way, the advantages of the former are drawbacks for the latter.

One of the main disadvantages of an overt observation is the necessity of obtaining permission to conduct observations in the setting chosen. Gaining such permission often requires the investment of a great deal of time and effort, as we will see in the next chapter.

One advantage of overt observation, however, is that the researcher does not have to perform a specific role or task so that, depending on the organization, he or she enjoys a certain amount of freedom. Finally, the researcher may find it difficult to manage the reactivity inevitably provoked by his or her presence.

6.5 On the border of ethnography: Studying internet communities

A new observation technique has recently come to the fore: so-called online, digital or virtual ethnography (Hine, 2000; Markham, 2005), which consists in studying internet communities in their various forms, such as chat rooms, forums, etc. In certain respects, virtual ethnography breaks with the traditional ways of doing ethnography because:

> all the data is usually collected online without meeting the people concerned face-to-face. The question that arises here is: does ethnography depend upon the physical presence of the ethnographer in the midst of the people being studied? Or does the assumption that an ethnographer must be physically present involve an outdated conception of what is required for ethnographic work? (Hammersley, 2006: 8).

The problem raised by virtual ethnography is both theoretical and methodological: can online cultures be sufficiently understood if only text analysis is conducted? For this is what the method amounts to: the internet ethnographer merely observes and analyzes the texts which appear on the screen, without being able to meet their writers, observe the circumstances and contexts that have produced the text, or have any perspective other than what the internet people write and say about themselves. These problems are obviously not insurmountable and they vary from case to case. But it is difficult to associate this research technique with ethnography when it more closely resembles conversation analysis, discourse analysis, or more generally, text analysis.

6.6 Managing a research project: Work planning and timing

Conducting ethnographic research is a long and complex undertaking. Regardless of the researcher's wishes, it may be subject to interruptions or delays (due to problems in gaining access to the field, for example), or it may suddenly accelerate. Hence, even some years of work may be necessary to bring a project to completion. It is therefore important for the researcher not to lose track of what he or she is doing. A useful tool in this regard is the Gantt chart, which is used to plan a project and to track its progress. The activities planned are defined temporally and depicted by bars of lengths proportional to their durations. Figure 6.1 shows the work planning and timing of an ethnographic action-research project on HIV counseling.

This type of chart was first developed by Henry L. Gantt (1861–1919), who introduced it in 1910. Gantt was an American mechanical engineer, management consultant and industry advisor. His charts were used as a visual tool to show scheduled and actual progress of projects. Accepted as a commonplace project management tool today, it was an innovation of world-wide importance in the 1920s.

6.7 Concluding remarks

In ethnographic research, the transition from concepts to fieldwork is a complex process which requires careful thought and the taking of numerous decisions. The most delicate stage in the process is indubitably the sampling procedure. It is this that gives solidity to the research, increases the generalizability of its findings, and makes them more easily defendable against criticism.

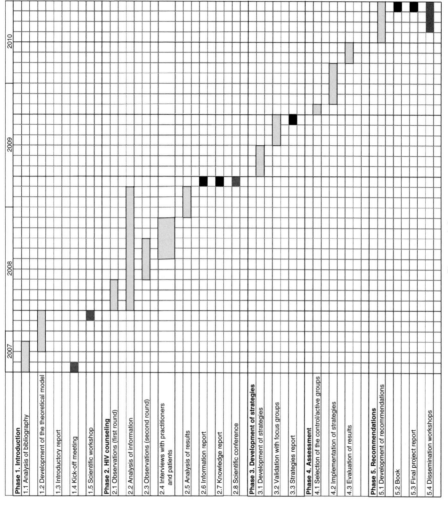

Figure 6.1

KEY POINTS

- Project management is the activity of defining and achieving targets while optimizing (or only allocating) the use of resources such as time, money, people, materials, etc.
- Sampling is unavoidable because, besides being scientific, it is an everyday activity.
- A sample is selected in two stages: conceptualization and definition of the units of observation.
- Representative samples are extremely useful in ethnographic research because they protect us against criticism about the scant generalizability of our research findings.
- It is important to distinguish between sampling settings and sampling incidents or individuals.
- However, representativeness must be reached on both levels.
- Theoretical sampling involves the selection of groups or categories to study according to their relevance to the research questions, the researcher's theoretical position and analytical framework.
- Sampling is a progressive, interactive and iterative process. It is never an automatic procedure.
- Covert research raises significant ethical problems: actors are entitled to their privacy and they have the right to know who they are dealing with, so that they can decide whether or not to take part in the research.
- Conducting ethnographic research is a long and complex undertaking. It is therefore important for the researcher not to lose track of what he or she is doing. A useful tool in this regard is the Gantt chart.

KEY TERMS

Case (see pp. 98–100) This is an instance or example of something. A case is always an item belonging to a more general category.

Covert research (see pp. 107–9) A situation where the actors are unaware of the researcher's identity and of the purposes of his or her research: the researcher acts 'incognito.'

Digital or virtual ethnography (see pp. 109–10) This is the study of internet communities.

Emblematic setting (see p. 103) It is a form of reasoned sampling. This may have up to features: *average* (the typical provincial hospital or the organization of a typical mountain village municipality); *excellence* (a well-known car manufacturing firm); and *emerging* (or avant-garde, like a recent juvenile fashion).

Gantt chart (see pp. 110–11)	A tool useful for planning and timing a research project.
Involvement (see pp. 105–7)	This concerns the emotional resources deployed by the researcher. It modulates among five different degrees: high, medium-high, medium-low, low or no involvement.
Opportunistic setting sampling (see pp. 101–2)	This is a convenience setting, the selection of which is made for practical reasons only. Nevertheless, the majority of the ethnographic studies which have shaped social theory's history have been based on convenience settings.
Overt research (see p. 109)	Indubitably the technique most widely used by ethnographers. All the members of the organization under study know the identity of the ethnographer.
Participation (see pp. 105–7)	By this is meant the degree of the researcher's identification with the group studied. It modulates among four different degrees: complete, active, moderate and passive.
Purposive setting sample (see pp. 102–3)	It is a form of reasoned sampling. It consists of settings with an extreme status on particular attributes, or settings which comprise a range of status such that all possible status are present.
Quota sampling (see p. 104)	It belongs to procedures for sampling individuals or groups. This is employed for topics which comprise a wide range of status. The sampling frame is divided into as many sub-sets as the attributes we want to observe, and the proportion of each sub-set in the sample is the same as it is in the sampling frame.
Reasoned setting sampling (see pp. 101–3)	It requires close scrutiny of existing settings and the choice of those best suited to the conceptualization produced during the research design.
Representative sample (see pp. 100–1)	A sub-set deemed to be a *miniature* of the sampling frame. The attributes of the sampling frame are therefore reproduced on a small scale in the sample.

Sample (see p. 100)	A sub-set of the sampling frame.
Sampling frame (see p. 98)	From the theoretical point of view, this corresponds to the extension of a concept. From the practical point of view, it is the set of single cases constituting a collective phenomenon subjected to study. Synonyms for 'sampling frame' are 'universe,' 'population' and 'complete list.'
Semi-covert research (see p. 109)	A situation where only some members of the group, organization or community studied, know the identity of the ethnographer.
Snowball sample (see p. 104)	It belongs to procedures for sampling individuals. This consists of some individuals who feature the necessary attributes and whose recommendations lead to other individuals with the same characteristics.

RECOMMENDED READING

For undergraduates:
Silverman, David (2005b)

For graduates:
Becker, Howard (1998b)

For advanced researchers:
Gobo, Giampietro (2008)

SELF-EVALUATION TEST

Are you ready for the next chapter? Check your knowledge by answering the following open-ended questions:

1. What is the difference between a sample and a representative sample?
2. What can one learn from Mitchell and Karttunen's survey of Finnish studies on 'artists'?
3. What is the confusion about sampling in which qualitative research is still entangled?
4. Why are interactive units more dynamic and preferable to individuals?
5. What is *theoretical sampling*?
6. Why are criticisms of *opportunistic (setting)* sampling too harsh?

Notes

1 The expression was first introduced by Glaser and Strauss (1967).
2 For details on case studies which have dealt with participation and involvement issues, go to www.sagepub.co.uk/gobo.

Part two
Collecting Materials

7

Entering the Field

LEARNING OBJECTIVES

- To understand the difficulty of field entry.

- To learn how to negotiate access to the field.

- To recognize the key figures in a group or organization.

- To know how to manage one's image and identity.

- To learn from one's errors and start again.

7.1 Introduction

Gaining access to the field is the most difficult phase in the entire process of ethnographic research. Unlike other types of inquiry (the survey, the focus group or the interview) where the researcher may inconvenience the organization, group or individual only briefly, ethnographic research requires a very much greater amount of co-operation from the participants. This requirement drastically reduces the number of organizations or groups on which ethnographic research can be conducted. Second, once access to the organization or group has been gained, the researcher must devote a great deal of time and energy to winning the trust of his or her interlocutors, and to maintaining that trust throughout the research. Otherwise, he or she will meet strong resistance, and his or her understanding of the phenomena observed will be deficient as a consequence.

CASE STUDIES
Lucky and unlucky accesses

In 2003 the Italian sociologist of organization, Attila Bruni, began ethnographic research on an association of volunteer doctors providing basic healthcare for illegal immigrants.

> The director had not replied to the letter from the regional administration, but it only took a telephone call from me to fix an interview and establish the ground rules for my observation. The meeting took place in the office that the director also used as a surgery, and on conclusion of the interview, he raised no objection to my observing the service's day-to-day work. He said that he would inform the personnel and only asked me to go to the center on the same day and present myself to one of his colleagues, responsible for scheduling shifts for the personnel.

> When I arrive at 16:50 (the center opens at 17:00), there are already a large number of people (around 20) waiting in the corridor, some of them sitting on a row of seats outside the surgery . . . I knock on the surgery door. It is opened by what appears to be a youth (a doctor, in fact, but he looks like a youth to me), who is immediately welcoming when he hears my name: 'Of course, I got the e-mail (sent by the chief surgery doctor to notify the personnel of my presence following our agreement), come in!'

> Never before have I begun ethnographic observation with such a welcome, but the surprise is not long in coming: Giuseppe (for this is the doctor's name) wants me to work! He explains that he is on his own (the secretary is absent and the other doctor is late), so if I can help with the administrative part, he can get started with the medical examinations. I am pleased to lend a hand, but I do not want to be a hindrance. However, Giuseppe's tone indicates that he is ordering rather than asking me to help (2006: 132).

David Silverman was not so lucky:

> I have failed to gain access, despite initial expression of interest, in two settings. In a pediatric clinic in the early 1980s, a very conservatively dressed physician, spotting my leather jacket, said I was being 'disrespectful of his patients' and threw me out! Fifteen years before that, as a novice researcher, I let slip over lunch that I was thinking of moving from the UK to North America when I had completed my Ph.D. This attitude was apparently viewed as improperly 'instrumental' by my host organization and the promised access was subsequently refused (2000: 199).

Cassell (1988: 93–5) has divided field access strategies into two phases: 'getting in' (achieving physical access to the place) and 'getting on' (achieving social access).

7.2 The politics of access

A methodology handbook cannot encompass the entire range of the strategies with which access is gained to field sites. These strategies are designed and adjusted according to the characteristics of the organization or group observed, its type (company or institution), its size (large, medium, small or very small), and the aims of the research. They therefore spring from the contingent situation of the inquiry and from the researcher's creativity. Nonetheless, we can establish some guidelines which will help less expert ethnographers, and novices especially, find their bearings.

7.2.1 Physical access . . .

The first thing to bear in mind is the type of observation planned (see 6.4): that is, whether the intention is to conduct covert or overt research.

In covert research

If the researcher opts for the former type of inquiry, the strategies to access the field will differ according to the type of topic studied, and therefore according to the field's accessibility. When the field site is a work organization, the usual practice is for the researcher to get him or herself hired as an employee or as a consultant, doing so by registering with a temporary job agency or answering advertisements in newspapers. The main drawback to this strategy is that the researcher has scant 'bargaining power,' because it is the organization which chooses the researcher, not the other way round. Moreover, the hiree may be assigned tasks different from those described in the job advertisement. In other words, the research design cannot be drawn up until the researcher has been taken on by the organization and has joined its personnel.

In overt research

Overt research requires very different strategies. It first requires *negotiation* with the heads of the organization or the group. This phase may last for differing amounts of time, and it is not always crowned with success. Moreover, the *identities* of the researcher and of the group or organization are created processually during the negotiations. The researcher presents his or her academic credentials and promises to behave in an ethically proper way. The organization asks for *guarantees* that the researcher's obtrusiveness will not cause any slow-down in production. It then marks out the spaces where the researcher may go, and ensures that no problems will arise for the administration and the organization of work, and so on, thereby minimizing the costs of the researcher's presence. Also negotiated is the subject of the *beneficence*, or the advantage that the organization or group may derive from allowing an outsider to observe it. These multiple negotiations usually result in a series of formal pacts or tacit agreements whose function is to establish an initial frame within which to collocate 'reciprocal obligations and expectations' (to use Goffman's term), and to define the boundaries of the ethnographer's action. The pacts and agreements reached are not irrevocable. Rather, they are often purely indicative, because they will be modified during the course of the research as psychological defensiveness and mutual suspicion diminish. Precisely because of its processual nature, in fact, fieldwork involves the partial revision of agreements, pacts and guarantees.

Intermediaries and guarantors

The literature describes four typical figures among the various participants encountered by ethnographers as their research proceeds: the intermediary, the guarantor, the gatekeeper and the informant. The first two perform a leading role during the phase when the researcher gains physical access to the organization and the third and the fourth are of greatest importance during the social access phase. Obviously, this classification is only analytical, given that the intermediary and the guarantor also help foster the collaborative relationship between the researcher and the social actors.

An *intermediary* can be defined as the person who creates the contact, or establishes the communication, between the researcher and certain members of the organization or group.

CASE STUDY
Street corner society

In Whyte's research (1943a) this role was performed by a social worker at the 'settlement house,' a social service agency operating at the heart of Cornerville. When the social worker understood what Whyte wanted, he arranged him an appointment with Doc, a 29-year-old man resident in the neighborhood who had already worked at the settlement house, and to whom Whyte could explain the purpose of his research. Intermediaries are therefore of key importance at the initial stage of research, for without their help the inquiry may never get off the ground. Whyte also found a useful intermediary in the person of the editor of an English-language weekly for the local Italo-American community, who helped him find lodgings in the neighborhood. The editor sent him to the Martini family, who ran a restaurant and rented out rooms above their establishment. But when Whyte arrived at the restaurant, the owner told him that he had no rooms free. The magazine editor then telephoned the Martinis' son, who immediately found a room for Whyte.

The *guarantor* is the person who sets up the relation between the ethnographer and the group or organization. Unlike the intermediary, he or she belongs to the group and is trusted by its members. In Whyte's study Doc was the leader of a local gang (the 'Corner Boys'). Well-known and respected in the neighborhood, he introduced Whyte into Cornerville society, reassuring him that: 'Just remember that you're my friend. That's all they need to know. I know these places, and, if I tell them that you're my friend, nobody will bother you' (1955: 291).

The ideal guarantor is someone who has solid ties with both the cultures involved in the ethnographic interface – that of the researcher and that of the participants – and who knows the latter with sufficient intimacy. In local communities and informal groups, the guarantor is usually a leader, someone exercising authority, a respected professional like a doctor, pharmacist, notary, lawyer or a priest. In formal organizations, instead, the guarantor is the immediate superior of the person in charge of the organization being studied (the 'gatekeeper'): for instance the director of a local health board in the former case or the head of a walk-in service for drug addicts in the latter.

7.2.2 Social access: Gatekeepers

In order to gain the co-operation of the social actors (or participants), ethnographers must be able to get consensus on their projects and win trust. They may therefore be subjected to close scrutiny by the gatekeepers, these being individuals who supervise the organization or group's territory:

> there is in every setting certain persons from whom one needs acceptance in order to gain access to the setting and its participants. [They] control who can be where and what they can hear or see (Schwartz and Jacobs, 1979: 53).

Gatekeepers are part of the culture observed by the ethnographer, and they perform a role of prime importance. They are worried, despite the guarantor's reassurances, that the research may damage the organization's image, and that the researcher's presence may alter its internal relationships. Ethnographers must therefore pay particularly close attention to organizational gatekeepers.

By means of the strategies deployed to gain acceptance by the gatekeepers and the other participants, the ethnographer processually and interactively constructs his or her identity. Not only his or her own identity, though, the participants also construct and reconstruct their own identities in relation to the researcher's. In doing so, they are guided by the desire described by Goffman to furnish a particular image of themselves, to show that they agree or disagree with the values of the organization in which they live or work. As the research proceeds, therefore, the identities of the researcher and of the subjects he or she is studying are reciprocally constructed.

7.3 The researcher's roles and identities

Whatever the ethnographer does in the group or organization, he or she is forced to *assume a role*. He or she is identified with this role by the social actors, and it gives meaning to his or her presence in the community. As Schwartz and Jacobs (1979: 52) stress, 'only one's social role gains one access to persons, situations, and kind of information that other social roles make unavailable.' The researcher can only partially influence the role and identity attributed to him or her because the participants creatively modify the information that they receive. When Barley (1990) was negotiating access to do research in a hospital radiology department, he introduced himself to the managers as an anthropologist, preferring this label to 'sociologist,' which was his actual profession. His identity changed again during the course of the research, because the hospital staff preferred to introduce him to patients as a student, rather than as an anthropologist.

The researcher's roles and identities are therefore constantly constructed during the research process, regardless of his or her intentions and efforts. Whilst it is obvious that, as Goffman points out, although 'each individual is responsible for the demeanor image of himself' (1956b: 84), it is also true that his contribution to that image may be entirely marginal, because he 'must rely on others to complete the picture of him which he himself is allowed to paint only certain parts' (1956: 84). Moreover, identity is not a stable ascribed property that persists for the entirety of the research: face, which is the 'positive social value a person effectively claims for himself . . ., is only on loan to him from society; it will be withdrawn unless he conducts himself in a way that is worthy of it'

(Goffman, 1955: 5 and 10). Finally, the line of behavior with which the ethnographer constructs and claims his or her image tends to assume an institutional character: 'he will find a small choice of lines will be open to him and a small choice of faces will be waiting for him' (1955: 7).

Goffman's acute observations should not alarm us, however. Instead, they should make us aware of the resources (on which we can draw) and the constraints (with which we must comply) during our observation work. In other words, we know that our identity is not attributed to us once and for all. Any errors, lapses or 'false starts' can be repaired interactionally with the cognitive mechanism whereby the present tends to rewrite the past.

In overt research, the ethnographer's presence is almost always obtrusive because it produces embarrassment, unease, stress and alarm in the community of participants. This happens at the beginning of the research, but it may persist until its completion. Yet the emotional, cognitive and social disruption caused by the ethnographer's presence is understandable: the ethnographer is a stranger who approaches the members of the group or organization to observe them. But his or her obtrusiveness and the consequential reactivity of the participants varies from group to group and from organization to organization, according to how receptive the host community is to outsiders. Although the effects of obtrusiveness are often unavoidable, they can be reduced. Let us consider a particularly complicated case: the presence of an adult ethnographer in a community of children.

CASE STUDY
Peer culture at pre-school age

The American ethnographer and sociologist of childhood, William A. Corsaro conducted research in Italian and American nursery schools. Corsaro's research topic was peer culture at pre-school age, and he had to solve a somewhat paradoxical methodological problem: he did not want the children to consider him a teacher or a parent, because this would make them behave towards him just as they behaved towards any adult. Instead, in order to gain profound entry into the children's culture, he had to be considered a non-adult. And yet he was very much a grown-up – with a beard and spectacles to boot. So how could he differentiate himself from an adult? Even if he learned to behave entirely like a child, banal esthetic differences would have constantly reminded the children of his different status. As a consequence, he might experience the hostility that children sometimes show towards adults; or alternatively he might be subject to the demands, expectations and affection that children also frequently express towards grown-ups. In short, his problem seemed insoluble.

EXERCISE 7.1

- What would you have done?
- Try to think of some strategies to solve Corsaro's methodological problem.
- Discuss them among yourselves or with your teacher.

In order to reduce his obtrusiveness and to differentiate himself from adults, Corsaro (1985) devised various strategies whereby he *did the opposite* of normal adult behavior:

(1) he adopted a 'passive' stance in interactions;
(2) he went into places almost exclusively frequented by the children;
(3) he granted all the children's requests;
(4) he sat very close to them, keeping silent and communicating non-verbally;
(5) he answered their questions and refrained from asking any;
(6) he never tried to initiate or terminate an interactional episode;
(7) he did not intervene to re-start interrupted activity;
(8) he did not settle disputes; and
(9) he did not co-ordinate or direct activity.

Corsaro's strategy is very similar to the approach used by other ethologists: Dian Fossey (1932–85), for instance, who studied a group of mountain gorillas in Rwanda for 18 years until she was murdered by poachers. Fossey's method (1983) – revolutionary at the time because gorillas were considered extremely dangerous and unapproachable – consisted in gradually getting close to them, adopting a passive posture, and waiting for the gorillas to approach her in their turn. She was the first person to have voluntary contact with a gorilla when one of them touched her hand. She was able to sit amongst them and play with them and their young (see the movie *Gorillas in the Mist: The Story of Dian Fossey* directed by Michael Apted).

Testifying to the success of Corsaro's strategies is the fact that his identity gradually changed from that of an adult into some sort of hybrid whom the children saw as a 'big kid,' a semi-adult or an older brother. There were five main indicators of this change:

- the nickname ('Big Bill' in the United States; 'Billo' or 'Billone' in Italy) given to him by the children;
- the fact that the children did not stop playing when Corsaro appeared on the scene;
- the children's perception of him as having no authority (on the few occasions when he tried to give orders, the children responded with expressions like 'shut up, you're not our teacher');
- the fact that on birthdays the children made him sit with them in a circle (while the teachers and parents stood at a distance); and
- his teasing by the children (in Italy) for his poor language skills.

7.4 Researcher's influence

Although a variety of strategies can be devised to reduce the researcher's influence, they can only be eliminated to a partial extent. According to the 'indeterminacy principle,'[1] what we see is not *the* reality, but a specific reality generated by our intervention. For example, in a study on nudism, Warren and Rasmussen (1977, quoted in Silverman, 2000: 206–7) realized that when the participants were asked by a person of the opposite sex why they went to nudist beaches, they answered that they did so for reasons of 'freedom and naturism.' But when the conversation was between people of the same gender, the reason given was more likely to be interest of a sexual nature (for another case study, go to www.sagepub. co.uk/gobo).

The presence of the ethnographer may also stimulate courses of action which perhaps would not have taken place if he or she had not been present.

CASE STUDY
Police work

When reflecting on his various studies of urban police organizations, the American anthropologist John Van Maanen asked whether he himself had not been the co-author of many of the events that he had witnessed. In fact, he could not rule out that they had happened *as a consequence of* his presence and the police offi-cers' desire to show him, for example, how they conducted searches, how they got suspects to respect them or how they earned a reputation as 'tough guys.'

This is the well-known mechanism termed the 'Hawthorne effect,' an expression coined by the Australian psychologist of work, George Elton Mayo (1880–1949), according to whom the researcher's presence almost always affects the behavior of the subjects observed.[2] As Schwartz and Jacobs stress, the identity of a person and the position that he or she occupies in a world, 'have a role in creating that world and in fashioning the colored glasses through which you see it and it sees you' (1979: 50).

The unavoidable influence exerted by the researcher should not be regarded as a defect of observation, but rather as a characteristic intrinsic to it. As the researcher observes, he or she alters the field of observation by virtue of the reflexivity principle, which states as follows:

> Descriptions about some aspect of the social world are simultaneously within (part of) the very world that they describe. As a result . . . there is no room in the social world *merely* to describe anything. [Descriptions] simultaneously affect social relationships, execute moral evaluations, produce political, moral, and social consequences, and so on. Descriptions are almost 'doing' many more things in a social situation than simply 'reporting' a set of facts (1979: 51).

Ethnographers exchange not only information with participants but also social moves; they gather both information and instructions on how to co-ordinate their interactions with informants.

CASE STUDY
Inmates' culture

During his interactions with inmates of the East Los Angeles Halfway House, Wieder (1974) realized that they were not only describing their moral code but applying it to him. As the inmates told Wieder about their code, they did not simply describe the rules in force in the halfway house, they simultaneously (owing to the reflexivity of discourse) `did' things as well, among them sanctioning the behavior of a researcher seeking to obtain information which they judged inappropriate. If they told him that the rule of `don't snitch' (1974: 169) applied, they were simultaneously depriving him of valuable information by imposing the code on him as well.

Likewise, Duranti found that some Samoans invariably talked to him in 'good speech,' the phonological repertoire which they used with strangers, while other Samoans addressed him in 'bad speech,' the register used among the natives:

> in my everyday reactions with the inhabitants of the village, it was not always possible to predict how they would speak to me. Some of them never stopped using 'good speech' with me. But I cannot say with certainty that this was a way to keep me at a distance, to remind me of my origins, and of how I had come to be among them. For some, it was a way to keep my social persona distinct from that of the others present, but for reasons that were not necessarily hostile towards me. In other cases, good speech was used to demonstrate mastery of the register and thereby to affirm a social identity associated with the use of that speech (being a teacher, or an influential member of the local religious congregation). My presence was therefore simply an occasion to flaunt a particular aspect of individual communicative competence (1992: 97).

On this view, therefore, the aim of the researcher is not so much to alter as little as possible the field of observation (though this should be the intention anyway) as to activate good strategies to gain the best possible understanding.

7.5 In the field

Contrary to appearances, the transition from gaining access to the field to actual observation is not a linear and uninterrupted process. From the cognitive point of view, the shift is intermittent, like the change from being a stranger to being familiar to a community. As the theoreticians of *Gestalt* (Wolfgang Köhler, Max Wertheimer and Kurt Koffka) noted, understanding does not proceed linearly, but rather in cognitive jumps which recast the knowledge hitherto acquired. For this reason, the ethnographer should optimize the first two or three weeks of presence at the field site while he or she is still a stranger (see 9.2). It is therefore advisable to devote these first weeks entirely to research, principally to observation and note-taking, while avoiding any commitments unrelated to the ethnographic work. In fact, when the first weeks have passed, the researcher's cognitive schemas will begin to resemble those of the participants.

7.5.1 The informants

Jordan's Law

An informant who never produces misinformation is too deviant to be trusted.

Besides the intermediary, the guarantor and the gatekeeper, an ethnographer will encounter another key figure during his or her research: the informant. To stay with the example of the drug addict service, possible informants are the nurses who administer methadone to the addicts and attend to their welfare, the security guard stationed in the unit to prevent violence and the addicts themselves. Unlike gatekeepers, who exist before the research begins, informants emerge as the research proceeds: they are actors whom the ethnographer *discovers* in the field *during* the research. Informants are vital for the researcher because they accelerate his or her understanding of the group or organization's culture. Researchers must construct a network of relationships with reliable informants who enable them to grasp the meanings of actions, words and symbols, who aid their comprehension, and who reveal new observation schemas. Although all the members of a community are potential informants, the community leaders, or the senior management of a company – those, that is, whose roles give them an overview of the entire organization – may not be the best of them. Anthropologists stress that informants may sometimes be marginal actors who use the interaction with the researcher to get someone to listen to them and to receive support. Finally, it should be borne in mind that it is not always the case that the persons most willing to co-operate are also those who are best informed.

Ambivalence

The relationship with informants is complex. Although on the one hand they are an essential resource for the researcher, on the other they may impede his or her fieldwork: whilst a privileged relationship with one particular native opens some doors to the society, it may close others. In other words, if the researcher chooses as his or her informant a person with little respect in the community, the fieldwork may suffer. Consequently, it is wise for the ethnographer to consolidate the relationship with an informant only after he or she has spent some time in the host community and has understood the social position of the interlocutor, and above all the latter's reasons for collaborating. There is an ever-present danger that the researcher will be manipulated. Moreover, given the inevitable partiality of informants' points of view, it is advisable to select them from all the various components of the organization or group. Communities are usually stratified by opinions, social positions, tasks and roles, so that if privileged relationships are established with only some informants, particular positions or cognitive schemas may be over-represented. It is accordingly advisable for the ethnographer to sample the various cognitive perspectives present in the setting in order to produce a 'plurivocal' or 'polyphonic' account[3] giving voice to community's various levels, dissenters included. Finally, it should be borne in mind that the attitude of informants may change as the research proceeds: people who were initially helpful may gradually retreat (Dalton, 1959), while subjects who were at first suspicious and hostile may become co-operative.

7.5.2 The participants

Of all the relations discussed thus far, the one with the social actors is perhaps the most important, not only because of its frequency (the gatekeepers and the informants are not always present), but also because it determines the quality and quantity of the information that the ethnographer is able to gather. Cicourel has frequently pointed out, research with suspicious or hostile actors is almost certainly doomed to failure. The participants use their relationship with the ethnographer both to exchange information and to decide the most appropriate behavior to adopt in subsequent interactions with the researcher:

> they will try to gauge how far he or she can be trusted, what he or she might be able to offer as an acquaintance or a friend, and perhaps also how easily he or she could be manipulated or exploited (Hammersley and Atkinson, 1983: 78).

In fact, sometimes the ethnographer may find him or herself having to maneuver among rival or conflicting groups (Dalton, 1959) within an organization. He or she may even be asked to arbitrate disputes (Lofland, 1971: 96) because he or she is thought to be well-educated and therefore likely to be impartial. Because of his or her intellectual status, the ethnographer must therefore assume a variety of identities, among them adviser, therapist, expert, and friend. Usually the best strategy is *not to do* what actors normally do: express opinions, intercede to settle disputes, react to insults or mockery (Corsaro, 1985; Barley, 1990). Instead, the ethnographer should be as non-reactive as possible and absorb all disagreeable behavior or language. He or she should therefore 'bounce back' the actors' questions, thereby inducing them to respond. Sometimes, however, this deliberately neutral stance intended not to influence the subjects' behavior may provoke their hostility. The actors may come to regard the ethnographer as untrustworthy, or as devoid of opinions, or even worse, as someone who thinks they are inferior and not worth talking to. In fact, being non-reactive (admitted that it is impossible to be completely impassive) is a form of behavior at odds with normal interactions, where people instead take up positions, decide that one or other participant is right, and so on. Consequently, there is no optimal form of behavior that can be recommended to the researcher: he or she should only bear in mind that 'there is no *time out* in field relations and that the most apparently informal occasions are times when you will often be judged' (Silverman, 2000: 199).

Attempts by the ethnographer to gain acceptance by the group studied may or may not be successful (for a case study, go to www.sagepub.co.uk/gobo).

External factors beyond the ethnographer's control may also cause the relationship between him or her and the actors to deteriorate. Given the prolonged nature of ethnography, it may happen that the organization or community being studied is simultaneously under scrutiny by other professionals (typically journalists, but also psychologists, political scientists, economists, etc.). If the reports of these professionals are published while the ethnographer's research is still in progress, the participants' possible negative reaction to them may influence the ethnographer's work, perhaps forcing him or her to abandon the project because the participants fear further damage to their image.

7.6 The invisible historical context

Just as fish do not see the water in which they swim and we do not see the air that we breathe, so the ethnographer hardly notices the effects exerted on the setting by the historical period in which his or her research takes place. Ethnography develops in the present, in a circumscribed period of time, and as Burawoy et al. (2000) stress, it finds the historical and social processes which surround the setting difficult to grasp (see 16.6).

CASE STUDY
The role of history in field research

Section 3.8 discussed the film *Kitchen Stories*. The Swedish researcher, who worked for an ergonomics company which was also Swedish, encountered great difficulty in entering the field, the house of an elderly bachelor living in a rural area of Norway. The man had initially agreed to be observed as he went about his everyday activities in his kitchen, but then changed his attitude, causing difficulties for the researcher. When the relationship between the two protagonists began to change and they started to communicate, there emerged (among the various reasons for the man's coldness) a certain rancour felt by Norwegians towards Swedes. This was the early 1950s and the Norwegians had not forgotten how the Swedes had collaborated with the Nazis during the war. Whereas the Norwegians had been occupied militarily by the Germans (with all the consequences that an occupation brings), the Swedes had preferred to co-operate. This the Norwegians had seen as a betrayal.

Ethnography is not always able to grasp the deeper underlying influence of history (even less so can the survey or the in-depth interview). Nevertheless the influence is present, albeit invisibly.

7.7 Finding documents

It is difficult to determine precisely what it is that constitutes an organization: some say it is rituals and ceremonies (Goffman), others cite social practices (ethnomethodology), yet others discursive or conversational practices (speech act theory, discourse analysis, conversation analysis) or cognitive processes (Karl Weick with his concept of 'sensemaking'). All these views are probably correct to some extent. Yet organizations are also constituted by texts, whereby 'texts' is meant process-based information created by the ordinary activities of people or private and public organizations. This is information which is 'produced, shared and used in socially organized ways' (Atkinson and Coffey, 1997: 47) by participants, instead of being created by the researcher – in the form of fieldnotes for example. The researcher does no more than select among these texts and adapt them to the purposes of his or her analysis.

There are three main types of text:

- those conventionally called *public documents* (files, databases, forms, official statistics, company reports, official proceedings, restaurant menus, and so on);

- *personal documents* (letters, diaries, autobiographies, suicide notes, post-it messages, and so on); and
- images, photographs, symbols, timetables, signs, notices, warnings and prohibitions, web pages, intranet and extranet communications (e-mails), television programs.

These materials are subjected to 'nonreactive techniques' or 'unobtrusive measures' for the study of groups or individuals, because they can be collected while minimizing the 'researcher effect.'

Organizations and institutions are full of texts which are not merely appendices or annotations to practices, but instead constitute integral and important parts of organizations. Consider a hospital: a doctor examines a patient, and then asks the latter to describe his symptoms while he takes notes. The doctor converts the information obtained from the interaction into a written record (a chart, a file, a case history). Thereafter his colleagues and assistants (doctors and nurses) base their decisions on this medical record, for they cannot again access the source of the data, namely the original doctor/patient interaction. The clinical record thus becomes an entirely autonomous agent which produces and constructs reality. It is therefore evident that documents, depending on the type of organization concerned, are important for its production and reproduction.

The documents and texts of an organization can be analyzed (as we shall see in 13.3) in a variety of ways.

(1) We can study their *content* in search of values, stereotypes, or ways of thinking. The texts thus become indicators of the organizational culture.
(2) Or we can analyze the *accomplishments* of the documents as non-human agents autonomously constructing a reality, as in the above example of the medical record.

Or again, we can examine the 'medium' of the document: that is to say, not the content but the container. In other words, the type of medium chosen for communications within an organization may be indicative of that organization's policies, its treatment of personnel, the organizational culture. For example, if a management uses a brusque e-mail (or the company intranet) to inform staff that the company is about to be merged with another one, this may be indicative of a top-down or technocratic managerial style, in a setting which lacks a participative culture. Likewise, if one day the employees discover that their firm has been taken over by another company (and has even changed its name) from the fact that their entry badges no longer work, what conception of human resources does the top management have?

Like ethnographic interviews (see Chapter 10), documents cannot be used as substitutes for observation – 'as surrogates for other kinds of data' (Atkinson and Coffey, 1997: 47). Rather, (a) they can help us to identify elements and topics on which to re-focus our observation; (b) they can be used to test our hypotheses; (c) they can be cited in support of our observations ('triangulation': see 13.3); or (d) they can furnish information which improves our understanding of what we have observed.

7.8 Concluding remarks

Handling field relations is a very complex and stressful undertaking for the researcher. Not surprisingly, numerous social scientists prefer to do their research using other methodologies (survey, in-depth interview, document analysis, discourse or conversational analysis and so on) which do not require them to spend lengthy periods in the field or to maintain prolonged contacts with participants. Gaining access to the field is therefore one of the most delicate aspects of ethnography: 'a field many claim to be the most scientific of the humanities and the most humanistic of the sciences' (Van Maanen, 2006: 13).

KEY POINTS

- Gaining access to the field is the most difficult phase in the entire process of ethnographic research.
- Field access strategies can be divided into two phases: 'getting in' (achieving physical access to the place) and 'getting on' (achieving social access).
- During negotiations it is advisable to define the *beneficence*, or the advantage that the organization or group may derive from allowing an outsider to observe it.
- Among the various participants encountered by the ethnographer are the intermediary, the guarantor, the gatekeeper and the informant. The first two perform a major role during the phase when the researcher gains physical access to the organization; the third and the fourth acquire greatest importance during the social access phase.
- The identities of the researcher and of the group or organization are created processually and reciprocally during negotiations on access, but above all subsequently during the day-to-day course of research.
- Because the researcher's identity is not attributed once and for all, any errors, lapses or 'false starts' can be repaired interactionally with the cognitive mechanism whereby the present tends to rewrite the past.

KEY TERMS

Document (see pp. 129–30)	Process-based information created by the ordinary activities of people, or of private and public organizations.
Face (see pp. 122–3)	According to Goffman, face, the 'positive social value a person effectively claims for himself . . ., is only on loan to him from society; it will be withdrawn unless he conducts himself in a way it is worthy of it.'
Gatekeeper (see p. 122)	A person embedded in the culture observed by the ethnographer and performing a role of prime importance.

	Despite the guarantor's reassurances, the gatekeeper is worried that the research may damage the organization's image, and that the researcher's presence may alter the organization's internal relationships.
Getting in (see pp. 120–1)	Achieving physical access to the place.
Getting on (see p. 122)	Achieving social access.
Guarantor (see p. 121)	The person who reassures the group or organization about the ethnographer's good reputation and his or her trustworthiness.
Hawthorne effect (see p. 125)	Phenomenon discovered in the 1920s and analyzed and interpreted by Elton Mayo. The implication of this discovery is that the presence of the researcher almost always affects the behavior of the observees.
Identity (see p. 122)	Self-image. According to Goffman, although 'each individual is responsible for the demeanor image of himself,' it is also true that his contribution to that image may be entirely marginal, because he 'must rely on others to complete the picture of him of which he himself is allowed to paint only certain parts.'
Indeterminacy principle (see p. 124)	Formulated in 1927 by the German physicist Heisenberg, the principle which states that what researchers see is not *the* reality, but a specific reality generated by their intervention.
Informant (see p. 127)	Informants are insiders within the culture observed. They are vital for the researcher because they accelerate his or her understanding of the group or organization's culture. Unlike gatekeepers, who exist before the research begins, informants emerge as the research proceeds: they are subjects whom the ethnographer *discovers* in the field *during* the research.
Intermediary (see p. 121)	The person who creates the contact, or establishes the communication, between the researcher and certain members of the organization or group.
Obtrusiveness (see pp. 120–1)	Phenomenon whereby the researcher's physical presence produces changes in the behavior of the subjects being observed.
Participants (see p. 128)	The social actors who populate the research setting.

Plurivocality and Polyphony (see p. 127)	Concepts introduced by Bachtin and adapted to social research. They signify that voice must be given to all the components of the community, dissenters included.
Reactivity (see p. 125)	The response by the participants to obtrusiveness. It ranges through embarrassment, unease, stress, fear, etc., to the display of highly artificial behavior.

RECOMMENDED READING

For undergraduates:
Bruni, Attila (2006)

For graduates:
Fielding, Nigel (2004)

For advanced researchers:
Back, Les (2004)

SELF-EVALUATION TEST

Are you ready for the next chapter? Check your knowledge by answering the following open-ended questions:

1. Why do many claim that ethnography is 'the most scientific of the humanities and the most humanistic of the sciences' (Van Maanen, 2006: 13)? What is implied by this play on words?
2. What was the innovation made by the American ethologist Dian Fossey?
3. Why, according to David Silverman, is there no 'time out' in ethnographic research?
4. How can we determine whether, as ethnographers, we have been accepted by the group or organization; or in other words, how can we know that we have been successful in 'getting on'? What indicators can we consider?
5. What is meant by 'there is no room in the social world *merely* to describe anything'?

Notes

1 Formulated in 1927 by the German physicist and Nobel prize-winner Werner Karl Heisenberg (1901–76), the indeterminacy principle is a cornerstone of quantum mechanics.

2 The Hawthorne effect is a phenomenon discovered by Roethlisberger, Dickson and Wright (1939) in the 1920s. These researchers, who belonged to a team headed by Mayo, were conducting experiments in industrial psychology at a Western Electric plant when they noticed that improvements in productivity or quality resulted merely from the fact that workers knew they were being studied or observed.

3 The concepts of 'plurivocality' and 'polyphony' were introduced by the Russian philologist and literary critic Michail Bachtin (1895–1975). Bachtin in maintained that numerous voices resound in every word, which consequently has polysemous meanings deposited by those who have previously used it.

Ethical Dilemmas

LEARNING OBJECTIVES

• To understand the difference between morals and ethics.

• To recognize the various forms of research ethics.

• To know the main ethical principles that guide and constrain research.

• To learn how to handle ethical dilemmas.

• To acquire a method-sensitive ethical stance.

8.1 Introduction

Many of our everyday actions are guided by moral customs: we must not lie to our partners, parents or children; we must not deceive them, nor hurt them; and we must seek to respect their wishes. We must comply with further ethical principles in the workplace: we must be loyal to the company or our colleagues and polite to customers and users. We are subject to moral conventions even in the street: we must try to give information to those who ask for it, or help people in difficulties rather than ignore them. Matters are little different in the scientific enterprise, so in this case too there is continuity between everyday life and science.

CASE STUDY
Ethical dilemmas

In the mid-1980s I was about to begin a research study on juvenile delinquency, and social workers at the Ministry of Justice had given me lists of youths with criminal records to contact as possible informants. However, the lists were furnished in exchange for my promise that I would not tell the future interviewees how I had obtained their names. The reason for this secrecy was that the youths had 'paid their debt to society' and were therefore of no further concern to the social services. If they had found out that their names were still on the social workers' lists they may consider themselves branded for life. Consequently, when I contacted the youths and they asked me how I had got hold of their names, I was faced with a dilemma: tell them a lie or break my promise to the social workers. In either case, I would have breached a norm of my professional code of ethics.

To deal with such topics we need to use two important terms: 'morals' and 'ethics.' Although the two words are often used interchangeably, morals are concerned with the set of customs which orient our behavior in public and private places, while ethics concerns customs that regulate behavior in the professional sphere.

During the various phases of the research process, therefore, the researcher in his or her capacity as a scientist and a professional must make decisions with regard to his or her code of ethics. For example, in the section on covert research (see 6.4.1), we encountered the ethical problems raised by that particular type of observation. Like other professionals, 'ethnographers have a responsibility not only to protect research participants from harm, but also to have regard to their rights' (Murphy and Dingwall, 2001: 339). Not only may participants suffer anxiety and stress during data collection, they may also be treated unfairly or unjustly. Accordingly, professional ethical codes have been drawn up to apply these abstract principles and to help researchers cope with concrete situations (see, for example, the Social Research Association Ethical Guidelines at www.the-sra.org.uk/documents/pdfs/ethics03.pdf: – the site also offers an excellent bibliography, as well as assistance with ethical problems from experienced SRA members). However, the ethical codes of professional associations do not always achieve their purpose: all too often they provide only general guidelines, or they lay down abstract rules of little help to researchers in solving their practical problems. The difficulty – namely the irresolvable clash between the rule (which is always general) and the situation (which is always particular) – is well known and has been amply treated by ethnomethodology (see 3.7). The two sides seem entirely at odds with each other. Moreover, as numerous authors have stressed (the list is so long that citing only some authors would be an injustice to those excluded), mechanical transposition of ethical codes to ethnographic research has encountered two main problems: 'first . . . [they] are not method-sensitive [and] may constrain research unnecessarily and inappropriately. Secondly . . . [they] may not give real protection to research participants but actually increase the risk of harm by blunting ethnographers' sensitivities to the method-specific issues which do arise' (Murphy and Dingwall, 2001: 340).

8.2 Competing ethics

The topic of research ethics is evidently very complex, and researchers have taken up very different positions on the question.

Utilitarianism

Some maintain that actions should be judged according to their consequences, more than the intentions behind them, and therefore in terms of the extent to which they increase or decrease the overall well-being of the participants. Hence there is a tendency to minimize the moral harm that may be caused to the participants because it is off-set by the benefits derived from the increase in scientific knowledge. This view gives legitimacy to forms of deception and mendacity used with participants, provided that the moral damage does not exceed the advantages foreseen, and that no single individual can claim to have been harmed by the research or by the publication of its findings. The opportunism of researchers is thus justified, and they may make instrumental use of the trust and friendship relations that develop in the field. This utilitarian doctrine that the ends justify the means is the basis for covert research and experiments. However, it is difficult to maintain, for it is impossible to predict beforehand whether the research will contribute significantly to scientific knowledge, or whether it will merely be bad research, an ethical wasteland. Moreover, one may ask, who is it that decides what the acceptable rate of harmfulness or the hurt-fulness threshold should be?

Postmodernism and feminism versus ethicism

Opposed to this utilitarian doctrine is the stance which privileges the rights and prerogatives of the participants and subordinates scientific interests to them. However, this position comprises two contrasting epistemological perspectives: feminism and ethicism.

- Postmodernism and feminism (Ellis, 1995; Denzin, 1997) argue that the time has come to break with traditional ethnography and its defects (objectivism, naturalism, colonialism, exploitation of the participants, and so on) and change to a *participatory ethnography* based on the concept of 'care' in which researcher and participants jointly define certain aspects of the research design, discuss the findings, and sometimes write the final report together.
- Ethicism is instead based on the concept of 'justice.' It adopts a strongly nor-mative and absolutist stance which is well represented by deontological ethi-cal codes (with all the harmful consequences that we saw in the previous section).

Given this variety of positions, it is clear that in the doing of his or her research, a researcher is confronted by numerous dilemmas, or problems for which there is no optimal solution, and that the decision taken will almost invariably be a second-best. Perhaps the best way to acquire an ethical attitude is to consider the main dilemmas faced by earlier ethnographers and to learn from their experi-ence. Accordingly, I now outline the dilemmas that most frequently arise in ethnographic research.

8.3 On the objectives of research

Ethical codes prescribe that the participants must be given complete information about the aims of the research, so that they can decide whether or not to give their consent to it. Although this principle seems self-evidently correct, when one tries to put it into practice, it becomes problematic. For example, covert research (see 5.4.1) is immediately prohibited. But even without going to this extreme, those who do overt research are well aware that it is not always advisable (in research on the attitudes and behaviors of certain professionals like lawyers, judges, politicians, police officers, etc.) to explain the purpose of the research, for on the one hand the participants may be made unnecessarily suspicious of the researcher's real motives, while on the other they may behave differently from normal and thus contaminate the findings. But even researchers who try to be crystal-clear in their behavior with participants may run into difficulties: it is not easy to give a complete explanation of a scientific objective 'without sending informants and cohabitants to graduate school' (Brewster Smith, 1979: 14, quoted in Murphy and Dingwall, 2001: 342). For non-social scientists, anthropological and sociological interests are shrouded in impenetrable opacity (Glazier, 1993). One should also bear in mind the well-known maxim 'expect the unexpected,' because the research may suddenly change its focus and catch the researcher unawares. Consequently,

> recent work has recognized that the distinction between covert and overt research is less straightforward than sometimes imagined . . . all research lies on a continuum between overtness and covertness' (Murphy and Dingwall, 2001: 342).

8.4 On loyalty and lies

It may happen that the ethnographer is forced to make a moral commitment to people occupying different roles, and possibly representing conflicting interests. As said at the beginning of the chapter, I myself have been caught up in a conflict between intermediaries and participants.

Sometimes, therefore, researchers find themselves forced to violate a pact of *trust* with their subjects, or not to tell them the whole truth, or to *conceal information* from them. In some kinds of research (for example, with alcoholics, drug addicts, the mentally ill, the handicapped or former prisoners) it is not always possible to tell the subjects why and how they have been selected for interview. How can we say to someone 'you interest me because you're an alcoholic' or 'I want to interview you because you've been in jail'? And if we did say so, would not this induce the person to behave according to the stereotype given to him or her by society (Goffman's 'sad tales')? Not saying so would instead give the person a chance to abandon the stereotype of the alcoholic or former prisoner and relate differently to the researcher, in the belief that the latter did not know their story.

Anonymity

Another apparently obvious principle is that the *anonymity* of participants and research settings must be guaranteed. The usual practice is to use pseudonyms and to alter details so that places and persons cannot be identified. This does not ensure complete anonymity, however, for several reasons: on reading the research report, the participants may recognize themselves or other people; or the setting may be so distinctive that it can be identified by journalists, the police or experts.

CASE STUDY
On anonymity

Vidich and Bensman (1958) studied a small rural town (given the pseudonym 'Springdale') in New York State. Despite the pseudonym, the town was recognized, and the towns' citizens protested vociferously that the book was a derogatory portrait of their community. Their protest even dragged in nearby Cornell University, where Vidich and Bensman worked, and they were also criticized by some colleagues. Similar controversies had previously been sparked by the celebrated *Middletown* (see 1.8 and 6.2.4) and the first books in the *Yankee City* series (see 6.2.4). Generally speaking, participants are never satisfied with their descriptions by researchers, even when the latter have told the truth. But for that matter how do we ourselves react when someone points out our defects?

Consequently, the researcher's intentions notwithstanding, publication of his or her findings may cause (and sometimes does cause) hurt and offence to participants – also because (if the research is particularly interesting) the findings may be used by the mass media to denigrate the organization or the group studied, and its members. It may also happen that the researcher is accused of revealing cultural codes and practices to the advantage of those who exercise social control and repression. A case in point is Laud Humphreys (1970), a former Protestant pastor and then sociologist who conducted covert research on male homosexual encounters in the public toilets of a large American city: transient, impersonal and clandestine sex between apparently upstanding citizens. Laud's descriptions were so accurate that he was accused of writing an excellent manual for the police to use in repressing gay encounters in public places.

Confidentiality

As ethnographers do their fieldwork they may learn personal details about participants or be privy to confidences from them. Ensuring that this information does not contaminate the ethnographer's relations with informants is more easily said than done. Just as it is important not to betray the trust of informants, who may at times expose themselves in order to help the ethnographer, so it is important not to betray the trust of the gatekeepers, guarantors, intermediaries and participants whose consent has ensured the success of the research. This aspect is particularly evident when the research report is being written, for it is then that a difficult balance must be struck between what the researcher would like to say, what he or she can say, and what he or she must say – as we saw in the case (among the many citable) of Vidich and Bensman (1958).

8.5 Informed consent

Stewart's Law of Retroaction

It's easier to get forgiveness than ask permission.

An instrument now essential in ethnographic research – from a legal point of view as well – is *informed consent*. This consists of a set of practices designed to give participants the information they need to decide whether or not to take part in the research. The researcher must then make sure that participants have understood the information and that their participation is voluntary. Finally, if the participants are minors or incompetents, the researcher must obtain permission from their guardians. For example, when Corsaro (1985) was doing his research in the nursery school, before he could film the children's interactions he had to obtain formal permission from their parents. Because he did not obtain it for all the children, when one of those without permission appeared in the video camera viewfinder, Corsaro had to stop filming.

The advent of informed consent has been the most evident signal that the people being studied are *subjects* of research (indeed, the most appropriate term has recently become 'participants'), not *objects* of observation. Informed consent is usually obtained by having participants sign a consent form which explains the aims of the research and asks for permission to handle their personal information. The American sociolinguist, Susan Ervin-Tripp, has drawn up a very detailed form which lists the possible uses that may be made of the collected data (for research purposes, for publication, shown at scientific meetings, broadcast on television or radio). The actors are asked to sign this form and give or refuse their permission for each of these uses (see Silverman 2000: 202, Table 15.2, now on www.sagepub.co.uk/gobo). However, it should be borne in mind that the initial consent given by a participant may not be enough, especially when a recording is made – a procedure which the researcher may decide to use only after the research has begun. In this case, it is advisable to obtain further formal consent for use to be made of participants' personal information. However, nor is this device entirely reliable, because in large settings it is difficult to obtain the consent of everyone present, some of whom may be there by chance (Ryan; 2004).

8.6 Self-disclosure, exploitation and reciprocity

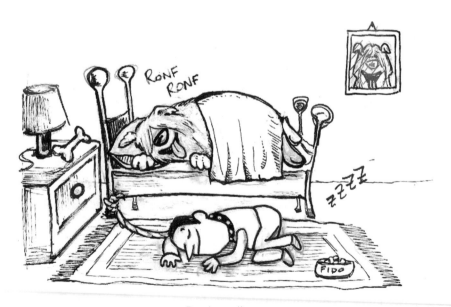

Reciprocity

More recently, a number of scholars – feminist and post-colonial anthropologists in particular – have addressed the problem of self-disclosure and the reciprocity of behavior. The question may be stated as follows: is it ethical for the researcher to conceal or to lie about (to his or her informants) certain aspects of his or her identity, such as religious affiliation, political preferences or sexual orientation? If the informants and participants instead declare these aspects, does not the researcher's deception breach the principle of reciprocal expectations and behavior? More generally, does this not create a power asymmetry between the researcher and the researched? And finally, is this not a situation where those studied are being exploited? Once again, if the problem is treated philosophically it is difficult to solve. But if we instead look at it in practical terms, according to a specific case and specific setting, the problem is easier to handle. As Marjorie Wolf (1996) has pointed out, from a feminist point of view, the word 'exploitation' is rather extreme and can be applied to only some kinds of research, typically experimental, which adopt the utilitarian model (now formally banned by professional ethical codes which provide severe sanctions on those who do not apply them). Moreover, the researcher's power and authority should be scaled down and contextualized: it may be that in some settings the researcher has considerable power, but increasingly often (because of the spread of ethical codes) he or she is beholden to powerful actors who obstruct and boycott, or define the conditions for access to the field. Finally, the image of the powerful researcher pertains to a pre-World War II conception of the ethnographer. Today, the modernization processes ongoing in even the most exotic and remotest of countries have empowered local populations. Of this anthropologists are well aware, as their informants correct even their most minor grammatical errors (Duranti, 2002: 161), teach them how to behave decorously in social exchanges with natives, and sanction any requests that they deem inappropriate.

8.7 On neutrality

The researcher should maintain a position of impartiality towards all the participants they meet in the course of research. This principle, too, is obviously impossible to apply in practice. Our emotions and inclinations make us prefer some relationships to others: we find some participants more likeable than others; we feel affinities with some of them but may be entirely indifferent to the rest. We may also be faced by more complicated and awkward dilemmas, as happened to the American anthropologist of organizations, John Van Maanen (1983).

CASE STUDY
Loyalty dilemmas

Between 1970 and 1973, Van Maanen conducted research on the police of 'Union City' (a pseudonym). During one of the many police patrols Van Maanen accompanied as an observer, he saw the patrolmen (after being called by members of the public) violently attack a drunken black man resisting arrest. The case was given prominence in the local press on the initiative of a journalist who hung around the local police precinct. The journalist made friends with Van Maanen and obtained confidential information from him (even ethnographers sometimes feel they must confide in someone!). In 1974 the case came to trial and Van Maanen received two subpoenas: one summonsing him to court as a witness, the other ordering him to hand over his ethnographic notes. He was therefore caught on the horns of a dilemma: should he testify and thus betray the trust of the police officers who had generously let him watch them at work, or should he remain silent and risk arrest? But more generally, to whom did he owe his loyalty: to his informants or to the community? Van Maanen went to court but refused to hand over his field notes, claiming his right to research confidentiality. The newspaper's lawyers then sued Van Maanen on the grounds that the community's right to know the truth outweighed his right to protect his sources. Luckily for Van Maanen, whose refusal put him at risk of arrest and possible imprisonment, the judge dismissed the case and the affair concluded.

Although Van Maanen's case may seem extreme, dilemmas of this kind, albeit usually of lesser seriousness, occur with a certain frequency.

EXERCISE 8.1

Discuss among yourselves or with the professor the following case, which happened to Patricia A. Adler (1985). It represents a dilemma between loyalty to a (future) informant and responsibility to the community.
You discover that a neighbor and friend is a drug trafficker (not a simple pusher). What do you do? Celebrate because you have found an excellent insider with whom to start research on drugs trafficking or report him to the police?

8.8 On beneficence: The repayment

'Beneficence' can be defined as the advantage that accrues to the organization or group from permitting the researcher to study it. In fact, we must always ask why an organization should allow itself to be observed by an outsider. Any kind of research is a potential risk for the group's identity: it may convey an image different from the one desired; it may bring to light conflicts and divisions; or the researcher's presence may impede the organization's day-to-day activities. Moreover, organizations sometimes make spaces and services available to the ethnographer – an office, a desk, or access to the cafeteria, for example. To use the language of psychology, what motivations and rewards can we offer to our participants to compensate them for our intrusion? It is not enough to give good reasons, we must also offer something. This entails a deal, a pact or a contract whereby both actors (the researcher and the group) benefit.

EXERCISE 8.2

Imagine that you must negotiate access to the field. What *objects* would you offer the host organization or group?

A wide variety of beneficences can be offered, with much depending on the ethnographer's creativity. However, not all of them will be suitable for the participants, and care should be taken to ensure that the beneficence is appropriate to them and the setting. There follows a list of (decontextualized) examples of what the researcher can do: offer post-research consultancy; provide training for the participants based on the researcher's expertise and the research findings; use the latter for within-organization analysis; present a copy of the video recordings; or organize an event on the research topic and invite the organization's representatives to express their opinions.

8.9 Ecological heritage and the future of the participants

The problem of 'ecological heritage' has received little attention in ethnographic literature. But just as it is now an accepted moral principle that parents should bequeath the environmental heritage to their children in at least the same condition as they inherited it, so the ethnographer should not 'burn' the field for subsequent research. This topic will be dealt with more thoroughly in Chapter 16 on 'Leaving the Field,' but some preliminary treatment is required here. It may happen that the participants' experience with the ethnographer has been so bad that they refuse to co-operate with any other researcher in the future. A typical case is that of broken promises: the ethnographer pledges to discuss the results with the participants or the intermediaries, to give them feedback or free consultancy, or to send a copy of the research report. When the participants see none of this transpiring, even though they may have devoted time to the research and helped the ethnographer deal with various practical problems, they may feel exploited and reluctant to repeat the experience with another researcher.

The ethnographer should also consider the potential effects of his or her research on informants, these being the people with whom he or she has had the longest contact. Predicting these effects is obviously impossible, but the researcher should nevertheless try to anticipate them.

CASE STUDY
Disrupting participants' life

One of the best-known examples of disrupting an informant's life is the case of Doc (whose real name was Dean Pecci), who was Whyte's principal informant for his celebrated study (1943a). According to Boelen (1992), who interviewed Doc's children, friends and acquaintances, and for 20 years (from 1970 to 1990) periodically visited Cornerville, Doc died in 1967 after having left the neighborhood and obsessed with guilt over betraying his people to help Whyte. The research and the book's subsequent success changed Doc-Pecci's life and personality. Although he was famous in academy (judging from his many invitations to lectures and seminars at the University of Massachusetts), he had lost the trust of his friends (because of his revelations to Whyte), who considered him a traitor and a snitch. Perhaps for these reasons he lost the leadership of the Norton Gang, and this probably caused his nervous exhaustion and numerous mental problems – which Whyte scrupulously documented, thus making them public and disgracing Doc even further. In short, Doc was no longer able to be what he was: he had become famous but he was no longer a leader; he had become a celebrity in the city, but he was stigmatized as a traitor in his neighborhood. Finally, he had refined his natural sociological sensibility, but he had not become a sociologist, even if (given his numerous descriptions and analytical interpretations for Whyte) he can be considered a co-author of *Street Corner Society*.

This case highlights how ethnography (much more than any other methodology) may disrupt the life and identity of the community observed.

EXERCISE 8.3

Discuss the case of Doc-Pecci among yourselves or with your professor. With the methodological and ethical sensitivity that we have acquired in recent years (it is all too easy to criticize with hindsight a study carried out in the 1940s), what would you have done, what measures would you have taken, to prevent what happened to Dean Pecci after Whyte's book was published?

8.10 Concluding remarks

We have seen in this survey of the ethical principles which should guide ethnographic research that they are not easy to apply. Should we therefore discard them as useless? No, we should not. Rather, we should remember that there are problems for which there are no ready-made solutions – not least because specific problems due to specific aspects of a setting often arise in the field and require contingent responses. All that the ethnographer can do is draw on a 'situational ethics' to invent ethical solutions which at least fulfill the criterion – perhaps somewhat moralistic but nevertheless useful – of not doing to others what you would not want them to do to you.

KEY POINTS

- Like our actions in our everyday lives, research also is subject to moral conventions.
- Like other professionals, ethnographers have a responsibility not only to protect research participants from harm, but also to have regard to their rights.
- However, the ethical codes of professional associations do not always achieve their purpose: all too often they provide only general guidelines or lay down abstract rules that are of little help in solving the researcher's practical problems.
- Moreover, professional ethical codes are not method-sensitive and may constrain research unnecessarily and inappropriately. They may not give real protection to research participants but actually increase the risk of harm by blunting ethnographers' sensitivities to the method-specific issues which do arise.
- There are various research ethical codes whose principles are sometimes in conflict. For example, the 'utilitarian ethics of consequences' model prioritizes the goodness of outcomes, so that the ends justify the means. Opposed to this model are postmodernism and ethicism.
- In the process of research, the ethnographer is confronted by numerous dilemmas, or problems for which there is no optimal solution. Hence the decision taken is almost invariably second-best.
- Because there are ethical problems for which there are no ready-made solutions (not least specific problems due to specific aspects of a setting often arise in the field and require contingent responses), all that the ethnographer can do is draw on a 'situational ethics' to invent solutions which at least fulfill the criterion of not doing to others what you would not want them to do to you.

KEY TERMS

Deontology
(see p. 137)

A discipline concerned with the obligations of certain categories of people, typically professionals, and the rights of their clients, users, or interlocutors. Deontology starts from the assumption that there exist *a priori* moral obligations, which do not change merely as a result of a change in circumstances (i.e. situational ethics). One of the most important implications of deontology is that praiseworthy goals can never justify immoral actions, in contrast to doctrines which claim that *the ends justify the means*. Deontology is directly in opposition to consequentialism (p.136).

Dilemma
(see pp. 135–6)

A situation or problem for which there is no optimal solution. Any decision that a researcher takes in regard

	to a dilemma will be unsatisfactory. Game theory has developed an array of models based on dilemmas. The best known of these is the prisoner's dilemma.
Ethical code (see p. 137)	Every professional association (psychologists, anthropologists, sociologists, but also engineers, architects and so on) have drawn up a deontological code which states the principles that should guide their associates in their dealings with participants and clients.
Ethicism (see p. 137)	An ethical approach based on justice. It adopts a strongly normative and absolutist stance well represented by deontological ethical codes.
Ethics (see p. 136)	Ethics concerns the set of norms that regulate behavior in the professional sphere.
Informed consent (see pp. 139–40)	A set of practices designed to give participants the information they need to decide whether or not to take part in the research. Informed consent is usually obtained by having participants sign a consent form which explains the aims of the research and asks for permission to handle their personal information.
Morals (see p. 136)	Morals concerns the set of customs which orient our behavior in public and private places.
Postmodernist and feminist ethics (see p. 137)	An ethical approach based on the conceptof 'care.' It promotes a *participatory ethnography* in which researcher and participants jointly define certain aspects of the research design, discuss the findings, and sometimes write the final report together.
Situational ethics (see p. 144)	Also known as 'situationism,' this states that the morality of an act is a function of the state of the system at the time it is performed. Abstract standards are considered to be far less important than the ongoing processes in which one is personally and physically involved. Situational ethics is an applied, teleological and consequential approach which is concerned with the outcome or consequences of an action; it does not consider an action as being intrinsically wrong as in the deontological perspective. In the case of situation ethics, the ends *can* justify the means.
Utilitarian ethics of consequences (see pp. 136–7)	An ethical approach which tends to minimize the moral harm that may be caused to the participants because they are off-set by the benefits deriving from the increase in scientific knowledge. According to consequentialism, the ends can justify the means because decisions are judged primarily in terms of their consequences.

RECOMMENDED READING

For undergraduates:
Cohen, Martin (2003)

For graduates:
Murphy, Elizabeth and Dingwall, Robert (2001)

For advanced researchers:
Edwards, Rosalind and Mauthner, Melanie (2002)

EXERCISE 8.4

Go to the website of the Social Research Association (www.the-sra.org.uk/documents/pdfs/ethics03.pdf). Its Ethical Guidelines cover a wide range of aspects of ethical practice. Emphasized in particular are four 'obligations' to:
(1) society
(2) funders and employers
(3) colleagues
(4) subjects.
Imagine that you are in a situation where you are unable to fulfill your obligations to all four of the above actors, but you must neglect one of them. To which of these actors do you feel the greatest ethical commitment? And to which do you feel the least?

SELF-EVALUATION TEST

Are you ready for the next chapter? Check your knowledge by answering the following open-ended questions:
1. What are the main weaknesses of ethical codes?
2. What is informed consent?
3. What is the difference between the ethics of care and the ethics of justice?
4. How can the exploitation of informants be prevented?
5. What is situational ethics?

How to Observe

The real voyage of discovery consists not in seeking new landscapes, but in having new eyes.

Marcel Proust

LEARNING OBJECTIVES

- To understand the aims of a phenomenological gaze.

- To grasp the advantages of estrangement.

- To learn how to observe.

9.1 Introduction

As the English sociologist of education Sara Delamont has stressed, 'the biggest problem novices find when preparing for ethnographic fieldwork is that the method books are not explicit enough about what to observe, how to observe and what to write down' (2004: 225). In fact, as we watch the activities that go on in a setting, we are tempted to record everything we see: all hints, particulars and details. But our enthusiasm soon wanes when we realize that there is an immense quantity of information that could be written down. To forestall this natural feeling of distress, it is advisable to narrow the observational field down from the outset. A good research design is therefore the best remedy against later difficulties; and anyway, just one piece of research should not set out to deal with too many things. Consequently, before ethnographers begin their fieldwork they should decide not only *what* to observe, but also *how* to do so. 'How' or 'what' (as we saw in 5.6 on conceptualization) are not questions to which there are straightforward and general answers, for these depend on the theoretical perspective that the researcher decides to adopt.

9.2 How to observe: Techniques of estrangement

At some time or another, all of us have felt an odd sense of being alienated from a social setting. We may be at a party, having dinner with friends, or in someone's company, and we suddenly have the eerie sensation of being on another plane.

We also feel ourselves separated and isolated within ourselves. The others with us seem to be aliens. This emotional isolation (namely 'estrangement') is an elementary form of distancing from reality. But estrangement is not always associated with discomfort. When we are abroad, we may enjoy watching the strange (for us) things that the natives do. Other forms of distancing from reality are *rêverie'* (letting our thoughts wander freely), fantasizing (the 'dreaming with eyes open' whereby introverted or creative children and adults withdraw from reality), autogenic training and yoga. Another form of estrangement is social embarrassment (Goffman, 1956b). Estrangement, *rêverie* and fantasizing are normal phenomena which show us that the ordinary perception of reality is a mental construct. Illness, too, may become an experience of estrangement.

CASE STUDY
Illness as estrangement

In *The Magic Mountain* (1924), the novel by the German novelist and Nobel prize-winner Thomas Mann (1875-1955), illness is an element that estranges and separates the protagonist (suffering from tuberculosis and confined to a sanatorium in Davos, high up in the Swiss Alps) from the world of industry, work and war. It guides him through philosophical-existential reflections on the human condition and helps him to mature internally. Finally, in this process of individual maturation, illness takes the form of a rejection of order and authority; an escape from the perverse organization of socio-economic relationships. It becomes symptomatic of an inner malaise, of the individual's alienation from society.

We can understand from these examples that ethnographers have at least two ways to approach their object of study:

> if we want to find something, one way to do it is to look for it out in the world in different places. Another way is to change our method of looking at the world in order to discover it. Traditional participant observation is primarily concerned with the first procedure (Schwartz and Jacobs, 1979: 247).

De-naturalizing

Changing our way of looking at things means switching from the layman's attitude inspired by an ingenuous realism, which sees the scene as natural, normal, obvious and taken-for-granted, to that of the researcher who sets him or herself the task of *de-naturalizing* the social world under investigation. The most appropriate cognitive attitude for a researcher engaged in phenomenologically-informed ethnography is what Schutz has called the attitude of the 'stranger': 'the adult individual of our times and civilization who tries to be permanently accepted or at least tolerated by the group which he approaches' (1944/1962: 91). Schutz includes a wide variety of individuals in the category 'stranger':

> the applicant for membership in a closed club, the prospective bridegroom who wants to be admitted to the girl's family, the farmer's son who enters college, the city dweller who settles in a rural environment, the 'selectee' who joins the Army, the family of the war worker who moves into a boom town (1944/1962: 91).

The immigrant is the most striking example of strangerhood.

What does a stranger do? Because he or she does not know many aspects of the group that he or she is trying to enter, by means of observation and attention to details he or she seeks to understand the group's conventions so that he or she can act as a competent member of it. He or she is able to notice details which for the other participants are banal and irrelevant, or are invisible to them. This is the attitude required of the ethnographer to gain access to the underlying structures of a culture.

The researcher finds this cognitive attitude easier to adopt, the greater his or her distance from the group observed – as in the case of the early anthropologists who sometimes knew little about even the language of the communities that they studied. Unfortunately, the situation of the sociologist, who often studies institutions and organizations of his or her own society (as I have repeatedly pointed out), is very different. Besides the difference from the classic anthropologist, who changed cognitive schemes much more slowly, the sociologist's feelings of curiosity and surprise may rapidly deteriorate (because he or she is never completely extraneous) once he or she has got close to the group.

What this entails is the researcher inventing a (necessarily artificial) cognitive style that enables him or her to maintain this de-naturalizing attitude as long as possible. Schwartz and Jacobs have called this cognitive style 'the cultural stranger device. [It] is a particularly nice device for exploring competences in a culture that everybody learns without ever having been explicitly taught' (1979: 250).

Behaving as a stranger (or foreigner) during research means constantly suspending – or 'bracketing' as the German philosopher Husserl terms it – the natural attitude. Unfortunately, because ethnographers are often not, nor could be, strangers in the settings that they observe, this suspension is difficult to accomplish. How can they remedy this difficulty? One way is to use 'estrangement techniques,' namely practical methods which suspend the natural attitude and force the ethnographer to see *sets of activities* in (supposedly) 'social facts.' For example, 'to the ordinary eye, a tree or a star is an object which exists [facts], while to the physicist they are events which are happening' (Schwartz and Jacobs, 1979: 261).

Garfinkel invited his students to perform 'revelatory actions' (see 3.4) so that they could estrange themselves from the scene observed and detect the tacit conventions which structure interactions. Goffman also performed revelatory actions – though less disruptively than ethnomethodologists – to test the hypothesis of his mental hospital study that there was a correlation between the hierarchical structure of elderliness and the ethological concept of personal territory.

CASE STUDY
Revelatory actions

In the ward, one of the large wooden chairs, positioned close to the light and to the radiator, was regularly occupied by an elderly and respected patient, to whom the other patients and the staff had granted this right.

> As an experiment, I waited for an evening when the second good chair had been moved to another part of the room and then, before this patient arrived, sat in his chair, attempting to give the appearance of someone innocently reading. When he arrived at his usual hour, he gave me a long, quiet look. I attempted to give the response of someone who didn't know that he was being looked at. Failing in this way to remind me of my place, the patient scanned the room for the other good chair, found it, and brought it back to its usual place next to the one I was in. The patient then said in a respectful, unantagonistic tone: 'Do you mind, son, moving over into that chair for me?' I moved, ending the experiment (Goffman, 1961: 247, note 100).

However, an ethnographer can only rarely perform these actions in the course of research, for otherwise he or she may harm the relationship with the participants and alienate him or herself from the community under study. This concerns ethical issues.

There are therefore two complementary strategies which can be used to deconstruct the scene observed and to make familiar things strange. One of them is mental, the other is practical.

9.2.1 Thought experiments

The first mental estrangement strategy is a sort of thought experiment consisting in the (virtual) reversal of the situations observed. The expression 'armchair or thought experiments' is the translation of the German term *Gedankenexperiment*, coined by the physicist and philosopher Ernst Mach. A thought experiment is an attempt to solve a problem using the power of the human imagination and the head as a laboratory. Many thought experiments involve apparent paradoxes about the known or accepted that with time have led to the reformulation or refinement of theories.

Thought experiments have been used to pose questions in philosophy at least since Greek antiquity; a famous example is Plato's cave, but others pre-date Socrates. They are used in contemporary philosophy as well. In physics many famous thought experiments date from the nineteenth and especially the twentieth century, but examples can be found at least as early as Galileo: his rejection of Aristotle's law of gravity was based on conceptual arguments only, because he never performed the associated experiment of the tower of Pisa. The term was popularized by Einstein, who relied heavily on *Gedankenexperiments* both in his derivation of relativity and in his arguments with Bohr about quantum mechanics. Conceptual experiments are also used in mathematics and economics.

In cognitive science the famous book *Scripts, Plans, Goals, and Understanding* (1977) by Roger C. Schank and Robert P. Abelson is based upon insightful thought experiments (for the famous thought experiment called 'the Chinese Room' and designed by the American philosopher John Searle, go to www.sagepub.co.uk/gobo).

This virtual reversal of a real situation observed is achieved by means of various cognitive devices. Among them is the 'counterfactual conditional' (see Van Dijk, 1977: 79–81), which is a phrasal operator used to envision possible or alternative worlds. We may use an 'if-clause' to ask, for example, whether the participants involved in the action had been younger, the same age, or older than the interlocutor, would we have witnessed the same ritual or reaction? It is thus possible to deconstruct and reconstruct the tacit interactional foundations of power and gender relations, of social stratification, and so on. Historiography has made much use of historical counterfactuals to imagine what might have happened if events had turned out otherwise: What if Hitler had won the war? If Nelson had lost the Battle of Trafalgar? If the Great Wall of China had never been built? If petrol had never been discovered? If human beings were allergic to meat? (see Cohen, 2005).

The same deconstructive function is performed by 'WHY-clauses,' where the adverb 'why' is used in imitation of how children pester their parents with tiresome questions. 'Why is that man speaking to that woman like that?'; 'Why does he keep on interrupting her?'; 'Why has he raised his voice?' The child's cognitive attitude is like that of the stranger, in that they are both extraneous to the culture of their interlocutors.

9.2.2 Observation of marginal subjects

Crespin's law of observation

> The probability of being observed is in direct proportion to the stupidity of ones actions.

The second strategy is more real and less virtual. It consists in observing culturally and organizationally marginal subjects who seek acceptance by a group or a community. Their access practices resemble (in certain respects) Garfinkel's revelatory actions, with the important difference that they are spontaneous. There are five main kinds of marginal subjects: foreigners, novices, cultural misfits, cultural troublemakers (Schwartz and Jacobs, 1979: 249 ff), and people with *low* education. Careful observation of these participants furnishes the ethnographer with vital information about the tacit foundations of the culture under study.

Foreigners
Recent immigration into Europe has given rise to large inflows of foreigners into organizations, institutions and social groups. It is therefore quite easy for ethnographers to encounter strangers in the settings that they study. Hence, if ethnographers find it impossible to behave like foreigners themselves, they can observe those who really are foreigners and learn a great deal from them.

CASE STUDY
Chinese diplomats visit England

In the second half of the nineteenth century, and specifically between 1866 and 1877, a group of Chinese diplomats were sent on an official mission to Europe and the United States. They were instructed by China's equivalent of what we would today call the Ministry of Foreign Affairs to keep detailed diaries on uses and customs, technological discoveries, production systems, to draw topographical maps, and to gather all information useful for the understanding of Western civilization – rather like ethnologists used to do when they studied so-called primitive cultures. The travel accounts of these diplomats, the astonishment with which they observed everyday Western life, reveal the tacit foundations and cognitive categories of European cultures.

The diplomat Liu Xihong visited England in 1876. This is how he saw the situation of English women at the time:

> In this country women are more esteemed than men . . . the rules regulating family life honor the wife and give scant importance to the husband . . . Great significance is given to the birth of a baby girl and little importance to the birth of a baby boy.

Moreover, women traveled on trains together with men, they attended receptions, they were free to walk the streets, they could travel unaccompanied, and go to the Opera. When the Chinese delegates paid a visit to an official, they were astounded when he introduced his wife to them. This they considered a breach of the Confucian code, which stipulated that a woman must be confined to the household's private quarters, and not enter the public ones, which were the prerogative of the man. Patterns of female participation were viewed as scandalous:

> The young and beautiful women do not avoid men, not even if they meet for the first time. They eat together with men at dinner parties, when they leave the house they sit in the same carriages as the men, they exchange toasts, they cross their legs without it being considered wicked . . . Men and women choose their spouses by themselves. When a man finds a woman pleasing, he invites her to his home, where he entertains her as a guest. In Western customs women are dissolute, while men are chaste. If a woman likes a man, she often asks him if he is married; if he is not, she brazenly proposes to him. The man dare not make the first move.

Liu Xihong (1876–77), Selections from *Personal Records of Travels in Britain*, in *Renditions* nos. 53/54 (*Special Issue: Chinese Impressions of the West*), Journal edited by Chinese University of Hong Kong.

Novices

Another type of actor of particular interest to the ethnographer is the novice: that is, someone learning an occupation (an apprentice, an intern, a

newly-hired worker) or who has recently acquired new status (a university freshman, army recruit, newly-admitted hospital patient or prison inmate, etc.). Both categories require training in the natural attitude (what Schutz [1944: 95] called 'thinking as usual'): that is, the cognitive schemas, communicative competences, and social skills necessary to interact appropriately in the new environment. A novice's difficulties of adjustment are an extremely important source of information for the researcher.

CASE STUDY
A novice in a concentration camp

Primo Levi (1919–87), an Italian chemist and non-religious Jew, was interned in Auschwitz (Poland) in February 1944 and remained in the concentration camp for 11 months until its liberation by the Russian army. This extreme experience prompted Levi to write a book, *If This is a Man*, in which he recounted the tragedy of millions of men, women and children whose only fault was that they had been born Jews, gypsies or homosexuals, or happened to be communists. The book is a detailed, lucid, and harrowing account of Levi's experiences from his arrest to his liberation. The extract which follows describes the social organization of the concentration camp as seen through the eyes of a novice forced rapidly to learn tacit conventions, classifications, rules and norms if he was to have any hope of survival.

We had soon learned that the guests of the Lager are divided into three categories: the criminals, the politicals and the Jews . . . And we learnt other things, more or less quickly, according to our intelligence: to reply "Jawohl," never to ask questions, always to pretend to understand. We have learnt the value of the food; now we also diligently scrape the bottom of the bowl after the ration and we hold it under our chins when we eat bread so as not to lose the crumbs. We, too, know that it is not the same thing to be given a ladleful of soup from the top or from the bottom of the vat, and we are already able to judge, according to the capacity of the various vats, what is the most suitable place to try and reach in the queue when we line up . . . In addition, there are innumerable circumstances, normally irrelevant, which here become problems. When one's nails grow long, they have to be shortened; which can only be done with one's teeth (for the toenails, the friction of the shoes is sufficient); if a button comes off, one has to tie it on with a piece of wire; if one goes to the latrine or the washroom, everything has to be carried along, always and everywhere, and while one washes one's face, the bundle of clothes has to be held tightly between one's knees: in any other manner it will be stolen in that second (1958/1959: 28–9).

Cultural misfits

Cultural misfits are marginal subjects who try, 'more or less successfully, to pass' (Schwartz and Jacobs, 1979: 260) in the group. Garfinkel (1967) provides the example of Agnes, a transsexual who claimed to be a woman. The description of how Agnes coped with everyday situations reveals important aspects of the work required to create and maintain a social role.

CASE STUDY
The social construction of gender

In October 1958 Agnes, 'a nineteen-year-old, white, single girl, who was at the time self-supporting and working as a typist for a local insurance company . . . appeared at the Department of Psychiatry at the University of California, Los Angeles . . . Agnes's appearance was convincingly female (however) until the age of seventeen she was recognized by everyone to be a boy' (Garkinkel, 1967: 118–20).

The author of the study was not morbidly interested in discovering whether Agnes was really a woman born with a rare disorder (a normal-sized penis and testicles on the body of a woman) or a hermaphrodite ('a freak of nature' as Agnes called herself) or simply a transsexual, and in this case a man being changed into a woman by surgery (as the doctors who examined Agnes maintained). Garfinkel was instead interested in the strategies used by Agnes to 'pass' as a woman.

Garfinkel conducted interviews with Agnes for a total of around 35 hours of tape-recorded conversation.

During these interviews Agnes described, amongst other things, her 'passing devices,' the circumstances in which her identity could be doubted by interlocutors, and her techniques for 'managing impressions.' Of interest to Garfinkel were not Agnes's excuses or evasions (strategies 'to get out from under'), or the outright lies, of 'episodic character,' which she was forced to tell in order to conceal the fact that she was not a real woman. Of interest instead were the actions, of 'a continuing and developmental character' (p. 146), whereby Agnes could seem a real woman, constantly perform that role, and 'pass' as a female. Agnes described the excuses which she used to avoid intercourse with her boyfriend Bill; and then 'how to cook . . . dishes to please Bill, . . . dressmaking and materials . . . which clothes she should wear . . . the skills of home management' (p. 146), not to sunbathe at five in the afternoon when men were coming home from work, because this 'was offensive to him (Bill), but attractive to other men' (p. 146).

The experiences of Agnes, a cultural misfit, reveal that gender is anything but an objective feature that can be taken for granted. It is not enough to say 'I am a man' or 'I am a woman' to be recognized as such: one must constantly certify and exhibit masculinity or femininity. This display requires the deployment of details, particulars, trifles, and therefore of material and symbolic resources, which constitute the foundations of a culture and which only a stranger can grasp.

EXERCISE 9.1

Go to a public place (an open-air café, an open space in shopping mall, a street, a park, or similar) and observe people smoking. Describe this action and then answer the following questions:
1. How do smokers hold their cigarettes? How many different ways are there?
2. How do they hold cigarettes in their mouths? How many different ways are there?
3. What do smokers do with their other hand, the one not holding the cigarette?
4. What do smokers do with the other parts of their bodies? What is the posture of their legs and arms? What do they lean against?

Now relate these actions to gender. Obviously, in Western countries, sex cannot be directly 'determined' in public places by physical examination. So, in order to be recognized/classified as the person they want to be recognized/classified as, people must continuously display their gender through 'passing devices.' Now, on the basis of your observations, try to answer these two final questions:
1. What must a smoking member do to 'pass as a woman'?
2. What must a smoking member do to 'pass as a man'?

You will discover things that you have never noticed before.

Cultural troublemakers

> You always have to explain things to grown-ups . . . Grown-ups never understand anything for themselves and children are forever explaining things to them.
>
>   A. de Saint-Exupéry, *The Little Prince*, 1943, Ch. 1

Cultural troublemakers are

> people who have been identified as defective in some area of social life and who, for one reason or another, are considered incapable of performing some of the tasks falling to the normal, natural adult member of the society. We might include in this category children, the mentally ill, the retarded, and certain types of criminals. These people are interesting in two ways – the way they deal with society, and the way society deals with them (Schwartz and Jacobs, 1979: 262).

CASE STUDY
The world through the eyes of the children

Children have a formidable talent to reveal the tacit knowledge of adults. The French writer and aviator, Antoine de Saint-Exupéry (1900–44), was an acute observer of children's behavior, which he exemplified as follows:

> Grown-ups love figures. When you tell them that you have made a new friend, they never ask you any questions about essential matters. They never say to you, 'What does his voice sound like? What games does he love best? Does he collect butterflies?' Instead, they demand: 'How old is he? How many brothers has he? How much does he weigh? How much money does his father make?' Only then do they think that they know him (*The Little Prince*, 1943: Ch. 4).

(For a case study of a disabled person, go to www.sagepub.co.uk/gobo.)

Several sociologists have made observation of cultural misfits their preferred approach. Goffman (1964) studied psychotic behavior in order to uncover the fundamental rituals (deference, embarrassment, demeanor) of the social order: he observed infringements so that he could infer the rule, and breaches to deduce the norm. Or he analyzed the accounts of secret agents (1969), describing the subterfuges they used to imitate the identity-construction strategies of 'common mortals'. Cicourel and Boese (1972) observed deaf or sightless children in order to understand socialization and language acquisition. The cultural misfit approach is founded on the relativist conviction that normality and deviance are inextricably intertwined and can only be defined in terms of each other.

EXERCISE 9.2

Alone, or in a group, choose a play or a concert for children. They are usually scheduled at weekends. Go to the show and observe the behavior of the children: how do they sit? How and when do they laugh? How and when do they applaud? Do they sit still? Do they interrupt while an actor is speaking? Then compare your observations with what happens at a theater performance for adults.

Draw up a list of the conventions governing a theatrical or musical event for adults based on your observations of the behavior of the children.

The minor incidents that marginal subjects (more or less consciously) provoke afford the ethnographer insight into the underlying social structure. As Schwartz and Jacobs write:

> cultural troublemakers are a continual source of naturally occurring disruption, for they break rules that are seldom broken, they say things that are never said, and they have technical problems that others do not. Such people provide us with the provocative contrasts to the normal and the ordinary (1979: 263).

EXERCISE 9.3

Find or borrow a wheelchair. Sit in it for ten minutes. Do not get up for any reason. Do all the things that you usually do, but sitting in the wheelchair. When the ten minutes have passed, reflect on the experience.

Now go with the wheelchair to a place where nobody knows you (a large supermarket, a post office, etc.) and try to do one of the many things that people go to that place to do. Observe how people behave towards you, how the social organization changes when you arrive, how they construct disability. Reflect on this experience as well.

People with low education

Although education levels have risen considerably in recent decades, there are still people who are relatively uneducated: dropouts, certain poor people, nomads, some residents of rural or mountain areas, etc. (for a really amusing case study, go to www.sagepub.co.uk/gobo).

In Chapter 11 we shall see that the illiterate have difficulty in forming abstractions, in generalizing, and in introspecting.

EXERCISE 9.4

Watch the film 'Born Yesterday.' There are two versions: the 1950 original directed by George Cukor and the 1993 remake by Luis Mandoki. Take the first that you find because both are serviceable, given that the script of the remake, with its wisecracks, is a 'photocopy' of the original. The comedy tells the story of a businessman in love with a dumb show-girl, of whom he is terribly ashamed when they are together in public. He consequently hires a journalist to teach the girl how to behave in society.

Because the show-girl is extraneous to the society frequented by the business-man, she acquires interesting tacit knowledge about that culture, just as Moravia's Ciociara did.

Now you should:

(a) discover from the show-girl (played by Judy Holliday, or by Melanie Griffith in the remake) the tacit assumptions of that society and make a list of them;

(b) transcribe the eight set phrases that the show-girl must utter on every social occasion in order to seem a competent member of that society. The phrases are suggested to her by her tutor, the journalist (played by Broderick Crawford, or by Don Johnson in the 1993 version).

What have we learned from these five case studies? At least this: when an ethnographer enters an organization or group, he or she must immediately seek to identify its marginal actors, because they are inexhaustible sources of information. Their actions abound with creativity and hypotheses about reality which are much more counter-intuitive than any sociological imaginings.

However, comprehension of a culture is not achieved with detached observation alone. For 'it is of the utmost importance that the researcher be both a stranger to a scene *and* enmeshed in it in practical ways. He must continually be in the position of having *do* to things' (Schwartz and Jacobs, 1979: 248). The well-known gap between *knowing* and *knowing how* suggests that exclusive reliance on observation and informal interviews with participants may be an obstacle against full understanding of their activities. There are obviously many ways to do such things without becoming a non-observing participant and thus lose the necessary distance.

If the researcher is studying a judicial authority, he or she may apply for a certificate and thus uncover (in the guise of a user) the paradoxes of the justice system. When studying an educational institution, he or she may try to borrow a book from the library. In a health facility, the ethnographer may help in an emergency situation without this affecting his or her identity as a researcher. In short, the best way to understand a practice is to do it, because this compels the investigator to draw on the tacit knowledge of the investigated:

> The big payoff in situations like this is finding oneself confronted with endless puzzles, problems and issues where others in the same place hardly see anything worth mentioning (nor do they even know how to mention it) (Schwartz and Jacobs, 1979: 249).

For this reason, 'the investigator must be placed in situations where real practical success and failures are all but unavoidable' (1979: 250). In case of failure, the researcher cannot resort to the excuse 'I am an ethnographer, not an expert on the subject,' although any lack of success should be reflected upon. For these experiences to emerge with all their richness, they should be practised at the beginning of the investigation, when the researcher is still a stranger, before the bulk of the information has become familiar (1979: 251–2).

EXERCISE 9.5

Get hold of a baby buggy and push it around the streets for a while. It will be even better if you can put a (relative's or friend's) baby in the buggy, as this will make the experience even more realistic. Try to follow a route well-known to you, so that you can note differences. Then answer these questions: for what kind of pedestrian are the streets and sidewalks of your town designed? Who is the ideal pedestrian? What are his or her attributes?

9.3 Concluding remarks

Social theory is very often a refinement and a specification of common-sense theories already present in public opinion. If social theory wants to emancipate itself from 'folk theories,' if it wants to make a qualitative 'leap,' it must assume a methodological attitude that helps it denaturalize situations and society. A phenomenologically-oriented ethnography may be of great help in this regard.

KEY POINTS

- To engage in phenomenologically-informed ethnography, the most appropriate attitude is that of the 'stranger.'
- The cultural stranger device helps to explore competences in a culture that everybody learns without ever having been explicitly taught.
- Behaving as a stranger (or foreigner) during research means constantly suspending – or 'bracketing' as the German philosopher Husserl terms it – the natural attitude.
- Unfortunately, because ethnographers are often not, nor could be, strangers in the settings that they observe, this suspension is difficult to accomplish.
- We can find help in so called 'estrangement techniques,' namely practical methods which suspend the natural attitude and force the ethnographer to see *sets of activities* in (supposedly) 'social facts.'
- To deconstruct the scene observed and to make familiar things strange we can adopt two complementary strategies: one of them is mental (thought experiments), the other is practical (observation of marginal subjects).
- There are five main kinds of culturally and organizationally marginal subjects who seek acceptance by a group or a community: foreigners, novices, cultural misfits, cultural troublemakers and people with low education.

KEY TERMS

Estrangement (see pp. 148–9)	A cognitive state where the natural attitude, 'thinking as usual,' is suspended and the ethnographer is forced to see *sets of activities* in (supposedly) 'social facts.'
Estrangement techniques (see p. 148ff)	These are practical ways to suspend the natural attitude.
Thought experiments (see p. 151)	These consist in the (virtual) revelation of the situations observed. They can be performed using various cognitive devices, among them counterfactual conditionals (IF-clauses) or WHY-clauses.

RECOMMENDED READING

For undergraduates:
Silverman, David (2007)

For graduates:
Mehan, Hugh and Wood, Houston (1975a)

For advanced researchers:
Cohen, Martin (2005)

SELF-EVALUATION TEST

Are you ready for the next chapter? Check your knowledge by answering the following open-ended questions:

1. In what way can an illness be an experience of estrangement?
2. What is meant by Marcel Proust's statement: 'The real voyage of discovery consists not in seeking new landscapes, but in having new eyes'?
3. What is a 'stranger' for Schutz?
4. Why in the past have some authors studied disabled people in order to understand how people without particular disabilities communicate?

What to Observe: Social Structures, Talks and Contexts

LEARNING OBJECTIVES

• To understand the main aims of observation.

• To learn what to observe.

• To uncover the ideologies lying behind objects.

• To appreciate visual ethnography tools.

• To grasp the differences among contexts.

10.1 Introduction

The principal purpose of estrangement is to render tacit knowledge explicit. Such knowledge is embodied in the routines which participants repeatedly perform without giving importance to them. Estrangement reveals the architecture on which society rests and whereby it reproduces itself. From this perspective, ethnographers should focus on three aspects constantly and simultaneously present in social scenes: social structures, the common-sense interpretations/ explanations given by participants in their talk, and the context of the action.

10.2 Uncovering social structures

The term 'social structure' is highly ambiguous and may denote many things. In a phenomenologically informed ethnography, structures are essentially social conventions. What is a convention? To understand the term, do the following exercise in class with your instructor.

EXERCISE 10.1

Imagine that a young Senegalese manager is about to arrive in London. He is an expert on African financial markets, and has an appointment with his English counterpart. This is the first time that he has been to London and has previously had few face-to-face interactions with English colleagues. He is consequently rather nervous because he is not sure how he should behave. You are invited to give him instructions on how to behave as a competent actor during the *first three minutes of interaction* with his English colleague. What is your advice? Be careful, though, for if the set of instructions is incomplete, the beginning of the meeting may be disastrous from an interactional point of view. So think carefully about the instructions that you give the Senegalese manager. Try to envisage a situation in which, if he could conceal his skin pigmentation, eliminate his accent and change the timbre of his voice (as in an interaction where the interlocutors cannot see each other because they are separated by a screen), his English colleague would not realize that he was talking to a foreigner. So what do you suggest? What should the Senegalese manager do to behave appropriately? Make a list of instructions, which your instructor will write on the board.

After ten minutes of discussion in class . . .

Now leave your seats and form pairs. You should do what I tell you. Are you ready? Have you chosen a partner?
Right. Now move the tips of your shoes so that they touch the tips of your partner's shoes. Have you done that?
How did you feel? Why were you laughing? Were you reminded of *Don't Stand So Close to Me*, the 1980 hit single by the British pop group The Police? Why did you feel embarrassed or uncomfortable?
(For details about this case study, go to www.sagepub.co.uk/gobo.)

Social conventions are not directly observable, but they assume material form in actors' rituals and ceremonies, in the social practices and routines that produce and reproduce the group or organization's culture. Social practices are made up of minor actions, of apparently banal and superfluous ceremonials, which day after day sustain organizations and sometimes alter them. For this reason, an ethnographer should never neglect the details, for these may sometimes be crucial for understanding. An illuminating example is provided by Schwartz and Jacobs' (1979) description of a treatment facility for drug users.

CASE STUDY
A treatment facility for drug users

Both the researchers and the outreach workers were interested in what attracted drug users to the center. If they were to follow the recommendations of scientific sociology they would look to social facts. If they were to follow the recommendations of symbolic interactionism, as outlined in Chapter 3, they would look at morals, meanings, and motives. Yet none of these did much to explain why users come to the center. In fact, it turned out to be the public bathroom that was behind the youthful 'rush' to the center (because it was) the only downtown public john. A lot of kids came to the center for no other reason than to go to the bathroom. Obviously the bathroom was not the sole attraction of the center, but it was a major one (Schwartz and Jacobs, 1979: 180).

Attention to detail is the practical correlate to the recommendation of treating banality seriously. As Schwartz and Jacobs point out:

> while age, sex, marital status, and occupation are all well-recognized independent variables in sociology, the presence or absence of toilets has yet to achieve this status. Along with many similar factors, this 'variable' is ordinarily considered too mundane, silly and 'unsociological' to receive much attention by social scientists. Yet such mean details of practical existence may turn out to have more significance than the factors which currently strike us as [apparently] so much more serious, important, and scientific (1979: 180).

Rituals and ceremonies afford important insights into conventions, and thence into social structures (for another interesting case study, go to www.sagepub.co.uk/gobo).

10.2.1 Three ways to study rituals
As Durkheim pointed out, rituals constitute the essence of society: they furnish actors with meaning for their actions, and they set the cadence of social and interior life. Rituals can be studied in three main ways.

1. Classifying activities
The researcher can start with activities which he or she separates and classifies. For example, Goffman (1961: 93ff) described 'institutional ceremonies' at the mental hospital which he studied: group meetings, editing of the in-house newspaper, the institute's open day, charity shows and sports events.

CASE STUDY
Natural scientists at work

Latour (1995) conducted meticulous analysis and classification of the various phases in the everyday activities of social actors. He followed the investigative practices of a team of French pedologists carrying out a survey in the jungles of Brazil. The purpose of the expedition was to determine whether the jungle was encroaching on the savannah, or the other way round. A pedologist is an expert on the surveying, classifying, mapping, analyzing and conserving of soil (from the Greek *pedon:* soil, earth). Latour photographed many of the expedition's routine practices, among them a moment when a member of the team, René Boulet, took a sample of soil with his right hand and put it in a small square container (a 'pedocomparator') held in his left hand. Latour thus immortalized the moment when the lump of earth, on passing from the right hand to the left, changed its status: the earth became a sign, it acquired a geometric shape, it began a career as a numerical code, and it was soon thereafter classified by a color (1995: 165). In other words, it became science.

2. Starting from a key-concept

The researcher can operate in the reverse direction by starting from a key-concept of a particular organization, or 'what could be called *parent activity* [for example in hospital]: *making a dead* or dying person [and observing all the activities that rotate around him or her like those consisting] of *seeing death, announcing death, suspecting death,* and the like' (Sudnow, 1967: 8–9).

CASE STUDY
The social construction of dying in hospital

A very common one that entails the 'improper' use of interward transfers. A patient who comes into the Emergency Ward whose condition is such that his death is expected shortly, will occasionally be transferred to a medical or surgical ward, the presumed motive being that he is terminally ill and not properly a person for emergency care. The actual motive is suspected by the receiving ward's personnel to be the removal of a patient who is about to die so as to avoid having to care for his body. One evening a patient in quite critical condition was transferred from the Emergency Ward to the men's medical ward. The head evening nurse refused to accept the obviously dying patient, and complained that the Emergency Ward clerk simply sent him over to die on her property. She angrily instructed the orderly to return the patient to the Emergency Ward, with this message, 'You tell Mrs. Smith to wrap her own bodies'. . .

A patient who is admitted to the hospital in what is considered to be near-death state: with, for example, extremely low blood pressure, very erratic heart beats, and a nonpalpable or very weak pulse, is frequently left on the stretcher on which he is admitted and put in the laboratory room, or large supply room. In such cases, a nurse explained, they don't want to mess a bed up and, since the patient would soon die, there was no need to assign a bed (upon death, the complete bedding must be stripped, the room thoroughly cleansed, disinfected, etc.). In several cases, patients were left throughout the night to die in the supply room, and, if in the morning they were still alive, nurses quickly assigned them beds, before the arrival of physicians and/or relatives (Sudnow, 1967: 83).

So-called 'comatose' patients are treated as essentially dead. Considering a person in a coma is warrant for talking about him in his 'presence' in ways that would not be permissible were he awake (Sudnow, 1967: 88).

3. Following an object

The researcher can select and follow a particular participant, letting his or her action define the boundaries of the context of observation. Or the researcher can choose an object with a certain importance in the organization under study and follow its trajectory. In policy analysis, for example, a rule, regulation or a new law is selected, and then its implementation is observed. It usually turns out that the measure is not applied as the political decision-maker intended; instead, as it passes from central government to the local authorities, from office to office, from interpretation to interpretation, from negotiation to negotiation, it undergoes numerous changes. But the object can be something much more concrete and much smaller . . . a shoe, for example.

CASE STUDY
Shoes in the life of a concentration camp

If a shoe hurts, one has to go in the evening to the ceremony of the changing of the shoes: this tests the skill of the individual who, in the middle of an incredible crowd, has to be able to choose at an eye's glance one (not a pair, one) shoe, which fits. Because once the choice is made, there can be no second change.

And do not think that shoes form a factor of secondary importance in the life of the Lager. Death begins with the shoes; for most of us, they show themselves to be instruments of torture, which after a few hours of marching cause painful sores which become fatally infected. Whoever has them is forced to walk as if he was dragging a convict's chain (this explains the strange gait of the army which returns every evening on parade); he arrives last everywhere, and everywhere he receives blows. He cannot escape if they run after him; his feet swell and the more they swell, the more the friction with the wood and the cloth of the shoes becomes insupportable. Then only the hospital is left: but to enter the hospital with a diagnosis of *'dicke Füsse'* (swollen feet) is extremely dangerous, because it is well known by all, and especially to the SS, that there is no cure for that complaint (Levi, 1958/1959: 29–30).

EXERCISE 10.2

Watch the film 'Train de vie' (1998) by the Romanian director Radu Mihaileanu.
The film is set in 1941. News has reached the inhabitants of a Jewish village in Eastern Europe that the Nazis have started to deport and murder the Jews living in nearby villages. In a desperate search for a solution which will save their lives, they come up with the almost insane idea of organizing a fake deportation train. They themselves will be simultaneously the deportees, train crew, soldiers and Nazi officers. In this way they will be able to cross the German lines and reach safety.
At various moments during the film, the fake Nazis are nearly discovered. How does the bogus Nazi officer in charge of the train perform his role? On which material and symbolic resources does he rely? What communicative and linguistic strategies does he use to interact with the real Nazis without being discovered?

10.3 Listening to talk

Observing behavior is very important: indeed, it is crucial. But observation in itself, without concomitant listening to the speech that precedes, accompanies or follows the behavior observed may be the cause of errors. In 'Hollywood Ending,' a 2002 film by the New York director Woody Allen there are a number of episodes that illustrate this issue well. The film is set in a studio, to which full access is granted to Andrew Ford (Jodie Markell), a backstabbing reporter for *Esquire*, a well-known magazine for men. The film's producer has allowed the journalist access so that she will file a report with the magazine and induce its readers to see the film. Instead, the journalist snoops around the set (inexplicably, with head office permission) looking for a story. Nevertheless, she rarely talks to the director, who keeps her at a distance because he distrusts her. On the basis of observation alone, without linguistic access to the director's point of view, she misunderstands numerous situations and commits various blunders.

Hence, behaviors have diverse meanings for those who watch them. Listening to the 'talk' of participants may be of help in resolving this natural semantic ambiguity.

CASE STUDY
Punks, swastikas and the polysemy of signs

When you see a swastika on a banner or a jacket, or tattooed on a person's arm, what do you think? That the person flaunting the swastika is a Nazi sympathizer? This may be the case, but it is not necessarily so. Signs (in this case the swastika) are polysemous, and they may be the hardware (the physical support) of diverse meanings. Meaning and sign combine to create the symbol.

For example, Dick Hebdige, a leading representative of the cultural studies school (see Chapter 3), noted in a book on the esthetics of English youth subcultures that the punks who wore a swastika on their clothes did not regard it as a Nazi symbol (as the dominant culture considered it, consequently classifying the punk subculture as pro-Nazi). Instead, they saw it as a symbol of opposition and open hostility:

> Conventionally, as far as the British were concerned, the swastika signified 'enemy.' Nonetheless, in punk usage, the symbol lost its 'natural' meaning – fascism. The punks were not generally sympathetic to the parties of the extreme right . . . the swastika was worn because it was guaranteed to shock . . . 'punks just like to be hated'. This represented more than a simple inversion or inflection of the ordinary meanings attached to an object. The signifier (swastika) had been wilfully detached from the concept (Nazism) it conventionally signified, and although it had been re-positioned . . . within an alternative subcultural context, its primary value and appeal derived precisely from its lack of meaning: from its potential for deceit. It was exploited as empty effect (Hebdige, 1979: 116).

Many youth subcultures are in fact constituted by a series of (deliberately) shocking transformations made to objects, values, attitudes, or practices of the dominant culture in order to flaunt symbolic forms of resistance. But how can we understand all this? Observation is certainly not enough: we must listen to the talk of the participants.

10.3.1 Discovering meanings

Signs (as we have seen in this example but also in 5.2) may be polysemous. So too (if not even more so) may be *words* (if we consider them from the strictly phenomenological point of view) in that they are nothing but *sounds* (if spoken) or *signs* (if written).

Take the word 'sister': how many meanings does it have? At least five:

(1) a collateral relative of the first degree as the child of the same parents;

(2) used in the plural, it is said of people who closely resemble each other ('they look like sisters');

(3) with regard to an intimate but chaste relationship ('they love each other like brother and sister');

(4) with regard to things with close affinities ('sister civilizations'); or

(5) as a noun denoting a nun.

Hence, the same word is used to convey a variety of meanings. This is a problem, because misunderstandings may arise and sometimes (though obviously not always) trigger conflict. Studies on road directions, and the relative misunderstandings, provide numerous examples. For instance, the instruction may be given: 'go straight on until you pass a bridge and then turn right.' Yet the social representations of 'bridge' are highly diverse (viaduct, overpass, flyover, footbridge, causeway, etc.) and those of the two actors may not coincide.

This is due to the fact that the conceptual stock (meanings) of a culture is much larger than its terminological stock (words or terms). It would be fine (perhaps, but not always, given that ambiguity has appeal for its own sake) if there were one single term for each meaning, so that misunderstandings would be almost impossible. However, the actual situation is very different, and in ethnography attention to the polysemy of words plays a fundamental role in the understanding of cultures.

CASE STUDY
The concepts/meanings of an organization's customers

Some years ago, a student of mine conducted an ethnography in two large sportswear stores for his masters dissertation, the aim of which was to study organizational cultures. To this end, the student sought, amongst other things, to identify the principal key-words and key-concepts/meanings present in the two organizations, as this would yield useful insights into their cultures. As he listened to conversations among the staff at one of the shops, he realized that they had at least three concepts of 'customer.'

For example, when the *managers* used the word 'customer,' they were thinking of a highly abstract and intangible individual (as evidenced by statements like 'the company's success depends on its customers' or 'the customer always comes first.' They therefore had an idealized conception of the customer, which also served as a useful rhetorical device with which to impose their decisions on the employees.

By contrast, when the *department heads* talked about the 'customer,' they were referring to a more concrete individual: the one who enabled them to win the daily competition against the other departments. In fact, the organizational culture of the store (by will of the management) provided for examination of the accounts at the end of each day, with a productivity bonus being awarded to the department with the highest sales.

Finally, for the *sales assistants*, the 'customer' was essentially a nuisance, someone who distracted them from more important (for them) tasks, like tidying up the items on display, attaching prices to products, checking stock on the computer, and so on. Obviously the sales assistants were not so foolish as to prefer an empty shop with no customers: they knew very well that the customer was the (indirect) source of their wages. Nevertheless, while for the department heads the more customers the better (because they would win the daily competition with the other department heads), of importance for the sales staff was that the daily number of customers did not fall below the threshold ensuring the company's survival while they were left to get on with their work in peace.

10.3.2 Discursive practices

It should by now be clear that without concepts there is no perception; even less is there understanding (see 5.1). Without understanding, observation is stunted, as exemplified by the descriptions by Chinese diplomats on a mission to Europe in the nineteenth century.

CASE STUDY
Chinese diplomats and Christian religious practices

Zhang Deyi was an intelligent 19-year-old student selected to accompany the first Chinese fact-finding mission to Europe in 1866. During his voyage on a French ship, on 8 April 1866 he noted in his diary as follows:

> There are missionaries on the ship, and when Sunday comes they arrange four rows of chairs and stools on the deck. In the middle they erect a cross, light candles, and then muster the passengers. Those who go, men and women, carry the Bible with them, and standing or seated they recite the holy texts in low voices. Sometimes they point to their shoulders and orifices with a hand, or they strike their faces and seem to weep. On the dais, a man called 'father', wearing a long gown and a white hat, reads the texts and the people respond in chorus. When on terra firma, upon the appointed day, they gather together in churches (Zhang Deyi (1869)) *Strange Tales from Over the Ocean*, in *Renditions* Nos. 53 & 54 Spring & Autumn, 2000).

In this case, the Chinese observer is unable to grasp the meaning of the scene because he does not possess the concepts of *mass* and *sign of the cross*. This account is, as the philosopher Gilbert Ryle would put it, a 'thin description.'

It is a phenomenalistic 'snapshot observation' which, if it sees a rapid blinking of the right eyelid cannot distinguish an involuntary tic from a wink, that 'a classic device for establishing byplay' (Goffman, 1963: 184, note 7). What this observation lacks is a 'thick description' which reproduces the *meanings* of actions.[1] In other words, it perceives but does not comprehend; it watches but does not see.

Instead, if an ethnographer is to understand, he or she must listen to the talk of actors as they interact. The majority of social actions are preceded, accompanied or followed by comments. Indeed, comments ('accounts' as ethnomethodologists would call them) are part of the action itself. If language is a form of action, as the English philosopher of language John L. Austin theorized, then discourses produce and reproduce the social structure, besides helping us to understand action. The comments of participants explain and describe the meaning of action. Indeed, according to Garfinkel, action and description coincide:

> the activities whereby members produce and manage settings of organized everyday affairs are identical with members' procedures for making those settings 'account-able.' . . . When I speak of accountable my interests are directed to such matters as . . . situated practices of looking-and-telling (1967: 1).

Members' comments are therefore not independent or separate from the social practices in which they are produced. Thus manifest is the *reflexive relation* between action and comment: the one explains the other, and vice versa. This crucial point is made clear by the following example.

CASE STUDY
The convict code

Wieder quotes the phrase 'You know I won't snitch' (1974: 168) as the response by a resident of a halfway house to a researcher's question which he deemed inappropriate. This seemingly innocuous phrase was instead simultaneously 'multi-formulative and multi-consequential' (p. 168).

In the former case, the inmate communicated the meaning of his refusal, and specifically (i) how he perceived the conversation at that point (as a request for inside information); (ii) his state of mind in responding; (iii) the reasons why he might cut the conversation short; (iv) the role and social status that differentiated him from the researcher; and (v) his adherence to the convict code.

In the latter case (multi-consequential) the comment was also *an action*, in that (i) it sanctioned the researcher's behavior (that 'you know' signified 'you know very well that there is a rule against snitching so why do you insist on asking these questions?'; (ii) it interrupted the conversation; (iii) it left the researcher without the information he was looking for; (iv) it warned him that the conversation could turn unpleasant if it did not get back to normal; (v) it hinted at the risk that the inmate was running ('you understand' also meant: 'you know very well that if I talk, they're going to beat me up or brand me a rat fink,' and (vi) it pointed out that, because it was the wardens' duty to protect the inmates, if he was assaulted the conversation would cause trouble for the staff as well. Wieder acutely points out:

> conversations . . . instructed one another on how to *see* the behavior of residents . . . By naming, explaining, justifying, and even requesting to do an act, residents taught both staff and researcher how to see the sense of residents' circumstances and residents' conduct *from the standpoint of the resident* (1974: 219).

Conversations have another peculiarity: that of reproducing the organization. If an attendant serving behind the counter at a university cafeteria is asked by a student for 'some more spaghetti' and he replies peevishly: 'how many times do I have to tell you that the portions are fixed,' he is communicating a convention and simultaneously reproducing a part of the cafeteria-system.

> On this view, the social structure is therefore 'constituted' by acts and by the interpretations that these acts furnish to social actors . . . For example, the use of certain linguistic expressions like addressals (Professor! Hi buddy! Hey, you!) or the way in which two people initiate a telephone conversation, not only presuppose a certain social relationship (of subjection, intimacy, power) but also reinforce it, or even create it through the use of particular expressions. In other words, it is partly the way in which we talk to people that defines our relationship with them (note that this is a criticism of the distinction traditionally drawn in behavioral science between dependent and independent variables) (Duranti, 1992: 29).

We may therefore say that the social structure reproduced in social interactions is constituted by precisely those interactions (see also the 'theory of interaction ritual chains' developed by Randall Collins, 2004).

Discourses therefore afford access to the interpretations of participants; they also act as 'hooks' on which to hang social representations. Hence, language is an excellent means with which to penetrate both the interpretations and the actions of social actors (see Figure 10.1).

Figure 10.1   Relations between thought, language and action

10.4 The main context of action: Space

Full understanding of discourse-actions (or if one wishes, action-discourses) requires a third dimension: the context. Social practices are always situated practices, in that they take place in an organized situation comprising an array of both resources for action and constraints upon it. Neglecting these constraints may cause the ethnographer to misinterpret the meanings of the linguistic practices observed. For example, the American linguistic anthropologist Elinor Ochs (1988: 1), in her study of language acquisition at home by children in Western Samoa, noticed that the verbal behavior of the participants changed among different zones in the house, besides depending on where the researcher was positioned. In the zones of the household considered public, the natives adopted a formal language style (what the Samoans call 'good speech'). Instead, in the zones considered private, they switched to a more informal style (called 'bad speech'). Consequently, language development had to be studied within a broader context comprising, amongst other characteristics, the social organization of space in a Samoan house.

Considering the context, therefore, means above all observing the physical space or setting. And this is represented mainly by the furnishings and artifacts amid which actions take place. We shall examine artifacts later. To be considered now is the role of furnishings in enabling (and at the same time restricting) actions; without forgetting that furnishings are also indicators of their designer's ideology.

EXERCISE 10.3

As long as I have frequented university classrooms, first as an undergraduate and then as a lecturer, I have been struck by how infrequently students intervene (with questions, comments, criticisms) during lectures. This scant participation has always been a mystery to me.

You are now invited to discover the causes (the independent variables) of this phenomenon by discussing them in class with your instructor's guidance. We shall thus move along a path which, step by step and using (on occasion) a kind of thought experiment, will lead us to solution of the mystery.

First step. Look at your classroom; look at its furnishings. How is the seating arranged? Where do the students sit? Where does the teacher stand? Does everything seem normal to you? Do you notice anything odd? Formulate an answer.

Second step. Of course everything is normal. It has always been. This arrangement of the furnishings appears natural to us; we take it for granted. But let us try to estrange ourselves for a moment, pretending that we are aliens entering a university lecture room for the first time. Begin with a thought experiment. Why are the students sitting over there? And if they were sitting next to the lecturer? And if the lecturer took the place of a student and sat in the middle of the room, what would happen? Try to answer.

Third step. Lecture rooms do not come into being ready-made, so to speak. They are designed and constructed by someone, usually an architect or an engineer. Look at your lecture room: according to you, what idea of the teaching process did the architect have in mind when designing the room? What did he consider the requirements of good teaching to be? In what surroundings can it take place? Answer.
(For my view and explanations, go to www.sagepub.co.uk/gobo.)

EXERCISE 10.4

Go to http://www.flickr.com/search/?q=university+classroom and search a classroom like the one described in step seven. At which university is it located? Of the 1,000 or more photographs published on the site, how many fall within the category described in step seven? What do you deduce from this?

The description of classroom interactions has conveyed well the concept of 'situated action,' much used in *Practice-based studies* and *Workplace studies*: cognitive activities are not only mental; in order to be performed, they necessarily require material supports, which end up guiding the reasoning process. As 'organizational symbolism' (Turner, 1990) has theorized, furnishings perform an important function in structuring interactions (for a case study on space and social relations in a psychiatric hospital, go to www.sagepub.co.uk/gobo).

Observation of spatial settings helps one find more specifically sociological explanations for human behaviors by reducing the role traditionally assigned to the intentionality of action.

CASE STUDY
Reducing the explanatory function of the concept of intentionality

The social sciences are still strongly influenced by a voluntarist theory of action which, since Max Weber, has explained behaviors in terms of the concepts of 'interest,' 'intention,' 'value orientation,' 'rationality,' 'motivation,' 'conscience,' and so on (see 2.4). Nobody would deny the importance of these concepts, yet (as ethnomethodology has stressed) their explanatory capacity has been decidedly overestimated. I provide two examples showing this from my own experience.

I.
When I was hired by my university department, I was assigned an office very close to the toilets. Moreover, it was of such small size that it was more of a broom

cupboard than an office. I consequently always left the door open to fend off claustrophobia. Seeing that the toilets were frequently visited by my colleagues, and because my door was always open, I soon made acquaintances in the department and joined its community. The toilets were also used by the director of the department, whose office happened to be on the same floor as mine. So a day did not pass when I did not meet my director and have a brief chat with him. Day after day, casual conversation after casual conversation, he came to know my research interests, my intellectual concerns, the publications I was working on, and many other things. I, for my part, learned a lot about him, and we even did some research together. If I had been assigned a different office, or one on a different floor, this particular relationship with the director would never have come about. That said, however, it would be an exaggeration to say that I became a professor merely by lavatorial merit!

II.

Some years later, owing to renovation work, the department moved temporarily to another building. Because this building was smaller and had only a few large-sized offices, these were occupied by groups of four department members. I ended up in an office with three other colleagues whom I knew only slightly because in the old building they had occupied offices on different floors from mine. But in the new situation, because of physical proximity, we got to know each other well, even becoming friends, and then began to collaborate academically. We remained in the temporary premises for a couple of years and then returned to the department building when its refurbishment was complete.

Each of us was assigned a single office, and ones moreover located on different floors. Since then, our relationships have cooled, contacts have become increasingly rare, and now weeks can pass without our even seeing each other. In the meantime, I have formed new relationships, especially with colleagues in the offices adjoining mine.

So, we may ask, to what extent is it happenstance that determines actions, and to what extent is it intentionality? Is not the concept of 'situated action' more suitable?

10.5 Artifacts

It is not only furnishings that provide resources for action and set constraints on it. So too do artifacts; that is, the objects with which we perform actions. In highly technological societies like ours, interactions are increasingly mediated by artifacts. In normal settings we usually have three types of artifact available to us:

- technological;
- cognitive; and
- organizational.

Technological artifacts are instruments which perform, boost, or supplement *physical* action (examples are a lathe, a conveyor belt, an assembly line, but also a pencil, a microphone or a telephone).

Cognitive artifacts are objects constructed in order to augment cognitive capacity: a knot in a handkerchief, a calendar, a shopping list, a notebook, a diary, a visual or acoustic signal, an abacus, a notice board, a blackboard, a data matrix, a photograph, a film clip, the display on a cash dispenser or a computer terminal. Norman (1991) extends the notion of cognitive artifact to include products of the human mind (proverbs, memorization techniques, and so on). Cognitive artifacts are artificial systems which store and process information useful for reasoning and decision-making.

Organizational artifacts instead boost the human capacity to predict and to plan. They enable actions to be distributed in time and space so as to produce complex activities with internal co-ordination and coherence. Examples are the procedures of a work organization, but also the distribution of roles in a team game.

These artifacts do not merely support action; they increasingly structure and condition it. In the organizational spaces of contemporary societies, technologies and actors are no longer the two terms of a dichotomy, but rather an integrated form of meaning production. Indeed, Actor-Network Theory conceives organizations as the combined action of 'actants,' by which they mean both human and non-human actors (for example, artifacts and technologies).

CASE STUDY
Non-human agents

Actor-Network Theory (ANT) is a distinctive approach to social theory and research which originated in the field of science studies. Developed by two leading French Science and Technology Studies (STS) scholars, Michel Callon and Bruno Latour, British sociologist John Law, and others, it can more technically be described as a 'material-semiotic' method. This means that it maps relations that are simultaneously material (between things) and 'semiotic' (between concepts). It assumes that many relations are both material and 'semiotic' (for instance the interactions in a bank involve both people and their ideas, and computers. Together these form a single network).

ANT tries to explain how material-semiotic networks come together to act as a whole. In the ANT approach, for instance, a bank is both a network *and* an actor that hangs together, and for certain purposes acts as a single entity. As a part of this it may look at explicit strategies for relating different elements together into a network so that they form an apparently coherent whole.

Although it is called a 'theory' ANT does not usually explain *why* a network takes the form that it does. It is much more interested in exploring *how* actor-networks get formed, hold themselves together, or fall apart.

It assumes that all the elements in a network, human and non-human, can and should be described in the same terms. This is called the principle of *generalized symmethnography*. The rationale for this is that differences between them are generated in the network of relations, and should not be presupposed.

Broadly speaking, it is a constructivist approach in that it avoids essentialist explanations of events or innovations (for example, explaining a successful theory by saying it is 'true' and the others are 'false') (http://en.wikipedia.org/wiki/Actor_network_theory).

From the methodological point of view, ANT performs a double somersault. It disrupts and overturns standard assumptions, thereby causing difficulties for both the interpretativist and positivist approaches. On the one hand, ANT criticizes as obsolete the distinction between (what were once called) the 'sciences of culture' (the social sciences) and the 'sciences of nature' (the physical and biological sciences) because human and non-human beings no longer exist, only 'actants.' On the other hand, it argues that both scientific and social facts can be studied using the same methodology. But this not the methodology of the measurement (or quantitative) paradigm long propounded by positivists, but rather that of the semiotic paradigm.

Although at first sight the premises of ANT resemble the physicalism of August Comte, their outcomes are entirely different.

One of the best-known studies conducted using the ANT approach is that by Latour (1985) on the discovery, rise and spread of vaccinations (in late nineteenth-century France) brought about by the French chemist and biologist Louis Pasteur (1822–95). Latour argues that if a scientific fact is to become established, it must have 'allies' both in the laboratory and outside it. In Pasteur's case, his discoveries of the vaccines for anthrax and rabies were opposed by none other than doctors themselves. However, Pasteur's victory was not *solely* the result of his genius, which in the end triumphed over adversity, it was *also* due to his ability to construct a complex network of alliances and troops 'enlisted' in support of his ideas and consisting (according to Latour) of veterinarians, hygienists, farmers and the bacteria themselves!

In the same way, as Gherardi points out,

> our authorship of a book is the outcome of the alignment of human and non-human materials: paper, word processor, co-authors, manuscript, publisher, funding, printing press, printers, copy editors, readers, reviews, citations, etc. Our authorship is made up as much by configurations of human and non-human materials as by our desire and ability to write and thereby mobilize this set of human and non-human materials (2000: 56).

Consequently, no interaction is fully comprehensible if the role of artifacts is ignored. It is accordingly useful for the ethnographer to take photographs, obtain diagrams, or make sketches or drawings of the place being studied, so that he or she can reflect on the situated nature of interactions and convey their 'flavor' to the reader.

10.6 The support of visual ethnography

If we compare a book on social sciences with one on architecture, engineering, medicine or biology, we are struck by an obvious difference between them: the massive use by the latter of photographs, figures, drawings and sketches. Why do social science texts have so few images in them? The reasons are probably numerous and complex, and there is no space to discuss them here. Yet I would stress that these cognitive artifacts are powerful means to increase understanding of our descriptions, or to support a theory or an explanation. After all, as the saying goes, a drawing is worth a thousand words. A clear example is provided by Coffey, et al. (2006: 200), who describe the exhibits hall of an interactive science discovery center in Wales. As you can see, their fieldnote consisted of 129 words:

When you enter . . . you see a huge, well-lit hall in front of you with high ceilings and a gallery above. It is a white space with big white pillars and vast windows, but there's also lots of colour, noise and movement. On entering, immediately ahead of you is a plastic ball, suspended seemingly by magic in front of a bright yellow solid pyramid. Beyond are more yellows and reds and greens and blues. All around are a variety of different brightly-coloured devices or machines, housed in brightly coloured casings and consoles. Many of them move, produce sounds, create visual effects, and so forth when activated by a user. There are lots of children moving around excitedly, flitting from exhibit to exhibit, sometimes bumping into each other.

While the photograph (Photograph 10.1) is much more informative and rich in detail.

10.6.1 Drawings

Sometimes it is not possible to photograph places, even less to visually record the behaviors of participants. Numerous organizations dislike being filmed, and obtaining formal permission to do so may greatly prolong the research. Paper and pencil are among the least invasive of tools, and making sketches and drawings may therefore be an acceptable alternative.

Photograph 10.1   The exhibits hall (source: Coffey, Renold, Dicks, Soyinka and Mason (2006: 22)).

CASE STUDY
Interactions among the sales assistants in two sportswear stores

Longoni and Decathlon are two sportswear companies: the former Italian in origin, the latter French, both with outlets around the world. For his masters dissertation, Andrea Paranchini conducted an ethnography on the organizational cultures of the two companies. One interesting finding of his study was the relationship between decor and the behavior of sales personnel.

LONGONI

In this shop, the goods were displayed on lozenge-shaped display units, no more than two meters in height, known in the Italian retail trade as 'gondolas.' The sales assistants said that the shop resembled a 'Native American camp,' because it was apparently chaotic but had an underlying, and not immediately visible, order. Customers followed a marked walkway through the store (called the 'path' by the personnel, again using the metaphor of the Native American camp), from which they wandered when their attention was caught by an item displayed on the gondolas (see Figure 10.2).

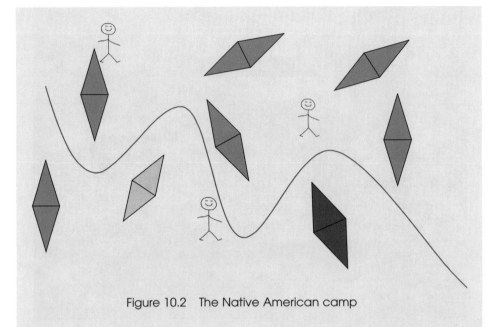

Figure 10.2   The Native American camp

The store was a large open space, and the particular way in which it had been furnished had the following consequences (certainly unforeseen by the designer):

1. The sales assistants could always see each other: this encouraged interaction among them and fostered a group spirit.
2. The lack of precise boundaries among the sections of the store furnished a more complete overview of the organization and a less strictly task-based and isolated conception of the job: 'gray zones,' ever-present in a work flow, could thus be more easily covered.
3. 'Trespassing' on another sales assistant's section was very frequent, but it was not seen as invasive.
4. Collaboration among sales assistants was more frequent because they could see when a colleague was in difficulties (for example, had too many customers waiting to be served) and go and help him or her.
5. The sales assistants were able to signal each other: hence they had no need to use the telephone.
6. High visibility encouraged knowledge distribution, sharing and management.
7. The open space layout favored greater social control by the management, which could monitor work visually.

DECATHLON

This store had an entirely different organizational esthetic. Some staff described it using the metaphor of a 'Roman military camp': a broad central aisle divided the store into two large blocks, with numerous side-aisles forming its various sections.

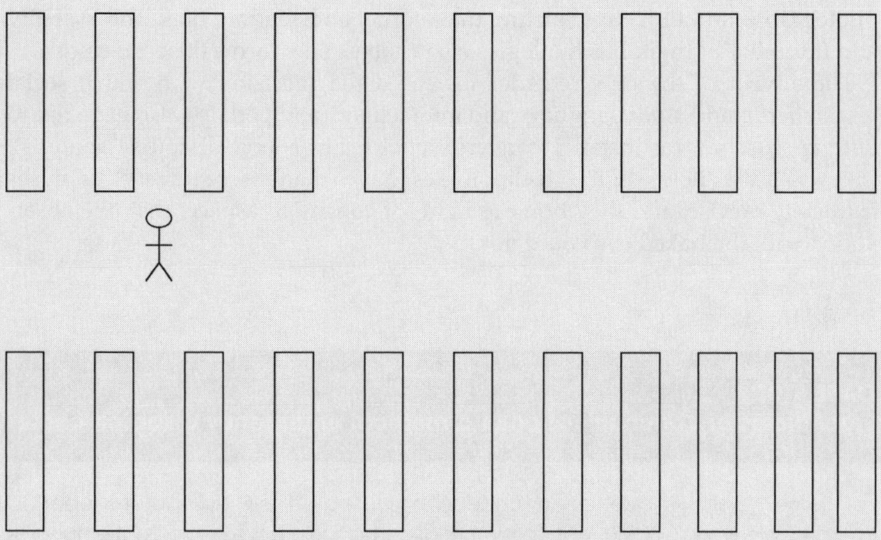

Figure 10.3   The Roman military camp

Goods were arranged on 3 to 4 meter high display units, which interrupted sight-lines. With this kind of spatial organization:

1. Interaction at a distance among the sales assistants was only possible in the central aisle.
2. Other forms of communication, by telephone or via intranet, were used, rather than the non-verbal and semi-verbal communication pervasive at the Longoni store.
3. Because of the way in which spaces were arranged, it was difficult for the sales staff to enter other sections. Consequently both relations and 'trespasses' were of lower intensity, and were always intentional: the result was less knowledge sharing.
4. Face-to-face communication could only take place in the central aisle.
5. Each section of the store was an independent subsystem, unlike the more organic organization at Longoni. A sales assistant commented: 'my section is like a little store within the store,' we have everything we need, from computers to telephones.'

10.6.2 Maps, photographs and videos

Today, mass technologies cost increasingly less. So a student should not find buying a digital camera, a video camera or a tape recorder prohibitively expensive. Digital technologies allow research to be conducted in ways inconceivable only a decade ago. Moreover, recording techniques are much less intrusive: consider how many things can be done with a videophone – taking photographs and film clips, surfing the internet and sending files. The usability and flexibility of digital technologies also enables new forms of social research.

The advent of the tape recorder increased the precision with which social researchers could study language and interactions (and perhaps also gave rise to new approaches, for instance conversational analysis and discourse analysis). Likewise, the new digital technologies have made researchers' analyses extremely precise, and they bring to light (or construct) aspects that live observation with the naked eye could not see.

CASE STUDY
Ergonomics of communication in a medical emergency dispatch center

For some years I have been conducting research on computer-supported co-operative work (CSCW). With a number of colleagues I have carried out ethnographies in medical emergency dispatch centers (Gobo, et al., 2008). These handle calls to an emergency telephone number which varies according to the country: 999 in the UK and Ireland; 911 in the USA and Canada; 118 in Italy, and so on.

The photograph and plan below (Figure 10.4) depict the call center and the various functions performed by its personnel.

There are 15 work stations in the call center. There are six stations in the figure are occupied by the call-takers. The operators at the three ISDN workstations handle the return to base of ambulances (on completion of their missions) or communications with agencies (the police, fire fighters, etc.) whose intervention may be required in the case of especially serious accidents. The three BRV stations are manned by the medical staff, who maintain constant contact with the Basic Rescue Vehicles (mainly ambulances) sent to the scenes of accidents. Finally, another medical team sits at the ARV stations but this team is in constant contact with the Advanced Rescue Vehicles (generally helicopters) sent to deal with the most serious emergencies.

While observing the interactions of the call-takers among themselves and with the medical staff, we noticed that some call-takers tended to communicate more frequently than others with the medical staff. Using the techniques of ergonomic ethnography developed in the 1950s (see 3.8), we set about counting the number of verbal exchanges that took place in a given time span. The result of this observation is shown in the following figure, where the broader stripes represent high frequencies of exchanges (see Figure 10.5).

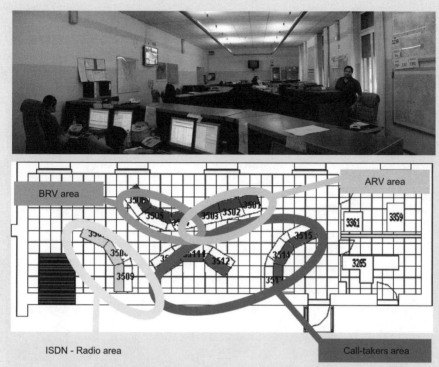

Figure 10.4   Photograph and plan of the medical emergency
dispatch center

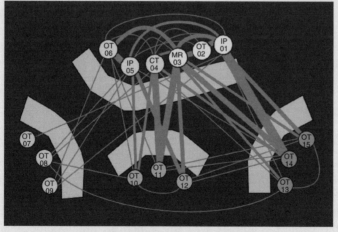

Figure 10.5   Map of the interactions

We then inquired why some call-takers interacted more frequently than others with the medical staff. Having discarded emotional explanations (sympathy, the pleasure of conversation for its own sake) and psychological ones, we concluded that the phenomenon could be explained in more strictly structural (cognitive and logistical) terms to do with the constraints imposed by visual orientation (see Figure 10.6).

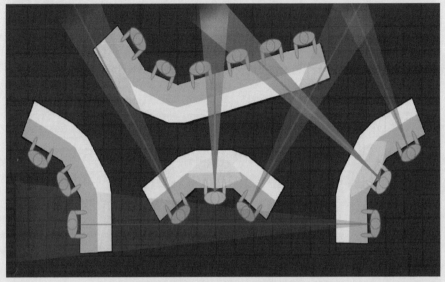

Figure 10.6   Visual orientation

Figure 10.6 shows the 'foveal vision' cones corresponding to the visual angles of greatest attentive concentration in the call center. These visual orientations of the call-takers resulted from a specific logistical situation (put banally: where the call-takers sat).

The angles of vision that biologically restrict human beings thus explain why there were privileged relations among certain call-takers and certain members of the medical staff. This example clearly shows the concept 'situated communication.'

There are many ways to use these technologies. In 'participatory video research' (see Lunch and Lunch, 2006), for example, the researcher gives the participants a camera or a video camera and asks them to take photographs or make video recordings, the purpose being to see reality from their perspective. One of the earliest examples was the American anthropologist Sol Worth (1922–77), who gave movie cameras to the Navajos so that they could film life in their village (Worth and Adair, 1972). However, these technologies should be used prudently, because there are public places (like the subway, supermarkets, and so on) where taking photographs is prohibited. The ethnographer may be mistaken for a terrorist gathering information for an attack, or for a robber, if he or she is caught photographing banks, post offices, and so on.

10.7 Other contexts

Rituals, discourses and spaces are the elementary referents of observational practice. Starting from these referents, the ethnographer can creatively follow other paths and focus on proxemics, relational networks, an organization's documents, and so on.

There are obviously other contexts as well. Within an organization, for example, the practices of its members take place in an *organizational* setting that can be reconstructed from the organization chart showing the functions and tasks of the personnel and marking out the participants' ranges of action. We can likewise determine a *normative* setting of regulations, laws or employment contracts. There follows an example of how a shortage of personnel (an economic aspect) was the main independent variable for a practice:

> in some of the worst wards, housing up to 60 patients, many 'regressed', the problem of reduced personnel on the evening (4:00 to 12:00 P.M.) shift was met by herding all the patients into the day room and blocking the entrance . . . at that time a pall fell on what was already a pall, and there was an intensification of negative affect, tension, and strife (Goffman, 1961: 238).

The intensification described by Goffman would be misunderstood without reference being made to the normative context. Strauss and Corbin (1990) place the *action* at the center of a diagram (what they call a 'conditional matrix') with seven concentric circles or levels (see Figure 10.7).

Moving outwards from the center of the diagram, we encounter the various contexts that influence the central action, and are in their turn influenced by it.

There are therefore extra-situational variables, material and symbolic resources, which participants bring to the interaction from *outside*. However, it is not advisable for the ethnographer to immediately concentrate on these cross-situation components; rather, he or she should focus on the three components of the situation: practices, talk and space. Analysis that instead starts from other, so to speak, more external contexts tacitly and prematurely assumes (takes for granted, the ethnomethodologists would say) that these are influential even before the empirical observation begins. The risk that the researcher will resort to his or her own stereotypes is therefore high. It is therefore recommended that:

> no assumptions are made regarding the participants' motivation, intentions, or purposes; nor about their ideas, thoughts, or understandings; nor their moods, emotions, or feelings; except insofar as this can demonstrably be shown to be matters that participants themselves are noticing, attending to, or orienting to in the course of their interaction (Psathas, 1995: 47).

For example, the status, authority or power of social actors should not be asserted beforehand on the basis of pre-established independent variables.

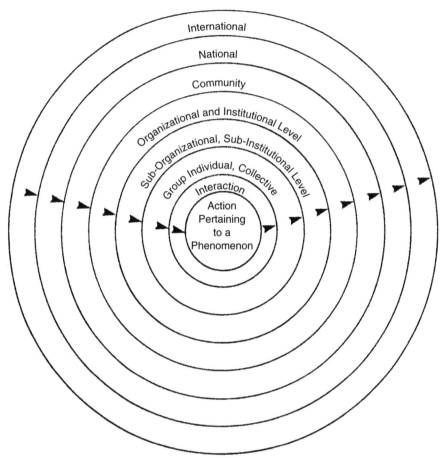

Figure 10.7   The conditional matrix (Source: Strauss and Corbin, 1990: 163)

Rather, they should be sought in the furnishings and the space (i.e. size) of the offices occupied by those actors, the responsibilities given to them, their presence at important meetings, the attention given to their opinions, the extent to which their recommendations are applied, and so on. Extra-situational materials and symbolic materials should therefore be identified according to the situation,[2] for the social structure is not detached from the local situation: 'settings and actions are mutually and inextricably interrelated. Social actions are actions conducting-the-affairs-of-a-social-order' (Sharrock and Button, 1991: 171). Even though social structure and action are interrelated for sociologists, the ethnographer should initially avoid making this assumption. From the methodological point of view, this means avoidance of:

> terms such as 'doctor's office', 'courtroom', 'police department', 'school room', and the like, to characterise settings . . . [which] can obscure much of what occurs within those settings . . . if and how interactants themselves reveal an orientation to institutional or other contexts (Maynard and Clayman, 1991: 406–7).

Because '"the field". . . is itself the product of "disciplinary technologies"' (Turner, 1989: 13) used to examine individuals and groups, it is necessary first to identify the set of local, contingent and situational features that constitute the setting of the study, and only subsequently place them in an institutional framework and have other settings interact.

10.8 Concluding remarks

Our human-centered perspective drives us always to focus primarily on the participants and only then on the contexts of their actions. This is the reason why social actors' actions are often overloaded with intentions, interests and motivations. We need to reverse this perspective and reduce human-centrism, as already suggested by Goffman with his famous statement: 'not . . . men and their moments. Rather moments and their men' (1967: 3). By changing our observation perspective we will start to notice furniture, artifacts, technologies and many other objects we previously neglected. This will allow a re-balance of our analyses and a better symmetry between human and non-human agents.

KEY POINTS

- When observing actions, ethnographers should focus on three aspects constantly and simultaneously present in social scenes: social structures, the common sense interpretations/explanations given by participants in their talk, and the context of the action.
- In a phenomenologically informed ethnography, by 'structures' what is essentially meant is the social conventions that guide rituals.
- Rituals can be studied in three main ways:
  (1) starting from activities, which are separated and classified;
  (2) proceeding in reverse by starting from a key-concept of a particular organization and then observing all the activities that rotate around it; and
  (3) selecting and following a particular participant or object, letting his, her or its action define the boundaries of the context of observation.
- Observing behaviors is very important; yet observation in itself, without concomitant listening to the speech that precedes, accompanies or follows the behavior observed, may be misleading. This is why it is equally important to analyze participants' talk.
- Full understanding of discourse-actions (or if one wishes, action-discourses) requires a third dimension: the context. Social practices are always situated practices, in that they take place in organized situations comprising an array of resources for action, but also constraints upon it.
- Fixtures and furnishings perform an important function in structuring interactions.
- Not only do furnishings provide resources for action and set constraints on it, so too do artifacts. In highly technological societies like ours, interactions

are increasingly mediated by artifacts: these do not merely support action, they increasingly structure and condition it.

- Fully and accurately depicting rituals requires the use of drawings, photographs and videotapes.
- As well as the setting, there obviously exist extra-situational contexts: organizational, normative, social, political and economic.
- However, when analysis begins, it is methodologically advisable not to examine these settings and leave them in the background, so as not to furnish predetermined explanations.

KEY TERMS

Actor-Network Theory (see pp. 176–7)	This is a distinctive approach to social theory and research which originated in the field of science studies. It assumesthat all the elements in a network, human and non-human, can and should be described in the same terms. This is called the principle of *generalized symmethnographery*.
Artifacts (see pp. 175–8)	These are objects with which we perform actions or which boost or supplement our capacities. In highly technological societies, interactions are increasingly mediated by artifacts, of which there are three kinds: technological, cognitive and organizational.
Conditional matrix (see pp. 185–6)	A diagram depicting the seven different settings or levels in which an action takes place: (1) the *interaction*, (2) the *group*, (3) the *sub-organizational* level (physical space), (4) the *organizational* level (the normative structure), (5) the *community* of which the organization is part, (6) the *national* level of the law and the economy, and finally (7) the *international* level.
Organizational symbolism (see p. 174)	A theoretical approach which studies the esthetics of organizations and how furnishings give sense to action.
Proxemics (see p. 163)	The study of humans' appreciation and use of space. The term was coined by Edward T. Hall in 1963.
Situated action (see p. 184)	Cognitive activities are not only mental; in order to be performed, they necessarily require material supports, which end up guiding the reasoning process.
Thin description (see p. 170)	A rough, phenomenalistic, quasi-objective, snapshot-type description of an action. For example: 'a person lays his hand on another person's shoulder.'

Thick description (see p. 171)	A description that produces the *meaning* of the action observed. To continue the previous example: 'a gesture of (a) affection, (b) love, (c) comfort, (d) sexual harassment, or (e) comradeship is made.'
Visual ethnography (see p. 178ff)	Integration of the documentary methodology with ethnographic methodology. Ethnographies are conducted using visual media (photographs and film clips), also in order to document the analysis more graphically.

RECOMMENDED READING

For undergraduates:
Tuchman, Gaye (1972)

For graduates:
Heath, Christian (2004)

For advanced researchers:
Callon, Michel (1986)

SELF-EVALUATION TEST

Are you ready for the next chapter? Check your knowledge by answering the following open-ended questions:

1. Consider the extract from Primo Levi's novel *If This a Man* (10.2.1). Why can such an apparently insignificant object like a shoe be an important starting-point for observation?
2. What is meant by saying that language (talk) is 'situated'?
3. Why are furnishings a resource for and a constraint on action?
4. What is a cognitive artifact?
5. Why are members of the animal, vegetable and mineral kingdoms (what ANT calls *non-human actors*) so important for the study of social action?

Notes

1 For a discussion of Ryle's distinction see Geertz, 1973: 6–7.
2 This methodological caveat is recurrent in the more general discussion of the micro/macro link.

Ethnographic Interviewing

LEARNING OBJECTIVES

- To know the main characteristics of the ethnographic interview.

- To understand its strengths and weaknesses.

- To learn how to conduct an ethnographic interview.

- To recognize that its findings are a co-construction.

11.1 Introduction

The feature that distinguishes ethnography from other methodologies is its use of observation as the principal source of knowledge about social phenomena (see 2.4). However, this is not to rule out that an ethnographer may not occasionally use other methodologies during his or her research, the purpose being to clarify aspects which observation alone fails to make completely comprehensible. The researcher may accordingly conduct interviews, organize focus groups (Agar and MacDonald, 1995), collect and analyze documents produced by the organization, or transcribe everyday conversations or verbal exchanges among actors. Discursive interviewing and document analysis are two other methodologies frequently used by ethnographers. For example, when discussing his study of professional dance musicians, Becker recounts: 'I seldom did any formal interviewing, but concentrated rather on listening to and recording the ordinary kinds of conversation that occurred among musicians' (1951/1963: 84).

When used as part of an ethnographic study, therefore, these methodologies perform only an ancillary role, in the sense that the researcher resorts to them to obtain further information or data. Conversely, research conducted using the discursive interview methodology, or the survey methodology, may benefit from ethnographic observation.

Like 'ethnography,' also the term 'ethnographic interview' has been recently stretched. In marketing research, for instance, the expression 'ethnographic interview' commonly denotes the practice of interviewing a person (the target) at home rather than on the premises of the agency. However, in light of the themes treated previously, this practice cannot plausibly be considered ethnography, but rather a variant of the discursive interview (see 2.4). Doing ethnography means staying longer than a couple of hours in the field.

11.2 Discursive interviews in ethnographic contexts

An 'ethnographic interview' is a particular type of discursive interview conducted by the ethnographer during his or her ongoing research in the field (Spradley, 1979). Its purpose is to reveal the cultural meanings used by actors, and to investigate aspects of the culture observed which are still unclear or ambiguous even though they have been subject to close observation.

CASE STUDY
Punishment at school

In a study on schooling, Mehan, Hertweek and Meihls (1986: 80) noted that a teacher had punished a boy for giving a playful slap to one of his classmates. But identical behavior had not been punished on other occasions. Why not? Mehan interviewed the teacher and showed her the film he had taped of the incident in the classroom. The interview revealed that the teacher envisaged two different 'language game' situations involving the playful slapping of hands: one during lessons, the other during recreation. The former was punishable, she said, the latter was permissible. The ethnographic interview thus helped the researcher grasp meanings and interpretations not directly observable or easily recognizable (see also 14.4).

Ethnographic interviews differ from conventional discursive interviews in various respects. First, in the ethnographic interview, the interviewer and the interviewee already know each other and have previously talked together. This gives rise to a different emotional climate between the two parties. Second, ethnographic interviews are not normally scheduled but are held impromptu during the course of the participant observation. Third, they are likely to be briefer than discursive interviews and more closely focused on specific topics. The interviewer may ask a few brief questions about a scene observed in order to understand the reasons for a particular reaction, or the meaning of a particular act or gesture. Finally, the interviewer is less concerned to achieve his knowledge objective with one single interview, because doubts, ambiguities and interpretative uncertainties can be resolved by subsequent interviews over the entire span of the research. An ethnographic interview conducted at the beginning can be used as a strategy to gain acceptance, or it can be used to 'break the ice' and establish trust and a co-operative relationship with the gatekeepers.

11.3 The benefits and shortcomings of the ethnographic interview

The ethnographic interview may be of great help to the researcher. It may be especially so during the intermediate phase of the inquiry, when the ethnographer begins gradually to acquire the actors' mental schemas and to identify the meanings of rituals and behaviors; and then during the member validation. In the first phase of the research, however, it is instead preferable for the researcher to concentrate solely on observation, for otherwise he or she may seem aggressive to the social actors,[1] and may be misled by the intrinsic shortcomings of the interview.

The gap between the interviewee's declared state and his or her actual state

The first of these shortcomings is the oft-encountered gap between the interviewee's *declared* state and his or her *actual* state. This raises the problem of the fidelity of data (see 14.6). The interview technique may be appropriate when these two states are presumably close to each other. But it is not particularly useful when there is a considerable mismatch between the two states, because the interviewees are unaware of the reasons for their actions, and of their more banal or routine effects.

CASE STUDY
Mathematics in everyday life

An example of this unawareness is provided by the educationists Hoyles, Noss and Pozzi (2001), scholars of mathematics in everyday settings, who carried out ethnographic research to study, among other things, the strategies used by nurses to calculate the drug dosages to administer to their patients. Because Hoyles and his colleagues wanted to study these strategies first hand, they went into hospital wards and watched the nurses as they prepared the dosages and asked for information about the kind of calculations they were performing. The researchers observed a group of 12 expert pediatric nurses, aged between 26 and 35 and with at least three years of ward experience. Each nurse was observed between two and seven times, and each observation session lasted between one and three hours, for a total of more than 80 hours of observation. The researchers then conducted formal interviews with the nurses and discovered that they used a wide array of tacit calculation strategies (largely based on proportional scalar procedures) different from the algorithm taught to them during their training courses. However, the nurses were convinced that they used the 'propositional calculus' learned at school, without realizing that they acted very differently in practice.

Projective interviewing

In the same way, the classic question 'describe your typical day' used in studies on work is likely to receive stereotypical replies which omit the micro-rituals or important details on which, according to Simmel, Goffman and the ethnomethodologists, the social order is founded. In this regard, Schutz suggested that those investigating the structures of everyday life should badger their interviewees with detailed questions like those used in the phenomenological interview: What time did you get up this morning? What was the first thing you did? Has anything unexpected happened today? Have you eaten anything? How did you choose the clothes you're wearing? What have you said today to your family members? In social psychology this mode of gathering information about routines has been codified in the technique known as 'interview with the double' (see Oddone, Re and Briante, 1977).

CASE STUDY
The interview with the double

In organizational research it has been used for example by the Italian sociologist of organization, Silvia Gherardi, in two ethnographic studies conducted in a battery factory and a large publishing house:

> The interviewee was asked to imagine the interviewer as his double and give him all the information that he would need to take over his job the next day without anybody noticing the switch. It was assumed that interviewee and interviewer possessed the same knowledge of the work process (after the first phase of the research), and therefore that the double had the requisite technical knowledge but was ignorant of the relational knowledge that he needed to pass himself off as a competent member of the community. The interviewer did not intervene (during the interview) . . . and on its conclusion asked (the interviewee) to list the most important instructions for the double. The intention was to give the interviewee a task . . . which would stimulate him to interpret that task, structure it, and present himself and his discourse according to his order of priorities (1995: 13–14).

The gap between the researcher's and interviewees' cognitive interests

The second drawback to the interview derives from the gap between the researcher's cognitive interests and practices and those of the interviewees. Social actors sometimes find it difficult to understand the purpose of an ethnographer's questions, so that their replies manifest a certain surprise and embarrassment, or mockery of the ethnographer as a crackpot.

Moerman (1974), an American anthropologist and linguist who long studied the dialect of the Lue, a Thai people, recounts that the questions 'who is a Lue' or 'what is appropriate Lue behavior,' which he frequently asked the natives, caught them by surprise because they required definitions that the natives thought were entirely obvious and irrelevant. In other words, they could not say who a Lue was, although they knew how to behave like a Lue.

CASE STUDY
Interviewing illiterate people

Similarly, when in the early 1930s the Russian psychologist Alexander R. Luria (1902–77) and his assistants interviewed the illiterate peasants of Uzbekistan, a Central Asian region of the former Soviet Union,[2] they realized that when questions requiring 'abstraction, generalization, imagination' were put to their subjects, they were unable to provide definitions, only descriptions of concrete details. They responded in the same way to 'self-analysis' questions:

Subject: Murza Shiral, age fifty-five . . . illiterate

. . . Well, what are you like? Describe your character.

'My character is very good-natured. Even if it's a youngster who's before me, I use the polite form of address and speak courteously . . . You have to understand everything, and I don't.'   Description of own behavior.

Still, do you have shortcomings?

'I have many shortcomings, food, clothing, everythings.'

(Luria, 1974, transl. 1976: 148–9).

The limits of human memory

A third shortcoming of the interview resides in the limits of human memory. As we saw in 5.2 in regard to the processes of remembering and recalling information, people have limited capacities to remember. Consequently, as scholars who use the life history method well know, it is unwise to place too much reliance on statements by participants as factual witnesses or informants. In fact, things may go awry for the ethnographer if he or she considers the informant's memory to be a store or a kind of database that can be drawn upon at will. This is the view of memory that has to date prevailed in cognitive psychology. But it is gainsaid by a fact pointed out by the Italian ethnologist Giorgio R. Cardona (1943–92):

> informants who know hundreds of plants with great assurance, and demonstrate that they have all of them in mind when making comparisons,

[during interviews] are unable to list eight or ten plant names in a row (1985: 25).

The mentalist conception that has developed within cognitivism conceives memory as the outcome of a process which takes place largely in people's heads. But this is to overlook the fact that, as the American cognitivist Donald A. Norman writes,

> much of our everyday knowledge resides in the world, not in the head . . . people certainly rely upon the placement and location of objects, upon written texts, upon the information contained within other people, upon the artifacts of society, and upon the information transmitted within and by a culture. There certainly is a lot of information out there in the world, not in the head (1988: xix).

Remembering is therefore a contingent activity, a form of practical reasoning. More precisely, it is the result of interaction between knowledge present in the memory as mental schemata (schematized knowledge) and knowledge present in the specific social situation of the interview (local knowledge) (Cicourel, 1988: 908). As a consequence, the information collected by the ethnographer must be contextualized, and the informants and the social actors must be helped to remember it.

The meaning of the interview

A fourth shortcoming of the interview may derive from the significance that the interviewee attributes to the interview. If the research has been commissioned by a social service, a municipality, or a public corporate body furnishing a service, the interviewee (especially if suffering from hardship) may perceive the ethnographer as someone with the power to improve his or her situation. Hence participants may reply to questions attributing a frame of reference to the interview which differs from that attributed to it by the ethnographer. Consequently, conformist replies (the concept of social desirability is well-known) will not be infrequent, or replies intended to please the interviewer. In other words, the participant forms a certain idea about the interviewer which may condition his or her replies to a greater or lesser marked extent (for a case study on the difficulty – for a white researcher – on interviewing a black child, go to www.sagepub.co.uk/gobo).

To conclude: we should not expect the discursive interview to deliver what it cannot. It is useful (but only to a certain extent) in recalling events from the past which, as such, are not directly observable to the researcher. And it can help in the identification of thought patterns, schemas or cultural categories and shared meanings (McCracken, 1988: 7). Finally, it can enable the researcher to reconstruct discourse models, speech patterns and argumentative structures. But it is of little use in describing rituals, codes of behavior and actions, or in reconstructing decision-making processes. Ethnographic interviews are only useful as participants' accounts rather than as reality reports (Atkinson and Coffey, 2001). The discursive interview is suited to the investigation of conscious states, explicit knowledge, and social processes of which the interviewee has a good degree of awareness. But, as already argued in 2.4, when the researcher's interest focuses on action, it is difficult to envisage any valid alternative to observation.

11.4 Conducting interviews

An ethnographer may select his or her interviewees in two different ways: by contacting the participants in a specific scene previously observed, or by contacting members of the community being studied. In the latter case, the ethnographer can use more or less sophisticated sampling procedures (see 6.4) according to his or her research requirements (for a case study on researching radical religions, go to www.sagepub.co.uk/gobo).

Another ploy is to make each cognitive task (imposed by the question) as familiar to the interviewee as possible. With the exception of certain professionals (doctors, journalists and social workers, for instance), most people are interviewed only very infrequently in their lives. Consequently, trying to turn what is an intrinsically unnatural interaction into a 'natural' one may seem paradoxical and perhaps impossible. The strategies used by Luria are illuminating:

> These talks were frequently held in groups; even in interviews with one person alone, the experimenter and the other subjects formed a group of two or three, listening attentively and sometimes offering remarks. The talk often took the form of an exchange of opinion between the participants . . . Only gradually did the experimenters introduce the prepared tasks, which resembled the 'riddles' familiar to the population and thus seemed like a natural extension of the conversation (1974, transl. 1976: 16).

When possible, interviews should be recorded, firstly because the tape recorder has the indubitable merit of furnishing a more reliable document, and secondly because the ethnographer does not have to take notes while the interviewee is speaking, and is consequently more closely focused on the latter's discourse.

The request to use a tape recorder should be made repeatedly, but also casually, as if it was an entirely natural thing to do. Conversation analysts have noticed that when a request is made politely and unexpectedly, in the majority of cases it is granted ('preference format') – this being one of the structural characteristics of conversation intended to aid the 'maintenance of social solidarity' (Heritage, 1984: 265 and 269). However, the use of a tape recorder should be considered very carefully beforehand, as interviewees tend to censor their speech when it is being recorded.

11.4.1 Probes

Not all questions are intended to obtain information. The interviewer may accompany his or her main question with 'probes,' which can be used without interrupting the interlocutor (Spradley, 1979). Probes have various functions: (a) encouraging interviewees to talk; (b) breaking down their defenses; (c) helping them make themselves clear; (d) checking that the ethnographer has correctly understood the replies; and (e) getting the interviewee to elaborate on stereotypical answers. Probes may be verbal, para-verbal (interjections like 'mm,' 'ah,' 'uh'), or non-verbal, i.e. bodily expressions like nods of the head or smiles. There are various kinds of probe, some of them observable in everyday interactions:

- *reformulation of the question* if the interviewee has not understood it;

- *comment* ('ah, interesting,' 'really!'), which manifests participation and interest in the account, prompting the interviewee to continue;
- *repetition of replies* to encourage him or her to continue with a description;
- *summaries* ('so you're saying that . . .') which give the ethnographer's interpretation of what the interviewee means, so that it can be corrected if necessary;
- *request for clarification* ('in what sense?,' 'what do you mean by . . .?,' 'could you explain . . . a bit better?') aimed at deepening a topic, understanding a definition better, clarifying a term used by the interviewee; and
- *control* by giving the interviewee deliberately altered or inaccurate summaries, or pretending to have misunderstood replies, so that the interviewee is prompted to confirm or revise previous statements. Do this only for important information, and not too often; otherwise the interviewee will think you are an idiot!

Questions should be balanced in form. In other words, they should not already contain one or several opinions ('do you think that the director shouted at the secretary because he'd lost his temper or because he wanted to reprimand her in front of the other staff?'). Nor should they be designed to elicit a specific reply ('leading questions'). The ethnographer should also be careful to avoid 'cues,' expressions which condition the interviewee's answers. Pauses and silences should be managed wisely, not hastily plugged as if to eliminate a cause of embarrassment, because they may give the interviewee a moment to reflect and gather his or her thoughts. Silences, too, are actions (see also Rapley, 2004 regarding the issue of careful transcription).

When framing questions, it is better not to employ terminology taken from the ethnographer's scientific jargon ('motivation,' 'identity,' etc.), but instead to acquire and use the interviewee's own language as early as possible. Preference should be given to questions focused on the description of social processes (on 'how'). When the subject manifests embarrassment or difficulty in expressing inner states (feelings, emotions, opinions) revealing the interviewers intimate self, it is advisable to ask for a description of the inner states of colleagues, thereby inducing projection.[3]

If the research is more markedly anthropological in its purpose and aimed at reconstructing 'cultural domains' (Spradley, 1980: 102), the ethnographer may use dyadic contrast questions (1980: 125) – for instance 'what is the difference between a teacher and a social worker?' – or triadic ones (1980: 126) like 'if you talk to a doctor, a nurse and a psychologist, which two of the three conversations are most similar, and which is most different from the other?'

It should be borne in mind that questions are always 'moves' (Goffman, 1976: 24–5), in the sense that they are real and proper actions which occupy positions in an interactive exchange and which have pragmatic effects according to the interpretation given to them by the interviewee. In other words, questions are never simply informative, but may be interpreted as attempts to snoop, as acts of insolence, invasions of privacy, or criticisms of the community's rituals.

11.5 Concluding remarks

The ethnographic interview is a method with a long history behind it. Indeed, members of the First Chicago School were already using it to grasp and clarify meanings not directly construable by observation alone. However, it should be remembered, as the feminist and postmodern approaches stress, that what emerges from an interview is a 'co-construction,' in the sense that it does not belong entirely to the interviewee but is the outcome of interaction with the interviewing researcher. The opinions of interviewees are not invariant. Rather, they are adapted to the interlocutor at hand, to the social setting of the interviewee, and to the frame imposed by the interviewee on the exchange.

EXERCISE 11.1

- Choose an ethnic group with which you are familiar (for example, Pakistanis, Anglo-Saxons, West Indians, Kurds, Armenians, Romanians, Albanians, Tamils, Somalis or Afghans).
- Write down on a piece of paper what you think about the ethnic group (habits, character, good qualities and defects).
- Now imagine that you give an interview.
- In fact, imagine that, on the same morning, you are interviewed about what you have written on the piece of paper by very different interviewers: a close friend, a parent, your teacher at university, a right-wing extremist, a conservative, a socialist, a liberal, a left-wing extremist and . . . a member of the ethnic group you have chosen.
- Would you say exactly the same things, on the basis of what you have written on the piece of paper, to all the interviewees? Why? Why not?

KEY POINTS

- The feature that distinguishes ethnography from other methodologies is its use of observation as the pivotal source of knowledge about social phenomena (see 2.4). However, this is not to say that an ethnographer may not occasionally use other methodologies during his or her research. Discursive interviewing and document analysis are two such alternative methodologies frequently used by ethnographers.
- The ethnographic interview may be of great help to the researcher in clarifying aspects not entirely comprehensible with observation alone, and in bringing out hidden meanings.
- However, it has a number of shortcomings. First, an interview is unlikely to reveal tacit knowledge, that essential resource for the understanding of action. Second, the memory is not always accurate in recalling events. Third, exactly what the researcher wants to know is sometimes difficult to convey to the interviewee, with the risk that questions may be misunderstood.
- In addition the people interviewed in the research setting constitute a sample, and there exist various strategies for sampling them.
- The interviewer should pay attention to various aspects of the interview: he or she should conduct interviews in the most suitable places

provided by the research setting; employ appropriate communicative strategies; and make shrewd use of probes.

- It should always be borne in mind that what emerges from an interview cannot be attributed entirely to the interviewee. It is always a co-construction, a product of the interaction between interviewee and interviewer which takes place in a particular social context and setting.

KEY TERMS

Dyadic contrast question (see p. 197)	Used in anthropology to uncover general cultural domains. 'A "dyad" refers to two items, a pair. A dyadic contrast question takes two members of a domain and asks, "In what way are these two things different?"' (Spradley, 1980: 125).
Ethnographic interview (see p. 190)	A method, a variant of the discursive interview, which the ethnographer employs in the setting of his or her research.
General cultural domain (see p. 197)	An anthropological tool denoting 'categories of cultural meaning that occur in almost every social situation' (Spradley, 1980: 102).
Interview with the double (see p. 193)	A method or variant of the discursive interview. The interviewee is asked to imagine the interviewer as his or her double and give the latter all the information for him or her to take over the interviewee's job the next day without anybody noticing the switch.
Preference format (see p. 196)	Response behavior in a turn-taking sequence. Conversation analysts have noticed that when a request is made, in the majority of cases it is granted – this being one of the structural characteristics of conversation intended to aid 'the maintenance of social solidarity' (Heritage, 1984: 265 and 269).
Probe (see pp. 136–7)	A supplementary question with a more phatic than knowledge-gathering purpose. It performs various functions: (a) encouraging the interviewee to talk; (b) relaxing his or her defenses; (c) helping him or her to be clear; (d) checking that the ethnographer has correctly understood the replies; and (e) getting the interviewee to elaborate on stereotypical answers. Probes may be verbal, para-verbal (interjections like 'mm,' 'ah,' 'uh') or non-verbal, i.e. bodily expressions like nods of the head or smiles. There are various kinds of probe, some of them observable in everyday interactions.

Triadic contrast question (see p. 197)	'This type of question uses three terms or categories at the same time. It takes the following form: "Which two are the most alike in some way, but different from the third?" This kind of question involves looking for similarities and contrasts at the same time. It is especially useful for uncovering tacit contrasts that are easily overlooked' (Spradley, 1980: 127).

RECOMMENDED READING

For undergraduates:
Rapley, Tim (2004)

For graduates:
Heyl, Sherman Barbara (2001)

For advanced researchers:
Atkinson, Paul and Coffey, Amanda (2002)

SELF-EVALUATION TEST

Are you ready for the next chapter? Check your knowledge by answering the following open-ended questions:

1. What is an ethnographic interview?
2. What are the three main shortcomings of the ethnographic interview?
3. What can we learn from the experience of Luria (1974)?
4. What are the six types of probe?
5. What is meant by saying that an interview is a 'co-construction'?

Notes

1 Whyte recalls the following methodological rebuke by Doc for his excessive invasiveness: 'Go easy on that "who," "what," "why," "when," "where" stuff, Bill. You ask those questions, and people will clam up on you. If people accept you, you can just hang around, and you'll learn the answers in the long run without even having to ask the questions' (1943a: 303).

2 It is interesting that Luria, who spent two years in the field, changed his methodology to one better suited to his subjects. His original intention was to conduct psychological tests, but soon realized that these set the subjects 'unusual problems, unrelated to their habitual activities . . . Thus we used no standard psychometric tests, and we worked only with specially developed tests that the subjects found meaningful and open to several solutions, each indicating some aspect of cognitive activity' (1974, transl. 1976: 16–17).

Luria therefore opted for the clinical interview together with a series of experiments: 'we emphasized preliminary contact with the population; we tried to establish friendly relations so that the experimental run-throughs seemed natural and unaggressive . . . As a rule our experiments sessions began with long conversations (sometimes repeated) with the subjects in a relaxed atmosphere of a house – where the villagers spent most of their free time – or in camps in the fields and mountain pastures around the evening campfire' (1974, transl. 1976: 16–17).

3 The concept of *projection* was first introduced in the 1920s by the Viennese psychopathologist Sigmund Freud. It can be defined as a defense mechanism whereby a person protects him or herself against awareness of his or her own undesirable traits by attributing them to others

Crafting Ethnographic Records

LEARNING OBJECTIVES

• To understand the usefulness of fieldnotes.

• To learn how to write ethnographic notes.

• To grasp the importance of ethnographic statistics.

• To find one's way among an organization's numerous documents.

• To manage audiovisual materials.

12.1 Introduction

The methodological literature has often considered ethnography as lacking rigor and systematicity, and as being excessively sensitive to the researcher's biases. Ethnography's main weaknesses, it is alleged, are that its empirical bases are difficult to verify and that the information it collects can be easily manipulated. If the output from a survey is cross tabulation statistics, the output from an interview is a text, and that from a conversation analysis is a transcript, what is the output from an ethnography? Moreover, as Corsaro and Heise point out,

> the great exemplars of sociological ethnography – like the work of Whyte (1955), Becker (1963), Goffman (1961, 1971) – certainly are theoretically rich, but they do not tell us how to focus ethnographic data for sociological presentation or how to articulate ethnographic data with theories of sociological concern (1990: 1–2).

For some time, however, rigorous and systematic (as well as refined) techniques have been available for the collection and analysis of ethnographic data. They are able to remedy some of the methodology's shortcomings.

CASE STUDY
Access rituals in an American pre-school

Children not involved in ongoing play desire entry and want to be part of shared activities. Because their entry bids are continually resisted, they realize they must be persistent. Over time most children meet the challenge of resistance and develop a complex set of *access strategies*. Consider the following case study involving three four-year-old girls in an American pre-school.

Jenny and Betty are playing around a sandbox in the outside courtyard of the school. I am sitting on the ground near the sandbox watching. The girls are putting sand in pots, cupcake pans, and teapots. Occasionally the girls bring me a sand cake to pretend to eat. Debbie now comes up to the sandbox and stands near me, observing the other two girls. After watching for about five minutes she circles the sandbox three times and stops again and stands next to me. After a few more minutes of watching, Debbie moves to the sandbox and reaches for a teapot. Jenny takes the pot away from Debbie and mumbles, 'No.' Debbie backs away and again stands near me, observing the activity of Jenny and Betty. Then she walks over next to Betty, who is filling the cupcake pan with sand.

Debbie watches Betty for just a few seconds, then says, 'We're friends, right, Betty?'

Betty, not looking up at Debbie, continues to place sand in the pan and says, 'Right.'

Debbie now moves alongside Betty, takes a pot and spoon, begins putting sand in the pot, and says, 'I'm making coffee.'

'I'm making cupcakes,' Betty replies.

Betty now turns to Jenny and says, 'We're mothers, right, Jenny?'

'Right,' says Jenny.

The three 'mothers' continue to play together for about twenty more minutes, until the teachers announce clean-up time (Corsaro, 1997: 124–5).

In this example the author describes what he has seen. Yet his account (as should be clear by now) is not a description of reality. Rather, it is an interpretation of reality made by the researcher: a description mediated by his cognitive interests, stereotypes and, maybe, his prejudices. As the American anthropologist James Clifford has put it, fieldnotes are 'inscriptions,' that is, actions whereby 'the flow of action and discourse has been interrupted, *turned* to writing' (1990: 51). As the English sociologist Paul Atkinson also stresses, 'there is no datum that exists independently of its inscription in conventional forms; some are visual (film, video, photography), but the great majority of representations are textual' (1992: 16).

Every description, and in general every process of documentation, is by definition partial because it necessarily assumes a partial point of view. The American conversation analyst Emanuel A. Schegloff has neatly illustrated this point by showing the various ways in which a state of affairs can be described:

> Were I now to formulate where my notes are, it would be correct to say that they are: right in front of me, next to the telephone, on the desk, in my office, in the office, in Room 213, in Lewisohn Hall, on campus, at school, at Colombia, in Morningside Heights, on the upper West Side, in Manhattan, in New York City, in New York State, in the Northeast, on the Eastern Seaboard, in the United States, etc. Each of these terms could in some sense be correct . . . were its relevance provided for (1972: 81).

Not only are fieldnotes constructs, but also

> 'the field'. . . is itself the product of 'disciplinary technologies'. Prisons, schools, hospitals, clinics can no longer be treated as self-limiting sites available for scientific inquiries into their everyday life (Turner, 1989: 13).

12.2 Three methodological principles for preserving linguistic variability

According to the anthropologist Spradley, ethnographic protocols should be compiled with particular rigor. This applies especially to those who conduct research in the society to which they belong and whose language they already know. In fact:

> when anthropologists do ethnographic research in non-Western societies, they encounter striking language differences . . . [and] the first task is to learn the native language. Fieldnotes soon become filled with native terms, and it is easy to distinguish the ethnographer's language in the fieldnotes from the language of the people studied.
>
> When doing ethnography in your own society, however, it is easy to overlook language differences and thereby lose important clues to cultural meaning. The central question faced by every ethnographer when taking fieldnotes is *what language shall be used in making an ethnographic record*? (Spradley, 1980: 65).

Spradley then invites researchers to respect three criteria or principles when they take ethnographic notes.

12.2.1 The first principle: The language identification

To introduce the first principle Spradley describes the problems that he encountered when researching the 'skid row men' of Seattle (Spradley, 1970). These men were tramps, often alcoholics, whose drunken brawling or rowdiness frequently landed them in court. During his fieldwork, Spradley met police officers, judges, social workers, journalists, and obviously several 'urban nomads.' Because all these actors spoke English, Spradley set about writing summaries of their interactions in which he occasionally included words or expressions that struck him as particularly curious. But in doing so he forgot that each professional category has its own code, made up not only of peculiar usages but above all of particular kinds of discourse organization: a hierarchy of topics, an account of events deemed significant, expressed judgments, classifications and categorizations.

By reducing conversations, either held or heard, to a summary written in his or her own language, the ethnographer reduces the linguistic variation among participant categories (see Figure 12.1) and produces an 'amalgamated language.'

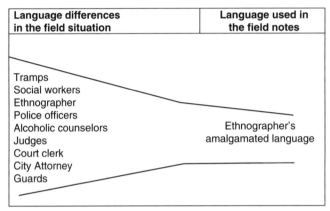

Figure 12.1   Types of language (Source: Spradley, 1980: 66, Figure 10)

Besides being imprecise, ethnographic notes written in an amalgamated language become unusable after some time. When the researcher re-reads them some months later, he or she is no longer able to establish relations between categories of participant and discourse contents. He or she may therefore introduce serious distortions when analyzing the materials: for instance, attributing the thought of one social category to another. It is therefore advisable to write interviews down on separate sheets of paper and then group them by occupational category.

12.2.2 The second principle: The verbatim

Consider the following example taken from Spradley's study (1970s).

CASE STUDY
Tramps' culture

Informant's actual statement: 'I made the bucket in Seattle one time for pooling; I asked a guy how much he was holding on a jug and he turned out to be a ragpicker and he pinched me.'

Fieldnote entry: 'I talked to Joe about his experience of being arrested on skid row when he wasn't drunk.'

At that time, this condensed entry appeared sufficient; I certainly did not feel it was a distortion of what Joe said. I didn't fully understand all his words but I thought I knew roughly what they meant. However, this entry lost some of the most important clues to the informant's culture, clues that came from such folk terms as *pooling* (a complex routine for contributing to a fund for purchasing something), *the bucket* (city jail), *ragpicker* (a certain kind of policeman), and *pinched* (arrested) (Spradley, 1980: 67).

We gather from this passage that, besides identifying the speakers, we should also accurately record what they say. Faithfully transcribing the words (verbatim) used by actors to describe, classify, comment upon, and justify an event may be useful for reconstructing the meanings attributed to actions. Metaphorically, terms are hooks which anchor meanings (concepts), and we can use them to investigate the mental schemas and thought patterns of participants.

But what should the ethnographer transcribe from the immense flow of words that make up a conversation? It is not easy to answer, given that ethnographers, as members of the language community which they are studying, rarely encounter peculiar words, or ones entirely unknown to them. Only in the latter case are ethnographers not required to make a special effort, for words in some way impose themselves upon their attention (for another case study on addict ethnomethods to deceive the doctor, go to www.sagepub.co.uk/gobo).

Researchers, therefore, more frequently encounter words with which they are already familiar. But they tend to ignore these words, failing to recognize them as terms in the participants' communicative code which denote specific practices. Researchers may therefore be deluded that they know what is being talked about.

Collecting verbatim

During the first phase of fieldwork, when situations still seem 'new,' the ethnographer must therefore note down terms, phrases and idiomatic expressions which may initially not seem worth bothering about. For terms which at first were not particularly significant may become so as the research proceeds; or they may reveal meanings different from those that the researcher initially assumed. In particular, the researcher should pay attention to the *definitions* – that is, sentences containing the verb 'to be' – which actors produce. These are usually used to classify an event, i.e. to establish a link between a term and a concept.

The practice followed by ethnographers of reformulating conversations in their own words, rather than complying with the verbatim principle, may prevent them from achieving the goal of describing and itemizing the participants' code – as we saw in the example of Spradley and the tramps' culture. Consequently, a 'condensed' or 'amalgamated' ethnographic note may introduce distortions; or it may lack important information which is difficult to recover once the researcher has left the field.

Without an audio or video recording of the scene, it is difficult to transcribe exactly what has been said: not only because after a few minutes certain terms have already been forgotten, but also because in some situations it is not possible immediately to transcribe what has been seen or heard. As Goffman advises, learn to

> fake off-phase note taking. That is, don't write your notes on the act you're observing because then people will know what it is you're recording. Try to discipline yourself to write your notes before an act has begun, or after it has started so that people won't be able to detect from when you start taking notes and when you stop taking notes what act you're taking notes about (1989: 130).

The anecdotes abound on this process, and the most unlikely places in organizations have been used as 'bolt-holes' to note down an observation or a dialogue: the organization's bathroom, bar or stairwell for example. Likewise, if the researcher lacks a notebook, his or her jottings end up on any surface available: paper tissues, tablecloths, napkins, newspapers, doors or even bathroom walls. Or the ethnographer may take a different approach and explicitly tell the participants that he or she wants to take notes, perhaps backing the request with a reassuring comment: 'What you're telling me is very interesting. Would you mind if I write it down? Otherwise I'll forget it.'

When withdrawing from an interaction to make notes, it is best to do so in the ways, and following the rituals, used by the organization (for example, with the excuse of going to the bathroom or taking a coffee break) so that the exit is culturally appropriate. It may sometimes be useful to carry a tape recorder and, when the observation session has ended, record your comments on your way back home or to the office.

12.2.3 The third principle: Describe basic practices

The culture of a group or organization is manifest in everyday basic social practices. Perceiving and recognizing these practices requires greater effort from the ethnographer-member-of-the society-studied than is usually required of an anthropologist (see 2.4). If the researcher is to describe participants' activities accurately, he or she must transcribe the micro-events and micro-actions that make up each of the social practices observed. When writing up ethnographic notes, therefore, the researcher should adopt, to use Spradley's expression, 'a concrete language' (1980: 68), as exemplified by the following extract.

CASE STUDY
Firefighter's culture: receiving the alarm

Before the first hit of the gong has faded away, men are already stepping out of shoes and into boots, pulling on coats and helmets . . . The man who has caught the watch for the day (or night) picks up the fire phone, gives the number of the engine house, and writes down the location and any other information the dispatcher gives him. The fire phone is connected to the intercom so that everyone can hear the dispatcher. Within twenty to thirty seconds, the captain has checked to see if his men are ready and the driver has sped off the platform leaving the garage doors to close automatically on twelve deserted pairs of shoes where three shining rigs stood before (Judy Woods, 1972: 225).

The narrative style used for this ethnographic note pertains to what has been called 'naturalistic' or 'thin' description (see 10.3). This is the necessary basis (Brekhus, Galliher and Gubrium, 2005) for 'thick description.' Thick and thin descriptions, therefore, are two chronologically and cognitively distinct phases: the first involves the collection of information; the second its analysis.

So that the use of concrete language is ensured, ethnographic notes should not include terms taken from the linguistic and cognitive code of the social sciences like *roles, social interaction, actor, ritual, class, status, system, strategy, social situations, culture, symbols, mental schema, socialization, ceremonial, inequalities, genders*, etc. Besides being part of a conceptual and terminological stock extraneous to participants' practices, these terms are generalizations of *particular* actions or events:

> although you will want to make generalizations during your research, it is necessary to begin with concrete facts that you see, hear, taste, smell, and feel. If your fieldnotes become filled with the abstract jargon of social science, you will find it difficult to make generalizations from generalizations (Spradley, 1980: 68–9).

If it is true, as Geertz (1973) says, that the ethnographer inevitably works with 'interpretations of interpretations,' 'explanations of explanations,' and so on, it is all the more necessary to avoid using sociological concepts when making fieldnotes. As Schutz puts it, these are 'constructs of common-sense constructs' or 'second level concepts.'

EXERCISE 12.1

Silverman (2007: 22) narrates an anecdote by the great American songwriter of the 1940s, Sammy Kahn, about a question he was often asked: 'when you write a song, what comes first – the words or the music?' To which Kahn replied: 'no, not the words or the music – first comes the phonecall!'
What is the serious significance of Kahn's joke?
(For Silverman's answer, go to www.sagepub.co.uk/gobo.)

12.3 Four kinds of ethnographic notes

After a few days of fieldwork, the scrupulous ethnographer – especially if he or she has followed Spradley's three principles – will have already accumulated several pages of jottings and notes. The material will then rapidly grow even further, and after some weeks have passed a sense of bewilderment will set in: 'And now,' says the ethnographer, 'what am I going to do with all these notes?' The fear of being submerged by an enormous mass of jottings, scraps of paper and notes is justified. Those who have done ethnographic research know this anxiety very well. As Goffman recalls:

> there is an issue about when to stop taking notes. Usually when you are merely duplicating what you've already got. Remember, you'll get, in a year, between 500 and 1,000 pages of single-spaced typed notes and this is too much to read more than once or twice in your lifetime. So do not take *too* many notes (1989: 130–1).

To avert chaos, Schatzman and Strauss (1973: 99–101) and Corsaro (1986: 295) suggest that fieldnotes should be divided among four different files, each containing a particular type of material. Schatzman and Strauss identify three categories: 'Observational Notes (ON), Theoretical Notes (TN) [and] Methodological Notes (TN)' (1973: 99). To these Corsaro adds a fourth; what he calls 'personal notes' but which would be more correctly termed 'Emotional Notes' (EM). This classification will enable the researcher to organize his or her observations and reduce the complexity of the work.[1]

12.3.1 Observational notes

First Law of Applied Terror

When reviewing your notes before an exam, the most important ones will be illegible.

Observational notes are thin and detailed descriptions of events and actions directly seen or heard by the researcher. The writing of observational notes should comply strictly with the three principles described in the previous section. They should therefore contain the smallest possible amount of interpretation by the researcher.[2] This means that (as far as possible) observational notes should be no more than plain and simple descriptions of events, and that they should avoid, for example, qualifying adjectives (the parts of speech that give information about the qualities of nouns).[3] Moreover, the ethnographer should take down plain notes of this kind during observation sessions, or just after they have finished. He or she should not worry about spelling or grammar: there will be time later for polishing. As Atkinson writes:

> the more *comprehensible* and readable the reported speech, the less 'authentic' it must be. The less the ethnographer intervenes, the more delicately he or she transcribes, the *less* readable becomes the reported speech (1992: 23).

There follows an example taken from Corsaro (1985: 24–5) concerning a routine (a game) at a nursery school.

Observational notes

Date: October 29
Morning – Episode #5
Scene: Outside Sandbox
Participants: Rita (R), Barbara (B), Jack (J), Bill (Bi), Linda (L), Richard (Rich).

Five children (R, B, J, Bi and L) are playing around the outside sandbox. The children are pretending to make cakes, pies, etc., by placing sand in pans and other cooking utensils. There is a toy sink with faucet and a toy oven near the sandbox. Most of the time the children seem to be involved in parallel play, but there is verbal negotiation when the children need to share utensils or props.

B-Bi	I need to get some water.	Bi is standing near front of sink and moves to one side as B approaches.
Bi-B	There's no water in there.	Referring to fact that faucet is not real.
B-Bi	Well, it's *pretend water.*	
Bi-B	Ok.	
B-Bi	We all have to share the only one.	

Later another instance involving co-operation and sharing occurred.

B-J	Jack?	
J-B	What?	
B-J	I'm putting this in the oven.	
J-B	OK.	B puts pan in the oven.
B-J	Here, this is mine, Jack.	J now holds pan as B puts sand in it.
		J now reaches for a scoop in the sandbox.
J-B	Mine.	
B-J	No. You can have this.	B hands a spoon to J.

(Shortly after this exchange B leaves the area with no verbal marking and goes inside the school.)

Now only R, J and L remain playing around the sandbox. Rich now approaches and watches the other children for a few minutes. Rich then walks near J and says:

Rich-J: It's clean up time.

Richard then reaches for Jack's pan filled with sand and tries to dump it out. J resists Rich and dumps the sand himself, J then goes inside the school. Rich remains a few minutes and plays in sandbox and then leaves. R and L play (there are several verbal exchanges) until a teaching assistant announces that it is clean-up time.

Emerson, Fretz and Shaw (1995) suggest that observational notes should also include the researcher, specifying his or her spatial position and relationship with the actors at the time of observation.

Fieldnotes can be made even more rigorous by compiling 'systematic observation sheets': as did Laud Humphreys (1970) in his study on men's homosexual activity in a city park restrooms ('tearooms'). An example of such a sheet is reprinted in *Tearoom Trade* (see Humphreys, 1970: 35):

> A range of data are recorded: the date and day of the week, the weather, the number and type of people in the parks, the estimated volume of gay activity, the place, the tearoom participants (observer, principal [sexual] aggressor, principal passive participant, other participants, law enforcement personnel), the time an encounter began and ended, a diagram of moves within an encounter, and a narrative description of the action (Brekhus, Galliher and Gubrium, 2005: 8).

12.3.2 Methodological notes

While conducting research, an ethnographer may encounter various difficulties that hinder or restrict his or her observation. Sometimes these difficulties are resolved as the research proceeds; but sometimes they still remain when the research has concluded. Methodological notes are essentially questions or reflections about how to remedy the difficulties that arise in the field. They may therefore include questions to which the answers are not yet known, as well as specific evaluations, recommendations and strategies to improve the research method used:

> a methodological note is a statement that reflects an operational act completed or planned: an instruction to oneself, a reminder, a critique of one's own tactics; [this type of annotations are] notes on the researcher himself and upon the methodological process itself (Schatzman and Strauss, 1973: 101).

Methodological notes therefore represent constant feedback among the activity observed, the method used and the reaction of the participants. To continue with the above example taken from a school setting, Corsaro's methodological notes (1985: 25) run as follows.

Methodological notes

I will want to observe interaction around the outside sandbox when I begin participant observation. This should not be difficult, since I could sit down by the sandbox and be at the same height as the children. Obtrusion would be less of a problem around the sandbox than in the playhouses or climbing bars.

12.3.3 Theoretical notes

Ideas, hypotheses or interpretations spring to the ethnographer's mind right from his or her first entry into the field. In order that these intuitions can be kept separate from more specifically factual observations, theoretical notes develop the more general theoretical meaning of observational notes: the researcher 'develops new concepts, links these to older ones, or relates any observation to any other in this presently private effort to create social science' (Schatzman and Strauss, 1973: 101). Theoretical notes signal elements that warrant further exploration, or they invite the researcher to recognize that the action observed is an empirical example of a concept, a hypothesis or a sociological theory.

Theoretical notes

(1) The fact that the children moved from seemingly parallel play to social interaction to negotiate sharing of objects is interesting and should be investigated further. It suggests the importance of contextual factors in the children's use of social and egocentric speech.

(2) As in earlier episodes, the children did not verbally mark leave-taking, and after they departed they did not seem to be missed by the other children.

(3) Play around the outside of the sandbox is similar to play in the play-houses in that the children go through or produce household routines (i.e., cooking, cleaning, etc.). However, specific roles (mother, father, baby, etc.) are not assigned in the play around the sandbox, as they often are in the role play in the playhouses (Corsaro, 1985: 26).

Theoretical notes also plot the researcher's cognitive path. On reading them diachronically after some months of fieldwork, the ethnographer is able to reconstruct how his or her hypotheses, interpretations, and cognitive schemas have changed in the course of time. A useful way to capitalize on these reflections is to ask oneself, after every observation session, 'what new things have I learned today?'

12.3.4 Emotional notes

Positivism and scientism long denied a role to the emotions in scientific activity. Fortunately, in the social sciences, this stance has now largely given way to the view that the emotions are not only important but ineliminable. The cognitive sciences have shown: (i) that observed events, theoretical assumptions, and pre-understandings are inextricably condensed into an interpretation; and (ii) that we learn on the basis of our emotions. The emotions (empathy, for example), are therefore essential resources for understanding. Or conversely, they may be the cause of misunderstanding.

Corsaro (1985: 295) writes that the purpose of emotional notes is to capture the researcher's feelings, sensations and reactions to the specific features of the event observed. In other words, emotional notes should report the outcomes of a kind of self-analysis. Cicourel (1986: 51–2) furnishes some example of this analytical attitude:

> If, for example, on reading the file of a juvenile you find that her parents are divorced, what do you think? How might this influence you when you begin to turn your attention to this girl?. . . If the girl offends you or treats you badly, how does this influence the way you analyze the information? We must recognize and clearly define all the conditions that may influence the researcher . . . How do our reactions to data . . . reflect our mental models of people in general and of particular persons with whom we come often in contact?

Emotional notes, which remain the researcher's private materials, aid awareness (as far as is humanly possible) of the stereotypes and prejudices, the fears and beliefs that the ethnographer may harbor towards the actors studied. They may also include the researcher's frustrations, as illustrated by the following example from Corsaro (1985: 26).

Emotional notes

I found earlier that any attempt to record everything the children said was fruitless. As a result, I often relied on summaries here. It seemed Richard said it was clean-up time so that he could dump Jack's sand, but it was apparent that Jack did not fall for his ploy.

If read diachronically, emotional notes inform researchers about the extent of the emotional change that has taken place within themselves during the research process, marking the distance between their initial and final self.

12.3.5 Summarizing

The note-taking procedure can be summed up in the following stages:

(1) for the first two or three weeks, immerse yourself full-time in the setting observed (Schwartz and Jacobs, 1979: 251). This will yield the benefits of the cognitive attitude of the stranger. As Goffman stresses: 'there is a freshness cycle when moving into the field. The first day you'll see more than you'll ever see again. And you'll see things that you won't see again. So the first day you should constantly take notes all the time' (1989: 130). From the third week on, however, this sensitivity rapidly declines, and the setting with its rituals starts to become familiar;

(2) immediately jot down (Emerson, Fretz and Shaw, 2001: 356) what you observe, your strongest emotions, the ideas that spring to mind, your intuitions: 'write [your fieldnotes] as lushly as you can, as loosely as you can, as long as you put yourself into it' (Goffman, 1989: 131); to make easier the task of collecting theoretical, methodological or emotional notes, you can

carry a small audio-recorder and talk into it as FBI Special Agent Dale Cooper, in the American TV serial drama *Twin Peaks*, does tape-recording his thoughts during the investigation;

(3) then re-read your notes, sort them out, summarize them in short phrases (Corsaro, 1985: 295) and key words, and put them into the four files containing observational notes, methodological notes, emotional notes and theoretical notes;

(4) plan to allocate time during the day for writing up and organizing your notes. This should take up as much time as you have devoted to observation (Lofland, 1971: 104): 'every night you should type up your fieldnotes. [And] you have to do it every night because you have too much work to do and you'll begin to forget' (Goffman, 1989: 130). If the observation is so demanding that little time is left to write up your notes, it is preferable 'to alternate periods of observation with periods of writing' (Hammersley and Atkinson, 1983: 150) so as not to neglect the latter. A suggested schedule is: 25% of your time allocated to observation; 25% to writing up fieldnotes; 20% to analysis of the empirical documentation; and 30% for writing the research report;

(5) after some time, re-read your notes, which have now been divided and stored in different files, and try to enrich them with reflections or new details.

12.4 Selecting useful documents

Law of the Office

Vital papers will demonstrate their vitality by spontaneously moving from where you left them to where you can't find them.

Organizations, associations and groups are full of documents that either they have produced (brochures, regulations, letters, etc.) or that has been written about them (press reviews, advertisements, and so on). These documents are stored in archives (both digital and paper-based), or they are retrievable on the internet. If the organization or group has only a few documents, reading them will not be difficult. But if there are hundreds, how can you find your bearings among them? Always start from the research topic and look for documents relating to it. For example, if your subject is the work practices of the operators at a call center, it may be useful to get hold of the response scripts that they follow when taking calls from clients (inbound activity) or when contacting clients to sell the product (outbound activity). It may also be useful to read the contract setting out the operators' rights and duties. Announcements, advertisements, and information posted on notice boards may also be very useful; likewise trade-union documents or company reports and statistics (for example, on turnover among the operators, the number of telephone contacts, etc.). Finally, the company organization chart may be a valuable source of information. Note, however, that it is always better to read these documents *after* you have conducted several observation sessions, and *after* you have tried to comprehend the organization's social conventions and culture: this way you will not be influenced *a priori* (as we saw when discussing the concept of 'context' in 10.7).

So read organizational practices (which are often informal) through documents (which are often formal). Because fieldnotes and documents are different kinds of texts, you should use the latter to interpret your fieldnotes, not to substitute them. In this way, the documents will help contextualize your observations and inferences, and to confirm or refute your hypotheses.

12.5 Ethnographic statistics

Ethnographic researchers construct their databases mainly by observing and writing up their observational notes. They may keep their fieldnotes as written texts, or they may convert them into the narrative form typical of descriptive statistics.

The American psychologist, David L. Rosenhan, and his colleagues conducted a number of small-scale experiments to produce their study (see 5.8) on the organizational construction of mental illness. One of these experiments centered on 'staff [i.e. psychiatrists, nurses and attendants] responses to patient-initiated contact' (1973: 132) and tested the following hypothesis:

> It has long been known that the amount of time a person spends with you can be an index of your significance to him. If he initiates and maintains eye contact, there is a reason to believe that he is considering your requests and needs. If he pauses to chat or actually stops and talks, there is a reason to infer that he is individuating you (1973: 132).

To observe the attention paid by staff to patients, Rosenhan and his colleagues (who had gained admittance to various hospitals on the pretence of being mentally ill) would approach members of staff and politely ask concrete questions appropriate to the situation: for example, when they would be presented to the meeting with the staff or when they would be discharged.[4]

Table 12.1 compares the contacts initiated by the pseudopatients (Rosenhan and colleagues) with the psychiatric staff and contacts with other professional groups (university faculty, and Stanford University medical center physicians).

The table shows that the psychiatric staff paid almost no attention to their patients:

> The encounter frequently took the following bizarre form: (Pseudopatient) 'Pardon me, Dr. X. could you tell me when I am eligible for grounds privileges?' (Physician) 'Good morning, Dave. How are you today?' (Moves off without waiting for a response) (1973: 133).

It is believed that professors at large and eminent universities are so busy that they have no time for students. Yet a female pseudostudent who approached individual faculty members apparently walking purposefully to some meeting or teaching engagement and asked them appropriate questions (which sometimes required long answers), always received, without exception, a response: 'no matter how rushed they were, all respondents not only maintained eye contact, but stopped to talk. Indeed, many of the respondents went out of their way to direct or take the questioner to the office she was seeking . . .' (1973: 135). In conclusion,

> the general degree of co-operative responses is considerably higher for these university groups than it was for pseudopatients in psychiatric hospitals. Even so, differences are apparent within the medical school setting.

Table 12.1 Self-initiated contact by pseudopatients with psychiatrists, nurses, and attendants, compared to contact with other groups

Contact	Psychiatric hospitals		University campus (nonmedical)	University medical center physicians		
	(1) Psychiatrists	(2) Nurses and attendants	(3) Faculty	(4) "Looking for a psychiatrist"	(5) "Looking for an internist"	(6) No additional comment
Responses						
Moves on, head averted (%)	71	88	0	0	0	0
Makes eye contact (%)	23	10	0	11	0	0
Pauses and chats (%)	2	2	0	11	0	10
Stops and talks (%)	4	0.5	100	78	100	90
Mean number of questions answered (out of 6)	*	*	6	3.8	4.8	4.5
Respondents (no.)	13	47	14	18	15	10
Attempts (no.)	185	1283	14	18	15	10

*Not applicable

(Source: Rosenhan, 1973: 134, Table 1)

Once having indicated that she was looking for a psychiatrist, the degree of co-operation elicited was less than when she sought an internist (1973: 135).

Ethnographic statistics versus survey statistics

It is important not to confuse ethnographic statistics with survey statistics. As already explained in more detail in 2.7.1, ethnographic research differs from survey methodology in that it rarely attempts to *measure* phenomena. More frequently it merely *counts* – as in the above example of visual contacts between staff and patients. Measurement is made of things which are continuous (for example, time, income, height, etc.), while counting is made of things which are numerable (for example, the people in a doctor's waiting room, the members of a gang, the books in a library, the files dealt with by an office). Measurements are rarely to be found in qualitative research. Although they sometimes crop up in conversation analysis when pauses and silences (generally the latter) are measured, they are nevertheless of little importance for such analysis.

In ethnography, counting is used to obtain information for two purposes:

(1) to determine the extent of the phenomenon observed; and
(2) to document hypotheses.

The phenomena counted may be interactive acts (for instance, the number of questions asked in an interview, the number of interruptions in a conversation, or the duration of a ritual).

CASE STUDY
Counting

Mehan, Hertweck and Meihls (1986: 145–50), when studying the social construction of academic failure by disabled students, collected the explanations or 'educators' theories' furnished by 15 teachers at the school observed. The authors then classified these 'educators' theories' into 12 categories (cognitive incapacity, psychological problems, physical state, etc.) and subsequently conducted a more detailed survey on the three categories most frequently mentioned by the teachers. The statistical survey helped the researchers focus on the explanations given greatest weight in educational practices.

Instead, in a study on the interaction between doctors and cancer patients, Silverman (1984) used counting to support his impression that interviews with private doctors were considerably shorter than those with doctors working in public hospitals. Silverman discovered that this difference did not depend on the professionalism of the private doctors (indeed, during treatment, private patients participated more in interactions, asking twice as many questions as normal in interviews with public-sector doctors). Rather, it was due to the appointments schedule, which fixed numerous interviews during surgery hours so that as many patients as possible could be treated: 'these quantitative data were a useful check on over-enthusiastic claims about the degree of difference between (public) and private clinics' (Silverman, 2000: 147).

Counting therefore enables ethnographers to document intuitions, sensations or first impressions more precisely.

Finally, counting also enables them to check the extent to which the phenomenon observed is representative of the organization studied.

12.6 Catching the fleeting instant: Collecting images

Contemporary ethnography makes increasing use of electronic technologies. Behaviors were once noted down with paper and a pen (fieldnotes, drawings, sketches). Then came cameras, followed by audio recorders and – later – video cameras. Today, electronic or digital recording devices are widely available. But they have not supplanted the old-style pen-and-paper fieldnotes; rather, they have supplemented and supported them. As the anthropologist Alessandro Duranti puts it:

> writing is a poor technology for describing the richness of the experience, [because] a good quality video recording or a film with a sound track of an event is going to have a lot more information than a written description of it. At the same time, it is also true that . . . we cannot make visual and sound records of everything . . . and there might be situations for which a written record might be more revealing than a visual one; . . . ethnographic notes can add dimensions of description that cannot be captured on tape not even on video tape (1997a: 113 and 109).

EXERCISE 12.2

Create this experience: watch a video recording of a place that you have never visited; then watch one of a place where you have spent some time. You'll have two very different sensations, because in the second viewing 'there is an experiential, subjective dimension of "having been there" that is not quite visible or audible on a tape' (Duranti, 1997a: 115).

As mentioned in the introduction to this chapter where the unavoidable selectiveness of descriptions was discussed, any medium can only yield a partial account. It is bound to grasp different aspects of the phenomenon that it wants to capture. What is more, it is bound to miss various aspects as well. Just as 'the strength of the thermometer . . . is precisely that it can ignore everything except the temperature' (Duranti, 1997a: 114), so the strength of a medium (a tape recorder, a camera or a video recorder) is also its weakness. For example, the tape recorder is certainly better at storing complete conversations than are memory or fieldnotes – however good we may be at listening and remembering. But the tape recorder is also a profoundly egalitarian and ultimately stupid instrument (in this case), because it reduces everything to the same level. It treats a participant's speech as just as important as the noise of his or her chair scraping on the floor.

For the tape recorder these are both noises (it is a great phenomenologist, it goes without saying), and it records them with equal intensity.

Video recordings can be used to grasp important but fleeting details of interactions so that they can be repeatedly re-viewed. While 'the writer [crafting a fieldnote] choos[es] what to highlight and what to neglect . . . there is less hierarchical ordering in the image' (Coffey et al., 2006: 22) – see the contrast between a fieldnote and an image in 10.5). However, many other important things may be going on outside the video recorder's viewfinder, because participants move behind it or simply go off to other places in the organization. As Duranti writes, 'I have found that fieldnotes contain crucial information which helps me contextualize what I have recorded on tape' (1997a: 116).

The advantage of giving due importance to each medium is that 'we don't have to engage in the hopeless search for the perfect recording tool or the perfect description . . . What we need to do instead is to understand the specific properties of such tools' (Duranti, 1997a: 114).

12.6.1 Tips and advice

The research practice of video recording began to spread in the early 1970s. Consequently, there is now a large body of literature on how naturally occurring interactions can be recorded on video.

Intrusivity

Two issues much debated when the video recorder first became widely available were its intrusiveness and its ability to induce artificial behavior in participants. However, with time these concerns subsided. Firstly, because the video recorder is no more intrusive than the ethnographer (perhaps less so, in fact). Moreover, in principle there is no such thing as 'natural' behavior: every behavior adapts to its setting, and attention should also be paid to the use that participants make of it (Wolfson, 1976). As Duranti points out:

> there is no question that our presence as observers is more intrusive in some situations than in others. There is a difference between walking with a camera in our hands into a room where two people are having a conversation and bringing a camera to a public event that involves dozens of people (1997a: 118).

In addition, compared to the 1970s, our society is highly technological, and the video camera has become familiar, readily available, and used by non-researchers as well. Research practice has also discovered that participants feel the video recorder to be intrusive when the first recording sessions take place. Thereafter, amid the flow of events and routines, they forget the presence of the 'indiscreet' device:

> perhaps with the exception of obvious **camera behaviors** (for example, certain types of camera-recognitions or salutations like staring into the camera and smiling), people usually do not *invent* social behavior, language included, out of the blue . . . most of the time people are too busy running their own lives to change them in substantial ways because of the presence of a new gadget or a new person (1997a: 118).

CASE STUDY
Detecting intrusivity

There are indicators that can reveal the extent to which the video camera is or is not intrusive. In the research recording of the emergency dispatch center, described in 10.6.2, there is a scene in which an operator passes in front of the video camera. He looks at the camera and then continues with his normal activities. On several occasions he scratches his crotch, a (vulgar) gesture customary among some men. The fact that the operator did not restrain himself, even though he knew he was being filmed, can be taken as a good indicator of the scant intrusivity, in that context, of the video camera.

A useful way to reduce the video camera's intrusiveness is to place it, switched off, in the setting as soon as observation begins, so that it gradually becomes as familiar to participants as an ornament or a piece of furniture (Corsaro, 1982). Finally, it should also be borne in mind that there are certain professionals (judges, lawyers, politicians, show business personalities, television journalists, etc.) for whom being observed is part of their work because they constantly act in front of watching audiences.

Gathering images

It is not always necessary to gather data at first hand (Silverman, 2000); likewise, it is not always necessary to take original video images. In fact, public and private organizations produce numerous documents in the form of images which can be analyzed. Today, video cameras have been installed in a large number of public places: streets and squares, parks, banks, post offices, airports, railway stations, and so on. And the researcher can get hold of this documentation for, at least, initial analysis.[5]

However, if the research topic requires original video recordings, you should draw on the past experiences of other researchers and follow their advice. First the video camera should be kept fixed, in the sense that it should remain stably trained on the scene. Television filming techniques are of little use in social research: the video camera should not be constantly panned to frame the speaker (as in talk shows) or zoomed in on details of the speaker's face or upper body.[6] Make a series of tests to find the best camera angle, the one which frames the setting most completely. In small rooms, use a wide-angle lens, and the camera should be kept fixed to record interactions in context. Establish the best distance for comprehensible sound recording. If the setting is large, get hold of external microphones or a portable tape recorder and place them close to the participants, as the microphones incorporated in video cameras are usually feeble.

12.7 The advent of hypermedia ethnography

Over time, ethnography has constantly enriched its array of information-collecting techniques. Traditional fieldnotes have been gradually supplemented with other forms of documentation:

> Rather than working with a single mode (for example, spoken, written or visual), ethnographers are beginning to integrate these different modes together by using different media (such as digital video audio recordings and photographs, as well as fieldnotes, documents and interview texts). However, mixing modes and media is a complex undertaking, and raises considerable methodological and practical challenges for qualitative work (Coffey et al., 2006: 15).

This transformation of ethnography is not yet concluded. Indeed, it is all the more dynamic, and discussion has recently begun on *hypermedia ethnography* (Coffey et al., 2006) or *multimodal ethnography* (Coffey et al., 2006: 15):

> Hypermedia combines two concepts: multimedia and hypertext. *Multimedia* refers to the use of, and often the integration of, diverse and multi-semiotic media (often including still and moving images, sound and graphics, as well as written text) into a single environment. *Hypertext* [navigating inside our ethnographic materials] through 'clickable' *hyperlinks*, make[s] possible to construct and 'read' [page by page, text by text] multi-linear networks of information . . . Hypermedia thus utilises the concept and practice of hyperlinking, with multimedia materials or data (Coffey et al., 2006: 17).

However, multimedia ethnography is not simply a mosaic, a melange of materials collected with diverse media. Instead, it can institute a new, multi-semiotic in which meaning is produced through the inter-relationships between and among different modes or forms of data. Will *hypermedia ethnography* maintain its promises, or will it prove to be merely a bluff? We shall see in the next few years.

12.8 Concluding remarks

Crafting ethnographic records requires patience, precision and systematicity. These are qualities at times lacking in contemporary ethnographies more concerned with the problems of fieldwork (entering, ethics, field relations) than with those of collecting and analyzing materials. Hence one should always bear in mind Clifford Geertz's warning in *Available Light*, one of his last works: 'the world being so full of a number of things, rushing to judgment is more than a mistake, it's a crime' (2000: 61).

EXERCISE 12.3 (GROUP)

Finagle's 8th Rule

Teamwork is essential – it allows you to blame someone else.

To apply the principles set out in this and the previous chapter, do the following exercise.

(1) Form groups of three students.

(2) Each group should choose an information collection unit. 'Collection unit' means a theoretical topic (for example, interaction between a barman and a customer, checking-in at the airport, queuing at the entrance of a club, cinema or concert). When the group chooses a collection unit, it should focus on a specific and circumscribed action (for example, a particular ritual or a brief ceremonial).

(3) Having decided the collection unit, the group should then choose the setting in which to do its observation. It is preferable to select at least two different settings (for example, a downtown cinema and one in the suburbs, two bars frequented by different ethnic groups) because comparison more readily reveals the distinctive features of a setting.

(4) When choosing the settings, it is better to opt for public places. It will thus not be necessary to negotiate access to the field. Because this is only an exercise (not a research project), it is not worthwhile bothering with long negotiations. There are dozens of organizations or institutions with 'open' access: bars, pizzerias, fast food outlets, restaurants, post offices, ticket offices at railway stations, trains, buses, supermarkets, large stores, shopping malls, airports, museums, hospital emergency departments, churches, squares, libraries, gyms, clubs, etc.

(5) Next to be decided is the sample, i.e. the events to be observed. If the ritual chosen is rapid (for example, purchasing a subway ticket from an automatic vending machine), numerous cases will be observed in just one hour. If instead the ritual (a religious ceremony, for example) is relatively protracted, only one, or at most two, cases will be observed in an hour.

(6) Each member of the group should devote two half-day sessions to observation. These sessions should preferably be a morning and an afternoon, so that the group can see whether the ritual changes according to the time of day.

(7) Each of the group's three members should be given a specific task: the first member should observe the conventions, rules and norms that govern the ritual; the second should listen to the conversations of the participants; the third should map and describe the main features of the physical place. It is not necessary for all three observers to be present simultaneously: rituals are fixed and recursive, so that different observers at different times see largely the same things. But if all three observers are simultaneously present, the exercise will be even more effective.

(8) While in the field, each of the three observers should take ethnographic notes according to his or her task. The writing of the *observational* notes should follow the language identification, verbatim and concreteness principles.

(9) *As soon as* each observation session has concluded, the ethnographer should re-read the ethnographic notes and sort them systematically into observational, theoretical (hypotheses, new concepts, etc.), emotional and methodological.

(10) If you think that you have identified a convention, and if you feel it appropriate, try to devise a breaching procedure to check the existence of the convention itself, and the extent to which it can be violated.

(11) Write a report no more than 15 pages in length.

KEY POINTS

- Ethnography is often considered to lack rigor. Its main weaknesses are that its empirical bases are difficult to verify and that the information it collects can be easily manipulated.
- Fieldnotes are *inscriptions*.
- Every description (fieldnote) is by definition partial, in the sense that it necessarily assumes a selective point of view.
- Not only are fieldnotes constructs, but also the field itself is the product of disciplinary technologies.
- Spradley suggests three criteria or principles to follow when taking ethnographic notes: the language identification, verbatim and concreteness principles.
- There are at least four kinds of ethnographic notes: observational, theoretical, methodological and emotional.
- Observational notes should be written bearing the three above principles in mind;
- Other kinds of notes can be written as one wishes.
- An organization's numerous documents should be examined, with only those most relevant to analysis being retained.
- The possibility of collecting ethnographic statistics should be borne in mind.
- Contemporary ethnography is a necessarily multimedia enterprise, in which traditional ethnographic notes (still extremely valid) are integrated with audiovisual materials.

KEY TERMS

Amalgamated language
(see p. 204)

The result of the researcher's simplification of linguistic variability into his or her language.

Emotional notes
(see pp. 221–2)

These seek to capture the researcher's feelings, sensations and reactions to the specific features of the event observed. In other words, emotional notes should report the outcomes of a kind of self-analysis.

Ethnographic statistics (see pp. 214–7)	The result of counting the occurrences of a given event and/or the number of people and objects present in a setting. Ethnographic statistics are useful for: (a) determining the magnitude of the phenomenon observed; and (b) documenting hypotheses.
Hypermedia ethnography (see p. 220)	An ethnographic style which integrates multimedia products (texts, sounds and images) with hypertext search.
Linguistic variability (see p. 203)	The various kinds of language, narrative structures, linguistic styles present in the settings observed by ethnographers.
Methodological notes (see p. 210)	These are essentially questions or reflections about how to deal with difficulties that arise in the field.
Observational notes (see pp. 208–10)	Observational notes are thin and detailed descriptions of events or actions seen or heard by the researcher.
The concreteness principle (see pp. 206–7)	Observational ethnographic notes should contain thin, naturalistic descriptions of basic practices.
The language identification principle (see pp. 203–4)	A principle which helps preserve linguistic variability. In practice, it consists of identifying the speaker alongside the noted-down texts of conversations or verbal exchanges.
The verbatim principle (see pp. 204–6)	Besides identifying the speakers, the ethnographer must make a faithful record of what they say.
Theoretical notes (see pp. 210–1)	Theoretical notes develop the more general theoretical meaning of observational notes.
Thin description (see p. 207)	A crude 'snapshot-type' phenomenological description.

RECOMMENDED READING

For undergraduates:
Ball, Mike and Smith, Greg (2001)

For graduates:
Emerson, Robert M., Fretz, Rachel I. and Shaw, Linda L. (2001)

For advanced researchers:
Duranti, Alessandro (1997b)

SELF-EVALUATION TEST

Are you ready for the next chapter? Check your knowledge by answering the following open-ended questions:

1. What did Geertz mean by saying: 'The world being so full of a number of things, rushing to judgment is more than a mistake, it's a crime'?

2. You already know that thick description is important. But why is thin description important as well?

3. What is 'an interpretation of an interpretation,' 'an explanation of an explanation'? How can they be avoided?

4. What is the difference between survey statistics and ethnographic statistics?

5. Have records collected using audiovisual techniques made fieldnotes obsolete? Why/why not?

Notes

1 This is certainly not the only classification of ethnographic notes. For example, the useful guide to the practice by Emerson, Fretz and Shaw (1995) talks of 'mental notes,' 'jotted notes,' 'asides,' 'commentaries,' 'in-process-memos,' and so on.

2 This advice should not be taken literally, because analytically it would be impracticable. From the cognitive point of view, in fact, we always interpret things, and even the most basic events are always our interpretations (see Chapter 4).

3 If we describe a room as 'tidy, clean, elegant,' and so on, this is not a factual description. These qualifying adjectives do not convey information about the room, but instead about the ethnographer's stereotypes. For example, instead of describing the setting as 'neat,' it would be better to describe the details of that neatness: 'the papers were arranged symmetrically on the table, all the chairs were arranged around the table, the furniture had been dusted,' etc.

4 For details on the methodology of this experiment see Rosenhan (1973: 132).

5 However, one should decide case by case. In fact, numerous video recordings are useless for the analysis of interactions. Video recordings of some organizations (banks, subways, etc.) do not reproduce the interactions among clients or consumers in their entirety but only a sequence of freeze-frames, as exemplified at http://www.earthcam.com/usa/newyork/timessquare/.

6 The same applies to the current fashion for filming episodes with wearable video cameras (see http://www.justin.tv/). The images collected are too unstable and too focused on one person alone (not on the interaction).

Part Three
Analyzing Materials

Coding and Analyzing Ethnographic Records

MaryAnn's Law
You can always find what you're not looking for.

LEARNING OBJECTIVES

- To gain an overview of the patient work that data analysis requires.

- To gain detailed knowledge of the three steps of data analysis.

- To learn how to code the materials collected.

- To familiarize yourself with the analysis of documents and images.

- To understand how to test hypotheses and to deal with deviant cases.

- To survey the limits and possibilities of the main softwares for the digital analysis of textual materials.

13.1 Introduction

Ethnography handbooks and books are usually devoid of instructions on how to conduct data analysis. They prefer to dwell on questions concerning the epistemology and philosophy of research, the relationship between the researcher and actors, or information collection techniques. Among the rare exceptions are the exponents of Grounded Theory (in particular Glaser and Strauss – see 3.5), who have made several original and significant contributions on the matter. I shall draw on these studies in describing this delicate phase of the ethnographer's work.

13.2 The analysis in three steps

It should be remembered that ethnographic data is never analyzed subsequent to its collection. According to many authors (among them Glaser and

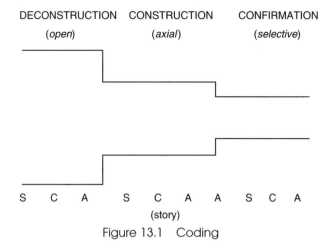

DECONSTRUCTION   CONSTRUCTION   CONFIRMATION
(*open*)   (*axial*)   (*selective*)

S   C   A   S   C   A   A   S   C   A
(story)

Figure 13.1   Coding

Strauss, 1967; Wiseman, 1970; Spradley, 1980; Strauss and Corbin, 1990; Charmaz, 2000), the collection and the analysis of data (fieldnotes, documents and visual materials) are not strictly distinct phases. Instead, they are closely intertwined processes which proceed circularly in reciprocal interaction because the data analysis drives closely-focused sampling and information collection.

Strauss and Corbin (1990: 59) propose a data coding procedure divided into three progressive steps: deconstruction (*open coding*), construction (*axial coding*) and confirmation (*selective coding*). This is a sophisticated procedure which enables systematic and efficacious analysis. It generates a spiral reflexive process in which sampling (S), collection (C) and analysis (A) are repeated with a progressively narrower focus in each of the three phases (see Figure 13.1).

The collection of data (fieldnotes, documents and visual materials) therefore takes place in all three of these steps, but in each of them it serves a different purpose: in deconstruction the ethnographer seeks to uncover the conventions regulating the interactions observed; in construction he or she devises a story (theory) about the phenomenon observed; in the confirmation the information collected is used to document precisely and systematically the hypotheses contained in the story (theory).

The American sociologist Kathy Charmaz (2000) has argued that the Grounded Theory must be emancipated from its original subtly positivist premises, released from its objectivistic underpinnings, and purged of certain 'strong' assumptions (causality, operational acts, testing hypothesis, verifiability, confirmation and disconfirmation, prediction, reproducibility, and so on). Of course, Grounded Theory must evolve in a more constructivist direction. Nevertheless, as I have argued throughout this book, there is a risk of throwing the baby out with the bath water: numerous terms can be very well recovered from the positivist lexicon, rather than eliminating them within a constructivist rationale.

13.2.1 Deconstruction (open coding)

Deconstruction is an exploratory phase in which the ethnographer examines the field for concepts (or categories) that can explain an observed phenomenon.

As we saw in Chapter 10, the ethnographer proceeds unsystematically in this phase, paying attention to all interesting events. He or she adopts a listening stance, ready to change focus whenever a noteworthy action or interaction occurs. Then, after spending some time in the setting, and having taken a certain number of ethnographic notes (mainly observational, but also theoretical, methodological and emotional), he or she sets about analyzing them.

There are three main strategies with which the ethnographer can begin the analysis of his or her observational notes:

(1) using a check list or conceptual grid to 'interrogate' them;
(2) using a framework; or
(3) classifying.

These three strategies involve different degrees of laboriousness. I shall therefore start with the simplest of them and finish with the most complex.

The check list

The first strategy has been suggested by Atkinson (1992: 455–9) and Silverman (1993: 39–41; 2006: 89–92). It consists of the use of a check list (coding sheet or coding form or conceptual grid) with a relatively small number of entries or items (around 20) eliciting information from the observational notes.[1] As Silverman (2006: 89) stresses, this coding form must *not* be drawn up *before* the fieldwork begins. Rather, it should be developed only *after* a sizable number of observations have been made and, if the research is being conducted with colleagues or co-workers, after extensive discussion.

This style of work entails that

> the data are inspected for categories and instances. It . . . disaggregates the text (notes and transcripts) into a series of fragments, which are then regrouped under a series of thematic headings (Atkinson, 1992: 455, quoted in Silverman, 2006: 92).

CASE STUDY
Doctor–patient interaction in a pediatric cardiology unit

In the early 1980s David Silverman carried out a study on doctor–patient interactions in a pediatric cardiology unit. During the research the focus was restricted to 'how decisions (or "disposals") were organized and announced. It seemed likely that the doctor's way of announcing decisions was systematically related not only to clinical factors (like the child's heart condition) but to social factors (such as what parents would be told at various stages of treatments)' (2006: 89).

After observation of more than ten outpatient clinics, Silverman and his co-worker Robert Hilliard developed the following coding sheet to record their observations, which is reproduced only partially (for the full coding sheet, go to www.sagepub.co.uk/gobo).

9 Stage of treatment:

>   First consultation
>
>   Pre-inpatient
>
>   Post-catheter (test requiring inpatient stay)
>
>   Post-operation

10 Outcome of consultation:

>   Discharge or referral elsewhere
>
>   Non-inpatient follow up
>
>   Possible eventual catheter or surgery
>
>   Catheter
>
>   Surgery
>
>   No decision
>
>   . . .

14 Scope of consultation:

	Family	**Doctor**
Prior treatment		
History		
Extra-cardiac		
Physical states		
Child development		
Child behavior		
Family's practicalities of treatment or attendance		
Doctor's practicalities of treatment or attendance		
Anxieties and emotional problems of family		
Social situation of family		
External treatment agencies		

15 Family's presentation of a referral history

16 Format of doctor's initial elicitation question (e.g. how is she? is she well?)

   . . .

19 Diagnosis statement:

      (a)   Use of 'well' (Dr/Family/Both)

      (b)   Use of 'normal' (Dr/Family/Both)

      (c)   Possible diagnoses mentioned (0/1/>1)

20 Decisions:

      (a)   Possible disposals mentioned (0/1/>1)

      (b)   Medical preference stated (Yes/No)

      (c)   Medical intention stated (Yes/No)

      (d)   Family assent requested (Yes/No)

      (e)   Family allowed to make decision (Yes/No)

      (f)   Family wishes volunteered (Yes/No)

      (g)   Family dissent from doctor's proposed disposal (Yes/No)

(Source: Silverman, 2006: 90–1, Table. 3.2)

This coding form enabled the researchers to identify some behavioral patterns:

> For instance, by relating Item 14 on the scope of the consultation to the decision-format (Item 20), we were able to see differences between consultations involving Down's children and others. Moreover, it also turned out that there were significant differences between these two groups both in the form of the elicitation question (Item 16) and the diagnosis statement (Item 19).

> . . . Obviously, in making fieldnotes, one is not simply recording data but also analyzing them. The categories you use will inevitably be theoretically-saturated – whether or not you realise it! So the coding form . . . reflected my interest in Goffman's (1974) concept of 'framing'. This meant that I tried to note down the activities through which the participants managed their identities. For instance, I noted how long the doctor and patient spent on social 'small talk' and how subsequent appointments were arranged.

> These concerns show how theoretically-defined concepts drive good ethnographic research . . . They also demonstrate how one can develop analysis of field data after a research problem has been carefully defined (Silverman, 2006: 92).

This strategy has two advantages and a shortcoming. The advantages are that it simplifies the analysis by reducing the complexity of the information, and that patterns can immediately be identified by cross-referencing information reported in the items. The shortcoming is that the coding form is a highly constrictive instrument from which it is difficult to escape (Atkinson, 1992: 459), so that the ethnographer is cognitively unable to grasp information and activities not immediately insertable into the grid. To remedy (partly) this drawback, it may be useful for the ethnographer occasionally to return to his or her fieldnotes and retrieve information on activities obscured or not considered by the grid (Silverman, 1993: 39). In the case of Silverman and Hilliard, moreover, they tape-recorded all interactions so that they could recode as their hypotheses developed.

The framework

The second strategy consists in using a framework to analyze organizational routines. As in the previous strategy, the framework is constructed only *after* several hours of observation have been conducted in the field.

CASE STUDY
Finding an ambulance

In 10.6.2, I discussed research that I have been conducting for some years, together with co-workers, at a number of Italian medical emergency dispatch centers. After a period of observation we devised an analytical framework to interpret the operators' activities (see Gobo et al., 2008). It consisted of six entries:

(a)   the operator's goal;

(b)   interaction strategy among the actors to achieve the goal;

(c)   operator's difficulties;

(d)   operator's needs;

(e)   inefficiencies of the computerized information system; and

(f)   theoretical notes or outcomes.

It sometimes happened that a call-taker requested the dispatch of an ambulance when none were available because all the center's vehicles were already dealing with emergencies. In this case, the framework was compiled with observational notes, as follows:

(a)   The operator's goal:

This situation arises whenever all the vehicles are already dealing with emergencies and the call-taker receives an urgent request for assistance. The situation may be extremely serious (classified as 'red code') but no ambulances are available.

If the call-taker's case is considered most urgent, his goal is to get an ambulance assigned to his case as quickly as possible. To do so, he must 'grab' an ambulance assigned to another case deemed less urgent (for example, one classified as 'green code').

(b)   Interaction strategies among the actors to achieve the goal

Strategy 1 – In a loud voice the call-taker asks a colleague call-taker to re-route the ambulance (which he had just dispatched) to the scene of the more serious emergency. This request is made when the call-taker realizes that the colleague has sent an ambulance to a location close to the one from which his high-priority emergency call has been made.

Strategy 2 – Again in a loud voice the call-taker asks the operators handling vehicles redeployment (they sit at the ISDN-Radio Area stations in Figure 10.4, 10.6.2) whether there are ambulances soon becoming available but not yet on his monitor.

There may sometimes be several simultaneous requests for ambulances. All of them are shouted out loud, and they overlap to increase the din in the operations room (Figure 13.2).

Figure 13.2   Call-taker's request to the ISDN-Radio Area operators

(c)   Operator's difficulties

(i)   The call-taker has difficulty in communicating his request to the colleague who has just dispatched the ambulance. The more physically distant the operators are from each other, the more they must shout their requests. Because of the height of the desk backs and the monitors, the call-takers must rise to their feet to see the faces of their colleagues.

(ii)   The call-taker has difficulty in communicating with the ISDN-Radio Area because of its distance away from him. He therefore has to shout to make himself heard.

(d)   The call-taker's needs

- To rapidly attract the attention of the colleague call-taker.

- To rapidly attract the attention of the ISDN-Radio operators.

- To get a rapid reply about the availability of ambulances.

- To know whether vehicles will soon be available, and which ones.

(e)   Inefficiencies of the computerized information system

- The interphone system (with headsets) and its SMS (Short Message System) backup for computer-mediated communication among operators is considered inadequate for urgent communications;

- consequently, the operators prefer face-to-face verbal communication;

- but this is hampered by the layout of the work stations.

(f)   Theoretical notes or outcomes

The observational notes highlight that the 'old' or analogical technologies (spoken, non-verbal, face-to-face) are anything but obsolete. Indeed, the operators prefer 'headsets-off' communication (with shouted requests, expletives, and so on) to the interphone system with its SMS backup, because they find it more rapid and reliable. Indeed, in a previously-observed incident, this 'headsets-off' type of communication – not foreseen by the computerized information system – enabled a nurse to intercept information decisive for successful conclusion of a rescue operation that she was monitoring via radio.

Hence, the information system can only function properly with the so-called 'soft technologies,' i.e. those with low formal and engineering content. And the design of systems and services based on the user's social knowledge, rather than the designer's, must necessarily envisage the integration of digital technologies with analogical ones, instead of excluding the latter.

The classification

The third strategy is to classify the observational notes applying a similarity/dissimilarity criterion. Assigned to each note is a code referring to a concept, and the same code is assigned to notes with similar content. However, the same notes may refer to several concepts, so that they may receive other codes and labels as well, and be repeatedly classified under different headings (Hammersley and Atkinson, 1983: 170).[2] Consider, for example, the following observational note taken by David Rosenhan (1973: 133) when he was a pseudopatient in a psychiatric hospital. The doctor's behavior can be classified with diverse codes or labels.

Table 13.1

Actors	Verbal exchanges	Body movements	Codes or labels
Pseudopatient	Pardon me, Dr. X. Could you tell me when I am eligible for grounds privileges?		
Physician	Good morning, Dave. How are you today?'	(Moves off without waiting for a response)	1. indifference 2. rudeness 3. non-person (considering patient as)

The aim of classification is to deconstruct the events and actions observed and segment them among a series of concepts. Depending on the researcher's preferences, there are three ways to select the codewords assigned to ethnographic notes:

(1) invent new terms;
(2) use terms taken from the literature; or
(3) use terms employed by the actors.

The first option is by far the most preferable because it stimulates the researcher's creativity and averts the danger of confusion with already-existing concepts or theories (Strauss and Corbin, 1990: 68). However, it should be borne in mind that assigning a code to an action is not a neutral act, for it immediately attributes a *function* to the action, and assigns it a frame.

Deconstructing a set of observational notes is to *denaturalize them*, i.e. dissolve their spatial and temporal wholeness. By means of classification, the researcher breaks up the natural flow of actions and events (still present in his or her ethnographic notes) in order to give them new sense.

This deconstructive activity can be performed in various ways, among them the use of counterfactual conditionals as discussed in 9.2.1.

13.2.2 Construction (axial coding)

In the second (constructive) phase, the researcher reassembles the concepts developed in the previous phase into a new pattern, the aim being to construct a first coherent framework. He or she does so according to the model proposed by Strauss and Corbin (1990), which comprises the following five components: causal conditions, intervening conditions, context, micro-actions, and consequences. In logical terms, we have the following sequence:

(A) CASUAL CONDITIONS $\longrightarrow$
(B) PHENOMENON (under study) $\longrightarrow$
(C) CONTEXT $\longrightarrow$
(D) INTERVENING CONDITIONS $\longrightarrow$
(E) ACTION/INTERACTIONAL STRATEGIES $\longrightarrow$
(F) CONSEQUENCES

Figure 13.3

A first logical framework can thus be constructed for every phenomenon. On the basis of these preliminary results, the ethnographer conducts a second sampling procedure, but this time focused only on the concepts which he or she has decided to explore further.[3] In this second phase, the data collection concentrates on each of the five aspects in Figure 13.3. The relative observational notes furnish the basis for constructive analysis which states the relations between the concept (usually of a ceremonial or ritual around which many other micro-actions rotate) and its attributes (see 5.6).

Fruitful use may be made in this phase of interviews and informal conversations conducted in the field (see Chapter 11). These aid the researcher to understand what he or she has observed, and to uncover meanings hidden within the rituals reported by his or her observational notes. This is an analytical procedure which has been used for some time. For example Humphreys (1970), in his already-mentioned study on men's homosexual activity (see 12.3.1), noted down the car license plates of the users of the city park tearooms, traced the names of the owners, contacted them, and then interviewed them. Notwithstanding the enormous ethical issues raised by Humphreys' behavior (which were much debated on publication of his book), his interviews gave him greater insight into the participants' practices. Indeed, as Brekhus, Galliher and Gubrium stress,

> the contrast between the focal thin description of tearoom participants and the thick description of the participants' personalities, families, and neighborhoods outside of the tearoom gives the new theme empirical punch (2005: 15).

13.2.3 Confirmation (selective coding)

In the third phase (confirmation), the ethnographer documents/checks the hypotheses formulated during the constrictive phase and anchors them to a theory. This final phase involves two stages of materials analysis (see Figure. 13.1) which integrate the data at a level of generality higher than in the previous two phases. The ethnographer constructs a '*story*, a descriptive narrative about the central phenomenon of the study' (Strauss and Corbin, 1990: 116) consisting of ten or so statements (though still taking the form of hypotheses) about the relations between the core concept and its indicators.

CASE STUDY
Managing risk factors associated with pregnancy

In the mid-1980s, the American health sociologist Juliet Corbin carried out a study 'focused on the issue of how 20 women with chronic illness managed their pregnancies. They were enlisted as subjects at the end of the first or beginning of the second trimester, and followed until six weeks after delivery' (Strauss and Corbin, 1990: 118).

In the advanced phase of his fieldwork, Corbin integrated the various phases of her previous analysis to produce a story entitled (or based on the core category) 'management of *risk factors* associated with a pregnancy/illness':

> The main story seems to be about how women with pregnancies compli-
> cated by chronic illness manage the risks they perceive to be associated
> with their pregnancies. Each pregnancy/illness can be said to be on-course,
> indicating that the risks are being managed, or off-course, indicating that
> they are not. Women are managing the perceived risks in order to have
> a healthy baby. This desired outcome seems to be the primary force
> motivating them to do whatever is necessary to minimize the risks. However,
> they are not passive recipients of care but play a very important role in the
> management process. They not only are responsible for monitoring their
> illnesses and pregnancies at home, but also make very active decisions
> about the regimes they are told to follow. In the latter case they consider the
> harm that might come to the baby from procedures like amniocentesis or
> from taking high doses of certain medication while pregnant. They carefully
> weigh the risks and make judgments about the right thing to do. If they think
> the doctor is wrong, then they do what they (the women) think should be
> done (1990: 119–20).

Having told his or her story, the ethnographer returns to the field and undertakes a final sampling procedure in order to collect further information with which to test his or her statements. The relationships, documented in a satisfactory manner, assume the form of distinct patterns representable in a non-numerical matrix (see Table 13.2, 13.7.4).

Strauss and Corbin (1990) stress that the distinction between the deconstructive, constructive and confirmatory phases is only analytical. In practice, the three phases interweave. Or they may be repeated at the end of the research, if the ethnographer realizes that some concepts are still unclear or some relations are still poorly defined (Strauss and Corbin, 1990: 58; Silverman, 1993: 46). Analysis strategies obviously differ according to the researcher's degree of knowledge about his or her topic of study. As noted in the section on conceptualization (5.6), the ethnographer may already have a well-defined theory (constructed through previous research or drawn from another author), so that he or she can start his or her research from the second phase (construction) straight, or the third one (confirmation). Besides the virtuality of each phase, one should not forget that the analysis of observational notes serves to deconstruct the data, conceptualize them, and then reassemble them in new form (Strauss and Corbin, 1990: 57), striking an appropriate balance among creativity, rigor, consistency and, above all, theoretical sensitivity. As Duranti points out,

> an *analysis is*, after all, *a selective process of representation of a given phenomenon with the aim of highlighting some of its properties*. An analysis that tried to reproduce a perfect copy of its object would not be an analysis, it would give it back to us the way it was. *Analysis implies transformation*, for some purpose (1997a: 114).

13.3 Using documents

As already said in 12.4, a researcher engaged in ethnographic inquiry should examine the documents collected, not in and of themselves, but rather in light of his or her observation plan. In other words, fieldnotes are the core of ethnographic research, and all other materials (documents and images) are ancillary or supplementary to them. For two reasons: first because we are dealing with an ethnographic methodology, not a documentary methodology (see 2.4); second because the documents have been produced, not by the ethnographer with his or her phenomenological and denaturalizing gaze, but by an organization or a group. They therefore have a status different from that of fieldnotes and must be deconstructed beforehand. How is this done?

First, the deconstruction can be performed by not treating the document in the usual or natural manner (i.e. by reading it from beginning to end). The document's unitariness can be 'fragmented': for example by analyzing pages extracted at random, or by photocopying the document and then mixing up the pages, or by reading it in reverse from the end to the beginning.

Second, an important exercise consists in answering the following series of questions proposed by Hammersley and Atkinson (1983: 142–3):

(1) 'How are texts written?
(2) How are they read?
(3) Who writes them?
(4) Who reads them?
(5) For what purposes?
(6) On what occasions?
(7) With what outcomes?
(8) What is recorded?
(9) What is omitted?
(10) What is taken for granted?
(11) What does the writer seem to take for granted about reader(s)?
(12) What do readers need to know in order to make sense of them?'

Answering these questions enables the researcher to deconstruct the document and bring out its ideological structures and rhetorical narratives, thereby avoiding simple content or textual analysis.

Third, the researcher must refrain from the 'autism' intrinsic to narrative analysis. As Gubrum has argued:

> much of [narrative] analysis has centered on the internal organization of stories. Less attention has been paid to their production, distribution, and circulation in society . . . I have found that the internal organization of stories, while important to understand in its own right, does not tell us very much about the relation of stories to the worlds in which they circulate (2005: 169).

As Lindsay Prior (2004) has rightly emphasized, not only do we do things with words (to paraphrase the title of Austin's famous book of 1962), we also do things with documents. Put otherwise: just as words are not separate from deeds, so documents are not separate from action. They themselves are actions in that they intervene in reality to modify and influence it. Seeing documents as non-human agents (see the ANT theory in 10.5) allows one to escape from purely linguistic analysis and switch to a pragmatic approach.

13.4 Analyzing images

The above recommendation on the use of documents applies to images as well: their analysis should serve to integrate observational notes, for otherwise, the research will expand to such an extent that it becomes never-ending.

CASE STUDY
Teachers' interpretations of students' behavior

An integrative approach has been used by Mehan, Hertweek and Meihls (1986) in their study on decision-making in elementary school students' educational careers (see Case Study in 11.2). Their specific purpose was to grasp the teachers' interpretations of students' behavior. After long periods of observation of the 'referrals' of students in different elementary-school classes (on the basis of psycho-attitudinal tests, intelligence tests, medical diagnoses, etc.), Mehan and colleagues showed the teachers various episodes that they had video recorded in the classroom. An example follows:

> Similar behavior was displayed by a referral student and a non-referral student in another classroom. 'Eddie' has been referred for many reasons, one of which was 'hitting other people'. At the opening of the videotaped reading lesson he began hitting the student seated beside him. During the viewing session the teacher stopped the tape at the point and cited this as an example of the behavior for which Eddie had been referred. Later in the same reading lesson, another student who had not been referred struck Eddie on the head. The teacher did not stop the tape or comment on the incident (1986: 80).

This episode revealed to the researchers that:

> teachers are not reacting to discrete pieces of information; they do not seem to be separating student's behavior (for example hitting a child or saying,

'it's too hard for me') from the circumstances surrounding it. Instead of attending to behavior in isolation, teachers are attending to action in context. The context, in turn, includes the student, the task, the lesson, and the situation in which the action transpires . . . a piece of behavior is not the same when it is conducted by different contexts. 'Johnny hitting Mary during math' is not the same as 'Mary hitting Billy at recess' . . . In this way a 'slap in the face' takes on different meanings when embedded in different classroom contexts (1986: 80–1).

Precisely because they preserve the participants' actions in time, video recorded materials lend themselves better to intersubjectivity than do observational notes, and they are particularly useful for team research. Indeed, as Duranti remarks,

> such a record can be viewed by different people and subjected to analysis in ways that are quite different from the ways in which a narrative by an observer of the same event would allow (1997: 119).

As for written documents, so for images, the first step in their analysis is deconstruction. Watching a video recording like a film may certainly be useful, but it does not fulfill the functions of a phenomenologically focused gaze. De-naturalizing a video requires fragmentation of its wholeness: partial use is made of the recording, and with timelines different from those of continuous and integral viewing. There are various ways to de-naturalize the social practices preserved in a video recording. An example provided by Christian Heath and Paul Luff, well-known English representatives of workplace studies, is 'transcribing the talk and then mapping out the visual conduct' (1993: 325). Or the researcher can read the transcripts *before* listening to the soundtrack; or again, he or she can switch off the video (or cover it) and conduct a first analysis listening only to the sound, and vice versa. It is in fact difficult to analyze a document in the real time of its production, because too much information simultaneously impacts upon the researcher, who must follow both the soundtrack and the video footage. Instead, slowing down or breaking up the natural rhythm of the document facilitates analysis and aids deconstruction. Moreover, to bring out the latent conventions regulating behaviors, a sequence-by-sequence analysis can be performed by viewing the same episode again and again (or, in the case of recorded interviews, listening and re-listening to the same episode). Only after repeated exposure does the researcher begin to feel a sense of estrangement and uncover tacit knowledge. As Duranti points out:

> the introduction of recording machines such as the tape recorder and the video camera (or camcorder) . . . has a number of advantages over the traditional method of participant-observation based on the researcher's skills at listening, seeing, and (most importantly) remembering – whether or not aided by written notes. The ability to stop the flow of discourse or the flow of body movements, go back to a particular spot and replay it allows us to concentrate

on what is sometimes a very small detail at the time, including a particular sound or a person's small gesture (Duranti, 1997a: 116).

Duranti concludes:

> Although at this point a video tape is, albeit limited, the best type of record we can have if we are interested in the integration of speech with body movements and, more generally, with visual communication, we are still trying to learn how to take advantage of such a tool (Duranti, 1997a: 115).

13.5 Documenting hypotheses

Murphy's Law of Research

Enough research will tend to support whatever theory.

Before we examine how hypotheses are checked, there is an epistemological issue to clarify. One often hears or reads the expression 'verifying a hypothesis.' Yet it pertains to an outmoded form of scientific reasoning (the 'inductivism' devised by the British philosopher Sir Francis Bacon) which maintained that hypotheses should be proved to be true (for details on this topic, go to www.sagepub.co.uk/gobo). Other expressions as well, like 'testing' or 'hypothesis checking' (although less neo-positivist) are not always suited to a constructivist perspective because they assume that it is possible to get at the truth.

Most recently, amid postmodernism and the reflexive turn, the epistemologically most suitable expression seems to be 'documenting a hypothesis.' Whatever the case may be, one should never use the expression 'verifying a hypothesis.'

13.5.1 Logical procedure for documenting a hypothesis

Many years ago, Becker and Geer (1960) suggested a logical procedure for hypothesis testing. It moved through four phases:

(1) compare the hypothesis within different groups of subjects;
(2) ensure that the hypothesis covers all events observed and deemed relevant;
(3) pay maximum attention to the 'deviant cases' or exceptions not adequately explained by the hypothesis; and
(4) conduct a statistical test (if the events have been counted) to calculate the extent of the deviance.

Mehan (1979: 21) and Silverman (2000: 180ff) have supplemented this procedure by suggesting that a hypothesis should first be tested on a restricted corpus of instances. If it does not work, it should be revised in order to encompass the deviant instances. According to the British methodologists Nigel Fielding and Jane Fielding, in qualitative studies

> there is no random error variance. All exceptions are eliminated by revising hypotheses until all data fit. The result of this procedure is that [in qualitative

research] statistical tests are actually *unnecessary* once the negative cases are removed (1986: 89).

These authors therefore adopt a more radical position by maintaining that all exceptions must be eliminated (see 13.8).

Hypothesis checking is a mix of inductive and deductive processes. It is facilitated if the ethnographer is able to formulate his or her hypotheses in a quasi-experimental form. This is what Rosenhan (1973) did when he designed a counter-research whose outcomes, for the hypothesis to be valid, had to be the reverse of the results of the previous research (see 5.8).

An alternative is to document hypotheses by conducting small-scale tests in the field, formulating *beforehand* (because, as the well-known proverb says, 'it is easy to be wise after the event') the consequences that should ensue if the hypothesis is valid.

Case Study
Conformist behavior at an art gallery

Some years ago three undergraduates conducted a small-scale ethnographic exercise at an art gallery. After some hours of observing the behavior of visitors, they formulated their hypothesis: 'when less expert visitors (i.e. those without a specialized knowledge of art) enter a room, they first head for the paintings which the largest number of people are looking at' (theoretical note). We may call this a 'hypothesis of conformism.'

To document this hypothesis, in a room chosen at random, the students positioned themselves in front of one of the pictures (also chosen at random) painted by a little-known artist. They inspected it carefully and with manifest interest, pretending to exchange their impressions and to take notes.

After a while a middle-aged couple entered the room. Without hesitating, they approached the picture of such apparent interest to the students and read the explanatory caption to find out the painter's name. They seemed disappointed. They even tried to peek at the students' notes, but being unable to do so, walked away. Then two further visitors entered the room. They too immediately went up to the picture that the students were studying. They gazed at it for a few seconds, and then one of them, with a bemused expression on his face, asked the other: 'Do you know him?' The answer was 'No.' They inspected the picture for a few more seconds and then strode off.

The logical procedure followed by the students can be summarized as follows:

1. Having checked the statuses on the two attributes considered by the hypothesis (level of art knowledge; density of visitors looking at a painting),

2. having checked for the possible presence of intervening variables explaining the visitors' behavior (for example, courting, the students' physical attractiveness, etc.),

3. having observed a sufficient number of individuals or instances, and

4. having also considered possible exceptions,

5. the hypothesis of conformism can be considered adequately documented.

6. A possible counter-test might be to observe 'expert' visitors, noting whether their behavior was less conformist, more self-directed.

(To see a complete research project conducted by one of Europe's best-known ethnologists, with detailed reconstruction of his hypothesis-testing procedure, go to www.sagepub.co.uk/gobo.)

The biggest risk run by a researcher when checking hypotheses is that he or she may reproduce his or her prejudices and pre-assumptions (see 5.5). To partly avert this risk, the researcher may find it useful to deliberately disseminate a 'cognitive trap' in order to slow down and make cautious her or his reasoning (Gobo, 1993), for example, by reversing the data chronologically, 'mixing' the observational notes, and so on. This has the function of 'blocking' the researcher's mental connections, and forestalling too hasty conclusions which may prevent him or her from expecting the unexpected.

13.6 Building a theory

The difference between 'hypothesis' and 'theory' is anything but clear in the literature. This is certainly not the place to deal with this intricate issue. For our practical purposes we may define a theory as a set of assertions which rest on concepts that have not been given operational definitions (see 5.4), and consequently have not been directly observed. From this it follows that theories, contrary to hypotheses, are not directly testable.

A theory therefore consists of a series of hypotheses which have been checked and documented. A theory has only a mediated (by the hypotheses) relationship with the empirical level. The relationship between theory and hypotheses is depicted graphically by the following Figure 13.4.

How can one build a theory? A concrete answer was provided in 13.3, when constructing a story was discussed. We may say that a story (which is a set of hypotheses) is a theory in the making. The main difference is that a story is a set of hypotheses still to be tested. But once they have been tested, the story becomes a theory.

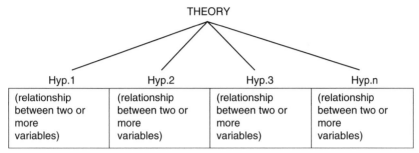

Figure 13.4   The relationship between theory and hypotheses

13.7 A research example: The organizational construction of blindness

In order to exemplify the procedures described thus far, I shall report the data analysis strategies used in a study on the organizational construction of blindness which I co-ordinated some years ago (Gobo, 1997). The research was conducted in a third-year class (16 pupils) of an Italian elementary school to which a sightless girl (named Yasmeen, aged 8) had been assigned. The initial (and therefore still generic) aim of the research was to study the difficulties of integration encountered by a disabled person in the school system.

13.7.1 Deconstruction (open coding)

After some weeks of closely observing the sightless girl's interactions with her classmates, and having collected and collated my ethnographic notes, I began to analyze the latter by classifying their content. This analysis yielded a preliminary list of categories (concepts) of rituals. I gave a label to each category: 'arrival at school,' 'getting ready to enter the classroom,' 'going to the washroom,' 'questioning pupils,' 'turn-taking strategies' to speak in class, 'choosing a playmate,' etc. For example, I assigned to this last category an episode – recorded by an *observational note* – when a boy asked the teaching assistant why Yasmeen (the sightless girl) could not join in a game. The teaching assistant answered as follows: 'because she can't see and so might hurt herself.' In a related *theoretical note*, I put the hypothesis that sightlessness is not nearly the self-evident phenomenon as one might believe. The fact that the boy had asked such an apparently obvious question suggested that children have mental schemas of sightlessness which differ profoundly from those of adults (and also researchers). At the beginning of the school year, Yasmeen's classmates probably had no precise social representation of a sightless person.[4] In other words, they did not know what a sightless person was (apart from the banal notion that he or she is someone who cannot see), and above all what a sightless person can or cannot do. This was evidenced by the fact that they initially asked Yasmeen to join in the same games that they proposed to other children. At this stage of the research, I therefore hypothesized that sightlessness (as regards its behavioral features) was primarily a 'process,' a conceptual product constructed in everyday interactions at school among pupils, teaching staff and non-teaching staff. I recalled a study carried out many years previously by Sudnow (1967) on the social organization of death in hospital, where he documented how death is a *social* phenomenon before it becomes a biological one. The death of the patient occurred well before his physical demise, when the hospital staff decided – more or less correctly – that he was dying. A series of organizational practices reserved for dying were then enacted, so that it was very difficult for the patient to 'save himself.'

13.7.2 Construction (axial coding)

Having formulated this hypothesis, based on the ethnographic material and suggested by Sudnow's study, I moved on to the next phase (construction) and collected further materials documenting organizational practices and environmental constraints in the school that contributed decisively to constructing a specific notion of disability, and especially the sightless girl's identity. I used the five components of Strauss and Corbin's (1990) model to construct a preliminary framework: causal conditions, intervening conditions, context, micro-actions and consequences. Thus the initial and generic research objective was made more precise. If the pupils formed their conception of sightlessness mainly through the organizational practices and rituals performed around the sightless child, then systematic observations would have to be made in the school premises indicated by my observations during the deconstruction phase as most significant: the entrance lobby, the staircases, the toilets and the classroom. I therefore assembled a more specific sample for the new category: the help practices (ethno-methods) enacted for Yasmeen by the teaching assistant in these five places. For each of them I identified the most recurrent actions, which were then sampled.

1. Recreation

For example, during recreation, the children were accompanied to the toilets before the next lesson began:

Observational note 23

Yasmeen usually took more time than her friends to finish her snack, and on occasion was urged by the teaching assistant to eat more quickly: 'Come on! You're always the last.' Consequently, Yasmeen got to the washrooms a little after the others. While her classmates were in the toilets, the class teacher waited at the door, leaving the children alone inside. By contrast, the teaching assistant always accompanied Yasmeen into the toilets.

Theoretical note 6

It is likely that this behavior altered the children's concepts of 'private' and 'body' with respect to Yasmeen.

Observational note 46

Whereas the children often playfully splashed each other with water while they were in the washrooms, they never played the same joke on Yasmeen. On leaving, the children held hands and filed back into the classroom. Yasmeen and the teaching assistant were left behind in the toilets and only got back to the classroom when the other children had settled down at their desks.

For me to state that the children 'never' played jokes on Yasmeen, or that she was 'always' accompanied into the washroom, I must have collected a certain number of substantially similar episodes. In this case, from the sampling frame of 216 recreations (as many as there were in the school year) I extracted a sample of 43 cases, which represented 20% of all episodes of the 'going to the toilet' ritual. Samples were similarly constructed of the most significant rituals (units of analysis) performed in the other places in the school.

2. The entrance lobby

At Yasmeen's elementary school, the cadence of organizational time was set by the ringing of a bell. At 8:20 the bell rang for a first time to tell the children to get ready to go up to the classrooms. At 8:30 it rang again: the children formed pairs and then filed into the classrooms to begin their lessons. During these organizational activities there occurred a series of behaviors which constructed Yasmeen's 'difference': (a) whereas the other children came to school on their own or were accompanied by their parents, Yasmeen was brought by an escort provided by the social services; (b) whereas the children had to arrive at the school before the first bell rang, lateness by Yasmeen was tolerated, and she sometimes arrived even after the second bell; (c) whereas the children played and joked among themselves while waiting for the second bell to ring, Yasmeen was taken aside by the teaching assistant, and they talked together separately from the class and the teachers; (d) whereas the children formed pairs to go up to the classroom, Yasmeen and the teaching assistant either preceded or followed them. It appears likely from these observational notes that Yasmeen's identity (and in particular what it means to be sightless in cognitive terms) was constructed organizationally.

3. The classroom

The children's work tables were arranged facing the teacher's desk. Yasmeen sat in the back row, next to the teaching assistant's desk. The children changed places during the school year so that they could interact with other classmates.

But Yasmeen stayed at the same work table throughout the year, because it was next to the teaching assistant's desk. I also noted that the children who showed the greatest friendliness towards Yasmeen were those who sat at the table closest to her: physical proximity bred affection. A further difference was apparent from the differing use of deference rituals (Goffman, 1956a): whereas the children addressed the class teacher as 'Miss', Yasmeen was allowed to use the teacher's first name.

The various subjects taught during the school day may have heightened the differences between Yasmeen and the class. During a geography lesson, for example, the class teacher described the morphological features (mountains, plains, rivers) of an Italian region. The pupils stood around the teacher's desk on which the map was displayed. Yasmeen stretched out her hands to touch the map. The teacher told her that in so doing she was preventing the other children from following the description, and that in any case the map did not have 'enough relief' for Yasmeen to be able to understand by touching it. The same thing happened while the teacher explained how the compass worked: Yasmeen tried to open the instrument.[5]

As the teacher was explaining a point, Yasmeen would sometimes raise her hand to ask questions or to make remarks, thereby interrupting the lesson and irritating her classmates. On other occasions she raised her hand to ask for the turn, but spoke before being explicitly permitted to do so by the teacher. This event was rather common: the convention that a pupil had to wait for a signal from the teacher before he or she spoke was often breached, because the children co-ordinated themselves differently; they looked at who had raised their hand first, or if there were still hands raised by pupils wanting to speak, they acted without waiting for the teacher's signal. These cognitive and social skills were obviously not available to sightless Yasmeen. It was grotesque for the teacher to reprimand her by saying: 'Wait your turn! Someone put their hand up before you did.'

Also the weekly lessons in religious (Catholic) education and English unjustifiably constructed a difference between Yasmeen and the class. The religious education teacher (a priest) adopted a protective and permissive attitude towards Yasmeen which he never showed to the other pupils. The English teacher was likewise over-indulgent with Yasmeen: indeed, a pupil exclaimed one day: 'Why does Yasmeen always get "very good" and we almost never do?' The teacher's explanation was that Yasmeen had to be helped because she was handicapped.

13.7.3 A framework
Using the suggestions of Strauss and Corbin (1990), I then constructed the following framework, with five aspects (see 13.2.2).

1. Causal conditions = The professional model used by the teaching assistant to interact with disabled pupils
The main features of the teaching assistant's professional model were the *principles* on which it is based. These included: never leave disabled pupils

on their own; always keep them beside you; give them affection; do not let them feel alone; support them; foster their relations with the other children; guide them in their movements; do not let them feel too diverse, etc.

As Strauss and Corbin (1990: 100) note, in reality a ritual rarely has only one cause: the etiology is usually more complex. For example, the type of training received by the teaching assistant, his or her religious beliefs and biography may be included among the causal conditions.

In my observational notes (given below in 5. *Action/interactional strategies*), causal conditions are signaled by the conjunction 'whereas,' which frequently occurs in the descriptions.

2. Phenomenon (main concept) = Teacher's supporting practices

I was interested in the following properties of the teaching assistant's support:

(a) the main aim of her supporting practices;
(b) the rhythm with which they were repeated; and
(c) their timing.

The indicator of the attributes 'aim' was the *degree of independence* that Yasmeen was able to acquire in the course of the school year. Given that this was an excessively general indicator, I concentrated on one of its (sub)indicators: the amount of initiative granted to Yasmeen by the teaching assistant.

The indicator of the attributes 'rhythm' was the *frequency* of the supporting action.

The indicator of the attributes 'time' was the *duration* of the supporting action.

The choice of the indicators had to be carefully thought-out, and it had to concentrate on highly significant aspects of the practice examined, because the indicators would subsequently be used as variables in the non-numerical matrices.

For the *degree of independence* indicator I selected a four-mode variable comprising none/low/medium/high. For the *frequency of support* indicator I used a five-mode variable: never/rarely/sometimes/often/always. Finally, for the *duration of support* indicator I restricted the variable to three modes: no action/brief action/prolonged action.

3. Intervening actions = The classroom teacher's mental model (or conception of sightlessness)

This model may have helped or hindered the micro-actions.

4. Context = Environmental constraints, the behavior of the other teachers, the school staff and Yasmeen's classmates as the school year proceeded, and of the children's parents

5. Action/interactional strategies = (a) Arrival at school, (b) Control of punctuality, (c) Waiting in the entrance lobby, (d) Forming the line

For example, I identified, sampled and systematically observed four micro-actions in the entrance lobby (my observational notes are in brackets):

(a) *Arrival at school* (whereas the children came to school individually or were brought by a parent, Yasmeen was accompanied by an escort);

(b) *Punctuality ritual* (whereas it was compulsory for the children to arrive at the school before the first bell rang – at 8.20 – lateness by Yasmeen was tolerated; indeed, she sometimes arrived after the second bell at 8.30);

(c) *Waiting in the entrance lobby* (whereas the children played and joked among themselves in the lobby, Yasmeen was met by the teaching assistant, and they talked together – separately from the class and the teachers – while waiting for the second bell to ring); and

(d) *Forming the line* (whereas the children lined up in pairs before going to the classroom, Yasmeen and the teaching assistant either preceded or followed the class).

6. Consequences = Concept of handicap acquired by Yasmeen's classmates

As said, Yasmeen's identity – and in particular what sightlessness signifies in cognitive terms – was organizationally constructed. The causal chain may have been as follows:

(1) the teaching assistant's professional model guided her supporting practices, which in their turn; (2) were the cause of Yasmeen's lack of independence; and (3) formed her classmates' conception of disability.

The three assertions were very strong hypotheses which had to be tested and documented with equally strong empirical evidence. The axial coding therefore formulated assertions about the concept (usually related to an action) and its properties.

13.7.4 Confirmation (selective coding)

The third phase began with the construction of a story (Strauss and Corbin, 1990: 119) consisting of a restricted number of hypothetical statements (around ten) which, once tested, constituted the framework of the theory. The aim of the research, in fact, was to produce a theory, not just descriptions. The story was

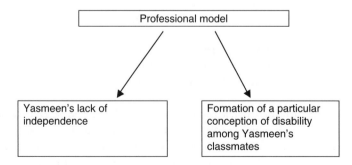

Figure 13.5   Professional model

entitled 'supporting practices' (the main category) and its hypothetical assertions were:

Supporting practices

1. *the teaching assistant had learned an assistive professional model;*

2. *this model tended (unconsciously?) to keep Yasmeen in a state of dependency;*

3. *in fact, towards the end of the school year Yasmeen had still not developed a significant degree of independence;*

4. *Yasmeen's independence was obstructed not only by the teaching assistant but also by environmental constraints in the school;*

5. *the supporting practices which rotated around Yasmeen contributed crucially to forming the concept of visual disability among her classmates, especially as regards what a sightless person can and cannot do;*

6. *the same function was performed (albeit to a lesser extent) by the sanctions and rewards distributed by the class teacher, and by the teachers of religion and English;*

7. *during the school year Yasmeen's classmates changed the way in which they related to her;*

8. *towards the end of the school year Yasmeen had not formed any meaningful or close relationships with her classmates;*

9. *her only close relationship was with the teaching assistant.*

Having outlined the story, the next step was to return to the field and sample (for the third time) the actions and events associated with each assertion, thereby collecting further information with which to document their validity. Obviously, the data collected previously was not neglected: given that ethnographic research is a long and laborious process, it is vital that the ethnographer exploit all information to the maximum extent, and especially information that has already been collected. I therefore returned to my 'old' notes with a new objective, that of confirming or disproving the assertions of the story.

Each assertion (which was no more than a statement) had to be supported by an accurate description. In other words, it had to be enriched with details and episodes which gave it solidity in the eyes of the reader (concept of 'thick description'). I thus expanded the story, constructed a complex model, and gave greater sophistication to my theory. In some cases, the relations confirmed were

Table 13.2 Patterns of behavior

SETTING	MICRO-ACTIONS	DEGREE OF INITIATIVE granted to Yasmeen	DURATION of the teaching assistant's action	FREQUENCY of the teaching assistant's action
Entrance lobby	Arriving at school	none	—	—
	Controlling punctuality	high	—	—
	Waiting	none	long	always
	Forming the line	none	long	always
Classroom	Turn-taking	high	no action	—
	Participating in activities at the teacher's desk	high	no action	—
	Question-asking	high	no action	—
	Rotating pupils among work tables	none	no action	—
	Writing compositions	high	brief	rarely
Washrooms	Entering the toilets	low	prolonged	always
	Water splashing	—	—	—
	Leaving the toilets	low	prolonged	always

Legend: — = not relevant.

outright patterns which could be represented in non-numerical matrices (see Table 13.2), like those proposed by componential analysis (cf. Spradley, 1980: 130ff) or produced by cross-classification.

The matrix furnishes a succinct representation of the pattern of relations. However, like all typologies, taxonomies and classifications, it is static. The researcher must consequently make it dynamic by describing processes. The information contained in the matrix must therefore be connected with actions so that the reader can perceive the indexicality and meaning of the interaction lying behind the succinct representation furnished by a matrix.

13.7.5 Operational proposals

Obviously, it is not necessary for a research study to finish with practical suggestions besides the theoretical conclusions (which are obligatory). However, it does no harm if young researchers propose applications which exploit the richness of their ethnographic observations. The point is very simple: if research has no social utility, should the public pay for it? This is obviously not to argue that all social research should be applied research; anything but. Yet conceiving social research only as pure basic research is deleterious to both research or society.

As regards the case examined here, I began to think of measures that could be designed to encourage the sightless girl's integration into the school. From this point of view, a variety of organizational changes could be proposed. First, individual intervention by the teaching assistant should have been reduced because it had harmful effects: by creating excessive dependency in Yasmeen, it hampered her progressive achievement of independence. Moreover, it did not encourage the development of relationships between Yasmeen and her classmates: rather than fostering solidarity and social integration, the teaching assistant was a factor in Yasmeen's social exclusion.

Second, the teaching assistant should have taught the whole class, and not Yasmeen singly. Functional differences can be designed for this purpose while avoiding overlaps between the roles of the two teachers.

Third, as regards the specific problem of blindness, a collective distribution of responsibility for Yasmeen could sensitize her classmates in practical terms. The emphasis on practical aspects is important. A study conducted by Siperstein and Bak (1980) in England, where children at an elementary school were given lessons to heighten their awareness of blindness, showed that purely technical instruction produces improvements in terms of politeness and carefulness towards sightless classmates, but it does not create friendship. The responsibilization of Yasmeen's classmates should instead have been developed on practical tasks: for example, many of the activities described in previous sections could have been entrusted to the children themselves, thus stimulating greater solidarity in the class.

Fourth, Yasmeen should have been given greater freedom of action so that she could develop intellective and psychomotorial autonomy. She could have gone to the toilets by herself, finding her way by touching the corridor walls, orienting herself by means of the voices and noises in the school, and by using the banisters on the stairs. Many other ergonomic devices could have been installed for her. It was also important for Yasmeen to learn certain falling techniques (forwards, sideways, etc.) in order to increase her autonomy.

13.8 Dealing with deviant cases (instances)

Maier's Law

If the facts do not conform to the theory, they must be disposed of.

Ethnographers often come across observations or instances that conflict with their hypotheses or theory (for a case study by the ethnologist de Martino, go to www.sagepub.co.uk/gobo).

Mehan (1979) and Silverman (2000: 181) argue that a theory must be reformulated so that *all* deviant cases are removed. This task can be made easier if you collect video or tape-recorded data; so you can return to them to check on apparently deviant cases which is very difficult if you only have fieldnotes.

This is certainly to be recommended, and researchers should make every effort in this direction. However, it is not always possible to resolve the discrepancy between hypothesis and instances. As Strauss and Corbin (1990: 140) point out, there may be numerous reasons for the gap: the presence of observations that differ markedly from the majority of cases (outliers); observations which represent transition states (both entry and exit) in the behavior studied; or the differing influences that intervening conditions may exert on the states of an attribute, without this invalidating the relation highlighted. Illuminating in this regard is the analogy proposed by Jerry Jacobs (to justify the fact that his formulation – relative to the phenomenon of suicide – was valid for almost all the 112 notes left by suicides with the exception of ten):

> consider the statement 'Light travels in a straight line,' except when it encounters an opaque object, except in the case of refraction, except in the case of diffraction, and so forth. One does not say of these *exceptions* that they tend to negate the principle of the rectilinear propagation of light. They simply work to narrow its scope and set its limits . . . To the extent that one is able to explain the 'exceptions' in such a way that the explanations are consistent with the evidence, the sum total of these explanations constitutes a more detailed and inclusive understanding of light (Schwartz and Jacobs, 1979: 159).

13.9 Using computers to analyze ethnographic data

The Law of Computer Programming

Any given program, when running, is obsolete.

As I have already mentioned, recent years have seen the spread of software programs which can be of great assistance in the analysis of materials. To draw a rather rough distinction, we may say there are two types of software on the market: qualitative (CAQDAS) and statistical.

13.9.1 Computer-Assisted *Qualitative* Data Analysis Software

Denoted with the acronym CAQDAS (Computer-Assisted Qualitative Data Analysis Software), programs as NVIVO, ETHNOGRAPH, ATLAS, QUALPRO and so on have been developed mainly for the analysis of texts (interviews and documents in particular).

They were initially electronic 'cut and paste' tools, but with the passage of time some of them (for example, NVIVO) have extended their capabilities to the analysis of visual materials as well, starting from the semiotic principle that images, too, are nothing other than texts.

Learning these programs obviously requires time and resources, but the investment is worthwhile.[6] Moreover, there are several excellent overviews (Seale, 2000; Fielding, 2001; Kelle, 2004) which explain the use of them. I only provide the references for these publications here, given that there is insufficient space to discuss them thoroughly.

What, bearing in mind that fieldnotes are nothing other than texts, are the principal advantages of these programs?

13.9.2 Five advantages of CAQDAS

First, they help researchers when sorting their ethnographic notes. It should be remembered that the analysis of ethnographic notes is not done in a day; instead it is a process that lasts for months. It is therefore easy to forget the details of work done previously. Manual sorting is always a complex operation: the codes previously used, or their original meanings, are forgotten; and the assignation of the codes to the fieldnotes is not always consistent. This gives rise to problems of reliability (see 14.3) in the classification, and to confusion in building a consistent theory.

With these software programs, instead, the researcher has a constantly present overview of the list of codes that he or she has invented (the master list), and their meanings. Moreover, ethnographic notes sorted under a particular code can be instantly retrieved and, if necessary, changed, renamed or revised. However, these capabilities and the relative ease with which codes can be assigned may be harmful, because they give rise to delusions of omnipotence. Various authors have warned that these programs (if used recklessly) may generate a plethora of codes difficult to handle in the subsequent phases of analysis (Bryman, 1988: 83–7; Silverman, 1993: 47). Hence the well-known Dykstra's Law – 'if de-bugging is the process of removing bugs, then programming must be the process of putting them in' – applies to these programs as well.

Second, starting from the basic codes, more refined CAQDAS can be used to enumerate codes (and therefore produce statistics as defined in 12.5), create co-occurring codes showing relationships among categories, and develop hierarchical category systems. These category systems are constituted by nodes which can be browsed.

Third, this way of working increases the transparency of the fieldnotes classification process and heightens intersubjectivity. This facilitates team research: the researchers can exchange codes and examples of sorting, and agree on the interpretation of certain incidents. All this considerably improves reliability.

Fourth, the more refined CAQDAS aid the process of 'building a theory.' The meaning of this expression must obviously be defined, for the theory is not automatically churned out by the program when it has sorted the ethnographic notes. If only this were so! What the software can do is assist the researcher in the more rigorous checking of hypotheses. For example, NVIVO has nine Boolean operators (AND, OR/XOR, NOT, IF, THEN, EXCEPT and so on) which, once the observational notes have been imported into the software, enable the hypotheses to be checked automatically by scanning the content of the observational notes. The outputs from this scanning are portions of text (in this case of ethnographic notes) assembled by the action of the Boolean operators and immediately visualized.

Finally, hypotheses and theories can be graphically depicted by means of diagrams.

Since the beginning of the 1990s, widespread use has been made of CAQDAS, fueled by an unconscious collective hope that at last software is available for the automatic and standardized treatment of textual data – rather like the statistical packages that have made such a major contribution to the success of quantitative research. Now, however, these hopes have faded: there is nothing miraculous about CAQDAS, and those who use such programs must be diligent and patient. Indeed, several criticisms have been brought against them:

> conventional approaches to CAQDAS have tended to naturalise divisions
> between data management, analysis and representation, and thus there has

been a tendency to neglect the potential of digital technology to transform all stages of the research process . . . And while some software packages now enable visual data to be included in the dataset, there remains little scope to integrate across data types within an interpretative analysis (Coffey et al. 2006: 18).

13.9.3 Statistical computerized systems for data collection and analysis

Recent technological advances have also led to the development of a number of semi-automated systems for collecting real-time observational data. They are especially widespread in ethnographic psychology, which since its foundation by the American social psychologist Robert F. Bales (1916–2004), has always played an important niche role in psychology.

These systems supposedly facilitate observation by improving the reliability and accuracy of recording compared to cumbersome paper and pencil methods, and by making data calculation and graphing more efficient. The use of computers to record and analyze data has consequently acquired ever greater importance in clinical work as well as in research.

These softwares are mainly used to analyze video materials. For instance, we can video-record the interaction between a mother and her child, or among children at play, and then classify what happens in an interval of time (three seconds, for instance). The operation is made easier by the fact that the video material and the software interact in an integrated manner.

These software programs enable the user to record up to 100 different responses during a session. They have the capability of recording response frequency, duration, intervals (variable duration), time samples, latency, inter-response time (IRT), antecedent-behavior-consequences (ABC), and discrete trials. A text feature enables the recording of notes for unique or atypical events. Moreover, a pause feature allows the interruption of observation sessions if necessary, and entry errors made while recording can be edited. The data analysis program gives the user the option of calculating response frequency (total number and rate), duration, latency, IRT, percentage of intervals, percentage of trials, and conditional probabilities. The user can also define subgroups that contain various combinations of responses (A or B, A and B).

The software also offers the option of calculating statistical measures as central tendencies (mean and median), variability (range and frequency distribution), and statistical significance (z score transformations). There are more than 20 in circulation: most notably *The Observer, Behavioral Evaluation Strategy and Taxonomy (BEST)* and *Behavior Observer System (BOS)*. For a complete overview of their features see Kahng and Iwata (1998) and for a demo of the program *The Observer*, go to http://www.noldus.com/site/doc200401012.

13.10 Concluding remarks

This chapter has shown how to conduct the analysis of ethnographic materials. Such analysis can be done manually, or by means of digital technologies, which are the cause of great optimism. However, we should not forget what happened in quantitative methods during the 1960s. As the Italian quantitative methodologist Alberto Marradi wrote:

> before the age of the computer, data analysis required large investments of time and ability. Researchers therefore saw accuracy in data collection as a guarantee that their efforts would not be wasted on distorted and unreliable data. Now that it is possible to produce hundreds of cross tabulations or correlation matrices in a few hours . . ., the psychological need for this guarantee has gone. [Indeed] on reading research reports, one gains the impression that increasingly sophisticated statistical techniques are applied to increasingly inferior or inadequate data (1980: 4).

It is therefore clear that we have only just begun to experiment with digital technologies, and that we are still far from understanding their potential. But it is certain that, as Duranti stresses,

> the invention of new tools that can be used for storing, replaying, manipulating, and reproducing information about human interaction not only offers new solutions to old problems, it also opens up the possibility of new analytical questions (1997a: 115).

KEY POINTS

- Data analysis moves through three main steps: deconstruction (*open coding*), construction (*axial coding*) and confirmation (*selective coding*).
- In the first step (deconstruction) three alternative strategies can be employed: (a) using a coding sheet; (b) using a framework; or (c) sorting the ethnographic notes.
- Constructed in the second step is a framework consisting of five elements: (causal conditions → phenomenon (under study) → context → intervening conditions → action/interactional strategies → consequences) which begin to outline the main features of what will subsequently be the story.
- The third step (construction) ends with the writing of a story which contains the main hypotheses generated by analysis of the materials and forms the core of the final theory.
- Analysis of the ethnographic notes can be usefully integrated with analysis of documents, and of audio or video materials.
- An essential part of the analysis is formulating hypotheses and documenting them with thin and thick descriptions.
- Theories consist of sets of hypotheses which have been adequately documented.
- Not all the incidents observed are appropriately explained by the hypothesis; so some are not covered by it and assume the status of deviant instances.
- The ethnographer must make the maximum imaginative effort to revise hypotheses so that the majority of deviant cases can be recovered.
- CAQDAS may be useful tools for sorting textual materials, constructing hierarchical category systems, testing hypotheses, and building theories more rapidly and accurately.

KEY TERMS

Analysis
(see pp. 234–40)

A selective process whereby a phenomenon is represented so that certain attributes can be emphasized. The aim of an analysis is not to produce a perfect copy of its topic, instead, it involves a transformation of, a cognitive intervention in, the reality observed.

Axial coding
(see pp. 234–5)

Construction is the phase when the ethnographer begins reassembling in different forms the concepts developed during the previous open coding stage, the aim being to construct a first consistent framework.

CAQDAS
(see pp. 252–4)

Computer-Assisted Qualitative Data Analysis Software used for textual analysis.

Coding sheet
(see pp. 228–31)

A conceptual grid with a relatively small number of entries or items (around) eliciting information from the observational notes.

Deviant instances
(see pp. 251–2)

Incidents and observations at odds with the hypothesis or the theory which seeks to encompass and explain them.

Framework
(see pp. 231–3)

A consistent schema made up of a restricted set of elements on which observational notes are collected.

Open coding
(see pp. 227–34)

Deconstruction is an exploratory phase in which the ethnographer examines the field for concepts (or categories) which can explain a phenomenon observed.

Selective coding
(see pp. 235–7)

The confirmation phase, in which the hypotheses emerging from the axial coding are tested and strongly documented, and then anchored to a theory.

Story (see pp. 235–7)

An account centered on the main research concept or topic. It consists of ten or so assertions (though still taking the form of hypotheses) about the relations between the core concept and its indicators. The story is a mock-up of the full theory.

Theory (see pp. 242–4)

A set of assertions resting on concepts that have not been given operational definitions and consequently have not been directly observed. Theories, unlike hypotheses, are not directly testable. Variously mutually consistent and appropriately confirmed hypotheses constitute a theory.

RECOMMENDED READING

For undergraduates:
Seale, Clive (2000)

For graduates:
Fielding, Nigel (2001)

For advanced researchers:
Emerson, Robert M. (2004)

SELF-EVALUATION TEST

Are you ready for the next chapter? Check your knowledge by answering the following open-ended questions:

1. Three strategies are proposed for the analysis of observational notes (coding sheet, framework and sorting). Which of the three do you prefer? Why?
2. What is the main difference between a theory and a hypothesis?
3. Should an analysis, and consequently a theory, seek to achieve a perfect match with the reality observed?
4. What is meant by the 'integrative use' of documents and visual materials?
5. Why is the expression 'documenting a hypothesis' preferable to the more common expression 'verifying a hypothesis'?
6. Are CAQDAS a genuine alternative to the traditional manual analysis of ethnographic data? Can you see any risks if they take over from the latter?

Notes

1 This strategy is very widespread in psychology and it has authoritative precursors in for examples, Bales (1951) and Sears, Rau and Alpert (1965), who drew up a short list of behavior categories and then determined their presence or otherwise (their importance and frequency) in incidents concretely observed.

2 Available for some time are software programs which provide very useful assistance with simple or multiple classification. They are discussed in more detail in 12.9.

3 Lofland (1971: 123) has called this process the 'drama of selection,' because the researcher is forced to restrict his or her focus. This entails that some of the materials must be discarded, perhaps those that the researcher is most attached to because they are rich with interesting details. The researcher must, however, make drastic choices, lest the topics proliferate and a consistent procedure be lost.

4 Goffman noted a similar phenomenon in the psychiatric hospital where he conducted his research: 'children of resident doctors were the only non-patient category I found that did not evince obvious caste distance from patients; why I do not know' (1961: 218, note 2).

5 After a lesson at the town museum, the teacher told the class to write compositions about their visit. Yasmeen introduced hers as follows: 'My composition is perhaps not as good as those by my classmates because I could not see the things in the museum very well because they were enclosed in the showcases.' Evident in Yasmeen's cognitive system is the equation 'see = touch.'

6 If you are interested in software planning seminars, free interactive introductions to several software programs, introductory workshops, special customized events, follow-up workshops, advisory helplines, CAQDAS bibliography, web links to other resources and so on, go to http://caqdas.soc.surrey.ac.uk.

Politics of Accountability

First Law of Debate

Never argue with a fool – people might not know the difference.

LEARNING OBJECTIVES

- To gain an overview of the debate on the legitimation of qualitative research.

- To understand why it is important to address the problem of evaluating and legitimating your research.

- To identify the main evaluation standards applicable to an ethnographic study.

- To review these standards from a 'practical' perspective.

- To learn how to generalize and defend your generalizations against criticism.

14.1 Introduction

Of all the themes addressed thus far, that of legitimation is probably the most complicated. It has provoked the most heated controversies, and found least agreement among experts on qualitative methodologies. But it is also perhaps the most important of issues, for upon it depends the reputation of ethnography, of qualitative research, and more generally, of the social sciences themselves. I shall seek to show why with a straightforward example.

CASE STUDY
How loud were the voices of the passengers?

A group of three of my students conducted an exercise. The first student was from Sicily (Southern Italy), the second from Florence (Central Italy), and the third from

Alessandria (a city in North Italy). They had observed the behavior and listened to the conversations of bus passengers in Siena (a city in Central Italy, close to Florence). In their report to the class they said that they had been unable to agree on how loud the voices of the more elderly passengers had been. For the Sicilian student the passengers had talked at low volume; for the student from Florence their speech volume had been loud; whilst for the student from Alessandria both the elderly and young passengers had spoken loudly. Evident in this case is the role played by the common-sense backgrounds of the three observers: in Sicily, the speech volume used in public conversations is probably louder, so that the Sicilian student thought that the elderly bus passengers of Siena were soft-spoken.

This example brings us straight to the crux of the problem: what degree of correspondence can exist between an ethnographer's interpretations and the phenomenon observed?

If the researcher lives somewhere remote with no outside contacts, this may not be a significant problem. But since most researchers must communicate with their community (for a variety of reasons ranging from narcissism, through the need to persuade the commissioners of their research, to the obligation to publish imposed on academics), at a certain point in his or her research, the ethnographer must address this problem.

If we abandon the positivistic idea that an objective reality exists independently of the observer, the problem of the correctness and veracity of the ethnographer's statements shifts to a broader dimension, where it is not so much the truth (which, as we shall see, is often impossible to ascertain) that matters, as the researcher's ability to persuade his or her audience of the credibility of his or her conclusions. In this epistemological framework, therefore, of crucial importance are rhetorical strategies, or in other words, the 'poetics and politics' of the validation of research results (see also Chapter 15).

14.2 The crisis of legitimation

Truman's Law

If you cannot convince them, confuse them.

In the standard methodological literature, the problem of legitimating research findings has usually been approached via two main concepts: *reliability* (of the measurement instrument) and *validity* (of data). These concepts originated in the hard sciences (in particular astronomy and psychometry), where they were intended to prevent both systematic and accidental errors. After long resistance, in the early 1980s they were introduced into qualitative research as well, with substantial adaptations by qualitative methodologists like Kirk and Miller (1986), Hammersley (1990 and 1992), and Silverman (1993 and 2000). This development was important because it helped qualitative research rebut criticism concerning its romanticism and excessive subjectivity, and to establish standards for the credibility and consistency of its findings. The entire debate has been well summed up by the expressions 'the quality of qualitative research' (Seale, 1999) and 'the credibility of qualitative research' (Silverman, 2006: 271ff).

This opening-up has been attacked as a 'mere positivist concern' by the feminist and postmodern critiques (see 4.3 and 4.4), which diagnose a 'legitimation crisis' (Denzin and Lincoln, 2000: 17), meaning by this expression that the qualitative research cannot be evaluated with conventional criteria.

Is there a way out of this impasse? There are good arguments on both sides. But what is lacking, and which I shall seek to describe in the next sections of this chapter, is a *practical approach* which treats these questions separately: incident by incident, case by case, study by study, methodology by methodology, method by method. For example, if the purpose of the concepts of reliability and validity is to prevent both systematic and accidental errors, ethnographic methodology already has an advantage over other types of methodologies, because some of these errors (precisely because of the circular nature of ethnographic research) can be corrected as the research proceeds.

The concepts of reliability and validity are certainly reductive, for they neglect a number of important questions concerning the process of materials interpretation. Moreover, if it were always possible from an ontological point of view to ascertain the validity (of data), there would be no need to check the reliability of the instrument used, because validity presupposes reliability. But validity can be verified only in certain incidents (see 14.6.1), and the legitimation of ethnography becomes the painstaking work of collecting evidence. In this it resembles doing a jigsaw puzzle, where each piece (or item of evidence) has little significance in itself but acquires meaning as part of a wider picture. It should also be borne in mind, however, that legitimation work resembles the construction of a jigsaw puzzle which may be impossible to complete because some of the pieces are missing. Nevertheless, piece by piece, the ethnographer furnishes his or her audience with the elements for evaluating his or her knowledge enterprise. Consequently, the debate on the legitimation of qualitative research would benefit greatly if a 'practical turn' came about.

14.3 The reliability of the gathering instrument

Segal's Law

A man with a watch knows what time it is. A man with two watches is never sure.

A first aspect to consider is the reliability or precision of the *instrument* (or method). When methodology handbooks introduce the concept of 'reliability,' they usually exemplify it with the thermometer, or with weighing scales. If we repeatedly weigh the same object and obtain similar results, and if the values are the same when a second set of scales is used, we may say that the first scales (and reflexively or tautologically, also the second) are reliable. Reliability therefore concerns our confidence in the consistency of a gathering instrument – its capacity to replicate results. The assumption underlying this concept of reliability is that the object does not change between the times of the two measurements (for details on the weakness of the concept of reliability, go to www.sagepub. co.uk/gobo).

This assumption does not seem appropriate to research conducted with the survey or the discursive interview methodologies, where opinions and attitudes may change over time. In fact, they may change both as an effect of the measurement instrument used (induced change), in that discussion of an issue during the interview interaction may change the interviewee's mind; and because opinions may be volatile and susceptible to the influence, for instance, of the mass media (natural change). This requires one to carefully consider the reliability of informants' accounts.

Hence, the risks attendant on the concept of reliability certainly exist in participant observation.[1] But (from a practical perspective) they should not be exaggerated. First, gathering is a long drawn-out process involving numerous observations. As a consequence, wrong information collected by the first observations can be corrected by subsequent ones. Second, unlike opinions, social practices (rituals, routines, ceremonials) are stable processes unlikely to change during the time-span of a research project, unless it lasts for years, or unless the ethnographer is perceived as a spy or an informer (which infrequently happens). Third, prolonged fieldwork allows elimination of the misunderstandings which certain questions may have produced, and which may have made the information imprecise. Finally, prolonged fieldwork also familiarizes the participants with ethnographic methodology. It thus reduces intrusiveness – although this is still the factor that most affects the instrument's reliability.

Information relative to the reliability of ethnographic observation can also be collected by means of *triangulation* procedures (Denzin, 1970; Jick, 1979; Fielding and Fielding, 1986). Taken from military strategy and navigation,[2] this term denotes in the social sciences the combined use of different methodologies in the analysis of a phenomenon. The data yielded by individual interviews, focus groups, questionnaires, or official statistics can be compared against the ethnographic data. Consistent results may confirm the reliability of the ethnography. But if the results are partially consistent, or not at all, one may conclude that: (a) the ethnography is unreliable; or (b) that the other methodologies are unreliable;[3] or (c) that the researcher has been careless.

14.4 The researcher's accuracy

Rule of Accuracy

When working towards the solution of a problem, it always helps if you know the answer.

Participant observation grants a great deal of autonomy to the researcher. He or she has broad discretion in choosing how to proceed, and when. However, it may not be certain that the observations reported by the ethnographer faithfully reflect the events observed. This doubt was raised, for example, by ethnomethodologists in regard to Goffman's studies. The audience may, therefore, question the researcher's accuracy and his or her ability to listen and understand. There is also the possibility that accidental errors have been committed.

There are two distinct aspects to the problem of researcher accuracy: one 'internal' and concerning the researcher him or herself; the other 'external' and concerning the reader and the scientific community.

14.4.1 Internal accuracy

The researcher can *improve* his or her accuracy by introducing rigorous procedures into each phase of the inquiry. The research design and operational definitions (Chapter 5), field access strategies (Chapter 7), observation proce-dures (Chapter 9), interview instructions (Chapter 11), information collection techniques (Chapter 10), and principles of conversation transcription, the logic of data analysis (Chapter 13), and write-up formats (Chapter 15) – all of these provide the researcher with constant help and referents. But these constraints should not be regarded as obstacles to ethnography's smooth progress, for they are also (and above all) resources on which researchers – especially novices – can constantly draw.

CASE STUDY
Are indicators really useful?

I described my doctoral thesis in 5.7.1 and how I operationalized the concept of 'difficulty in answering' a questionnaire.

Operationalizing this concept enabled me to analyse audio-recorded verbal exchanges (the question-reply process) with greater systematicity, rigor and precision. Was I then able to remain faithful to the operational definition when I analyzed my materials? This is what I wrote in long-ago 1992:

> constructing indicators to analyse the interactions had the purpose of disciplining my analysis and making it intersubjective for the reader. But I found it very difficult to remain faithful to the indicators. Thus my ideas sometimes (fortunately) arose independently of them: on some occasions because I buckled beneath the self-reflexive effort; on others because after analysis of few recorded interviews I felt sufficiently well-trained, and I had to force myself to continue referring to my list of indicators.

> The indicators therefore usefully reminded me to be systematic in my analysis. But they did not always lead my analysis as I wanted. So in the end an indicator became more a 'guardian angel' for observation and analysis than an inflexible martinet. Are (explicit) indicators useful, therefore? Are they not excessively burdensome on analysis? These are questions for the reader of this research report to answer. Personally, I believe that being constrained to systematicity helped me notice unexpected events, and it induced me to revise certain of ethnomethodology's assumptions, for example that everything is negotiable.

14.4.2 Accountability: Information for the audience's evaluation of research (external accuracy)

The reader sees things differently. He or she wants to know how to check the researcher's accuracy. This introduces the problem of the 'inspectionability' of databases: in the sense that, as Alan Bryman points out, 'field notes . . . are rarely available; these would be very helpful in order to allow the reader to formulate his or her hunches' (1988: 77). The solution to the problem is *accountability*, that is for the researcher to publish the empirical documentation on which his or her analysis has been based. He or she should therefore exhibit the main materials (observational notes, dialogue transcripts, photographs and drawings of the places observed) from which his or her conclusions have been drawn. Obviously, this can only be done to a partial extent, and only to support the most important findings, given the limited space made available for publications by book publishers and journals. However, in this way, ethnographers let themselves be judged by readers, and by the scientific community at large, on six main criteria:

(1) *completeness*: descriptions must be accompanied by details of the context;
(2) *saturation* of the categories: all events must be covered by the concepts proposed, with cognitive dissonances eliminated and the marginal utility of limit incidents evaluated;
(3) *authenticity*: the fieldwork must be certified as genuine;
(4) *consistency*: the extent to which events observed on different occasions are allocated to the same category;
(5) *credibility*: the consistency between descriptions and interpretations. The following requirements should be fulfilled: the results are consistent with the theory adopted; the concepts have been systematically correlated; the causal relations have been developed correctly; and
(6) *plausibility*: consistency between the researcher's conclusions and his or her scientific community's consolidated knowledge. This criterion should not be too rigorously applied, however, for otherwise the conclusions will merely replicate the disciplinary *status quo*.

According to Randall Collins, this last criterion is the most important of all:

> the most important way in which the validity of a theory can be established is by showing the coherence of its explanatory principles with other well-grounded theory . . . Qualitative microsociology, for example, or observation-based organizational studies, have not depended upon statistics. Their validity and their contributions to our knowledge – which I would say have been considerable – come from their degree of coherence with all our accumulated theoretical principles (1988: 504–5).

If a team is doing the research, the accuracy issue assumes different features: the presence of several researchers may be a problem but it is also an important resource. Although the problem arises of consistency in the allocation of events to the same category (Hammersley, 1992: 67), accidental errors and distortions can be corrected or reduced by comparisons among the researchers. Consistency among codes can be further increased if they are generated by CAQDAS programs. These provide greater transparency and facilitate intersubjective agreement among the researchers, thereby ensuring greater accuracy.

14.5 The appropriateness of conceptualization

Young's Corollary

The greater the funding, the longer it takes to make the mistake.

By means of conceptualization (see 5.6), the ethnographer establishes a relationship between the general concept and the indicators (or specific concepts). This reflexive process comes about through the 'documentary method of interpretation' (see 4.5).

CASE STUDY
Strategies of nursing staff at a rest home

After a week of observing the behavior of nursing staff at a rest home, the ethnographer decided that the strategy of keeping the elderly residents in bed as long as possible was a sign (a clue or an indicator) of the existence of practices designed to achieve greater social control. However, the next week, on talking with the manager of the rest home, and some nurses who had worked at the facility for some time, the ethnographer discovered that the practice had been introduced only recently, as an organizational response to a shortage of staff due to a cut in public funding.

Thus, the ethnographer first thought that the strategy was a suitable indicator for collecting information about a particular phenomenon (concept or category), but then realized that he had conceptualized it incorrectly.

Posing the problem of the appropriateness of a conceptualization means enquiring as to whether the indicators considered are valid expressions of the concept in question. As Carmines and Zeller (1979: 101) point out, this is less a technical question (as in the case of operational definitions) than an eminently theoretical one.

However, assessing the appropriateness of an indicator is difficult. The conceptualization takes place 'upstream' from the operational definition, and therefore cannot be verified by the latter. Consequently, any errors in the conceptualization cannot be detected by the gathering procedures, because they lie 'downstream' from it. In other words, a systematic bias in the conceptualization due to a prejudice or a pre-assumption has a knock-on effect throughout the gathering's progress. 'Cultural deprivation' theory is a classic example (see 5.5); but all theories, especially if they have strong ideological content, or are part of a dominant paradigm, run this risk (for a case study about the ideological debate, in the late 1960s, on why black children in inner-city schools showed low educational achievement, go to www.sagepub.co.uk/gobo).

Escaping from this ideological circularity is difficult (and sometimes impossible), although the reflexive ethnographer, receptive to signals from the field and expecting the unexpected, is able to modify his or her conceptualization *as the research proceeds*.

An alternative is, once again, *accountability*, that is to provide the reader with the documentation necessary to assess the appropriateness of the researcher's conceptualization. This alternative requires the researcher to justify his or her decisions and choices explicitly. Unlike in the objectivist orientation – the tendency to consider objects and indicators as 'things,' not as cognitive tools – the choice of one concept among innumerable others as an indicator is always a discretionary operation by researchers. They are consequently obliged to justify their choices, setting out the reasons for the relationship established between concept and indicator. This relationship must be transparent to criticism: the researcher is not allowed to use obscure metaphors or resort to picturesque evocations of atmosphere.

14.6 The fidelity of data and of interpretations

Brook's Law

If at first you don't succeed, transform your data set!

Let us suppose that the conceptualization (i.e. the indication relationship) has been appropriate; that the operationalization (i.e. the move from the indicators to the relative variables) has been correct; that the various techniques of participant observation have been reliable; and that the ethnographer has been precise and accurate. Can we be sure that he or she has correctly interpreted the situations observed? No we cannot, because two forms of imprecision can always occur:

(1) at the data level: a discrepancy between the state recorded and the actual state (Marradi, 1990: 82); and
(2) at the interpretation level: a discrepancy between the researcher's interpretations and the social phenomenon to which they refer (Hammersley, 1990: 57).

The assumptions underlying these two statements introduce a specifically epistemological issue. It concerns the conventional 'truth theory' grounded on the correspondence between observation and reality, and which assumes that:

> there is the real world of people, events and circumstances, on the one hand, and one's own observations and descriptions of this world, on the other hand. Competent observation and description depend principally on achieving certain formal relationships between the former and the latter – that is, by producing good 'pictures' of reality (Schwartz and Jacobs, 1979: 256).

This realist theory of truth, which has bred the concept of 'validity,' presupposes that an effectively knowable state exists: an assumption which the postmodernists have assailed for decades. Yet still absent from the debate is treatment of this important issue from a practical standpoint, case by case, and eschewing conflict waged solely on principles and partisanships. Let us therefore try to frame the problem of validity from a practical point of view.

14.6.1 Validity re-framed

First to be pointed out is that, *practically*, there are some situations where 'facts,' or an objective reality, exist; and there are some situations where 'facts' do not exist. In other words, there are different levels of 'facticity.' Hence, adopting a truth theory based wholly on correspondence is problematic in the social sciences, because, as Marradi (1990: 81) points out, it can only apply to a *few* (albeit important) individual attributes of the social world generally constructed by bureaucratic processes: for example, demographic attributes (nationality, place of birth and residence, educational qualification, and so on), and in general all those attributes like possessing a driving licence, being on the electoral register, having a criminal record, having paid a fine, and so on. The distinctive feature of these attributes is that the official record (produced by a bureaucracy) not only records their status but also *constitutes* it. As ANT theory maintains (see 10.5), whilst it is true that everything is an invention, when something is invented it becomes real, and it objectively conditions our actions. Consequently, although official records are certainly artifacts that someone has constructed, once they have been so constructed they become real. A realist theory of truth may therefore be appropriate for certain attributes, in that it is possible to check whether a respondent is lying about them: for instance, we cannot say (subjectively) that we are UK citizens if there nowhere exists a record which (objectively) constitutes this status of ours. This also means that the postmodern theories that oppose a realist theory of truth should temper the absolutism of their assertions.

A realist theory of truth, instead, does not apply to the majority of the properties with which ethnographers concern themselves, 'given that the actual statuses on some continuous property are not knowable to us, and discrete properties are not measurable in the strict sense of the term' (Marradi, 1990: 82). In other words, attitudes, motivations, opinions do not have effective statuses (for a case study on the weakness of the concept of 'discovery,' go to www.sagepub.co.uk/gobo).

The epistemologically uncertain status of a theory of truth involves a further problem. It concerns the gaps among: (a) the description of a social practice, (b) the list of instructions necessary to replicate it, and (c) performance of the practice itself. Schwartz and Jacobs – in regard to Mehan and Wood's (1975: 225–38) radical proposal that readers should be given instructions on the practices observed, not just descriptions of them – ask as follows:

> [why do] we give our colleagues a picture of other people's picture of reality?. . . Why not skip the translation? Why not create that reality directly, instead of merely describing it through symbolic data? Surely this is one of the strongest possible ways to communicate information about another reality (Schwartz and Jacobs, 1979: 257).

Describing and giving instructions involve two different levels of fidelity. The situation is complicated further by the well-known difference between 'knowing' and 'knowing how.' Geertz gives the following example:

> to make a trade pact in Morocco, you have to do certain things in certain ways (among others, cut, while chanting Quranic Arabic, the throat of a lamb before the assembled, undeformed, adult male members of your tribe) and to be possessed of certain psychological characteristics (among others, a desire for

distant things). But a trade pact is neither the throat cutting nor the desire, though it is real enough . . .' (1973: 12).

As Psathas (1995) points out, a person can learn a great deal about swimming from books on the subject, but he still cannot swim.

It is therefore necessary to abandon the concept of validity and replace it with two epistemologically more appropriate concepts: the fidelity of data, and the fidelity of interpretations. We shall now see how they are applied in practice.

14.6.2 Fidelity as successful prediction

Jaffe's Precept

> There are some things which are impossible to know, but it is impossible to know which things they are.

One criterion with which to evaluate the fidelity of a statement is its degree of success in predicting. As the English philosopher of science Mary Hesse argues, in her polemic against the radical constructivists, the fact that a certain number of fatal diseases have been reduced and controlled through the identification of something (a virus for example), which can be paraded, demonstrates the capacity of human beings to conform with an external reality. Success is proof of this adjustment. More generally, survival testifies to a success. It is proof that not all cognitive inductions and procedures are purely arbitrary or completely conventional.

Likewise, an ability to imitate the practices of participants to the point that one is regarded for all practical purposes a competent member of the community (like the anthropologist Richard K. Nelson, who learned how to hunt like the Eskimos) may be indicative of the fidelity of a researcher's statements. This also seems to be Goffman's opinion with regard to the study of mental illness:

> as Harold Garfinkel has suggested, we should be in a position (not desirable in itself but desirable as a test of theory) to program insanity, that is, reduce to a minimum the instructions you would have to give an experimental subject in order to enable him beautifully to act crazy (1964: 140).

There are two obvious objections to this position. The first has been raised by Geertz and the ethnomethodologists: it is never possible to furnish complete instructions, precisely because instructions are intrinsically vague and indeterminate (Mehan and Wood, 1975: 233–5; Schwartz and Jacobs, 1979: 258). The second is that research situations do not always permit this attempt. Nevertheless, it is still extremely useful, when possible, to make small-scale predictions and observe their results. The fulfillment of certain predictions or the confirmation of a hypothesis may increase the fidelity of the researcher's statements and heighten intersubjectivity with his or her readers. But they cannot guarantee certainty, because the success may be due to intervening variables unknown to the researcher.

14.6.3 Participant validation

A further criterion that reflexive ethnography ought to embrace in evaluating the fidelity of data or an interpretation (or a researcher's account) is to obtain confirmation or denial (verbal or written) from the participants. This procedure has been variously called *member verification, host verification, member test of validity, respondent validation, group feedback analysis and member validation*. For this purpose the researcher conducts individual interviews or organizes discussion groups with the actors. The procedure requires that the ethnographer's description or theory be expounded simply and clearly, in conformity with Schutz's (1953: 45) 'postulate of adequacy,' so that the scientific models of social action are understandable to the participants. This does not mean that there should also be higher-order concepts, because researchers and actors have different jargons and different stocks of knowledge.

Participants may be requested to validate both descriptive statements (the recorded data or status) and interpretative ones (an explanation, a hypothesis or a theory). These are two different epistemological problems. As a matter of fact in the latter because denial by the actors may trigger long and tortuous negotiations on the fidelity of the interpretative statements.

CASE STUDY
Member validation in a psychiatric organization

The American ethnographers Robert M. Emerson and Melvin Pollner (1988) conducted research on the management of psychiatric emergencies in a regional Community Mental Health Clinic in southern California. Over a period of six months, they observed the work of psychiatric emergency teams (PET), these being mobile units consisting of psychiatric personnel deployed in the community in response to calls.

About one year after conclusion of their field research, Emerson and Pollner had completed the drafts of two papers on PET. These they presented to an assembly of 35 people, of whom about ten belonged to the regional clinic. Their purpose was to elicit feedback from members of a directly-observed team. Contrary to Emerson and Pollner's expectation of receiving clear feedback, their attempt at member validation obtained very ambiguous results. The recording of the event enabled Emerson and Pollner to reconstruct the obstacles against transparent feedback in detail:

- the participants could not fully understand the two papers because they were unfamiliar with the researchers' language;

- they could not recognize themselves in the researchers' descriptions and explanations because they were unaware of the motives for, and consequences of, their behavior;

- they considered the two papers to be not only 'scientific' but also 'political,' and thought that their critical findings threatened the existence of their organization;

- some participants agreed with the researchers' accounts; others partially or totally disagreed with them; and

- the participants' responses were ambiguous, in the sense that they did not reject, but nor did they accept, the researchers' accounts; hence it was unclear whether they could be taken as confirming or confounding the researchers' interpretations.

Emerson and Pollner concluded that it was entirely natural that evaluation of a research report should mix interests of various kinds (scientific, political, personal, etc.), because validation never takes place in a vacuum, but always in a specific social and organizational context. However, they were still optimistic about the technique's usefulness:

> although these (verification) transactions are . . . problematic . . . it is because validation episodes often comprise intense moments of organizational and interactional life that they are capable of revealing aspects of the setting or organization in a new light (1988: 189).

As I pointed out when discussing the researcher's role (see 5.2), owing to the reflexive property of action, ethnographic accounts do not simply describe things; they also 'execute moral evaluations, produce political, moral, and social consequences, and so on. Descriptions are almost always "doing" many more things in the social situation than simply "reporting" a set of facts' (Schwartz and Jacobs, 1979: 51). Indeed, Bloor (1983) and Fielding and Fielding (1986: 43) argue that member validation is only a further source of information. Although it yields valuable *extra* information which enriches the empirical documentation collected by the ethnographer, it is not a means with which to evaluate the scientific validity of an ethnographic account.

The reason for the likely incomprehension between ethnographer and participants is practical, but it is also gnoseological: the incommensurability between the perspectives of the observer and the observed. As Schultz writes:

> The meaning of an action is necessarily a different one (a) for the actor; (b) for his partner involved with him in interaction . . . and (c) for the observer not involved in such relationship . . . The constructs of the observer are, therefore, different ones than those used by the participants in the interaction, if for no other reason than the fact that the purpose of the observer is different from that of the interactors and therewith the systems of relevances attached to such purposes are also different (1953: 24 and 26–7).

Given this impossibility, ethnographers need 'only' concern themselves with correctly grasping the common sense meaning that action has for participants; they should not persuade them of that meaning. As the anthropologist Moerman (1974: 68) has stressed, social scientists should describe and analyze the ways in which concepts are used by the participants, and not simply – as the natives do – use them as explanations. Although scientific explanations should not disregard the meanings expressed by actors, they lie at a different level from those meanings. The participants may accept or reject them, but this should not necessarily affect the researcher's interpretative statements. As Fielding and Fielding put it:

> there is no reason to assume that members have privileged status as commentators on their actions . . . such feedback cannot be taken as direct validation or refutation of the observer's inferences (1986: 43, quoted in Silverman, 2000: 208).

Also because, as Sudnow reminds us, ethnography is a way of observing peculiar to the middle-class observer, so that it is 'continually plagued by the import of such descriptive biases' (1967: 176).

14.7 The observational relation

The fidelity of data does not depend on the conceptualization, the operational definition, the researcher's accuracy, and the reactivity of the gathering instrument alone. It depends on other factors as well, ones which may be largely beyond the researcher's control: the image that the actors want to convey of themselves; bureaucratic restrictions on the researcher's work; or the extent to which the participants wish to be observed. In this case, after the ethnographer has attempted to remedy these difficulties in the course of his or her research, the only option is to give the readers information ('*impressionist tales*' as John Van Maanen calls them) about the observational relation so that they have further material for evaluation of the contingency of the data. This information may be about the conditions in which the research has been conducted; the constraints on the researcher which have restricted the observational field; the help and hindrances encountered, and which of the participants were responsible for them; the requests and permissions granted or refused; problems of adapting to the field; the particular interests emerging from interviews, from correspondence, from conversations or telephone calls. For example, when research was being conducted on the difficulties at school of a sightless girl (see 13.7), the management refused permission for her classmates to be interviewed. Consequently, it was not possible to test hypotheses on how the girl's classmates constructed the concept of disability. Cicourel (1968) recalls that it was only after he had published the results of his research on juvenile courts that he learned that the police-officer participants (notwithstanding their apparent frankness) had been invariably reticent. He recounts that after the police officers had read his book, they commented to him roughly as follows: 'if we'd known that this was the purpose of your research, we'd have told you a whole lot of other things . . . .'

Publication of this information is a sort of 'natural' history of research, to which one devotes a chapter of a report, as did Whyte (1955) the 'Appendix,' Cicourel (1974) with the chapter 'Notes on The Argentine Historical Context and Some Ethnographic Impressions of Buenos Aires' or Mehan, Hertweck and Meihls (1986) with the third chapter titled 'The ethnographic context of the study.' This natural history, like the aspects treated in previous sections, does not guarantee the authenticity of ethnographic descriptions, but it does give the reader, and more generally the scientific community, good grounds for deciding whether to accept or to reject these descriptions. Also pertaining to a natural history of research are, according to Strauss and Corbin (1990: 253), explanation of the criteria on which the sample has been selected; how and when both the categories and the main hypotheses were formulated; for what reasons other hypotheses were discarded. Finally, it is also as important to specify the rules followed in confirming the hypotheses.

14.8 The generalizability of findings

Generalizability is one of the most controversial (if not *the* most controversial) of issues within and about qualitative research. For at least 70 years it has divided methodologists, causing great embarrassment. Consequently, the work of the ethnographer (and therefore of the qualitative researcher as well) when drawing conclusions is fraught with embarrassment and uncertainty. I shall first outline the cause of the controversy and then make some proposals.

14.8.1 The original sin, according to the quantitative critique

As you will have certainly read in the methodology textbooks, for more than a century quantitative methodologists have contended that only studies using *probability* samples (simple random, systematic, proportional stratified, non-proportional stratified, multistage and so on) can generalize their results to the sampling frame. The argument typically runs as follows:

> the obvious disadvantage of nonprobability sampling is that, since the proba-bility that a person will be chosen is not known, the investigator generally cannot claim that his or her sample is representative of the larger population. This greatly limits the investigator's ability to generalize his or her findings beyond the specific sample studied . . . A nonprobability sample may prove perfectly adequate if the researcher has no desire to generalize his or her find-ings beyond the sample (Bailey, 1978: 92).

This conventional position has sought (unsuccessfully) to relegate qualitative research to the marginal role of furnishing ancillary support for survey. In Gobo (2008) I have argued and amply documented that this methodological denigration of qualitative research is overly severe and unjustified, for three main reasons, which I will briefly summarize. First, because the use of probability samples and statistical inference in social research often proves problematic (because of the frequent lack of sampling frames, non-responses, etc.). Second, because there are numerous disciplines (like paleontology, archeology, geology, ethology, biology, astronomy, anthropology, cognitive science, linguistics and experimental psy-chology), whose theories are based exclusively on research conducted on only a few cases. Third because, *pace* the methodological orthodoxy, the most signifi-cant part of sociological knowledge is idiographic, i.e. based on few cases or even on haphazard or convenience samples (see 6.2.3):

> much of the best work in sociology has been carried out using qualitative methods without statistical tests. This has been true of research areas ranging from organizational and community studies to micro studies of face-to-face interaction and macro studies of the world system (Collins, 1988: 502).

14.8.2 Generalization as seen by qualitative methodologists

Over the years, qualitative researchers have reacted in various ways to the pronouncement that those who do not use probability samples cannot generalize. There are at least five concepts of generalization (see again Gobo, 2008), which range from very radical positions to more moderate ones. Among the most radical are those assumed by Lincoln and Guba (1979) and Denzin (1983), who (paradoxically) end by accepting the traditional quantitative position (see Gomm, Hammersley and Foster, 2000: 98) that qualitative research is an idio-graphic account which lays no claim to generalization. Norman K. Denzin is very explicit on the matter:

> the interpretivist rejects generalization as a goal and never aims to draw ran-domly selected samples of human experience. For the interpretivist every instance of social interaction, if thickly described (Geertz, 1973), represents a slice from the live world that is the proper subject matter for interpretative inquiry . . . Every topic . . . must be seen as carrying its own logic, sense or order, structure, and meaning (1983: 133–4).

The more moderate positions instead claim that there are two types of general-ization (which they have termed in various ways): *enumerative* (statistical) versus *analytic* induction; *formalistic/scientific* versus *naturalistic* generalization; or *distributive* versus *theoretical* generalization. The first type of generalization involves estimating the distribution of particular features within a sampling frame or population; the second, eminently theoretical, is 'only' concerned with the relations among the variables in the sample. The two generalizations are therefore made in completely different ways.[4]

CASE STUDY
The two types of generalization

The distinction between the two types of generalization has been drawn with exemplary clarity by the Italian sociologist Alberoni and colleagues, who wrote in their *Introduction* to a study on 108 political activists of the Italian Communist Party and the Christian Democrat Party as follows:

if we want to know, for instance, how many activists of both parties in the whole country are from families of Catholic or Communist tradition, (this) study is useless. Conversely, if we want to show that family background is important in determining whether a citizen will be an activist in the Communist rather than the Christian Democratic Party, this research can give the right answer. If we want to find out what are and have been the percentages of the different 'types' of activists . . . in both parties, the study is useless, whereas if we want to show that these types exist the study gives a certain answer . . . The study does not aim at giving a quantitative objective description of Italian activism, but it can aid understanding of some of its essential aspects, basic motivations, crucial experiences and typical situations which gave birth to Italian activism and help keep it alive (1967: 13).

This moderate stance has been adopted by the majority of qualitative methodologists, some of whom have sought to underscore the difference between statistical and 'qualitative' generalization by coining specific terms for the latter. This endeavor has given rise to a welter of terms, you have probably already met: 'naturalistic generalization,' 'transferability,' 'translatability,' 'analytic generalization,' 'extrapolation,' 'moderatum generalization' and others besides.

14.8.3 Do we need two concepts of generalization or is one enough?

The defensive and moderate position that states there are two types of generalization has had the indubitable merit of cooling the dispute with quantitative methodologists and of legitimating two ways to conduct research. However, this political compromise has also had at least two harmful consequences.

First, it has not stimulated reflection on how to emancipate 'qualitative' generalization from its subordination to statistical inference. Traditional methodologists continue to attribute inferior status to qualitative research, on the ground that, although it can produce interesting results, these have only a limited extension.

Second, an opportunity has been missed to re-discuss the entire issue, address-ing it in more practical (and not solely theoretical) terms with a view to develop-ing a new sampling theory: an idiographic theory, joint and equal with statistical theory, and which remedies a series of entrenched misunderstandings:

> denial of the capacity of case study research to support empirical [distributive] generalization often seems to rest on the mistaken assumption that this form of generalization requires statistical sampling. This restricts the idea of representation to its statistical version; it confuses the task of empirical generalization with the use of statistical techniques to achieve that goal. While those techniques are a very effective basis for generalization, they are not essential (Gomm, Hammersley and Foster, 2000: 104).

But do we really need two concepts of generalization? Is not just one enough? The many disciplines which do research with samples based on only a few cases – such as (with apologies for the repetition) paleontology, archeology, geology, ethology, biology, astronomy, anthropology, cognitive science, linguistics and experimental psychology – do not have two concepts of generalization. Are they more parsimonious than the social sciences? Perhaps so. And if they use only one concept, why cannot we do it as well?

Let us therefore, see why just one concept of generalization is sufficient.

14.8.4 *Deus ex machina*: The variance principle

We saw in 5.2.3. and 5.2.5 how a representative sample is constructed. Now to be added is that, when this is being done, the (statistical) principle of variance should always be borne in mind. Yes, the word is 'statistical,' because statistics are not to be abandoned entirely.

Contrary to the probability principle's standardizing intent and automatist inclination, variance is a criterion which requires the researcher to reason, to con-duct contextual analysis, and to take local decisions. It states that in order to determine the sample size, the statistics must first know the range of variance that the researcher intends to measure (at least in sufficiently close terms), because it is likely that, if the range of variance of variable X is high, n (the number of individuals to interview) will also be high, whereas if the range of variance is restricted (for example, to only two modalities), n may be very restricted as well. Hence, it is more likely that a sample will be a miniature of the sampling frame (population) if it is tendentially homogeneous; and it is less likely to be so if the sampling frame is tendentially heterogeneous. Consequently, if the variance is high, the researcher will require a large number of cases (in order to include every dimension of the phenomenon studied in his or her sample). If, instead, the variance is low, the researcher will presumably need only a few cases, and in some instances only one. In other words,

> it is important to recognize that the greater the heterogeneity of a population the more problematic are empirical generalizations based on a single case, or a handful of cases. If we could reasonably assume that the population was composed of more or less identical units, then there would be no problem (Gomm, Hammersley and Foster, 2000: 104).

As also Payne and Williams point out:

> the *breadth* of generalization can be extensive or narrow, depending on the nature of the phenomenon under study and our assumptions about the wider social world . . . [hence] the generalization may claim higher or lower levels of *precision of estimates* . . . [and it] will be conditional upon the ontological status of the phenomena in question. We can say more, or make stronger claims about some things than others. A taxonomy of phenomena might look like this: 1° physical objects and their social properties; 2° social structures; 3° cultural features and artifacts; 4° symbols; 5° group relationships; 6° dyadic relationship; 7° psychological dispositions/behavior . . . This outline taxonomy demonstrates that generalizations depend on what levels of social phenomena are being studied (2005: 306–7).

The conversation analyst Harvey Sacks (1992, vol. 1: 485, quoted in Silverman, 2000: 109) reminds us of the anthropologist and linguist Benjamin Lee Whorf, who was able to reconstruct Navajo grammar by extensively interviewing only one native Indian speaker. Grammar usually has low variance. However, had Whorf wanted to study how the Navajo educated their children, entertained themselves, and so on, he would (perhaps) have found greater variance in the phenomenon and would have needed more cases. On this logic, the formal criteria that guide sampling are more informed by and embedded in sociological (rather than statistical) reasoning based on contingent reflection about the dimensions specific to the phenomenon investigated and the knowledge objectives of the research.

This means that it is possible to find cases which on their own can represent a significant feature of a phenomenon. Generalizability, thus conceived, concerns more general structures and is detached from individual social practices, of which they are only an instance. In other words, the scholar does not generalize the individual instance, which as Max Weber stressed is unrepeatable, but rather the key structural features of which it is made up, and which are to be found in other cases or events belonging to the same species or class. As Howard Becker pointed out:

> in every city there is a body of social practices – forms of marriage, or work, or habitation – which don't change much, even though the people who perform them are continually replaced through the ordinary demographic process of birth, death, immigration, and emigration (2007: 6).

On this view, the question of generalizability assumes a different significance: for example, in the conclusions to his study on the relationship between a psychotherapist and a patient suffering from AIDS, Peräkylä writes:

> The results were not generalizable as descriptions of what other counselors or other professionals do with their clients; but they were generalizable as descriptions of what any counselor or other professional, with his or her clients, *can* do, given that he or she has the same array of interactional competencies as the participants of the AIDS counseling session have (1997: 216, quoted in Silverman, 2000: 109).

Something similar happens in film and radio productions with noise sampling. The creak of the door (which gives us the shivers when we watch a thriller or a horror film) does not represent all creakings of doors, but we associate it with them. We do not think about the differences between that creak and the one made by our front door; we notice the similarities only. These are two different ways of thinking, and most social sciences seek to find patterns of this kind.

14.8.5 How to generalize

We have already seen that the construction of a representative sample is a progressive, interactive and iterative process (see 5.2.5):

> theoretical sampling is cumulative. This is because concepts and their rela-tionships also accumulate through the interplay of data collection and analy-sis . . . until theoretical saturation of each category is reached (Strauss and Corbin, 1990: 178 and 188).

This interplay between sampling and hypothesis testing is needed because:

(1) representative samples are not predicted in advance but found, constructed and discovered gradually in the field; and
(2) it reflects the researcher's experience, previous studies, and the literature on the topic. In other words, the researcher will come to know the variance of a phenomenon cumulatively, observation by observation, study by study. As Gomm, Hammersley and Foster acknowledge:

> it is possible for subsequent investigations to build on earlier ones by provid-ing additional cases, so as to construct a sample over time that *would* allow effective generalization. At the present, this kind of cumulation is unusual . . . the cases are not usually selected in such a way as to complement previous work (2000: 107).

(3) representative samples are used to justify the researcher's statements.

Many generalizations develop and deepen the theoretical notes (see 12.3.3) taken during observation. Stimuli from the field are the platform on which abstractions of increasingly narrow focus are built.

The generalization process involves inferences which strip ethnographic descrip-tions down into statements with a higher degree of generality. This process takes place through the elimination of indexical expressions – those which contextualize the phenomenon in question. For example, the scientists described by Bruno Latour (see 5.2) moved from *type 2 statements* (descriptions) to *type 4 statements* (specialized facts) by removing from them every reference to the laboratory's work.

CASE STUDY
Generalizing from few instances

Garfinkel did the same when he described the results of his research on decision-making by jurors (see 1.5):

> in the material reported here, jurors did not actually have an understanding of the conditions that defined a correct decision until after the decision had

been made. Only in retrospect did they decide what they did that made their decisions correct ones. When the outcome was in hand they went back to find the 'why,' the things that led up to the outcome, and then in order to give their decisions some order, which namely, is the officialness of the decision (1967: 114).

In the next paragraph Garfinkel moves to a more abstract plane over and above his concrete research on the jurors:

If the above description is accurate, decision making in daily life would thereby have, as a critical feature, the *decision maker's task of justifying a course of action*. The rules of decision making in daily life, i.e. rules of decision making for more or less socially routinized and respected situations, may be much more preoccupied with the problem of assigning outcomes their legitimate history than with the question of deciding before the actual occasion of choice the conditions under which one, among a set of alternative possible courses of action, will be elected (1967: 114).

Generalization therefore eliminates details of the context in which the observations have been made. As an example of this cognitive procedure, Howard Becker recounts an anecdote about his colleague Bernard Beck. When Beck's students wanted to extrapolate a theory from their data, he instructed them as follows: 'Tell me what you've found out, but without using any of the identifying characteristics of the actual case' (1998a: 126, quoted in Silverman, 2000: 87).

14.8.6 Representativeness and generalizability: Two sides of the same coin?

A final aspect to consider is the connection between representativeness and generalizability. The social science textbooks usually describe generalizability as the natural outcome of a prior probabilistic procedure. In other words, the necessary condition for carrying out a statistical inference is previous use of a probability sample. It is forgotten, however, that probability/representativeness and generalizability are not two sides of the same coin. The former is an attribute of the *sample*, whilst the latter concerns the *findings* of research. Put otherwise: between construction of a sample and confirmation of a hypothesis there intervenes a complex set of activities (as we saw earlier) which pertain to at least seven different domains:

(1) the trustworthiness of operational definitions and operational acts;
(2) the reliability of the data collection instrument;
(3) the appropriateness of conceptualizations;

(4) the accuracy of the researcher's descriptions, categorizations and/or measurements;

(5) success with observational (or field) relations;

(6) the fidelity of the data; and

(7) the fidelity of the interpretation.

These activities, and their relative errors (called 'measurement errors' in the literature), may impair the connection between probability/representativeness and generalizability – a not infrequent occurrence in a complex activity like social research.

But the existence of these difficulties does not mean that our research has to be abandoned. Only that we should adopt a more reflexive, cautious and, above all, humble attitude when we present our results.

14.9 Between Scylla (normativism) and Charybdis (postmodernism)

Scylla and Charybdis were two monsters in Greek mythology that guarded opposite sides of a narrow passage of water between Italy and Sicily. The two sides of the channel were so close to each other that sailors attempting to avoid Charybdis would pass too close to Scylla, and vice versa. The expression 'between Scylla and Charybdis' today means being caught between two dangers, so that avoiding one means moving into range of the other.

Calling for a 'practical turn' on issues concerning the legitimation of qualitative research does not entail abandoning every prescriptive claim, that is, renouncing all research conventions on how to do ethnography. Between the normative (rule-based) approach of conventional methodology and the libertarian (rule-free) attitude of postmodern radicalism, as it flirts with methodological anarchism, the practical approach argues that methodological conventions can indeed be constructed, but they must derive from careful observation of (and reflection on) research practices. Still too often, both the normative and postmodernist approaches address methodological issues solely at the level of abstract principle. Is it possible to combine a (partly) normative endeavor with methodological situationism? At first sight, it does not seem so. And yet there are a number of examples which indicate otherwise.

CASE STUDY
The Sudnow method for playing the piano

David Sudnow, after his ethnomethodological studies on hospitals (1967) and on criminal courts (1965), turned his attention to the ethnomethodology of music. He published two books – *Ways of the Hand: The Organizaton of Improvised Conduct* (1978) and *Talk's Body: a Meditation. Between Two Keyboards* (1979) – based on phenomenological analysis of his experiences in learning how to play jazz piano and to improvise until he was able to perform in public.

Sudnow says that music is a form of communication in which there are written instructions (the notes), and verbal instructions and explanations like those given by a teacher. However, to become a true performer, especially in jazz improvisation, the learner must abandon this guidance.

Sudnow reflects on the relationship between the musician and his instrument, describing in detail how even the (apparently) simplest activities are organized: pressing the piano keys in a manner *accountable* for a musician among musicians; the range of action of the pianist's hands on the keyboard; how a chord is sounded by arranging the fingers in a certain way; the proxemics of the musician's body with the keyboard; following a rhythm (fast or slow).

Sudnow is not interested in an analytical conception of 'music.' Rather, he gives a processual account centered on the body's doings: hence, not on the music in itself but the music-making, 'thinking, not thoughts; melodying, not melodies' (1979: 57). Expert pianists are those whose hands move on their own account (they 'know where to go'), going off on their own to find the extremely precise place where a sound lives: they can play even with their eyes closed, without thinking about what they are doing.

Sudnow's ethnomethodological work produced the *Sudnow Method,* an extremely successful 'technique for playing the piano' (see www.sudnow.com). Sudnow promises that after a couple of months, at the most, of half an hour's practice a day anyone aged 14 and over with no previous experience will be able to play their first tunes. In six to eight months, they will be playing a dozen tunes. Within a year a novice will be able to play at a party. And all this for the modest sum of only 74.95 US dollars, shipping and handling included.

14.10 Concluding remarks

The Sudnow example is illuminating for, by studying practices, he has been able to design a music-teaching method (and therefore a prescriptive artifact) much more useful than many other such methods. This is because he has invented, not de-contextualized rules or general principles which stand alone (for a detailed discussion see Seale, Gobo, Gubrium and Silverman, 2004: 1ff), but conventions based on tacit knowledge and observation of participants' practices.

This example teaches us that the crisis of legitimation, as rightly denounced by postmodernism, can be resolved with new politics of legitimation based on a different conceptualization of the validation process. The nihilist route – that of abandoning any reference to the credibility of qualitative research (which may appear to be liberating) – has hidden pitfalls, as Clive Seale stresses:

> Some [authors], in searching for new ideals . . . seek to substitute moral values and political positions as guarantors of standards: promoting dialogue,

emancipating the oppressed, empowering the weak become the purposes of social research. But the epistemological relativism that these writers often claim stands in marked contrast to their political absolutism. My view is that such attempts to resolve the problem of criteria by resort to political values are frighteningly weak – the kind of thing that, as European history has shown, can be swept away in a few nights of concentrated book burning. I am also impressed by the general observation that one person's liberation may be another's oppression, and that 'emancipatory' positions too often involve closed minds (2004: 409).

KEY POINTS

- The conventional normative standards used to legitimate research results are no longer suited to the new epistemological doctrine.
- This doctrine maintains that, in many cases, a truth theory based on the correspondence between the researcher's account and the reality observed is untenable.
- The crisis of legitimation therefore requires the invention of new ways to assert the credibility of ethnographic research (and qualitative research in general).
- The conventional concepts of reliability and validity are not sufficient for this purpose: on the one hand because they have uncertain epistemological status; on the other because they fail to cover at least seven other aspects: (1) the trustworthiness of operational definitions and operational acts; (2) the reliability of the data collection instrument; (3) the appropriateness of conceptualizations; (4) the accuracy of the researcher's descriptions, categorizations and/or measurements; (5) success with observational (or field) relations; (6) the fidelity of the data; and (7) the fidelity of the interpretation.
- Also the conventional concepts of generalizability (both quantitative and qualitative) must be re-framed in more practical and less abstract terms.
- Only in this way will it be possible to re-think the credibility of qualitative research, avoiding both the conventional normative (rule-based) approach and the postmodern (rule-free) one.

KEY TERMS

Authenticity
(see p. 264)
Certification of the researcher's actual presence in the field.

Completeness
(see p. 264)
Descriptions must be accompanied by a detailed depiction of the context.

Consistency
(see p. 264)

The uniformity with which events observed on different occasions are assigned to the same category.

Credibility
(see p. 264)

The outcome of the legitimation process.

Fidelity of data
(see pp.266–7)

The degree of discrepancy between the status recorded and the actual status.

Fidelity of interpretation
(see p. 268ff)

The degree of discrepancy between the researcher's interpretations and the social phenomenon to which they refer.

Generalization
(see p. 272ff)

The process by which the results relative to the sample are transferred to the population or sampling frame.

Induced change
(see p. 262)

Change in a participant's status on an attribute of a concept owing to effects exerted by the method used.

Internal accuracy
(see p. 263)

The researcher's accuracy in each phase of the research process.

Legitimation
(see pp. 260–1)

The rhetorical work by which researchers seek to persuade their audience of the soundness of their research findings. This legitimation work resembles doing a jigsaw puzzle when some of the pieces may be missing.

Natural change
(see p. 262)

Change in a participant's status on an attribute of a concept owing to causes unrelated to the method used to gather that status.

Participant validation
(see pp. 268–70)

Obtaining the participants' confirmation or denial (verbal or written) of the researchers' accounts and interpretations so that these are a closer match with the reality observed.

Plausibility
(see p. 264)

Consistency between the researcher's conclusions and the social phenomenon to which they refer.

Practical turn
(see p. 273)

A radical intellectual shift whereby epistemological issues and methodological problems are addressed in a contextual and practical manner, without ideological pre-emptions, on the basis of concrete research practices.

Reliability
(see pp.261–2)

The precision of the instrument or method used for measurement.

Saturation
(see p. 264)

This testifies that all the events have been allocated to the concepts proposed, with cognitive dissonances eliminated and the marginal utility of the limit cases evaluated.

Validity (see pp. 266–7)	The correspondence between a researcher's account and the phenomenon observed. It is a concept similar to that of truth.
Variance principle (see pp. 275–6)	This states that, in order to determine the sample size, we must first know the range of variance of the phenomenon. If the variance is high this means that the phenomenon is heterogeneous; hence the researcher will require a large number of cases (in order to include every dimension of the phenomenon studied in his or her sample). If, instead, the variance is low, this means that the phenomenon is quite homogeneous; hence the researcher will presumably need only a few cases.

RECOMMENDED READINGS

For undergraduates:
Gobo, Giampietro (2004)

For graduates:
Gobo, Giampietro (2008)

For advanced researchers:
Gomm, Roger; Hammersley, Martyn and Foster, Peter (2000)

SELF-EVALUATION TEST

Are you ready for the next chapter? Check your knowledge by answering the following open-ended questions:
1. Why was it important in the 1980s to introduce the concepts of reliability and validity into qualitative research?
2. What is meant by the expressions 'the quality of qualitative research' (Clive Seale) and 'the credibility of qualitative research' (David Silverman)?
3. Why are representativeness and generalizability not two sides of the same coin?
4. What can we learn from David Sudnow's experience and from his piano-playing method?

Notes

1. In non-participant observation (see 2.4), by contrast, this risk does not exist because the observer is not noticed by the participants.
2. In navigation, three fixes are usually made to determine a nautical position.
3. Hammersley and Atkinson (1983: 199), Silverman (1993: 156–8; 2000: 99), Mason (1996: 27), are highly critical of triangulation, doubting the methodological soundness of comparing data collected with different instruments and cognitive intentions.
4. Indeed, there are some who maintain that *generalizability* is perhaps the wrong word for what qualitative researchers seek to achieve: 'Generalization is . . . [a] word . . . that should be reserved for surveys only' (Alasuutari, 1995: 156–7).

Part Four
Audiences

Communicating Findings, Writing Ethnographies

LEARNING OBJECTIVES

• To understand the role of writing in literate cultures.

• To realize that writing is a practice done in all phases of research, not just at its end.

• To be aware of the two audiences problem.

• To invent ways to make the audience appreciate your work.

15.1 Introduction

We live in a literate culture of which two fundamental pillars are writing and printing. Not by chance, a large part of your activity as students consists of reading, taking notes and writing. And thus it will be for at least some time to come . . . Some theorists of the mass media, like the Canadian mass-mediologist Marshall McLuhan, used to theorize that the advent of the cinema, radio and television (media which involve few written texts) would engender a return to the oral culture – the one previous to literacy – which had contributed so much to our knowledge (consider that Socrates was illiterate and that Plato always had a love/hate relationship with writing).

However, the internet is bringing us back (if we ever left it) to literate culture. In fact, the internet (with all that it involves, from newsgroups to chat rooms) is a world in which texts predominate over images. This applies to universities, which are places dense with written texts. Academic careers are based on writing, in fact. The lecturers who teach you have attained their status more from having written articles, books and papers than from the conferences that they have participated in. And lectures, which some decades ago were almost entirely oral, with few transparencies or writing on the blackboard are now, since the advent of Powerpoint, also closely based on written texts. Writing is therefore (and will be at least for some time to come) a practice integral to scientific research.

15.2 Why write?

The first question may seem banal: what is the purpose of a written text? The question is so obvious and even trite that the topic of writing has been largely neglected since the birth of ethnographic methodology. Perhaps because it was thought that if all the phases of a research project were carried out correctly, the research report (with the relative papers, articles and books) would spring automatically from the data. Only anthropology, some 30 years ago, took the matter seriously (as we shall see) with important contributions (Rabinow, 1977; Clifford, 1988). It thereafter came to treat writing as a specific object of analysis (Clifford and Marcus, 1986). Writing is important for two main reasons:

- it induces us to provide graphic descriptions of the cultures observed to those who have not seen them, or have not experienced them;
- it gives legitimacy to the ethnographer's work and to his or her results.

15.2.1 The chickens and the roost

Everything discussed in the previous chapter relative to the credibility of the researcher's results takes material form in writing. We may say that the 'chickens' of credibility, reliability, validity, consistency, accuracy, authenticity, plausibility, and so on, now 'come home to roost' in writing. The written text thus becomes the yardstick for evaluation of the research. The researcher may have conducted what he or she feels to be outstanding research, but if it is described to an audience in an institutionally unsuitable manner, it will be discredited. Unfortunately, the reverse does not happen: if the report is attractive and convincing, it will give brilliance to the research as well – even if the data is bogus, or if the research procedure has been sloppy. This, as we shall shortly see, is the contradiction that has provoked much discussion among those who concern themselves with writing.

15.2.2 The two audiences problem

Social scientists have an additional problem with respect to their colleagues in the physical and biological sciences. They have to convince two audiences: the scientific community, and the participants in their research. Hence they have two types of reader and, consequently, two types of potential critic. Although the matter may seem trivial, it is the greatest difference between the social sciences and the physical and biological sciences. A physicist's theory will never be disputed by an electron. Likewise, a cell could never disown its biologist. Even less could a guinea pig hold a press conference to protest against the suffering caused by animal experimentation. Instead, it is not infrequent for social scientists to be contested, criticized, and even slammed by participants, or by those who deem themselves to be such. For example, the book by Vidich and Bensman (1958) was harshly criticized by the inhabitants of the small rural town (Springdale) which the authors studied. The same happened to Robert and Helen Lynd with *Middletown* (1929) and to Lloyd W. Warner and Lunt S. Paul with *The Social Life of a Modern Community* (1941), the first book in the Yankee City series (see 6.2.4).

The participants were dissatisfied with the researchers' descriptions and they voiced their disapproval.

As a consequence, the social sciences will never be able to compete (if they continue to remain anchored in the Western idiom) with the hard sciences, because they must constantly deal with a twofold complexity: persuading two audiences.

15.3 When to write

Another commonly-held belief, which has only recently been disputed, was that the report should be written only on conclusion of the research. First the research design had to be produced; then the researcher went into the field to gather the data (to use an agricultural metaphor); then desk analysis was conducted, in a closed-off room; finally, the results were written up. It is instead now widely agreed (Strauss and Corbin, 1990; Silverman, 2000) that writing is not an isolated act, and that it is better to write *constantly* (from the beginning of the research until its end), and not only on conclusion of the fieldwork.

15.3.1 Writing is thinking

EXERCISE 15.1

- Try to describe or explain a scientific concept (for example, 'role' or 'identity') to a friend.
- First do it orally (recording what you say).
- Then do the same thing but by writing an e-mail message (to another friend, obviously).

You will have noticed that the two texts are rather different. This means that speaking and writing are also two (different) forms of thought. When we write we are never satisfied: we write a sentence and then erase it; we try again with different words, adding details or examples because the text never seems sufficiently clear. Then we find new connections with other concepts, and so on. If, during the exercise, you needed only a few minutes to explain the concept orally, writing it instead took much longer. Not only because speaking is more rapid than writing, but also because of the slowness inherent to the writing activity, so that the writer can reflect on what he or she has written (reflexivity) and expand on its content. Writing is therefore the form of reasoning best suited to reflection, discussion, analysis and scientific activity.

15.3.2 Writing is communicating (virtually with the reader)

Although when people write they may be physically on their own, from the psychological and sociological point of view they are not so at all. When they write they have in mind, often unconsciously, a referent, a virtual reader, an audience. The Italian semioticist Umberto Eco (1979) has called this referent the 'Model Reader.' In order to write, one must imagine the future reader. For example I, while writing, am thinking of you young students so different from me, who am of an age that I could be your father. I have tried to be as comprehensible as possible, considering what your knowledge, tastes, and interests might be. And to do this I have offered many examples that may interest you, I have simplified some parts and I have deepened others. In doing so, I have lengthened the text considerably (thus infuriating my publisher). You do the same when taking a written examination that requires you to expound a concept or a theory. You think of the teacher who will appraise your work: what he or she expects from you, the examples that he or she would want you to provide, the type of expository style that he or she would expect, and his or her preferences. However, you know your teacher; but I do not know you. Mine is the situation in which researchers generally find themselves: they do not know their readers, but imagine them. In fact, the Model Reader is not the actual reader 'in flesh and blood,' but the reader-type, an abstract role: an imaginary audience, in whose regard the ethnographer chooses among several stylistic options, and among similar or dissimilar expressions.

The activity of writing therefore puts the researcher in communication with his or her Model Reader.

15.3.3 Writing is continuing to analyze the data

By using the written form of communication, and by constantly bearing the Model Reader in mind, researchers clarify their statements to themselves and to others. They develop new ideas, refine concepts, invent new hypotheses (eliminate others), construct pieces of theory, generalize some of their results, test their argumentative structure, and sometimes censor themselves so as to avoid baseless claims or faulty explanations. For this reason, we may say that as the ethnographer writes, he or she continues to interpret the data. Moreover, if he or she begins to write immediately (as advised in 12.3.3 and 13.2.2), he or she will also begin immediately to change his or her research design according to the emerging hypotheses and theories – as in the best tradition of Grounded Theory.

15.4 How to write

A large part of the reflection on writing has concentrated on the 'enunciative modalities' used by the author; in other words, the stylistic, rhetorical and communicative strategies employed by ethnographers to persuade their readers of the quality of their analyses.

15.4.1 Paper cultures

Most of the readers of a book (or an article) do not have direct knowledge of the culture of the group or organization being described. The reader (unless he or she is particularly expert) therefore learns about that culture through the text.

For the reader, the book is not one representation among the many possible of a culture; it *becomes* the culture. In other words, for the majority of readers, 'real' cultures end up by coinciding with textual cultures (the documents). And if we address the matter from a radically phenomenological point of view, we must agree that they are nothing other than *paper cultures*. For the same reason, the French sociologist Pierre Bourdieu (1987), when discussing theories of social stratification, termed the social groups identified by sociologists as 'paper classes.'

If this is how matters stand, we cannot but feel a certain bewilderment. A number of questions immediately arise: Does this mean that the cultures described in books do not exist? Does it mean that they are all inventions of ethnographers? Fakes? No, not exactly. What is being emphasized here is more simply the power and the persuasive force of the written text. And also the central role of argumentation. (For details on the New Rhetoric movement and the role of argument, go to www.sagepub.co.uk/gobo)

15.4.2 The contribution of post-colonial anthropology

At the beginning of the 1980s, certain American anthropologists continued – more radically and from a postmodern perspective – along the route marked out by the *new rhetoric*: some of their ideas were treated in 4.4). Their concern was with a particular form of writing: the ethnographic text. George Marcus and Dick Cushman (1982) invited anthropologists to conduct critical examination on how ethnographic texts had been constructed until that time. James Clifford (1986), amongst others, denounced the ethnocentrism of traditional anthropology and its inability to describe other cultures adequately. This endeavor produced collective reflection on how ethnographic texts are constructed and then led to the publication of the famous book with the telling title *Writing Culture: Poetics and Politics of Ethnography*, edited by Clifford and Marcus (1986). This book definitively situated anthropological knowledge within the limits and ideologies of the Western cognitive paradigm, and acknowledged that 'enduring power inequalities had clearly constrained ethnographic practice' (Clifford, 1986: 8). Thus, writing – like reading – was essentially a *political act of meaning construction*.

There are three main types of narrative: realist, processual and reflexive; these are discussed below.

15.4.3 Realist narrative

In spite of everything, the realist expository style is today the one most widely used in the sciences. It is used to furnish not so much a (subjective) interpretation of reality as a 'snapshot' of it. The 'snapshot' metaphor is powerful because it leaves no space for mediation and affirms an ostensive view of reality. Hence, what the realist style renders is not one among many possible accounts of reality but *the* reality: its only possible description.

The style complies with precisely-defined narrative conventions on how research results should be expounded: for instance, references should be made to authoritative scholars and to well-established theories, footnotes should be appended to pages, bionotes should be provided, and so on – the purpose being to demonstrate that the author is a competent (and if possible, authoritative) member of the scientific community. The story is told of how Harvey Sacks found it difficult to obtain approval of his dissertation because it did not abide with these stylistic patterns. The same happened, much earlier, to William F. Whyte: during the animated discussion of his dissertation by a board comprising such a distinguished academic as Louis Wirth, he was fiercely criticized for not having used the conceptual apparatus of the Chicago School.

Aware of the researcher's interpretative work, the realist narrative seeks to conceal this by presenting the ethnographer as an anonymous subject ('from nowhere'), on the margins of the scene in order not to contaminate it. The style of writing is characterized by the use of third-person, documentary and detached discourse. It endeavors to distinguish itself from the sensationalism of journalistic discourse, from the partiality of political discourse, from the ingenuousness of common-sense discourse, from the fancifulness of literary discourse. Realist texts also conceal the researcher's emotions, his or her personal involvement in the participants' affairs, his or her sympathies, dislikes, idiosyncrasies. And also all his or her failures during the fieldwork. Clifford (1986: 5) observes that such language seeks to exclude subjectivity (for objectivity), the rhetorical (for linearity and sobriety), the fictional (for the facts): not only the subjectivity of the ethnographer, but also that of the participants, who become representatives of a general category, typical subjects (out of time and history), not people in flesh and blood.

In order to reassure the reader that the report is not the result of personal interpretation but a faithful representation of 'the natives' point of view,' the author resorts to specific stylistic conventions, such as the presentation of excerpts, or interview extracts, whose subjectivity is introduced generically through demographic information about the interviewee: 'F., age 24, baccalauréat and a few months in an Arts faculty; father: private means' (cited in Bourdieu, 1979/1984: 151). The (so-called) 'voice of the natives' is graphically separated from the rest of the text by means of boxes, italics and smaller font size.

Details, precise and abundant, are textual instruments to legitimate the accuracy and thoroughness of the observation. But they are also a way to convey the researcher's actual presence in the place where observation was made (Van Maanen, 1988: 49).

The writings of the British social anthropologist Edward E. Evans-Pritchard (1902–73) are excellent examples of objectivity and impersonality; by contrast, those of the American postmodern anthropologist Vincent Crapanzano (as we shall see) are shot through with fragmentariness and subjectivity.

CASE STUDY
The realist narrative

In the 1930s Evans-Pritchard studied the *Nuer*, a confederation of tribes located in Southern Sudan and Western Ethiopia devoted to farming and cattle-raising. He published his study in 1940. It is a monograph that epitomizes ethnography 'authoriality.' The text is linear, transparent and assertive. A realist and self-assured style of writing.

Nuer tribes are split into segments. The largest segments we call primary tribal sections and these are further segmented into secondary tribal sections which are further segmented into tertiary tribal sections. Experience shows that primary, secondary, and tertiary are sufficient terms of definition, and in the smallest tribes probably few terms are required. A tertiary tribal section comprises a number of village communities which are composed of kinship and domestic groups (1940: 139).

Each segment is itself segmented and there is opposition between its parts. The members of any segment unite for war against adjacent segments of the same order and unite with these adjacent segments against larger sections (1940: 142).

In the diagram on p.144, (see Figure 15.1) when Z^1 fights Z^2, no other section is involved. When Z^1 fights Y^1, Z^1 and Z^2 unite as Y^2. When Y^1 fights X^1, Y^1 and Y^2 unite, and so X^1 and X^2. When X^1 fights A, X^1, X^2, Y^1, and Y^2 all unite as B. When A raids the Dinka A and B may unite (1940: 143–4).

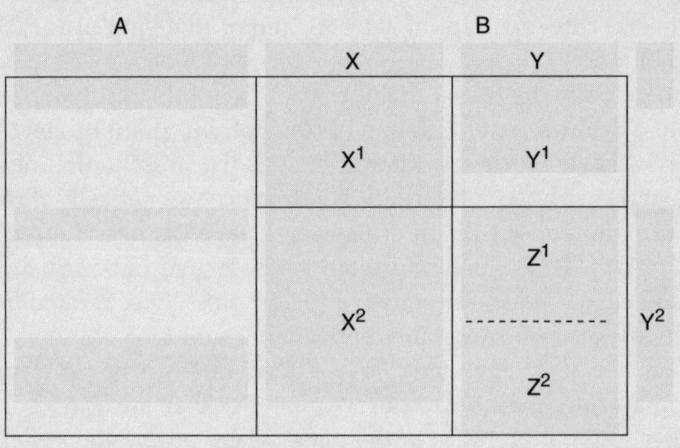

Figure 15.1

15.4.4 Processual narrative

The American anthropologist Paul Rabinow wrote about his book, 'an account of my experience in Morocco,' as follows:

I have tried to break through the double-bind which has defined anthropology in the past. As graduate students we are told that 'anthropology equals experience'; you are not an anthropologist until you have the experience of doing it. But when one returns from the field, the opposite immediately applies: anthropology is not the experiences which made you an initiate, but only the objective data you have brought back (1977: 4).

Processual narrative starts from this contradiction. And in contrast with realist narrative, it conceives the ethnographic text as an account of the experience of 'comprehension of the other' (1977: ix), of the researcher's cognitive evolution: the representation of the research process *in* the product itself of that process. The central metaphor is that of knowledge as a journey: at the beginning the ethnographer is completely lost, he or she has a baggage of knowledge (theoretical pre-assumptions and prejudices) of little use in understanding the meaning of events. Only participation in everyday rituals, conversations with the participants, the sharing of moments of sociality, involvement in banal events, apparently unproductive 'hanging around,' enables the ethnographer to discover, slowly and almost unconsciously, the social world in which he or she is immersed and absorb its meanings. The purpose is to achieve, by the end of the research process, coincidence between the point of view of the ethnographer and that of the natives, between the etic and emic accounts (see 2.7).

The account is littered with anecdotes, surprises, mishaps, incidents, dramatic turns of events, colorful conversations. Whilst realist narrative privileges the typical and the normal, processual narrative privileges the unusual and the exceptional. It seeks to immerse the reader directly in the world that it describes; have him or her perceive the sounds, smells, and tastes of that culture; involve him or her in it with all the senses. Contrary to the realist narrative, which is visual and the offspring of literate cultures or 'cultures of the eye,' processual narrative is auditory and more kindred to oral cultures, or those 'of the ear.'

In order to render a culture vivid, in order to evoke it in the mind of the reader (who does not know that culture), processual narrative uses instruments very similar to those of the literary genre. (For details on ethnography as a 'blurred genre,' go to www.sagepub.co.uk/gobo.)

Processual narratives make use of the first person singular. The author sometimes speaks (with self-irony) about him or herself, his or her emotions, errors, preferences, weaknesses, seeking to establish a direct and intimate relationship with the reader. The author dispenses with the aseptic and detached tone of the expert in order to place him or herself on the same level as the reader.

The validity of the researcher's findings is based not only on academic credentials or on direct evidence, but also on demonstration that he or she has been (at a certain point in the research process) accepted by the natives and recognized as competent in understanding their world. Description of the researcher's invitation to a ceremony from which he or she had been previously excluded, or the sharing of a confidence or a secret, are cited as evidence that the knowledge-gathering process has been successful. The concept of validity is thus replaced with that of *authenticity*.

The most widespread forms of processual narrative are the *dialogue*, the *diary*, *sociological introspection* and *heteroglossia*.

In the first case the text is a sequence of conversations between the researcher and the informants. An example is provided by *Tuhami: Portrait of a Moroccan* by Crapanzano (1980) about an illiterate Arab tilemaker who narrates his life in first person and answers brief questions put to him by the anthropologist. Tuhami's narrative constitutes a fragmented whole, with numerous loose ends and contradictions. Moreover, it is the story, not of a representative of Moroccan Arabic culture, but of a misfit who believes that he is possessed by spirits and married to a she-devil. A puzzle that requires the reader to contribute actively to its interpretation.

Crapanzano rejects the interpretative omnipotence of the researcher. Also because ethnographers tend to confuse what they believe natives think with what they actually feel. This error is due to attempts by authors to establish their authority over the accuracy of their texts. When an author fails to distinguish between his or her own view and that of the native, readers tend to forget that it is only the author's voice that they are hearing in the text. They consequently believe that the text is transmitting an objective reality, with no bias or interpretation by the author.

CASE STUDY
Dialogue

Crapanzano talks to Tuhami about the sexual attitudes of Moroccans:

Tuhami explained that the only proper way for a man to make love to his wife is in a prone, dominant position. With prostitutes, other positions are possible. (Unlike some of the Moroccan men I questioned, Tuhami did acknowledge the position in which the woman is astride the man. He told me it was called 'the vagina over the minaret.') When I asked him why a man can make love to his wife in only one position, he answered, 'Allah gave us our wives as he gave us a tree in front of our house. It is to be watered and left alone. Then it will bear fruit.' Women – even wives, he admitted – do get pleasure from sexual intercourse.

— They always get pleasure. Their muscles become so relaxed that you could throw them in the ocean and they wouldn't even cry out. All women in the world have only one thought: to make love to a man. At the time of the Prophet, a man could sleep with a woman forty times a night (1980: 110).

— A man cannot know if the woman he is making love to will conceive. The woman can tell. She feels it. She feels the child moving in her. The woman's stomach burns a little the night she is impregnated. She can be certain only after three days. She is always tired. She begins to hate her husband a month later. She gets angry at him and tries to scratch his face. She wants special foods: chicken and mutton. She always looks at what her husband has brought from the market. After three months she no longer wants special foods. There are women who make a lot of demands and refuse everything. Some women look at monkeys or pigs when they are pregnant; then their children – their faces only – will look like the animal.

— How is a baby made? — The male child is always on the right. The girl is always on the left. The girl in the mother's womb sees everything. She sees her father making love to her mother. The boy does not see. The boy turns to his side when his father makes love to his mother. The boy has already learned to be polite by the time he is born. A girl is always curious.

— Where does the child come from?

— When a man and a woman make love, a liquid comes out of the man and enters the woman. It is from this liquid that the child grows. God has made the liquid. When the liquid enters the womb of woman, the angels take care of it. They stretch it a little bit each month. Then God tells them to leave. The child is like a seed. The seed swells. You can say that it, the child, has been planted in the earth.

— What does the woman contribute?

— There is a pocket in her that stretches.

— Does the woman give anything to the child?

The child is already there in the man's liquid, but not in the shape of a child. On a night when a woman becomes more excited than usual, you can be sure she will become pregnant. They have been given a child because the angels on each side of them have reported to Allah that they have been good. The angels take a little of what the mother eats and gives it to the child (1980: 111–12).

A second form typically assumed by processual narratives is that of the *diary*. In sociology, an example is *Good Company* (1982) by the American Douglas Harper, an ethnography conducted among railroad tramps in the state of Washington. In anthropology, a by now classic example is *Reflections on Fieldwork in Morocco* (1977) by Rabinow. The book consists entirely of a diary in which the author notes down his experiences as a stranger 'initiated' into knowledge of the Moroccan Arab world: encounters, contacts, exchanges, (seemingly) insignificant episodes, `hanging around cafes drinking tea' (1977: 42), experiences of every kind. The diary form invites the reader to travel side-by-side with the author in his cognitive 'detour' in entering the unknown to emerge with new and unexpected knowledge. The diary has the reader participate, page after page, incident after incident, in this process of understanding the host culture.

**CASE STUDY
The diary**

In 1968 and 1969 Paul Rabinow conducted fieldwork in Morocco. He worked under the guidance of his advisor Clifford Geertz. Five years later he reconstructed the experience:

Driss ben Mohammed, a jovial, portly, and even-tempered young man, had consistently refused to work as an informant . . . As time wore on and my friendship with ben Mohammed deepened, I was learning more and more from him . . . we could spend many of the hot hours together . . . Casually . . . we had a meandering series of conversation . . . Although we talked of many things, perhaps the most significant set of discussions turned on our relations to our separate traditions. It would have been almost impossible to have had such conversations with either Alo or Malik (the informants) enmeshed as they were in the web of their own local world . . .

The fundamental tenet of Islam, for ben Mohammed, was that all believers are equal before Allah, even though pride, egoism, and ignorance obscure the fact. Very, very, few people, in his view, actually believe in Islam. Most take only a 'narrow' view: they think that if they merely follow the basic prescriptions then they are Muslims . . . For ben Mohammed the tensions of his world view turned on these two Moroccan alternatives. Morocco's future was far from bright . . . Moroccans could not ignore the West. This attitude required borrowing, integrating, and eliminating certain archaic and oppressive practices, but it did not mean merely imitating the West; and most important of all, it did not require the abandonment of Islam.

With most informants, I would have stopped at this point of generality. But with ben Mohammed I feel I could proceed further. Throughout my stay in Morocco I noticed that black was negatively valued in a variety of ways. In the broadest terms, white was generally equated with good and black with evil. Malik in particular seemed constantly concerned about color distinctions and their symbolism. Black was bad, according to his view, a color worthy of a dog. The lighter you are the better you are, the more you shone in the eyes of Allah. Malik was joking one day about a very poor villager. He said the man was so poor he would have to marry a black . . . When I showed him pictures of America he always made a point of saying that he could not tell if the blacks were men or women. He had been very upset when he found out that one of his favorite songs on the radio was by a black group. After that, he was careful to find out the color of a singer before offering any opinions on the music . . . He was quite sure of himself; his source of ultimate authority was the Koran (1977: 142–6).

The third type of processual narrative is *sociological introspection*, which also takes the name of *auto-ethnography* (see 4.4). This treats the researcher's life and the experiences as ethnographic material to analyze.

A final narrative strategy is *heteroglossia*. Introduced by the Russian literary critic Michail Bachtin, the term means that voice is given to all the members of the community, dissenters included. A heterogloss text is 'polyphonic' in that the researcher's voice and interpretation are flanked by the voices and interpretations of the informants and the participants. Thus, the voice of the ethnographer merges with those of the members, although the plurality of the voices speaking in the text does not call into question the authority of the author (the ethnographer) who has let them speak.

CASE STUDY
Heteroglossia

Between 1960 and 1969 the American ethnologist Donald M. Bahr studied the Pima's culture, a group of American Indians inhabiting an area of what is now central and southern Arizona (USA) and Sonora (Mexico). The name signifies 'river people,' who are closely related to the Tohono O'odham (meaning 'desert people,' formerly Papago). The name 'Pima' apparently derives from the phrase meaning 'I don't know' repeatedly used in their initial meetings with Europeans.

The topic of Bahr's research was native medicine, and in particular the 'Piman theory of sickness.' To this end, Bahr 'for a year and a half questioned a Papago shaman concerning the sickness of his people' (1974: 7). The result of this experience was a book jointly produced by a Papago Indian shaman (Juan Gregorio), a Papago Indian translator (David Lopez, a fluent bilingual), a Papago Indian linguist (Albert Alvarez), and a non-Indian explicator (Bahr). In another context, the first three collaborators would not have become co-authors. They might have been mentioned in the acknowledgements, but in most cases their names would not have appeared on the book's cover. Indeed, 'in many anthropological studies the role of the native informant is confined to stating facts while the functions subsumed under authorship devolve to the anthropologist. This state of affairs Bahr wished to reverse' (1974: 7). The book thus became a co-operative text all of whose creators had equal status. The anthropologist was only one of them and thus lost his monopoly over interpretation. A polyphonic, heterogloss text, therefore.

However, unlike postmodern ethnography, this is a substantive book whose central cognitive aim of understanding illness in the Pima culture is achieved through co-operative work.

Much criticism has been made of processual narrative. Latour (1988) maintains that in the heat of introspection, sight is lost of the research object. Geertz (1988) contends that putting the ethnographer's personal experience at the center of the analysis is a contrivance in the sense that the participants only enter into the representation in so far as they have effects on the observer. Moreover, this practice indulges in excessive complacency, narcissism and exhibitionism (Marcus and Fischer, 1986): the ethnographer becomes the center, whereas he or she instead should only be the periphery. In other words, the 'point of view of the native' becomes the 'point of view of the anthropologist.' In this regard, the American anthropologist Marshall D. Sahlins has written a comic dialogue between a postmodern anthropologist and a native, where the latter imploringly asks the former: 'but couldn't we talk a little bit about me as well'?

Finally, because readers are unable to check the accuracy of the researcher's analyses, they can only express a literary judgment on how the author has been able to render *his* or *her* personal experience vivid, interesting and stimulating.

15.4.5 Reflexive narrative

Is there, one may ask, an alternative way to write which steers a middle course between the Scylla and Charybdis of realist and processual narrative, taking the most interesting aspects of both? It is difficult to answer. And yet, in my view, anthropologists like Clifford Geertz and Michelle Rosaldo, sociologists like Bruno Latour and Steve Woolgar, and ethnomethodology in general, have been able to do so by adopting a narrative style which can be called *reflexive*. This style is on the one hand intended to reflect upon the intrinsically constructive nature of the methodology and methods used; and on the other to show the circumstances in which the analyses have been produced (Latour and Woolgar, 1979) – the backstage of the knowledge process as it were.

Explicitly stating the circumstances of the knowledge production process means that 'reports' on the following aspects of the research process should be included in the text. They should concern:

- *Theoretical interests*: what the researcher intended to investigate; if and how these interests changed in the course of the research, owing to what events and considerations; and what hypotheses guided (top downwards) the research.
- *Substantive interests*: why the researcher selected that particular topic, what concrete or contingent interests and aims induced him or her to pay attention to it rather than another; and what his or her extra-scientific intentions were.
- *Affective relations and the cultural and ideological background*: the researcher's emotional attitude to the topic studied; personal problems in adapting to the field. Obviously, there is an important private component in the researcher's reasoning which is not always opportune or necessary to make explicit. However, in some way revealing this private dimension allows the researcher to correct certain observations. For example, we can reasonably ask whether the fact that the researcher is a habitual drinker or smoker (or if he or she is not) has influenced his or her research on alcoholism and drug taking. If he or she is a Protestant, how would he or she react to such research topics as contemporary religious phenomena, sexual behaviors and customs, or belief systems? And likewise for innumerable other research topics.
- *Methodological notes*: how the researcher came to recognize particular replies, suggestions and details as congruent with his or her interests; why he or she believes that his or her interpretations are reasonable and convincing; and how he or she decided that the events selected were important and would enable him or her to accept or reject particular hypotheses and interpretations.
- *Theoretical knowledge*: the type of literature consulted, the theoretical approaches adopted, and the sociological categories used to codify events and classify them.
- *Techniques*: the techniques employed and the problems that arose in their application; the main materials used, so that other researchers can repeat the analysis.
- *The resources and constraints* that determined the range of his or her knowledge-gathering action: the conditions in which the research was conducted, how it was helped or hindered; requests for access or funding[1] granted or refused; reactions by colleagues, their encouragement or dissuasion.

- *Contacts*: casual contacts, informal interviews, correspondences and conversations, significant telephone calls and advice and criticism following the first writing-up of the results.
- *The indexicality of the research report*: recognizing the contingency of one's data, considering the discourses of social scientists as dependent on the context in which they are produced, that is, discourses tied to the *occasion* and subject to the same restrictions as apply to the participants' discourses.

Introspection versus accountability

Whilst the processual narrator introduces introspection into his or her texts, the reflexive one instead introduces accountability. The former maintains that, because it is impossible to describe 'external' reality, he or she has no alternative but to talk about his or her 'inner' reality, whereas the latter makes it his or her responsibility to express a point of view that does not merely replicate that of the participants. This move in some way comprises a sense of ethical obligation.

Whilst on the one hand reflexivity can be regarded as an astute strategic move to increase the authoritativeness of the description and to legitimate the ethnographer's omnipotence even further (Woolgar, 1988), on the other it wants to be an attempt to recognize the partiality of the researcher's point of view.

15.4.6 Transcribing, translating . . . betraying

Post-colonial anthropologists thus shift the attention to the text. But they are obviously not alone in doing so. Also Geertz, one of the foremost representatives of interpretative anthropology, expressly states that reality does not have 'its own idiom' (1988: 151). Hence the work of the ethnographer, like that of every researcher, consists in describing what he or she observes in the field in a manner intelligible to his or her audience. In other words, he or she has the difficult task of translating the culture observed (target or departure) into the culture of the reader (or arrival). Put in the terms of Actor-Network Theory (see 10.5), the ethnographer is forced to perform a 'translation' which inevitably alters the meaning. Every process of representation is intrinsically 'creative,' in the sense that it produces something different from the culture initially observed. It therefore (often involuntarily) performs a 'betrayal' on behalf of the observer.

15.4.7 The framing activity of metaphors, metonyms and analogies

On the wave of the new rhetoric, the late 1970s saw what has been called the 'linguistic turn,' among whose predecessors were Wittgenstein and analytic philosophy. However, it was with the American philosopher Richard Rorty, and subsequently many other influential theorists in diverse fields – philosophy,[2] economics (McCloskey, 1986), linguistics (Lakoff and Johnson, 1980), organizational studies (Morgan, 1986), and the social sciences in general – who demonstrated that language performs a fundamental role in constructing reality. The view that language 'constitutes' reality is contrary to common sense and to most of the Western tradition of philosophy. The traditional view was that words function like labels (see 2.2). However, the power of language, more specifically of certain rhetorical tropes, is more easy visible in historical discourse. For example, the fact that in the early 1600s the English doctor William Hurtley described the heart as a pump wrought a mechanist revolution in medicine. Or the term 'social class,' used to identify and distinguish groups (Gobo, 1993; 1995), conveyed a hierarchical, orderly and almost military idea of society. Again, in 1988 the American writer Susan Sontag showed that:

> modern medical thinking could be said to begin when the gross military metaphor becomes specific . . . military metaphors have inspired in increasing measure the description of medical pathology. Disease is seen as an invasion of alien organisms, to which the body responds by its own military operations, such as the mobilizing of immunological 'defenses', and medicine is 'aggressive', as in the language of most chemotherapies (2001: 97).

There is much talk in medicine of 'battles' among globules, 'war' on bacteria, 'weapons' to 'defeat' diseases, of virus that 'attack' and are considered 'enemies,' 'invaders,' 'threats,' 'antibodies,' 'command centers' of the immune system, and so on.

EXERCISE 15.2

The Swedish biologist Carolus Linnaeus (1707–78), the founder of modern botany, depicted nature as a sort of federation made up of three distinct worlds (animal, vegetable and mineral). Why did he call them 'kingdoms' and not 'republics'? And why did he place God at the head of this federation?

These examples show at least three things: that scientific concepts are often influenced by the historical period in which scientists work; that common sense has a great influence on science; and that metaphors are not simply forms of expressing, or better representing or disseminating, a concept. On the contrary, metaphors, like metonyms and analogies, are much more serious affairs: they construct an object cognitively and ideologically, they create a way to conceive and see the object itself (for some case studies on the use of metaphors in organization studies, go to www.sagepub.co.uk/gobo).

Metaphors are therefore not neutral rhetorical devices. Rather, they reflect a particular vision of the world, an ideology, shared by the scientists who use them. Furthermore, metaphors are not merely passive devices which reflect the way people think; they are also and above all active devices, because they constantly produce and reproduce that way of thinking.

15.4.8 The literary turn

According to Atkinson (1990), the linguistic turn paved the way for a 'literary turn' which inaugurated a different literary style, and a different way to write social science using *new literary forms*: ironic texts, the play, the limerick, the parody, the parable, the dialogue, the anti-preface, the anti-introduction, the parallel text-analytical and goal-analytical, the narrative collage, the lecture, the encyclopedia, the examination, and the press report. In addition to all these, occasional use has been made of such self-referential devices as the self-engulfing photograph, self-referring notes, and strange loops (on the authors who have used these devices see Ashmore, 1989: 66). However, these new literary forms are no more than attempts to frame reflexivity in terms of manipulation-deconstruction of the text. They consequently sometimes appear rather ridiculous and narcissistic, and they are not always beneficial to a reflexive style. Moreover, they also forget that there are institutional constraints on the form that texts can take to be accepted by the scientific community.

15.4.9 Tips for accountability, tricks of outing

It seems that those who propose the literary forms just described sometimes forget the original reason for interest in the rhetorical forms of text construction: the discovery that scientific writing is a complex of highly codified and institutionally defined strategies. Consequently, only a well-known author, with an established reputation, can dare not apply them and provocatively breach the conventions. But a student, or a young researcher, cannot disregard them without risking academic ostracism. So the *practical* problem is how to strike a balance between institutional requirements and reflexivity, how to comply with these conventions while also elegantly circumventing them.

Let us see some practicable alternative strategies or 'writing tactics' (Fischer, 1986: 207, 232 and 233).

First, one can adopt a *post-rhetorical style*. This aims less (or not only) to persuade the reader than to introduce materials which involve him or her in the creative process and to elicit hypotheses different from the author's. Essential for this purpose is an abundance of materials, a wealth of detail on rituals, and their thin description (see 10.3).

Second, the expository style can restrict the impersonal forms of expression ('one deduces that,' 'it is to be noted that,' 'from this it follows that'), certain visual metaphors ('it is clear that,' 'it is evident that') used to convey the idea of objectivity. Obviously, a prefatory note should explain why non-ostensive language will be used in the text; for otherwise the reader may think that the writer lacks confidence in his or her findings. It may likewise be useful to restrict the use of verbs in the indicative mood, since this conveys a sense of certainty that an incontrovertible deductive inference is being made.

When possible, the impersonal form may be alternated with the *first person singular or plural* (but in the latter case only when there is actually more than one writer, because the rhetorical device 'we' – often used by politicians – enables the researcher to transform his or her personal belief into a collective assertion). By writing 'I' or 'we,' researchers declare that the interpretations being made are *personal*: they are not the only ones possible, nor the only correct readings of the data. As the American anthropologist Harry F. Wolcott suggests,

> unless absolutely forbidden to do so by a stuffy editor or dissertation committee, write in the first person. Put yourself squarely in the scene, but don't take center stage. The world does not need more sentences of the sort that begin 'It appears to this writer . . . ' or 'What is being said here' . . . Try to avoid wordiness, passive or convoluted constructions, long words and pompous phrases (1990: 47).

The use of the first person can be accompanied by verbs revealing the presence of an author behind the text (Geertz, 1988). For this purpose, in order to avoid producing a realist narrative, expressions such as 'we believe that,' 'it appeared to us,' 'we think' can usefully preface the researchers' assertions.

Moreover, the indicative mood of verbs can be replaced with conditional forms conveying that the ethnographer's statements are uncertain, arguable or tentative. Or if the indicative mood is required, it can be used with verbs like 'seem,' 'appear,' 'look like,' rather than the verb 'to be.' This verb, which often semantically replaces 'to exist,' can be prefaced with modal auxiliaries ('can' and 'must'), which attenuate the sense of absolute certainty.

Adverbs of assertion ('in fact,' 'naturally,' 'exactly,' 'certainly,' 'undoubtedly,' 'specifically,' 'finally,' 'absolutely,' 'perfectly' and 'conclusively') can be replaced with adverbs of doubt ('perhaps,' 'probably,' largely,' 'approximately' and 'presumably'). Assertive terms like 'reality,' 'to discover,' 'to show,' 'to reveal,' 'to demonstrate,' 'to prove,' 'evidence,' 'truth,' 'true,' 'facts,' and 'given' can be used more parsimoniously and with greater caution, or replaced with 'document,' 'events,' 'phenomena,' 'information,' 'result' and 'interpret'.

One should avoid drawing outright 'conclusions' because, from the epistemological point of view, research does not 'conclude' but is only 'discontinued' according to a researcher's purposes and practical circumstances.

To all appearances, these literary forms are minor stratagems that do not affect the substance of the text. Instead, by modifying our vocabulary, they guide us in the transition from assertive language to a more tentative style.

Finally, if you submit your article to a journal published in the Commonwealth, the bibliography should not cite texts that have appeared in a language other than English, because this will reveal that you probably do not belong to one of the Commonwealth countries. The majority of the social scientists in those countries, in fact, very rarely cite publications not written in English. So your behavior will make the blind review more 'sighted.' Do so afterwards, when your article has been accepted.

EXERCISE 15.3

Look at the extracts in Exercise 3.8 from Becker, Goffman and Sudnow. Consider the following:
- The ways which the three authors document their statements. What rhetorical strategies do they use?
- How do they construct the authority of the ethnographic text?
- How do they construct its plausibility?
- What information do they give about the conditions in which the findings were produced?
- What strategies do they use to persuade the reader?
- What is the degree of detail and precision of their accounts?
- What purpose is the text supposed to serve?

15.5 Concluding remarks

Although we live in an age of blurred genres, a scientific text is not a novel. It is not so for many of the reasons examined in this chapter. But in regard to only the most structural ones, it should be borne in mind that the publishing houses that handle novels do not usually publish scientific texts. Yet reading novels can be of enormous help in writing scientific texts. As Silverman suggests,

> to do ethnography you don't need to enjoy reading novels of this kind but it certainly helps. At the very least, you will need to appreciate the value (and, ultimately, the beauty) of the fine details of mundane existence (Silverman, 2007: 11).

We often come across articles and books written in contorted and impenetrable prose; or in which the hypotheses and theories are poorly expounded, or the reasoning and explanations are convoluted. Instead, those who have read widely, preferably authors like Ernest Hemingway, Graham Greene, Ian McEwan, Paul Auster, Winfred G. Sebald, are also able to write well-constructed, clear, and convincing texts. So . . . read, read, read!

KEY POINTS

- If research results are to reach a wider audience, they must take the form of a written text.
- Social scientists must constantly deal with at least two audiences: their colleagues, and readers who identify with the participants.
- It is advisable to start writing straight away, without waiting until the research has nearly concluded. Writing helps you to think; it trains you in communicating with future audiences; it forces you to analyze the data constantly and recursively.
- There are at least three main types of narrative: realist, processual and reflexive.
- The most widespread forms of processual narrative are the *dialogue*, the *diary, sociological introspection* and *heteroglossia*.
- The processual author introduces introspection into his or her texts; the reflexive author instead introduces accountability.
- Any attempt to describe a culture with the interpretative categories of the ethnographer is always a betrayal. A necessary betrayal, though, because reality does not have its own language.
- The new narrative forms (processual and narrative) use novel literary forms and rhetorical devices.
- Innovative metaphors, analogies and metonyms are the most powerful devices to convey new theories and approaches.
- If you want to write in an effective and comprehensible way, reading good modern fiction will certainly be of help.

KEY TERMS

Analogy
(see pp.299–300)

A rhetorical figure which establishes a similarity between two dissimilar objects or facts. This cognitive process replaces comparison (using 'like') with identity (removing 'like'). For example, rather than saying 'AIDS is like a plague,' one says 'AIDS is a plague.' Note that these two apparently similar expressions have different effects. In the former we still perceive two distinct objects (AIDS and plague), but in the latter a single object.

Linguistic turn
(see pp. 299–300)

The view that language 'constitutes' reality.

Literary turn
(see pp. 300–1)

The advent of *new literary* experimental forms, including ironic texts, the play, the limerick, the parody, the parable, the dialogue and so on.

Literate culture
(see p. 286)

A culture where writing and printing are of fundamental importance.

Metaphor
(see pp. 299–300)

Replacement of one term with a figurative one following a transposition of images. In everyday language we frequently use expressions like 'I devoured the book' (as if I had eaten it). Of course, we can say 'I read the book with great interest,' but metaphors are handier and more expressive: that is, they convey our thoughts more immediately.

Metonymy
(see pp. 299–300)

A rhetorical figure which consists in reversing the roles of the referents, for example using the name of the container for the content ('drink a bottle'), the material for the object ('pumping iron'), the place of production or origin for the thing produced ('a bottle of Chianti'), the abstract for the concrete ('elude surveillance'), the brand for the content ('drink Guinness'), the author for his output ('read Kant').

Model Reader
(see p. 289)

Not the actual reader 'in flesh and blood' but the reader-type, an abstract role. An imaginary audience in whose regard the ethnographer makes specific stylistic choices in order to communicate effectively.

New rhetoric
(see pp. 300–2)

The study of discursive techniques that aim to provoke or to increase the adherence of minds to the theses put forward.

Oral culture
(see p. 286)

An illiterate culture.

RECOMMENDED READING

For undergraduates:
Silverman, David (2006)

For graduates:
Czarniawska, Barbara (2004)
Loseke, Donileen R. and Cahill, E. S (2004)

For advanced researchers:
Denzin, Norman (2007)

SELF-EVALUATION TEST

Are you ready for the next chapter? Check your knowledge by answering the following open-ended questions:

1. Why do we have to write?
2. What is meant by the expression 'paper cultures'?
3. The French sociologist Edgar Morin has recently said that the introduction of semiotics in schools has had disastrous effects: the grind of deconstructing texts, dissecting them to reveal stylist and rhetorical devices, has made students lose the interest and pleasure of reading. What do you think? Has it happened to you?
4. If you had to write a research report, which of the three narrative forms (realistic, processual or reflexive) would you choose? Why?
5. Those who criticize post-colonial anthropology argue that it has replaced the 'point of view of the native' with 'the point of view of the anthropologist.' Do you agree? Why?
6. There are those who argue that there is little difference between processual and reflexive narrative. What do you think?
7. Others maintain that the reflexive style is losing ground. The realistic style is much more effective and will never be ousted. What do you think?

Notes

1 In many countries there is a close connection between research and funding. Consequently, research topics are chosen less according to the interests of the researchers than according to the availability of grants, the pressures applied by governmental institutions, and the ruthless ambitions of some researchers who, for this purpose, choose intriguing or fashionable topics that can rapidly boost their reputations.

2 Belonging to the structuralist and poststructuralist tradition are, amongst others, the American philosopher Judith Butler, the French psychoanalyst and philosopher Luce Irigaray, the Bulgarian-French philosopher and literary critic Julia Kristeva, and the French philosopher Jacques Derrida.

Leaving the Field

16.1 Introduction

One of the most neglected problems in the literature on ethnography is how to leave the field. When we engage in an interaction, there are rituals and strategies with which to begin that interaction, keep it going, and then conclude it. For instance, conversation analysts have thoroughly studied such strategies in telephone interaction. By contrast, the literature on the ethnography comprises a huge amount of discussion on how to enter and live in the field, but it says very little about the process of disengagement.

16.2 Take the money and run

This neglect is very suspicious. It is probably due to the predatory mentality still prevalent among ethnographers and social researchers in general. They pay close attention to how to collect the data, but once they have filled their bags, they escape with the loot, never to be seen again.

Although the 'grab it and run' attitude is more common when methodologies like the survey and the discursive interview are used, ethnographers are not exempt from criticism. Only few of them reflect on the best way to leave the field; care about the feelings of the participants; and maintain relations with them after the research has finished. More prevalent instead is the 'colonial' attitude which exploits the informant like a mine (of information) and the participants as fruit trees.

This attitude can also have harmful consequences because it 'may strongly affect the efforts of future investigators in the same or similar settings' (Gallmeier, 1983). It raises the problem of the 'ecological heritage' (see 8.9): that is, the ethnographer's moral duty not to 'burn' the field for subsequent research.

The good news is that this attitude is changing and that there is a flourishing of studies that draw attention to the issue. These studies mainly derive from action-research, critical ethnography (see 4.2) and community studies.

16.3 When to go: Between duty and pleasure

When is the right moment to leave the field? The answer is easy enough for some methodologies, but more complicated for ethnography. Survey researchers leave the field (assuming that they have ever entered it, given that it is usually only visited by the interviewers) when they have collected the requisite number of questionnaires. Researchers who work with discursive interviews do more or less the same thing (though they may sometimes return for extra interviews). Experimenters conclude their research when they have fulfilled their research designs. Finally, in action-research the budget governs the timetable. But in ethnographic research everything is vaguer, more rarefied, subjective. This is why the question 'how do I know when it is time to leave' is anything but banal. Indeed, although the obvious answer is 'when enough data have been collected to sufficiently answer preexisting or emergent questions' (Snow, 1980: 101), as Snow himself shows, matters are otherwise.

16.3.1 When we have to go

Deciding when to leave the field is easy when . . . events take the decision for us. There are various reasons that may oblige us to conclude our presence in the field.

A first set of reasons are institutional: our grant has finished, our sabbatical leave is over, or we have no more time available and we must return to our institutional duties (teaching, publishing, co-ordinating, organizing events, etc.).

A second possible set of precipitants are interpersonal, 'such as role conflict between role of researcher and the role of spouse or parent' (Snow, 1980: 107). Because fieldwork is time-consuming, our families may become tired of not seeing us at weekends, in the evenings or holidays. Even worse is if they have been 'deported' to another country, far from friends and the comforts of home, to be close to you during months of fieldwork.

Finally, a third group of reasons are intrapersonal, 'such as sheer mental and physical exhaustion' (Snow, 1980: 107). It is irksome for your families to be deprived of your presence, it can be for you as well. Moreover, always being 'on stage' (see 7.3) and having to perform the role of researcher is fatiguing as time wears on. So that at a certain point you feel a physical need to close with the fieldwork and go back to ordinary routine, at least for a while:

According to Snow, whether these:

> pragmatic constraints and pressures . . . constitute the major reasons for
> disengagements in most field studies is difficult to say. Social scientists tend
> to be conspicuously mute about such matters . . . [However] I suspect that
> the[se] kinds of factors . . . are operative in most studies' (1980: 107–8).

16.3.2 When we can decide when to go

If we can decide when to leave the field, the music changes and everything
becomes even more . . . complicated. Yes, indeed. For although (apparently)
more rigorous criteria or more rigorous guidelines take over, they are not always
easy to interpret.

The first of them can be called 'taken-for-grantedness' (Snow, 1980: 102).
It consists of leaving the field when the organization or the group studied
begins to be taken for granted, in the sense that they no longer appear to us as
problematic, unfamiliar or interesting.

The second criterion is what Glaser and Strauss (1967: 61) call 'theoretical
saturation.' This expression denotes the point in the research process when no
new data is shedding any further light on the features of the category, group or
situation studied. Saturation is signaled by persistent observation of what is
already known, and by repetitive fieldnotes.

Glaser and Strauss cite a third criterion: what we may call 'heightened
confidence.' The researcher is nearing the end of his or her research when

> he is convinced that his conceptual framework forms a systematic theory, that
> it is a reasonably accurate statement of matters studied, that it is couched in a
> form possible for others to use in studying a similar area, and that he can
> publish his results with confidence (1967: 224–5).

These guidelines are very clear and are certainly to be borne in mind when one
decides when to leave the field. However, research is not always blessed
with simplicity and linearity. So that these guidelines are not always easily
implemented. When can we say, with reasonable certainty, that everything is by
now familiar or repetitive, or that we have a systematic theory to hand? Much
more often, even at the end of our research, we continue to find contradictory
data, or deviant instances which we still cannot explain satisfactorily. This compels the ethnographer to stay longer than he or she should in the field to collect
new data, further data, and yet more data besides. This attitude Glaser and
Strauss have aptly termed 'compulsive scientism' (1967: 227–8) and it induces
the ethnographer to collect much more data than he or she is then able to analyze (see 12.3). Instead, to my knowledge, the best researchers are those who
have conducted only a few researches (four or five) in their lifetimes, done them
well, and then analyzed the data for many years thereafter!

16.4 How to leave: Exit strategies

Whether our departure from the field is decided by us, or whether it is made
necessary by pragmatic constraints and pressures, in both cases we must devise
strategies to withdraw with professional dignity and honor. As we do so,
however, we may come up against various obstacles against our disengagement.

The first of them may be the fieldworker's close relationship with his or her informants. This is more typical of anthropologists, who are often totally immersed in the field and in the village community where they conduct their research.

If the participants have been very co-operative and the ethnographer has developed intense relations with them (or has even identified with the group), another obstacle is a sense of indebtedness or obligation. Especially if the participants suffer from hardship or social deprivation, leaving them may seem a 'betrayal'; or worse an 'exploitation' of people who have been simply used, or abused, as an exotic experience to recount to one's colleagues.

But leave-taking is certainly not always warm embraces and fond farewells. At times, the participants are very glad to see the back of the ethnographer – especially if he or she never integrated with them well, or if they have found his or her presence tiresome.

In any case, just as a theater actor takes care over the details of his or her exit from the stage at the end of a performance, so the ethnographer should carefully prepare his or her exit strategy. The literature is unfortunately not a great deal of help here, and a practical approach to the problem is far from available.

If the researcher has formed a positive relationship with the participants and informants, he or she can (some weeks previously) thematize his or her departure so as to prepare them for it. In some cases the researcher can help the participants examine and allow them to show their feelings about his or her departure, in keeping with the reciprocity and symmetry that should preside over the entire research process (see 8.6). The promise of feedback, or soft or light consultation, so that the participants too can benefit from the research results may also be useful. Another way to take one's leave is to promise to keep in touch, to continue the relationship at a distance.

When saying goodbye, one can also summarize what has happened during the fieldwork, identify positive aspects of the relationship with the participants, or express one's feelings about leaving them. If the researcher has had one informant in particular, he or she may give them a card or a photograph.

If the researcher makes any promises, for instance that he or she will come back to see the participants, or that the research will resume in the future, those promises should be kept, for they may be very important to the persons concerned. If it is uncertain that promises can be kept, they should not be made, so that any future visit will come as a pleasant surprise.

16.5 Keep in touch

There are many ways to keep in touch, and they are conditioned by various factors. At times, the relationship with participants is maintained out of scientific necessity, as in the case of longitudinal research. For example, Corsaro (1996) conducted a comparative longitudinal ethnography to understand children's transition from kindergarten to elementary school. Hence he periodically returned to the kindergartens which he had previously observed so that he could see the changes in both the children and the organization. Gallmeier (1983), who followed group of minor-league hockey players for a season, obtained one of his informant's address books. In this way he was subsequently able to contact the players and find out how their careers had progressed, and what social events had intervened. The informant also suggested that Gallmeier subscribe to *Hockey News* so that he could keep abreast of events in the world of hockey. He discovered that this publication performed a valuable networking function.

Keeping in touch is the best strategy to enable a return to the 'scene of the crime.'

16.6 Back to the field: Revisiting sites

Returning to ethnographic places is an ambivalent experience. On the one hand, seeing a familiar environment again is pleasurable; on the other, it may provoke a sense of extraneousness. The experience of Alessandro Duranti exemplifies the former case. From Los Angeles he returned to Falefâ (Samoa) ten years after his last fieldwork because of a tragic event: the funeral of the wife of Fa'atau'oloa Mauala, the Protestant pastor of the community and Duranti's principal informant. Unlike on previous occasions, 'the decision to depart was therefore, this time, dictated by affects and not by the logic of the research' (2002: 166). The inhabitants of the village were very moved by his presence at the funeral:

> everybody commented that my return for the funeral was true proof of my compassion (*alofa*) and also of the genuineness of my commitment to the 'Samoan family' and the religious congregation . . . I was their *pâlagi*, their foreigner who had not only studied them but now gave proof of compassion and respect, as required by such an important event as the funeral of their pastor's wife (2002: 167 and 177).

Gallmeier instead experienced extraneousness. When he returned to visit the hockey team the next season, he found some 'old' participants but also numerous new faces – as is typical of all sports teams, which must constantly renew themselves. Gallmeier consequently felt embarrassed, detached, and once again a stranger: 'the rapport I had worked so hard to develop was now missing' (1983: 405–6).

But returning to past ethnographic placements is an experience which has, above all, a *theoretical* significance. As Michael Burawoy argues, revisiting is the principal means to emancipate ethnography 'from the eternal present':

> sociologist-ethnographers, grounded theorists in particular . . . too often they remain trapped in the contemporary, riveted to and contained in their sites, from where they racket questions of historical change, social processes, wider contexts, theoretical traditions, as well as their own relation to the people they study (2003: 646).

Burawoy distinguishes the ethnographic revisit from other similar forms, viz.:

> *ethnographic reanalysis*, which involves the interrogation of already existing ethnography *without* any further field work . . . [the] *ethnographic update*, which brings an earlier study up to the present but does not reengage it . . ., [or the] *replication*, [which] is concerned with minimizing intervention to control research conditions and with minimizing the diversity of cases to secure the constancy of findings (2003: 646–7).

CASE STUDY
The focused revisit

Burawoy (1979) revisited a factory studied by the American interactionist sociologist of organization Donald Roy. He was:

> one of the great ethnographers of the Chicago School. Roy (1952) studied Geer Company in 1944–45, and I studied that same factory 30 years later in 1974–75, after it had become the engine division of Allied Corporation. Like Roy I was employed as a machine operator. For both of us it was a source of income as well as our dissertation field work . . . I discovered, indeed, a series of small but significant changes in the factory. First, the old authoritarian relation between management and workers was dissipated. This change was marked by the disappearance of the 'time and study men', who would clock operators' jobs when their backs were turned, in pursuit of piece rates that could be tightened. Second, if vertical tension had relaxed, horizontal conflicts had intensified. Instead of the collusion between operators and auxiliary workers that Roy described, I observed hostility and antagonism. Truck drivers, inspectors, crib attendants were the bane of my life (Burawoy, 2003: 650–1).

According to Burawoy (2003: 651–3), discrepancies between the findings of ethnographies conducted in different historical periods can be attributed to four types of differences, differences in:

(1) the relationship of ethnographer with participants,
(2) theory brought to the field by the researcher (Roy used the improvement of human relations theory, while Burawoy is Marxist),
(3) internal processes within the field site itself, as organizational and managerial changes, or
(4) forces external to field sites, like absorption of factories into the monopoly sector and secular national shifts in industrial relations.

For these reasons an *ethnographic revisit* can never be considered a replication.

In conclusion, the merit of long-term or diachronic field research in which ethnographers, working either as individuals or in a team, regularly revisit the field over many years (at least more than ten), in its endeavor to understand historical changes and continuities inevitably evades synchronic analysis.

16.7 Concluding remarks

Leaving the field is anything but an automatic procedure with no significant methodological aspects. On the contrary, it is a delicate operation that must be conducted with care. Especially if the intention is to return to the same field again later.

The return is not a simple journey through nostalgia. It may also be:

> an experience that reopens the interpretative horizon fixed in the memory and in our publications, undermining not so much the basis of our knowledge (commitment in the work of observing and documenting behaviors cannot be avoided or taken for granted) as some of the epistemological and ontological presuppositions that drive research in the social sciences (Duranti, 2002: 179).

Therefore, revisiting an ethnographic site is an opportunity to reformulate hypotheses and theories in more historical and less ephemeral terms.

KEY POINTS

- To avoid the 'colonial' mentality of simple exploitation of informants and participants, the ethnographer should carefully consider how to leave the field.
- Besides contingent ethical issues, leaving the field incurs the problem of the 'ecological heritage': the moral duty not to 'burn' the field for subsequent research by colleagues.
- There are two logics (often complementary) guiding the disengagement procedure: one is theoretical (taken-for-grantedness, saturation and heightened confidence), the other more pragmatic (institutional, interpersonal, and intrapersonal constraints and pressures).
- Because disengagement is not only a methodological and ethical problem but an emotional one as well, the fieldworker must devise suitable exit strategies.
- These strategies are particularly useful if the ethnographer intends to return to the field in the future.
- Although revisiting sites is a practice still relatively rare in sociology (but much more frequent in anthropology), it may be crucial if ethnography is to be emancipated 'from the eternal present' so that its findings can be framed within historical changes and wider contexts.

KEY TERMS

Compulsive scientism (see p. 308)	Obsessive insecurity about the consistency of one's data and findings. It induces researchers to stay longer than they should in the field and collect much more data than they are able to analyze.
Disengagement (see pp. 306–8)	Process by which the ethnographer disengages from the field, and in particular from informants and participants.
Exit strategy (see pp. 308–9)	An interactional and methodological technique for disengagement.

Revisiting sites (see pp. 310–1)	Returning to the places of previous ethnography.
Saturation (see p. 308)	The point in the research process when no new data can shed any further light on the features of the category, group or situation studied. Signals of saturation are persisting observation of what is already known and repetitive field notes.

RECOMMENDED READING

For undergraduates:
Whyte, William F. (1993)

For graduates:
Snow, David (1980)

For advanced researchers:
Burawoy, Michael (2003)

SELF-EVALUATION TEST

Check your knowledge by answering the following open-ended questions:
1. Burawoy criticizes contemporary ethnography for being uninterested in the historical and social processes that constitute the field observed. Do you agree? If so, why?
2. What is the most awkward aspect of disengagement?
3. What are the ethical issues involved in leaving the field?
4. If you had to go into the field with your family or partner, what would you do to make the research period less tedious for them, and their presence less stressful for yourself?

The 'Observation Society':
A Chance for Applied Ethnography

LEARNING OBJECTIVES

- To understand the connections between science and society in regard to observation.

- To be able to discuss a new tendency in contemporary societies: the observation society.

- To survey the main observational methods used in the professions.

- To gain an overview of the employment opportunities offered by ethnographic methodology.

17.1 Introduction

As 2.4 has shown more clearly, we acquire knowledge through our senses. Sight is one of these senses, and it is the basis of observation; and this in its turn is the basis of ethnography.

Watching, seeing, observing and ethnographing are obviously not the same things, even though they are interconnected. Ethnographing is certainly the most complex of these activities because it requires us not only to observe, but also to do so systematically (see Chapters 9 and 10), while also taking notes on our observations using specific narrative and stylistic techniques (see Chapter 11). Nor are watching and seeing the same things: the former is a passive activity (as when we watch television), while the latter is a more active one which involves recognition and discovery.

Evident from even these brief remarks is that observation is primarily a common-sense activity which only subsequently becomes scientific. In both spheres (those of common sense and science) observation has evolved with its own techniques. The aim of this chapter is to provide an overview of the observational techniques on which certain professions in contemporary society are grounded. Before it does so, however, discussion is required of how society is evolving in relation to observation.

17.2 From the interview society to the observation society

Many authors maintain that we live in a postmodern society. Nevertheless, still surviving are elements and aspects of modern and pre-modern society. Indeed, certain magical beliefs, several religious faiths, and numerous cultural attitudes, like scientism, masculinism and, in general, the absolutism of values (typical of modern and pre-modern societies), continue to coexist and interact with the components of postmodern society. One may likewise argue that we are now entering the 'observation society,' but this coexists with two other societies: that of the interview, and that of the conversation.

17.2.1 The interview society
Atkinson and Silverman (1997) have acutely noted that we live in an 'interview society,' a society in which interviewing has become a fundamental activity, and interviews seem to have become crucial for people to make sense of their lives. On the one hand, the interview (in the broad sense) is today one of the most widespread social forms of information-gathering: policemen, doctors, shop assistants, judges, social workers, managers, teachers, psychotherapists, priests, journalists, personnel recruiters and call-center operators all engage in some form of interviewing in their routine work. On the other hand, radio and television constantly and invasively transmit the expression (sometimes the flaunting) of the self into our homes: talk shows, variety shows, documentaries, the sound-bites elicited at the end of sports events, or the emotions stolen from victims at the scene of tragedies or disasters.

The ubiquity of the interview can be explained (reflexively) by the fact that most social research is based on the survey and the discursive interview, both of which (although very different in other respects) use the same technique to gather information: asking questions. Foucault (1975) pointed out that the interview shares many features with the Catholic confession and the psychoanalytic interview. Hence the interview and society are so mutually constitutive that we can state that we now live in an 'interview society.'

The 'interview society' is certainly the dominant societal model. However, it is not the only one, for there are other social forms which exist in parallel with it and which may, in the future, supersede it: to mention only two, the 'conversation society' and the 'observation society.'

17.2.2 The conversation society
As regards the conversation society, for some time notable in the press, and to a lesser extent on television, there has been an increasingly frequent presence of transcripts. These are not the products of interviews but of naturally occurring talk, and they are derived from overt recordings or from wire-taps (i.e. covert recordings). The general public grows increasingly wary and worried that private conversations may be listened to and recorded.

Overt recordings are made by 'black boxes' installed in aircraft, trains, ships, operating theaters – and in the future in private cars as well – to record data during movement and to preserve them. A black box is able to resist extremely high pressures and temperatures, and in the event of an accident the information which it contains is conserved intact. Black boxes are used mainly to conduct inquiries after crashes, when 'what really happened' is determined from the conversation recorded. Hence it is no exaggeration to say that in this case talk constructs the reality.

Besides overt recordings, numerous scandals and crimes are detected by covert recordings (ordered by the judicial authorities) obtained from fixed and mobile telephones or by means of concealed bugs and microphones (a thriving business). These forms of eavesdropping are increasingly widespread: indeed, it has been discovered that there exists a worldwide surveillance system (called ECHELON) created by a number of countries during the Cold War and now run by the United States, the United Kingdom, Australia, Canada and New Zealand.

17.3 The observation society

Besides interceptions, technological advances have made observation technologies more pervasive and flexible. Wherever we go (banks, shops, stadiums, parks, the streets or the subway) there is always a television camera ready to film our actions (unbeknownst to us). And camera phones, veritable digital eyes which capture the fleeting moment, which now support the current fashion for making video recordings of even the most personal and intimate situations and posting them on the internet. Or the trend to log on to webcams pointed at city streets, monuments, landscapes, plants, birds' nests (www.birdcam.it), coffee pots, maturing cheeses (www.cheddarvision.tv), freshly painted walls (www.watching-paint-dry.com), etc., to observe movements, developments and changes. There is the fad of webcams worn by people so that they can lead us virtually through their everyday lives (www.justin.tv). These are not minor eccentricities but websites visited by millions of people around the world.

Observing and being observed are two important features of contemporary Western societies. By means of observation, control can be maintained over a territory and its inhabitants, intimate behaviors can be spied upon (voyeurism), and actions deemed harmful can be prevented. Finally, there is an increasing demand in various sectors of society – from marketing to security, television to the fashion industry – for observation and ethnography. All of which suggests that ours is becoming an observation society.

17.4 The prototype of the 'observation society': The reality show

A reality show is a genre of television program which broadcasts dramatic and humorous situations which are not scripted, but rather enacted by the protagonists exactly as if they were part of their real lives.

The most interesting aspect of such programs is that they seem entirely unsuited to television. They unfold slowly (as does everyday life), and they feature everyday routines in which, for hours on end, nothing significant happens. Yet they have been the most important televisual novelty of the 2000s.

Their main characteristic is that they render people's everyday private lives public: in fact, documentaries and non-fiction programs like news bulletins and sports broadcasts are not usually classified as reality shows.

17.4.1 The origins of reality television

Although reality shows became unexpectedly popular towards the end of the 1990s, they had always been present in television schedules. The earliest television programs featuring people in unscripted situations date back to the 1940s. First broadcast in 1948, Allen Funt's *Candid Camera* depicted unsuspecting members of the public as they reacted to hoaxes perpetrated upon them. The program has been called the 'granddaddy of the reality TV genre.'

The watershed year – which in itself had little to do with reality shows but precluded the birth of a tendency – was 1969: between 20 and 21 July of that year two astronauts landed on the Moon, and 28 consecutive hours of worldwide telecasting were watched by more than 500 million people.

Since the 1970s we have witnessed the growth and then the explosion of reality shows in hundreds of countries around the globe.

Some commentators have maintained that the term 'reality television' is an inaccurate description of several styles of program included in the genre. In competition-based programs and other special-living-environment shows, the format of the show is designed, and the activities and the environment are controlled, to create a completely fabricated world in which the competition takes place. However, it is not authenticity that is of interest to us here, but rather the impact of these programs on society. For they are among the factors responsible for increasing interest in observation and the growing demand for ethnography.

EXERCISE 17.1

Watch a reality show. Try to understand why a company producing goods for the mass market would be very interested in using ethnography methodology for market research. Then discuss what you think with your classmates.

17.5 The new demand for ethnography and the professions of observation

Several professions are based on observation. Although less numerous than interview-based ones (see 17.2), some of these 'ethnography' professions are now proliferating and seem bound to increase even further.

17.5.1 New tools for marketing: Commercial ethnography

The success of reality television is beginning to impact on the marketing business. It is doing so, on the one hand, in mass marketing (i.e. the marketing of a product to a wide audience), and on the other hand, in market research institutes, which are constantly in search of new survey techniques. Companies producing mass consumption goods increasingly endeavor to enter the heads of consumers, to identify the meanings they attribute to goods and to the act of consuming, and to study their everyday behaviors. On the wave of reality television's success, they believe that all this can be done by means of ethnographic research. The new slogan seems to be *in vivo*, as opposed to *in vitro* and *in silico*. In other words, if the intent is to discover consumers' relationships with, say, biscuits, market researchers must go into people's homes and watch them eat breakfast: so that there, at the table, amid the early morning chaos, they can understand consumption motivators and the social uses of biscuits. Companies are increasingly dissatisfied with consumer panels or focus groups. These were the protagonists of market research in the 1980s and 1990s, but they are now in decline because their results are regarded as too superficial. Instead, ethnography is rightly or wrongly viewed as a new approach able to pick up contextual clues and unarticulated attitudes which elude the other methodologies.

Commercial ethnography is a tool with which to understand how products and people interact. It enables companies to engage with people in their 'natural' settings, to gather information about environments and cultures, to acquire concrete and actionable recommendations on how to improve both products and processes, and to gain insights into the so-called 'lived experience' and behavior of consumers.

The mystery shopper technique and its siblings

'Mystery shopping' means making purchases with one's identity disguised or concealed. However, the technique originally had nothing to do with shopping, but was used by private investigators to identify and prevent employee theft, especially in banks and retail stores.

The expression was coined only later, in the 1940s, by American consultants, who began using the technique to assess customer satisfaction and workplace conditions (with particular regard to health and safety issues). Since the advent of the 'services society,' mystery shopping has become a method to assess any kind of service. It works substantially as follows: a company which sells products (usually a large-scale retailer) wants to monitor how its sales personnel (both its own employees and franchisers) deal with customers. It commissions a market research company to visit its stores and to draw up a report. The market research company sends out a series of evaluators called 'mystery shoppers.' Pretending to be customers, these people visit the retail stores and go through all the stages of the typical shopping experience, from entry to the store to exit from it: they ask for information and help, and in some cases also make purchases. The researcher then compiles an evaluation form.

Mystery shopping is a highly effective tool with which to measure the performance of a store's sales staff; and it is probably the only technique simultaneously able to assess customer satisfaction and to identify the causes of such satisfaction – or conversely dissatisfaction. Hence, it may open new scenarios in enhancing customer loyalty.

There are various kinds of mystery evaluation, according to the field concerned:

- *Mystery shopper*: stores and catering establishments;

- *Mystery guest*: transport services (subways, local and national trains, airline companies) or the hospitality industry (hotels, restaurants, cruises);
- *Mystery client*: banks, insurance companies, postal services, car dealers, petroleum industry and large-scale retailers;
- *Mystery caller*: telephone customer services (call centers);
- *Competitive shops*: customer service and prices of competitors;
- *Trader evaluation*: companies distributing products and services to evaluate the loyalty of their dealers;
- *Sales performance evaluation*: assessment of the sales staff's ability to understand customer needs, propose solutions and conclude sales;
- *Internet angels*: customer care service for internet shoppers;
- *Mystery web*: evaluation of websites;
- *Mystery patient*: health care, clinics and hospitals;
- *Mystery public*: schools and universities – municipalities to evaluate compliance with supply contracts; and
- *Mystery inspector*: compliance with HACCP (Hazard Analysis Critical Control Point), etc., health and safety regulations.

EXERCISE 17.2

Watch the 1988 movie *Big* directed by Penny Marshall. At a certain point the movie introduces MacMillan (a character played by Robert Loggia), a toy manufacturer. While inspecting one of his stores, MacMillan meets Josh (played by Tom Hanks), a lowly employee who loves trying out the toys on sale. MacMillan is struck by Josh's childlike enthusiasm – he is in fact a child trapped in an adult's body – and gives him a new job, that of testing toys all day long, because he wants to discover 'what the marketing reports don't say.' With his insight into what sells to children, Josh quickly ascends the corporate hierarchy. The company also sets up a room where children can play with the prototypes of new toys, while being observed by the company's marketing experts – an extension of the focus group method.

When you have watched these scenes, can you say which things overlooked by the marketing reports are revealed by the observation methodology?

17.5.2 At the service of the fashion industry: The cool-hunter

Some years ago a new type of professional arose midway between marketing and fashion: the 'cool-hunter,' whose task is to spot emerging trends and translate them into innovative and marketable ideas. Cool-hunters operate at the interface between production and consumption. Cameras around their necks, with good powers of observation and creativity, they prowl the streets and clubs collecting flyers, exhibition and show programs, taking photographs, visiting markets, art galleries and shops, sampling food, and trying out new gadgets likely to become 'hip.' In short, cool-hunting is a profession (generally part-time) based on intuition and the ability to observe and interpret cultural and social trends.

The reports filed by the cool-hunters are used by companies to define their marketing strategies.

There are now courses and masters programs in cool-hunting. Those interested can obtain information from websites like www.coolhunting.com.

17.5.3 From management studies to action-research: Shadowing and other techniques

There is another broad area of research and study that uses techniques derived from observation and ethnography. It comprises diverse and interweaving disciplines: management studies, clinical sociology, organizational studies, evaluation research, action-research, and so on. There follows a brief survey of the main ethnography methods used by these disciplines.

The shadowing technique

Shadowing means following (like a shadow) a particular person in his or her natural environment while observing (without intervening in) his or her actions and interactions, how he or she does business, and so on. Because shadowing requires full disclosure of the researcher's presence and interests, it should be distinguished from other powerful field methods, such as eavesdropping and lurking (see Czarniawska, 2007).

This method has spread into various sectors (education, urban studies, consumer studies, etc.), in which management studies have somewhat altered its nature. It is used to teach novices their jobs more rapidly; to detect discrimination in work teams of executive managers; and to implement equal opportunities policies. The purpose of shadowing is to give a consultant access to people working in particular fields, so that he or she can watch them in their everyday settings. In a shadowing assignment, the observer does not do actual work, but watches the other person doing it. Shadowing provides the following benefits:

- an opportunity to watch someone 'in action';
- an opportunity to put questions to someone while they are actually working; and
- an opportunity for the consultant to check some of his or her assumptions about the field of work in question.

The observer will learn more about the job, the company and the industry; and he or she will also develop new network contacts.

EXERCISE 17.3

Read Truman Capote's *A Day's Work* (1975) or David Lodge's *Nice Work* (1988).
What did the shadowers in these books learn about the people they observed? Make a list of the items of knowledge and beliefs that they acquired from them.

17.5.4 Ergonomics, computer science, information and communication technology

As we saw in 3.8, after World War II ergonomics shifted to the study of users in their natural environments, doing so in response to criticisms of research conducted in the laboratory (also called 'white room research'). In fact, performing a task – for example, cooking food using the prototype of a domestic appliance – in an artificial environment is very different from performing the same task in the kitchen at home. More recently, ethnography techniques have been used in the fields of computer science and information and communication technology (ICT). These sectors have developed various methods for the study of users in their natural environments, most notably *flanking* and *focused ethnography*.

Flanking

This technique has been borrowed from managerial methods to facilitate new job entry. In some work settings, a novice (for example, a newly-hired employee) flanks an expert. The same technique, albeit for different purposes, is used in the computer science field in order to improve a software program or to test a new release. A sample of users are assigned tasks which they must perform using the software in question. The users are flanked by researchers who observe their performance and take notes (usually with a checklist) of all their difficulties: poor visualization of commands, failure to understand symbols, inability to perform the task, etc. Flanking has proved extremely useful in revealing users' tacit knowledge, interactive strategies with the computer and modes of reasoning; and also in the design of user-centered softwares, that is, ones that solve problems rather than complicating procedures.

Focused ethnography

The expression 'focused ethnography' (FE) was coined by the German sociologist Hubert Knoblauch (2005) to denote a specific type of sociological ethnography adopted especially in applied research. Focused ethnography involves relatively short-term field visits, their short duration being off-set by the intensive use of audiovisual technologies for data collection and analysis. In certain respects, focused ethnography can be likened to the commercial ethnography discussed in 17.5.1. Focused ethnography is not concerned with groups, organizations or milieux, but with settings, situations and activities (or performance) of importance to the actors themselves. It focuses on the particular, that is, the details of situated performance as it occurs naturally in everyday social interactions. FE therefore typically analyzes structures and patterns of interaction, such as those involved in the co-ordination of work activities, in family arguments or in meetings.

The goal of focused ethnography is to acquire the background knowledge necessary to perform the activities in question. However, it does not tap into the cultural stock of knowledge, but acquires certain of its (partly embodied) elements relevant to the activity. On studying technological activities, the focus is only on those elements relevant to understanding of the practices involved in handling the technology.

17.5.5 Other professional observers

The practice of observation is widespread in many other sectors and professions, and also in hobbies:

- observing is commonplace in the natural sciences, especially astronomy and zoology, but also in ethology (mammals) and ornithology (birds – associated with which is the hobby of birdwatching or 'birding');
- in the leisure industry, there are numerous professionals who watch over our safety: for instance, the lifeguards at swimming pools, water parks, or private or public beaches;
- in the news world there are various types of activity (such as investigative, evaluative and tabloid journalism) that rely primarily on observation;
- in numerous sports, umpires, players and . . . spectators base their actions on what they see in the field;
- in the security industry police, vigilantes, bodyguards, prison guards and secret services agents make a lot of use of observation techniques (tailing, patrolling, infiltrating, security rounds, surveillance, etc.) to prevent and repress crime; and
- criminals and terrorists do likewise in their politics of destabilization.

EXERCISE 17.4

DISCOVERING YOUR PREFERENCES

This chapter has surveyed the principal methods of applied ethnography; now answer the following questions:
- Which of these methods do you like the most?
- Which of them do you think you would find easiest to use?
- Which of the professions discussed would you like to do?

17.6 Concluding remarks

The professions have always used observation to perform or to improve their work. Just as they have made use of the interview. However, the tendency to use observation has considerably increased in recent times, and it has been accompanied by the birth of new observation-based professions.

This tendency has now spread into the world of fiction. We know that literature has often anticipated the advent of social phenomena and trends; and this has happened in the case of sociology as well. Indeed, Park, one of the founders of the Chicago School, made great efforts to persuade social scientists to do in their discipline what writers like Émile Zola (see 3.2) had done in their novels: provide vivid, participatory and analytical descriptions of society's problems.

Today we are witnessing the return of a realist narrative to supersede the postmodern genre represented by Don DeLillo, Thomas Pynchon and Kurt Vonnegut.

It uses participant observation to investigate worlds and phenomena of which we have only indistinct impressions. Writers and journalists convey powerful social images which arouse our indignation much more so than many political pamphlets and sociological analyzes are able to do, reviving the tradition of urban studies which began with the Chicago School. For example, the American journalist and writer Robert Neuwirth, in *Shadow Cities: A Billion Squatters, A New Urban World* (2005), describes his experiences when living in four squatter communities in large cities (Rio de Janeiro, Nairobi, Mumbai and Istanbul), for several months in each. Another American journalist and writer, Marc Cooper, in *The Last Honest Place in America* (2005) conducts a fascinating analysis of the city of Las Vegas (where he lived for six months), considered to be the best place to understand the true soul of the contemporary United States. Or, to conclude this brief survey, a book by the American journalist Adrian Nicole LeBlanc, *Random Family: Love, Drugs, Trouble, and Coming of Age in the Bronx*, (2004) recounts her ten-year residence in that notorious New York ghetto.

As I have sought to show in this chapter, observation and ethnography are acquiring renewed vitality and importance, perhaps because of a certain disillusionment with other methodologies. The question is are we going to make the most of them?

KEY POINTS

- Watching, seeing, observing and ethnographing are not the same things, although they are interconnected activities.
- Ethnographing is certainly the most complex of these activities because it requires us, not only to observe, but also to do so systematically, and also to take notes on our observations using specific narrative and stylistic techniques.
- We live in an 'interview society.' However, there are signs that two other types of society are developing, and may supersede it: the 'conversation society' and the 'observation society.'
- In contemporary Western societies, observation is associated with diverse social forms and relations: control, domination, voyeurism and the 'spectacularization' of ordinary behavior.
- The reality show is the prototype of the observation society.
- Many sectors and professions use observation (in the place of, or jointly with, the survey and the discursive interview): for instance, marketing, fashion, leisure, journalism, security, crime, management, action research, ergonomics, computer science, information and communication technology.
- These sectors have also developed their own techniques of observation-based inquiry.

KEY TERMS

Birdwatching
(see p. 322)

Involves the observation and study of birds with the naked eye, or using optical devices, most commonly binoculars. Most birders or birdwatchers pursue the activity for recreational or social reasons, unlike ornithologists, who are concerned with the formal scientific study of birds.

Commercial ethnography
(see pp. 317–19)

Commercial ethnography is a tool with which to understand how products and people interact. It enables companies to engage with people in their 'natural' settings, to gather information about environments and cultures, to acquire concrete and implementable recommendations on how to improve both products and processes, to gain insights into the so-called 'lived experience' and behavior of consumers.

Conversation society
(see pp. 315–16)

Emerging alongside the interview society is a 'conversation society' where naturally occurring talk (drawn from overt recordings or covert interceptions) are collected. There is increasing concern that people's conversations are being listened to and recorded.

Cool–hunting
(see pp. 319–20)

Professional activity in the fashion field. It involves spotting trends and interpreting emerging styles, so that they can be translated into innovative and marketable ideas.

Flanking
(see p. 321)

Method where a researcher flanks the user of a software program, observing his or her performance and taking notes of difficulties.

Focused ethnography
(see p. 321)

A specific type of sociological ethnography adopted in applied research, especially. It involves relatively short-term field visits, their short duration being off-set by the intensive use of audiovisual technologies for data collection and analysis.

Interview society
(see p. 315)

Atkinson and Silverman (1997) have acutely noted that we live in an 'interview society,' a society in which interviewing has become a fundamental activity and interviews seem to have become crucial for people to make sense of their lives.

Investigative journalism
(see p. 322)

A kind of journalism in which reporters conduct in-depth investigations of a news story, often involving crime, political corruption, or some other form of scandalous behavior in order to uncover the truth.

Lifeguard
(see p. 322)

A profession responsible for the safety of users of water-based recreational facilities, such as swimming pools, water parks, or private or public beaches.

Mystery shopping (see pp. 318–19)	Technique used to evaluate service and the performance of human resources at a retail store.
Observation society (see p. 316)	Observing and being observed are two fundamental features of contemporary Western societies. Wherever we go, there is always a television camera or a camera phone ready to film our actions.
Reality show (see p. 316–17)	A genre of television program which broadcasts dramatic and humorous situations which are not scripted but instead enacted by the protagonists exactly as if they were (allegedly) part of their real lives.
Shadowing (see p. 320)	Following (like a shadow) a particular person in his or her natural environment while observing (without intervening in) his or her actions and interactions, how he or she does business, and so on. As shadowing requires full disclosure of the researcher's presence and interests, it should be distinguished from other powerful field methods, such as eavesdropping, lurking or 'keeping one's eyes peeled.'

RECOMMENDED READING

For undergraduates:
Ereaut, Gill (2004)

For graduates:
Chambers, Erve (2000)

For advanced researchers:
Jordan, Brigitte and Dalal, Brinda (2006)

SELF-EVALUATION TEST

Check your knowledge by answering the following open-ended questions:
1. Why is ethnography becoming so fashionable?
2. Is it correct to classify ethnography among interpretative methodologies?
3. Why may ethnography become an instrument of social control?
4. Are observation-based professions more common than interview-based ones?

Finale

If you have managed to reach the end of this book, you are now able to start your own research. However, there are two issues which students sometimes raise and which I have not yet mentioned:

- Can any topic at all be studied with ethnography?
- Is anyone eligible to conduct ethnographic research?

These are complicated issues which textbooks and articles on methodology neglect entirely.

In theory, all topics can be studied with ethnographic methods. I remember being at a conference when someone in the audience provocatively asked the speaker if it was possible to study family life ethnographically – 'perhaps by hiding under the bed?', the questioner ironically inquired. The speaker coolly replied that the commonplace view that some research topics (for example 'family') can only be studied by interview methodology reflects the prejudice that families exist only in households. On the contrary, families do shopping and have picnics, go to the stadium, church, airport and so on. Moreover, a rhetoric of 'the family' is commonplace in many institutional settings (from soap operas to law courts). In conclusion, the speaker said, there are a multitude of sites where it is possible to observe 'familying,' that is family at work.

Hence any topic at all can be studied ethnographically. The real problem is perhaps another: that not all settings are accessible to everyone.

CASE STUDY
Gender and hockey

The identity attributed to us by the participants may make some settings and cultures particularly inaccessible. Read this ethnographic account drawn from research on a group of minor-league hockey players:

> The Rockets were extremely sexist, and I was tired of the continuous 'homosocial bonding process' (see Brod, 1987) that always occurred. The players would talk 'pussy talk' incessantly and would categorize women as 'pigs,' 'star-fuckers,' 'team girls,' 'blow jobs' and 'bimbos.' The Rockets were also preoccupied with what Brod (1987: 8) has labelled *homosociality*, homosexual behaviour without status. They delighted in displaying their genitalia . . . (Gallmeier, 1983: 403).

Now ask yourself: could a female ethnographer have carried out research in this homosocial culture? For instance, there are settings almost exclusively frequented by teenagers where a well-seasoned researcher would probably be ridiculous. It should therefore be recognized that, depending on the research topic, not all researchers may be eligible for an ethnography.

Moreover, the contingencies of life, our unavoidable family and work responsibilities, may radically restrict our ability to conduct ethnography directly. I suspect that there is a linear relationship between age and the possibility to conduct ethnography: the younger one is, the more one has chances (see Figure 18.1); however we can always co-ordinate ethnographic research with a team.

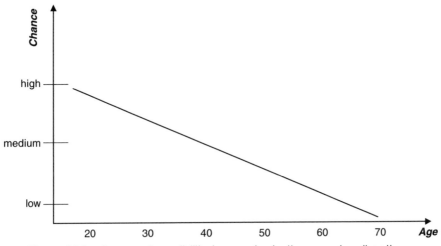

Figure 18.1   Age and possibility to conduct ethnography directly

So hurry, hurry, hurry. Don't waste time!

18.1 Common sense and prejudice about ethnography

Before we take our leave, I wish briefly to discuss some common place prejudices about ethnography. They consist of statements that you will have certainly heard or read.

18.1.1 Ethnography is highly subjective

There are many who argue that ethnography is a *highly* subjective method, in the sense that it is very sensitive to the researcher's attitudes and perceptions. In other words, if different researchers visit the same setting, they will see different things, and their ethnographic notes will record different aspects. Instead, a questionnaire or discursive interview, if conducted correctly, is more likely to obtain similar replies (reliability) regardless of who the interviewer is. And yet experience shows that this idea has scant empirical grounding.

A while ago, some students of mine conducted some ethnography in a pub. Two groups (formed of three students each) visited the same pub a few days apart from each other. The fact that they had chosen the same pub was absolutely coincidental, in the sense that they had not agreed on it beforehand. Nevertheless, the two groups had a specific research design: to study the rituals, ceremonials and behavior of consumption in pubs. They then produced a report. I discovered, to my great surprise, that they had observed and discovered practically the same things.

Hence the research design makes a greater contribution to discovery (or construction of data) than does the researcher him or herself. Ethnography, therefore, is anything but a *highly* subjective methodology (even if subjectivity is ever-present, as in all methodologies).

18.1.2 Behaviors are more consistent than attitudes and opinions

What does the experience just described tell us theoretically? In other words, why did six different observers in the same pub notice practically the same things? Because what ethnography mainly observes is behavior (rituals, routines and ceremonials), and these are much more stable over time than are attitudes and opinions (the privileged fields of inquiry for discursive interviews and surveys). Those who deal with organizations know very well that altering a behavior requires more time than altering an attitude, not to mention opinions, which are sometimes so volatile that they change from one day to the next.

18.1.3 Can ethnographic research be replicated, reproduced?

From this it follows that, because behaviors are temporally rather stable, the results of ethnographic research can be repeated and reproduced.

There are two requirements for this:

- the presence of a precise research design which has guided the research; and
- that no significant changes have taken place in an organization's routines between one research and the next.

18.1.4 Ethnography and generalization

For these reasons it is anything but odd to think that the results of ethnographic research can be generalized. If our focus is on behavior, and given that these are stable in time, then it is likely that generalizations are possible. Obviously, precise criteria must be followed in the choice of samples. Nevertheless (as we saw in 14.8), ethnography is not precluded from making generalizations.

18.1.5 Sampling cases or instances?

It will be clear by now that the term 'case' is used ambiguously in ethnographic research. In surveys and discursive interviews, the cases correspond to the number of persons interviewed (the sample), who are usually interviewed only once. Indeed, it is rather rare for several interviews to be conducted with the same person (during a single piece of research). Hence statistic calculations and analyses of the interview texts are performed on cases.

Ethnographic research is very different (see 6.2.2). What is usually referred to as the 'case' (the organization or the group studied) is in fact the setting. The cases are instead the hundreds of instances (pertaining to rituals, ceremonials and routines) that the researcher observes, or the dozens of individuals that he or she meets *dozens of times* during his or her presence in the field. The researcher is not interested in the organization (or the group) *per se* but rather in the behaviors which take place within it. Consequently, in order not to create confusion with the other methodologies, it would be better in ethnographic research to abandon the term 'case' and replace it with that of 'instance.'

18.1.6 Indicators, variables, samples and hypotheses: Can we really do without them?

Some qualitative researchers maintain that indicators, hypotheses, samples and variables belong to the baggage of positivism and therefore do not concern qualitative research. But, as I argued in Chapters 4 and 5, these are nothing other than cognitive tools, intrinsic components of the everyday thought processes of social actors. In other words, people normally reason with indicators and variables, they construct samples, and they constantly make hypotheses. Do ethnographers (and qualitative researchers in general) regard themselves as being so special and so different from the participants that they observe?

Chicholm's Law

If you explain so clearly that nobody can misunderstand, somebody will.

Bibliography

Adler, P. A. (1985), *Wheeling and Dealing*, New York: Columbia University Press.

Agar, M. (1986), *Speaking of Ethnography*, London: Sage.

Agar, M. and MacDonald, J. (1995), 'Focus Group and ethnography,' *Human Organization*, 54(1): 78–86.

Alasuutari, P. (1995), *Researching Culture*, London: Sage.

Alberoni, F. et al. (1967), *L'attivista di partito*, Bologna: Il Mulino.

Alexander, J. C., Giesen, B., Münch, R. and Smelser, N. J. (1987) (eds), *The Micro-Macro Link*, Berkeley: University of California Press.

Anderson, R. C. and Pickert, J. W. (1978), 'Recall of previously unrecallable information following a shift perspective,' *Journal of Verbal Learning and Verbal Behavior*, 17: 1–12.

Ang, I. (1991), *Desperately Seeking the Audience*, London: Routledge.

Ashmore, M. (1989), *The Reflexive Thesis: Wrighting Sociology of Scientific Knowledge*, Chicago: University of Chicago Press.

Atkinson, P. (1990), *The Ethnographic Imagination*, London: Routledge.

Atkinson, P. (1992), *Understanding Ethnographic Texts*, London: Sage.

Atkinson, P. and Coffey, A. (1997), 'Analysing Documentary Realities.' In D. Silverman (ed.) op. cit.: 45–62.

Atkinson, P. and Coffey, A. (2002), 'Revisiting the relationship between participant observation and interviewing,' In J. Gubrium and J. Holstein (eds), *Handbook of Interview Research*, Thousand Oaks, Ca.: Sage: 801–14.

Atkinson, P. and Hammersley, M. (1994), 'Ethnography and participant observation.' In N. K. Denzin and Y. S. Lincoln (eds), op. cit.: 248–61.

Atkinson, P. and Silverman, D. (1997), 'Kundera's *Immortality*: The Interview Society and the Invention of Self,' *Qualitative Inquiry*, 3 (3): 324–45.

Atkinson, P., Coffey, A., Delamont, S., Lofland J. and Lofland L. (eds) (2001), *Handbook of Ethnography*, London: Sage.

Back, L. (2004), 'Politics, research and understanding.' In C. Seale, G. Gobo, J. F. Gubrium and D. Silverman (eds), op. cit.: 261–75.

Bahr, D. M., De Gregorio J., Lopez, D. I. and Alvarez, A. (1974), *Piman Shamanism and Staying Sickness*, Tucson: University of Arizona Press.

Bailey, K. D. (1978), *Methods in Social Research*, New York: Free Press.

Bales, R. F. (1951), *Interaction Process Analysis*. Cambridge, Mass.: Addison-Wesley Press.

Ball, M. and Smith, G. (2001), 'Technologies of realism? Uses of photography and film.' In P. Atkinson, A. Coffey, S. Delamont, J. Lofland and L. Lofland (eds), op. cit.: 302–19.

Barley, S. (1990), 'The aligment of technology and structure through roles and networks,' *Administrative Science Quarterly*, 31: 61–103.

Becker, H. S. (1951), 'The professional dance musician and his audience,' *American Journal of Sociology*, 57(2): 136–44.

Becker, H. S. (1998a), *Trick of the Trade*, Chicago and London: University of Chicago Press.

Becker, H. S. (1998b), 'Sampling.' In H. Becker, op. cit.: 67–107.

Becker, H. S. (2007), 'Calvino, as urbanologist.' In H. S. Becker, *Telling About Society*, Chicago: University of Chicago Press.

Becker, H. S. and Geer, B. (1960), 'Participant observation: The analysis of qualitative field data.' In R. Adams and J. Preiss (eds), *Human Organization Research*, Homewood, Ill.: Dorsey: 267–89.

Becker, H. S., Geer, B., Hughes E. C. and Strauss, A. L. (1961), *Boys in White*, Chicago: University of Chicago Press.

Bell, C. and Newby, H. (1977), *Doing Sociological Research*, London: Allen and Unwin.

Benedict, R. (1934), *Pattern of Culture*, New York: Houghton.

Bloor, M. (1983), 'Notes on member validation.' In R. Emerson (ed.), *Contemporary Field Research*, Boston: Little Brown.

Blumer, H. (1956), 'Sociological analysis and the "variable",' *American Sociological Review*, 21: 633–60.

Blumer, H. (1969), *Symbolic Interactionism*, New York: Prentice-Hall.

Boelen, W. A. M. (1992), 'Street Corner Society: Corneville Revisited,' *Journal of Contemporary Ethnography*, 1: 11–51.

Bourdieu, P. (1979), *La distinction*, Paris: Les éditions de minuit, transl. *Distinction*, London: Routledge & Kegan Paul.

Bourdieu, P. (1987), 'What Makes a Social Class? On the Theoretical and Practical Existence of Groups,' *Berkeley Journal of Sociology*, 32: 1–17.

Brannen, J. (1992), *Mixing Methods*, London: Gower.

Brekhus, W. H., Galliher, J. F. and Gubrium, J. F. (2005), 'The Need for Thin Description,' *Qualitative Inquiry*, 11(6): 1–19.

Bruni, A. (2006), 'Access as Trajectory: Entering the Field in Organizational Ethnography,' *Management*, 9(3): 129–44.

Bryman, A. (1988), *Quantity and Quality in Social Research*, London: Unwin Hyman.

Bryman, A. (2001), *Ethnography*, London: Sage, 4-volume set.

Bulmer, M. (1984), *The Chicago School of Sociology*, Chicago: University of Chicago Press.

Burawoy, M. (1979), *Manufacturing Consent*, Chicago: University of Chicago Press.

Burawoy, M. (2003), 'Revisits: an outline of a theory of reflexive ethnography,' *American Sociological Review*, 68(5): 645–79.

Burawoy, M., Blum, J. A., George S., Gille, Z., Gowan, T., Haney, L., Klawiter, M., Lopez, S. H., Riain, S. O. and Thayer, M. (2000), *Global Ethnography*, Berkeley: University of California Press.

Callon, M. (1986), 'Some elements of a sociology of translation.' In J. Law (ed.), *Power, Action and Belief*, London: Routledge: 196–233.

Cardona, M. (1997), *Lo specchio, la rosa e il loto*, Roma: Seam.

Cardona, G. R. (1985), *La foresta di piume*: *Manuale di etnoscienza*, Bari: Laterza.

Carlspecken, P. F. (1996), *Critical Ethnography Research*, New York: Routledge.

Carmines, E. G. and Zeller, R. A. (1979), *Reliability and Validity Assessment*, Beverly Hills: Sage.

Cassell, J. (1988), 'The relationship of observer to observed when studying up.' In R. G. Burgess (ed.), *Studies in Qualitative Methodology*, Greenwich: JAI Press.

Chambers, E. (2000), 'Applied Ethnography.' In N. K. Denzin and Y. S. Lincoln (eds), op. cit.: 851–68.

Charmaz, K. (2000), 'Grounded Theory: objectivist and constructivist methods.' In Denzin and Lincoln (eds), op. cit.: 509–5.

Cicourel, A. V. (1964), *Method and Measurement in Sociology*, New York: Free Press.

Cicourel, A. V. (1968), *The Social Organization of Juvenile Justice*, New York: John Wiley.

Cicourel, A. V. (1974), *Theory and Method in a Study of Argentine Fertility*, New York: Wiley.

Cicourel, A. V. (1986), 'Intervista a Cicourel.' In F. Faccioli (ed.), *Dei delitti e delle Pene*, 1: 43–62.

Cicourel, A. V. (1988), 'Elicitation as a problem of discourse.' In U. Ammon, N. Dittmar and K. J. Mattheier (eds), *Sociolinguistics*, Vol. II, Berlin and New York: de Gruyter.

Cicourel, A. V. and Boese, R. (1972), 'Sign language acquisition and the teaching of deaf children.' In D. Hymes et al. (eds), *The Functions of Language*, New York: Teacher College Press.

Clifford, J. (1986), 'Introduction: partial truths.' In J. Clifford and G. E. Marcus (eds), op. cit.: 1–26.

Clifford, J. (1988), *Predicament of Culture*, Cambridge, MA: Harvard University Press.

Clifford, J. (1990), 'Note on (field)notes.' In R. Sanjek (ed.), *Fieldnotes: The Makings of Anthropology*, Ithaca, NY: Cornell University Press, 47–70.

Clifford, J. and Marcus, G. E. (eds) (1986), *Writing Culture: Poetics and Politics of Ethnography*, Berkeley: University of California Press.

Coffey, A., Renold, E., Dicks B., Soyinka, B. and Mason, B. (2006), 'Hypermedia ethnography in educational settings: possibilities and challenges,' *Ethnography and Education*, 1(1): 15–30.

Cohen, M. (2003), *101 Ethical Dilemmas*, London and New York: Routledge.

Cohen, M. (2005), *Wittgenstein's Beetle and Other Classic Thought Experiments*, Oxford: Blackwell.

Collett, P. and Marsh, P. (1974), 'Patterns of public behavior: collision avoidance on a pedestrian crossing,' *Semiotica*, 12: 281–99.

Collins, R. (1981), 'Micro-translation as a theory-building strategy.' In K. Knorr-Cetina and A. V. Cicourel, op. cit.: 81–108.

Collins, R. (1986), 'Reflections on the Death of Erving Goffman,' *Sociological Theory*, 4: 106–13.

Collins, R. (1988), *Theoretical Sociology*, San Diego: Harcourt, Brace, Jovanovich.

Collins, R. (2004), *Interaction Ritual Chains*, Princeton: Princeton University Press.

Comte, A. (1839), *Cours de philosophie positive*, Vol. IV, Paris: Bachelier.

Converse, J. M. (1987), *Survey Research in the United States*, Berkeley: University of California Press.

Corsaro, W. A. (1982), 'Something old and something new: the importance of prior ethnography in the collection and analysis of audiovisual data,' *Sociological Methods and Research*, 11(2): 145–66.

Corsaro, W. A. (1985), *Friendship and Peer Culture in the Early Years*, Norwood, N. J.: Ablex Publishing Corporation.

Corsaro, W. A. (1996), 'Transitions in Early Childhood: The Promise of Comparative Longitudinal Ethnography.' In R. Jessor, A. Colby and R. Shweder (eds), *Ethnography and Human Development*, Chicago: University of Chicago Press, 419–58.

Corsaro, W. A. (1997), *The Sociology of Childhood*, Thousand Oaks: Ca.: Pine Forge Press.

Corsaro, W. A. and Heise, D. (1990), 'Event structure models from ethnographic data,' *Sociological Methodology*, 20: 1–57.

Crapanzano, V. (1980), *Tuhami. Portrait of a Moroccan*, Chicago: University of Chicago Press.

Crapanzano, V. (1986), 'Hermes' dilemma. The masking of subversion in ethnographic descriptions.' In J. Clifford and G. E. Marcus, op. cit.: 51–76.

Creswell, J. W. (1998), *Qualitative Inquiry and Research Design*, London: Sage.

Czarniawska, B. (2004), 'Writing social science monograph.' In C. Seale, G. Gobo, J. F. Gubrium and D. Silverman (eds), op. cit.: 561–75.

Czarniawska, B. (2007), *Shadowing, and Other Techniques for Doing Fieldwork in Modern Societies*, Frederiksberg (Denmark): Liber / CBS Press.

Dalkey, N. C. and Helmer O. (1963), 'An experimental application of the Delphi Method to the use of experts,' *Management Science*, 9(3): 458–67.

Dalton, M. (1959), *Men who Manage*, New York: Wiley.

Davis, F. (1973), 'The martian and the convert: ontological polarities in social research,' *Urban Life*, 3: 333–43.

de Martino, E. (1961), *La terra del rimorso*, Milano: Il Saggiatore, transl. *The Land of Remorse: A Study of Southern Italian Tarantism*, London: Free Association Books, 2005.

Delamont, S. (2004), 'Ethnography and participant observation.' In C. Seale, G. Gobo, J. F. Gubrium and D. Silverman (eds), op. cit.: 217–29.

Denora, T. (2002), 'Music into action: performing gender on the Viennese concert stage, 1790–1810,' *Poetics*, 30(2): 19–33.

Denzin, N. K. (1970), *The Research Act*, New York: McGraw-Hill.

Denzin, N. K. (1971), 'Symbolic Interactionism and Ethnomethodology.' In J. D. Douglas (ed.), *Understanding Everyday Life*, London: Routledge and Kegan.

Denzin, N. K. (1983), 'Interpretive Interactionism.' In G. Morgan (ed.), *Beyond Method*, Beverly Hills, CA: Sage: 129–46.

Denzin, N. K. (1997), *Interpretive Ethnography*, Thousand Oaks, CA: Sage.

Denzin, N. K. (2007), 'Sacagawea's nickname, or the Sacagawea problem,' *Qualitative Research*, 7(1), 103–33.

Denzin, N. K. and Lincoln, Y. S. (eds) (2000), *Handbook of Qualitative Research* (2nd edn), Thousand Oaks, CA: Sage.

Denzin, N. K. and Lincoln, Y. S. (2000), 'The Discipline and Practice of Qualitative Research.' In N. K. Denzin and Y. S. Lincoln (eds), op. cit.: 1–28.

Deutscher, I. (1973), *What we Say/What we Do*, Glenview, Ill: Scott Foresman.

Dickens, L. (1983), 'Is feminist methodology a red herring?' Letter to the Editor of *Network* (Newsletter of the British Sociological Association): 26 May.

Duranti, A. (1992), *Etnografia del parlare quotidiano*, Roma: NIS.

Duranti, A. (1997a), *Linguistic Anthropology*, Cambridge: Cambridge University Press.

Duranti, A. (1997b), 'Appendix: Practical tips on recording interaction,' in A. Duranti, op. cit.: 340–7.

Duranti, A. (2002), 'Il ritorno come epifania etnografica: Samoa 1978–1999.' In L. Brutti and A. Paini, *La terra dei miei sogni*, Roma: Meltemi: 161–79.

Eco, U. (1979), *Lector in fabula*, Milano: Bompiani.

Edwards, R. and Mauthner, M. (2002), 'Ethics and feminist research: theory and practice.' In M. Mauthner, M. Birch, J. Jessop and T. Miller (eds), *Ethics in Qualitative Research*, London: Sage: 14–31.

Ellis, C. (1995), *Final Negotiations*. Philadelphia, PA: Temple University Press.

Ellis, C. and Bochner, A. (2000), 'Autoethnography, personal narrative, reflexivity: researcher as a subject.' In N. K. Denzin and Y. S. Lincoln (eds), op. cit.: 733–68.

Emerson, R. M. (2004), 'Working with "Key Incidents."' In C. Seale, G. Gobo, J. F. Gubrium and D. Silverman, op. cit.: 457–72.

Emerson, R. M., Fretz, R. I. and Shaw, L. L. (1995), *Writing Ethnographic Fieldnotes*, Chicago: University of Chicago Press.

Emerson, R. M., Fretz, R. I. and Shaw, L. L. (2001), 'Participant observation and fieldnotes.' In P. Atkinson, A. Coffey, S. Delamont, J. Lofland and L. Lofland (eds), op. cit.: 339–51.

Emerson, R. M. and Pollner, M. (1988), 'On the use of members' responses to researchers' account,' *Human Organization*, 47: 189–98.

Ereaut, G. (2004), 'Qualitative market research.' In C. Seale, G. Gobo, J. F. Gubrium and D. Silverman (eds), op. cit.: 504–20.

Fielding, N. (2001), 'Computer applications in qualitative research.' In P. Atkinson, A. Coffey, S. Delamont, J. Lofland and L. Lofland (eds), op. cit.: 453–67.

Fielding, N. (2004) 'Working in hostile environments.' In C. Seale, G. Gobo, J. F. Gubrium and D. Silverman (eds), op. cit.: 248–60.

Fielding, N. G. and Fielding, J. L. (1986), *Linking Data*, London: Sage.

Fischer, M. M. J. (1986), 'Ethnicity and the post-modern arts of memory.' In J. Clifford and G. E. Marcus (eds), op. cit.: 194–232.

Fossey, D. (1983), *Gorillas in the Mist*, Boston, MA: Houghton Mifflin.

Foucault, M. (1975), *Surveiller et punir*, Paris: Gallimard, transl. *Discipline and Punish*, Harmondsworth: Penguin, 1977.

Gallmeier, C. P. (1983), 'Leaving, revisiting, and staying in touch: neglected issues in field research.' In W. B. Shaffir and R. A. Stebbins (eds), *Experiencing Fieldwork*, Thousand Oaks: CA: Sage: 224–31.

Gans, H. J. (1968), 'The Participant-Observer as a Human Being: observations on the Personal Aspects of Fieldwork.' In H. S. Becker, B. Geer, D. Riesman and R. S. Weiss (eds), *Institutions and the Person*, Chicago: Aldine, 300–17.

Gans, H. (1999), 'Participant observation in the Era of "Ethnography,"' *Journal of Contemporary Ethnography*, 28(5): 540–8.

Garfinkel, H. (1962), 'Common sense knowledge of social structures: the documentary method of interpretation in lay and professional fact finding.' In J. M. Scher (ed.), *Theories of the Mind*, New York: The Free Press.

Garfinkel, H. (1967), *Studies in Ethnomethodology*, Englewood Cliffs, NJ: Prentice-Hall.

Geertz, C. (1972), 'Deep Play: Notes on the Balinese Cockfight,' *Dedalus*, 101: 1–37.

Geertz, C. (1973), *The Interpretation of Cultures*, New York: Basic Books.

Geertz, C. (1988), *Works and Lives*, Stanford: Stanford University Press.

Geertz, C. (2000), *Available Light*, Princeton, NJ: Princeton University Press.

Gelsthorpe, L. (1992), 'Response to Martin Hammersley's paper "on feminist methodology,"' *Sociology*, 26(2): 213–18.

Gherardi, S. (1995), 'When will he say: "Today the plates are soft?" Management of ambiguity and situated decision-making,' *Studies in Cultures, Organizations and Societies*, 1: 9–27.

Gherardi, S. (2000), 'Practice-based theorizing on learning and knowing in organizations: an introduction,' *Organization*, 7: 211–21.

Gilbert, N. and Mulkay, M. (1983), 'In Search of the Action.' In N. Gilbert and P. Abell, (eds) *Accounts and Action*, Aldershot: Gower.

Glaser, B. G. (1978), *Theoretical Sensitivity*. Mill Valley, CA: Sociology Press.

Glaser, B. G. (2002), 'Constructivist Grounded Theory?,' *Forum Qualitative Social Research*, 3 (3), www.qualitative-research.net/fqs-texte/3-02/3-02glaser-e.htm.

Glaser, B. G. and Strauss, A. L. (1964), 'The social loss of dying patients,' *American Journal of Nursing*, 64(6): 119–21.

Glaser, B. G. and Strauss, A. L. (1967), *The Discovery of Grounded Theory*, Chicago: Aldine.

Glazier, S. D. (1993), 'Responding to the anthropologist: when the spiritual Baptists of Trinidad read what I write about them.' In C. Brettell (ed.), *When They Read What We Write*, Westport, CT: Bergin and Garvey: 107–18.

Gobo, G. (1993), 'Class; stories of concepts. From ordinary language to scientific language,' *Social Science Information*, 32(3): 467–89.

Gobo, G. (1995), 'Class as metaphor: On the unreflexive transformation of a concept into an object,' *Philosophy of the Social Sciences*, 25(4): 442–67.

Gobo, G. (1997), 'La costruzione organizzativa della cecità.' In M. La Rosa (ed.), *Governo delle tecnologie, efficienza e creatività*, Bologna: Monduzzi, 65–8.

Gobo, G. (2004), 'Sampling, representativeness and generalizability.' In C. Seale, G. Gobo, J. F. Gubrium and D. Silverman (eds), op. cit.: 435–56.

Gobo, G. (2006), 'Set them free: Improving data quality by broadening an interviewer's task,' *International Journal of Social Research Methodology*, 9(4): 279–301.

Gobo, G. (2008), 'Re-conceptualizing generalization: Old issues in a new frame.' In P. Alasuutari, J. Brannen and L. Bickman (eds), *The Handbook of Social Research Methods*, London: Sage.

Gobo, G., Rozzi, S., Zanini, S. and Diotti, A. (2008), 'Routine dell'emergenza: il caso del 118.' In S. Gherardi (ed.), *Apprendimento tecnologico e tecnologie di apprendimento*, Bologna: Il Mulino.

Goffman, E. (1955), 'On face-work: an analysis of ritual elements in social interaction,' *Psychiatry*, 18(3): 213–31.

Goffman, E. (1956a), 'The nature of deference and demeanor,' *American Anthropologist*, 58: 473–502.

Goffman, E. (1956b), 'Embarrassment and Social Organization,' *American Journal of Sociology*, 62(3): 264–74.

Goffman, E. (1959), 'Preface.' In E. Goffman (1959), *The Presentation of Self in Everyday Life*, New York: Doubleday Anchor.

Goffman, E (1961), *Asylums*, New York: Doubleday Anchor.

Goffman, E. (1963), *Behavior in Public Places. Notes on the Social Organization of Gatherings*, Glencoe: The Free Press.

Goffman, E. (1964), 'Mental symptoms and public order,' *Disorders in Communication*, 42: 262–9.

Goffman, E. (1967), *Interaction Ritual*, New York: Doubleday Anchor.

Goffman, E. (1969), *Strategic Interaction*, Philadelphia: University of Pennsylvania Press.

Goffman, E. (1976), 'Replies and Responses,' *Language in Society*, 5: 257–313

Goffman, E. (1989), 'On fieldwork,' *Journal of Contemporary Ethnography*, 18(2): 124–32.

Gomm, R., Hammersley, M. and Foster, P. (2000), 'Case study and generalization.' In R. Gomm, M. Hammersley and P. Foster (eds), *Case Study Method*, London, Sage: 98–115.

Goodenough, W. (1957), 'Cultural anthropology and linguistics.' In P. L. Garvin (a cura di), *Monograph Series on Languages and Linguistics*, 9, Institute of Languages and Linguistics, Washington, DC.

Gouldner, A. W. (1954), *Patterns of Industrial Bureaucracy*, New York: The Free Press.

Gouldner, A. W. (1970), *The Coming Crisis in Western Sociology*, New York: Avon Books.

Grahame, P. R. and Grahame, K. M. (2000), 'Official knowledge and the relations of ruling: Explorations in institutional ethnography,' *Journal for Pedagogy, Pluralism, & Practice*, 5. www.lesley.edu/journals/jppp/5/grahame.html.

Guba, E. G. (1981), 'Criteria for assessing the trustworthiness of naturalistic enquiries,' *Educational Communication and Technology Journal*, 29(2): 75–92.

Guba, E. G. and Lincoln, Y. S. (1982), 'Epistemological and methodological bases of naturalistic inquiry,' *Educational Communication and Technology Journal*, 30: 233–52.

Gubrium, J. F. (1988), *Analyzing Field Reality*, Newbury Park: Sage.

Gubrium, J. F. (1988a), 'Field Reality: Orientations.' In J. F. Gubrium, op. cit.: 23–39.

Gubrium, J. F. (2005), 'Narrative Environments and Social Problems,' *Social Problems*, 52 (4): 525–8

Hammersley, M. (1989), *The Dilemma of Qualitative Method*, London: Routledge.

Hammersley, M. (1990), *Reading Ethnographic Research*, London: Longmans.

Hammersley, M. (1992), *What's Wrong with Ethnography*, London: Routledge.

Hammersley, M. (1992a), 'On feminist methodology,' *Sociology*, 26(2), 187–206.

Hammersley, M. (1996), 'The relationship between qualitative and quantitative research: paradigm loyalty versus methodological eclecticism.' In J. T. E. Richardson (ed.), *Handbook of Research Methods for Psychology and the Social Sciences*, Leicester: BPS Books: 159–79

Hammersley, M. (2006), 'Ethnography: problems and prospects.' *Ethnography and Education*, 1(1): 3–14.

Hammersley, M. and Atkinson, P. (1983), *Ethnography: Principles in Practice*, London: Tavistock.

Hammersley, M. and Atkinson, P. (1983a), 'Research design: problems, cases, and samples,' in M. Hammersley and P. Atkinson, op. cit.: 23–53.

Haraway, D. (1991), *Simians, Cyborg and Women*, London: Routledge.

Harding, S. (1987), *Feminism and Methodology*, Bloomington: Indiana University Press.

Hartley, J. (1987), 'Invisible fictions: television audiences, paedocracy, pleasure,' *Textual Practice*, 1(12): 121–38.

Hayek, F. A. (1949), *Individualism and Economic Order*, London: Routledge & Kegan Paul.

Heath, C. (2004), 'Analysing face-to-face interaction: video, the visual and material.' In D. Silverman (ed.), op. cit.: 266–82.

Heath, C. and Luff, P. (1993), 'Explicating face-to-face interaction.' In N. Gilbert (ed.), *Researching Social Life*, London: Sage: 306–26.

Hebdige, D. (1979), *Subculture: The Meaning of Style*, London and New York: Routledge.

Heritage, J. (1984), *Garfinkel and Ethnomethodology*, Cambridge: Polity.

Heyl, S. B. (2001), 'Ethnographic interviewing,' in P. Atkinson, A. Coffey, S. Delamont, J. Lofland and L. Lofland (eds), op. cit.: 369–83.

Hine, C. (2000), *Virtual Ethnography*, London: Sage.

Hobson, D. (1982), '*Crossroads:*' *the Drama of Soap Opera*, London: Methuen.

Holdaway, S. (1982), '"An inside job:" a case study of covert research on the police.' In Martin Bulmer (ed.), *Social Research Ethics*, London: Macmillan Press: 59–79.

Hoyles, C., Noss, R., and Pozzi, S. (2001), 'Proportional reasoning in nursing practice,' *Journal for Research in Mathematics Education*, 32(1), 4–27.

Hughes, E. C. (1971), *The Sociological Eye: Selected Papers*, Chicago: Aldine.

Hughes, J. and Sharrock, W. (2008), *Participant Observation*, London: Sage, 4-volume set.

Humphreys, L. (1970), *Tearoom Trade: Impersonal Sex in Public Places*, Chicago: Aldine.

Hymes, D. H. (1978), 'What is ethnography?' Sociolinguistics Working Paper #45, Southwest Educational Development Laboratory, Austin, Texas.

Jankowski, M. S. (1991), *Islands in the Street*, Berkeley: University of California Press.

Jarvie, I. C. (1972), *Concepts and Society*, London: Routledge & Kegan Paul.

Jick, T. D. (1979), 'Mixing qualitative and quantitative methods: triangulation in action,' *Administrative Science Quarterly*, 24: 602–11.

Jordan, B. and Dalal, B. (2006), 'Persuasive encounters: ethnography in the corporation,' *Field Methods*, 18(4): 359–81.

Kahng, S. W. and Iwata, B. A. (1998), 'Computerized systems for collecting real-time observational data,' *Journal of Applied Behavior Analysis*, 31(2): 253–61.

Kanter, R. M. (1977), *Men and Women of the Corporation*, New York: Basic Books.

Kasper, A. S. (1994), 'A feminist, qualitative methodology: a study of women with breast cancer,' *Qualitative Sociology*, 17(3): 263–81.

Keiser, R. L. (1969), *The Vice Lords*, New York: Holt, Rinehart and Winston.

Kelle, U. (2004), 'Computer-assisted qualitative data analysis.' In C. Seale, G. Gobo, J. F. Gubrium and D. Silverman (eds), op. cit.: 472–89.

Kincheloe, J. L. and McLaren, P. L. (1994), 'Rethinking critical theory and qualitative research.' In N. Denzin and Y. Lincoln (eds), *Handbook of Qualitative Research*, Thousand Oaks, CA: Sage: 138–57.

Kirk, J. and Miller, M. (1986), *Reliability and Validity in Qualitative Research*, London: Sage.

Kitzinger, C. (2004), 'Feminist approaches.' In C. Seale, G. Gobo, J. F. Gubrium and D. Silverman (eds), op. cit.: 125–40.

Knoblauch, H. (2005), 'Focused Ethnography,' *Forum: Qualitative Social Research*, 6(3), www.qualitative-research.net/fqs-texte/3-05/05-3-44-e.htm.

Knorr-Cetina, K. and Cicourel, A. V. (1981) (eds), *Advances in Social Theory and Methodology*, London: Routledge & Kegan Paul.

Korzybski, A. (1933), 'Science and sanity: an introduction to non-Aristotelian systems and general semantics,' Chicago: International Non-Aristotelian Library, Institute of General Semantics.

Kuhn, T. S. (1962), *The Structure of Scientific Revolutions*, Chicago: University of Chicago Press.

La Piere, R. T. (1934), 'Attitudes vs. Action,' *Social Force*, 12: 230–7.

Labov, W. (1972), 'Academic Ignorance and Black Intelligence,' *The Atlantic Monthly*, 6: 59–67.

Lakoff, G. and Johnson, M. (1980), *Metaphors We Live By*. Chicago: Chicago University Press.

Lather, P. (1988), 'Feminist perspective on empowering research methodologies,' *Women's Studies International Forum*, 11(6): 569–81.

Latour, B. (1988), 'The politics of explanation – an alternative.' In S. Woolgar (ed.), op. cit.: 155–76.

Latour, B. (1995), 'The 'pedofil' of Boa Vista: A photo-philosophical montage,' *Common Knowledge*, 4(1): 147–87.

Latour, B. and Woolgar, S. (1979), *Laboratory Life*, London: Sage.

Levi, P. (1958), *Se questo è un uomo*, Torino: Einaudi, transl., *If this is a man*, New York: Collier, 1959.

Lincoln, Y. S. and Guba, E. G. (1979), *Naturalist Inquiry*, Beverly Hills, CA: Sage: 27–42.

Lindeman, E. C. (1924), *Social Discovery*, New York: Republic.

Lofland, J. (1971), *Analyzing Social Settings*, Belmont, CA: Wadsworth.

Lofland, L. H. (1980), 'Reminiscences of Classic Chicago: "The Blumer-Hughes Talk,"' *Urban Life*, 9(3): 251–81.

Loseke, D. R. and Cahill, E. S. (2004), 'Publishing qualitative manuscripts: lesson learned.' In C. Seale, G. Gobo, J. F. Gubrium and D. Silverman (eds), op. cit.: 576–91.

Lull, J. (1980), 'The social uses of television,' *Human Communication Research*, 6(3): 197–209.

Lull, J. (1988), *World Families Watch Television*, London: Sage.

Lunch, C. and Lunch, N. (2006), 'Insights into participatory Video: a handbook for the field,' Oxford: Insight, www.insightshare.org/training_book.html.

Luria, A. R. (1974), *Ob istoricheskom razvitii poznavatel'nykh protsessov*, Moscow: Izdatelstvo "Nauka", transl. *Cognitive Development. Its cultural and social foundations*, Cambridge, Harvard University Press, 1976.

Lynd, R. S. and Lynd, M. H. (1929), *Middletown*, New York: Harcourt Brace and Company.

Lynd, R. S. and Lynd, M. H. (1937), *Middletown in Transition*, New York: Harcourt Brace and Company.

Madge, J. (1962), *The Origins of Scientific Sociology*, New York: The Free Press of Glencoe.

Malinowski, B. (1922), *Argonauts of the Western Pacific*, London: Routledge and Kegan.

Mann, L. (1969), 'Queue culture: the waiting line as a social system,' *American Journal of Sociology*, 75: 340–54.

Marcus, G. E. (1986), 'Contemporary problems of ethnography in the modern world system.' In J. Clifford and G. E. Marcus (eds), op. cit.: 165–93.

Marcus, G. E., and Cushman, D. (1982), 'Ethnographies as texts,' *Annual Review of Anthropology*, 11: 25–69.

Marcus, G. E. and Fischer, M. J. (1986), 'The Anthropologist as Hero.' In G. E. Marcus and M. J. Fischer, *Anthropology as Cultural Critique*, Chicago: University of Chicago Press.

Markham, A. N. (2005), 'The methods, politics and ethics of representation in online ethnography.' In N. K. Denzin and Y. S. Lincoln (eds), *Handbook of Qualitative Research* (3rd edn), Thousand Oaks, CA: Sage.

Marradi, A. (1980), *Concetti e metodi per la ricerca sociale*, Firenze: La Giuntina.

Marradi, A. (1990), 'Classification, typology, taxonomy,' *Quality and Quantity*, 24: 129–57.

Mason, J. (1996), *Qualitative Researching*, Newbury Park: Sage.

Matthew, D. (2005), *Case Study Research*, London: Sage, 4-volume set.

Maynard, D. (1989), 'On the ethnography and analysis of discourse in institutional settings.' In J. Holstein and G. Miller (eds), *Perspective in Social Problems*, vol. 1, Greenwich, CT: JAI Press: 127–46.

Maynard, D. and Clayman, S. (1991), 'The diversity of ethnomethodology,' *Annual Review of Sociology*, 17: 385–418.

Maynard, M. (1994), 'Methods, practice and epistemology: the debate about feminism and research,' in M. Maynard and J. Purvis (eds), *Researching Women's Lives from a Feminist Perspective*, London: Taylor & Francis.

McCall, M. M. (2000), 'Performance ethnography: A brief history and some advice.' In N. K. Denzin and Y. S. Lincoln (eds), op. cit.: 421–33.

McCloskey, D. N. (1986), *The Rhetoric of Economics*, Madison: University of Wisconsin Press.

McCracken, G. D. (1988), *The Long Interview*, Newbury Park: Sage.

McHugh, P. (1968), *Defining the Situation*, Indianapolis: Bobbs-Merrill.

Mehan, H. (1979), *Learning Lessons*, Cambridge, Mass.: Harvard University Press.

Mehan, H., Hertweck, A. and Meihls, L. J. (1986), *Handicapping the Handicapped:* Stanford: Stanford University Press.

Mehan, H. and Wood, H. (1975a), *The Reality of Ethnomethodology*, New York: Wiley.

Mehan, H. and Wood, H. (1975b), 'Becoming the phenomenon,' in H. Mehan and H. Wood, *The Reality of Ethnomethodology*, op. cit.: 225–38.

Merleau-Ponty, M. (1945), *Phénomenologie de la perception*, Paris: Gallimard, transl. *Phenomenology of Perception*, London: Routledge & Kegan Paul, 1962.

Miles, M. B. and Huberman, M. A. (1984), *Qualitative Data Analysis*, London: Sage.

Mitchell, R. and Karttunen, S. (1991), 'Perché e come definire un artista?' *Rassegna Italiana di Sociologia*, 32(3): 349–64.

Moerman, M. (1974), 'Accomplishing ethnicity.' In R. Turner (ed.) *Ethnomethodology*, Harmondsworth: Penguin: 34–68.

Moores, S. (1993), 'Approaching audiences.' In S. Moores, *Interpreting Audiences*, London: Sage: 1–10.

Morgan, G. (1986), *Images of Organization*, London: Sage.

Morley, D. (1992), *Television, Audiences and Cultural Studies*, London: Routledge.

Murphy, E. and Dingwall, R. (2001), 'The ethics of ethnography.' In P. Atkinson, A. Coffey, S. Delamont, J. Lofland and L. Lofland (eds), op. cit.: 339–51.

Norman, D. A. (1988), *The Psychology of Everyday Things*, Basic Books, New York.

Norman, D. A. (1991), 'Cognitive artifacts.' In J. M. Caroll (ed.), *Designing Interaction*, Cambridge: Cambridge University Press: 17–38,

Ochs, E. (1988), *Culture and Language Development*, Cambridge: Cambridge University Press.

Oddone, I., Re, A. and Briante, G. (1977), *L'esperienza operaia, coscienza di classe e psicologia del lavoro*, Torino: Einaudi.

Pascual-Leone, A., Amedi, A., Fregni, F. and Merabet, L. B. (2005), 'The Plastic Human Brain Cortex,' *Annual Review of Neurosciences*, 28: 377–401.

Payne, G. and Williams, M. (2005), 'Generalization in Qualitative Research,' *Sociology*, 39(2): 295–314.

Peräkylä, A. (1997), 'Reliability and Validity in Research based upon transcripts.' In D. Silverman (ed.), *Qualitative Research*, London: Sage: 201–19.

Platt, J. (1983), 'The Development of the "Participant Observation" Method in Sociology: Origin, Myth and History,' *Journal of the History of the Behavioural Sciences*, 19(4): 379–93.

Platt, J. (1996), *A History of Sociological Research Methods in America, 1920–1960*, Cambridge, Cambridge University Press.

Pole, C. (2004), *Fieldwork*, London: Sage, 4-volume set.

Pollner, M. and Emerson, R. M. (2001), 'Ethnomethodology and Ethnography.' In P. Atkinson, A. Coffey, S. Delamont, J. Lofland and L. Lofland (eds), op. cit.: 118–35.

Prior, L. (2004), 'Doing Things with Documents.' In D. Silverman (ed.), *Qualitative Research*, London: Sage: 76–94.

Psathas, G. (1995), *Conversation Analysis*, London: Sage.

Rabinow, P. (1977), *Reflections on Fieldwork in Morocco*, Berkeley: University of California Press.

Radcliffe-Brown, A. R. (1948), *A Natural Science of Society*, New York: Free Press.

Ragin, C. C. (1987), *The Comparative Method*, Berkeley: University of California Press.

Ragin, C.C. and Becker, H. S. (eds) (1992), *What is a case?* Cambridge: Cambridge University Press.

Ramazanoglu, C. (1992), 'On feminist methodology: male reason versus female empowerment,' *Sociology*, 26(2): 207–12.

Rapley, T. (2004), 'Interviews.' In C. Seale, G. Gobo, J. Gubrium and D. Silverman (eds), op. cit.: 15–33.

Reale, E. (2004), 'New perspective for women's health studies.' In F. Cantù and N. Serina (eds), *Women in Science*, European Conference Proceedings, Genova: Brigati: 95–110.

Reed-Danahay, D. E. (2001), 'Autobiography, intimacy and ethnography.' In P. Atkinson, A. Coffey, S. Delamont, J. Lofland and L. Lofland (eds), *Handbook of Ethnography*: 407–25.

Richardson, L. (1995), 'Co-Authoring "The Sea Monster": A Writing-Story,' *Qualitative Inquiry*, 1(2): 189–203.

Robbins, T., Anthony, D. and Curtis, T. E. (1973), 'The limits of symbolic realism: problems of emphatic field observation in a sectarian context,' *Journal of the Scientific Study of Religion*, 12: 259–72.

Roethlisberger, F. J., Dickson, W. J. and Wright, H. A. (1939), *Management and the Worker*, Cambridge, MA: Harvard University Press.

Rosenhan, D. L. (1973), 'On being sane in insane places,' *Science*, 179: 250–8.

Roy, D. (1952), 'Quota restriction and goldbricking in a machine shop,' *American Journal of Sociology*, 57: 427–42.

Ryen, A. (2004), 'Ethical issues.' In C. Seale, G. Gobo, J. F. Gubrium and D. Silverman, (eds), op. cit.: 230–47.

Sacks, H. (1992), *Lectures on Conversation*, Oxford, Blackwell: vol. 1.

Said, E. W. (1978), *Orientalism*, London: Routledge and Kegan Paul.

Schatzman, L. and Strauss, A. L. (1973), *Field Research*, Englewood Cliffs, NJ: Prentice-Hall.

Schein, E. H. (1988), *Process Consultation: Its Role in Organizational Development*, Reading, Mass.: Addison-Wesley.

Schegloff, E. A. (1972), 'Notes on conversational practice: formulating place.' In D. Sudnow (ed.), *Studies in Social Interaction*, New York: Free Press: 75–119.

Schutz, A. (1944), 'The stranger: an essay in social psychology,' *American Journal of Sociology*, 49(6): 499–507.

Schutz, A. (1953), 'Common-sense and scientific interpretation of human action,' *Philosophy and Phenomenological Research*, 14: 1–38.

Schutz, A. (1962), *Collected Papers I. The Problem of Social Reality*, The Hague: Martinus Nijhoff.

Schwartz, H. and Jacobs, J. (1979), *Qualitative Sociology*, New York: The Free Press.

Seale, C. (1999), *The Quality of Qualitative Research*, London: Sage.

Seale, C. (2000), 'Using computers to analyse qualitative data,' in D. Silverman, op. cit.: 154–74.

Seale, C. (2004), 'Quality in Qualitative Research.' In C. Seale, G. Gobo, J. F. Gubrium and D. Silverman (eds), op. cit.: 409–19.

Seale, C., Gobo, G., Gubrium, J. F. and Silverman, D. (eds) (2004), *Qualitative Research Practice*. London: Sage.

Sears, R. R., Rau, L. and Alpert, R. (1965), *Identification and Child Rearing*, Stanford, CA: Stanford University Press.

Sharrock, W. W. and Button, G. (1991), 'The social actor: social action in real time.' In G. Button (ed.), *Ethnomethodology and the Human Sciences*, Cambridge: Cambridge University Press: 137–75.

Silverman, D. (1984), 'Going private: ceremonial forms in a private oncology clinic,' *Sociology*, 18, 191–202.

Silverman, D. (1993), *Interpreting Qualitative Data*, London: Sage.

Silverman, D. (2000), *Doing Qualitative Research*, London: Sage.

Silverman, D. (2005), *Doing Qualitative Research*, London: Sage (2nd edn).

Silverman, D. (2005a), 'Selecting a topic.' In Silverman, 2005 op. cit.: 77–94.

Silverman, D. (2005b), 'Selecting a case.' In Silverman, 2005 op. cit.: 125–37.

Silverman, D. (2005), 'Choosing a methodology.' In Silverman, 2005 op. cit.: 109–23.

Silverman, D. (2006), *Interpreting Qualitative Data*, London: Sage (3rd edn).

Silverman, D. (2006a), 'Ethnography and observation.' In Silverman, 2006 op. cit.: 65–70.

Silverman, D. (2006b), 'The range of qualitative methods.' In Silverman, 2006 op. cit.: 18–29.

Silverman, D. (2006c), 'The ethnographic focus.' In Silverman, 2006 op. cit.: 70–8.

Silverman, D. (2006d), 'Research design: some broader issues.' In Silverman, 2006 op. cit.: 9–20

Silverman, D. (2006e), 'Writing your report.' In Silverman, 2006 op. cit.: 336–45.

Silverman, D. (2007), 'Innumerable inscrutable habits: Why unremarkable things matter.' In D. Silverman, *A Very Short, Fairly Interesting, Quite Cheap Book about Qualitative Research*, London: Sage: 11–36.

Silverman, D. and Gubrium, J. F. (1994), 'Competing strategies for analyzing the contexts of social interaction,' *Sociological Inquiry*, 64(2): 179–98.

Siperstein, G. N. and Bak, J. (1980), 'Improving Children's Attitudes Toward Blind Peers,' *Journal of Visual Impairment and Blindness*: 74(4).

Skeggs, B. (2001), 'Feminist Ethnography.' In P. Atkinson, A. Coffey, S. Delamont, J. Lofland and L. Lofland (eds), op. cit.: 426–42.

Smith, B. M. (1979), 'Some perspectives on ethical/political issues in social science research.' In M. Wax and J. Cassell (eds), *Federal Regulation: Ethical Issues and Social Research*, Boulder, CO: Westview Press, 11–22.

Smith, D. E. (1986), 'Institutional Ethnography: A Feminist Method,' *Resource for Feminist Research*, 15: 6–13.

Snell, B. (1953), *The Discovery of the Mind*. Cambrige: Harvard University Press.

Snow, D. (1980), 'The disengagement process: a neglected problem in participant observation research,' *Qualitative Sociology*, 3(2): 100–22.

Soloway, I. and Walters, J. (1977), 'Workin' the corner: the ethics and legality of ethnographic fieldwork among active heroin addicts.' In R. S. Weppner (ed.), *Street Ethnography*, Beverly Hills: Sage: 159–78.

Sontag, S. (2001), *Illness as Metaphor and AIDS and its Metaphors*, New York: Picador USA.

Spenser J. (2001), 'Ethnography after post-modernism.' In P. Atkinson, A. Coffey, S. Delamont, J. Lofland and L. Lofland (eds), op. cit.: 443–52.

Spradley, J. P. (1979), *The Ethnographic Interview*, New York: Holt, Rinehart and Winston.

Spradley, J. P. (1980), *Participant Observation*, New York: Holt, Rinehart and Winston.

Stanley, L. and Wise, S. (1983), *Breaking Out*, London: Routledge.

Strauss, A. L. and Corbin, J. (1990), *Basics of Qualitative Research*, Thousand Oaks: Sage.

Strauss, A. L., Buchner, R., Ehrlich, D., Schatzman, L. and Sabshin, M. (1964), *Psychiatric Ideologies and Institutions*, Glencoe: The Free Press.

Sudnow, D. (1967), *Passing On*, Englewood Cliffs: Prentice Hall.

Sudnow, D. (1978), *Ways of the Hand*, MA: Harvard University Press.

Sudnow, D. (1979), *Talk's Body*, New York: Alfred A. Knopf.

Travers, M. (2001a), 'Feminism and Qualitative Research.' In M. Travers, *Qualitative Research through Case Studies*, London: Sage: 133–50.

Travers, M. (2001b), 'Postmodern Ethnography.' In M. Travers, *Qualitative Research through Case Studies*, London: Sage: 151–72.

Tuchman, G. (1972), 'Objectivity as strategic ritual: an examination of newsmen's notions of objectivity,' *American Sociological Review*, 77: 660–79.

Turner, B. A. (1988), 'Connoisseurship in the study of organizational cultures.' In A. Bryman (ed.), *Doing Research in Organizations*, London: Routledge & Kegan Paul.

Turner, R. (1989), 'Deconstructing the field.' In J. F. Gubrium and D. Silverman (eds), *The Politics of Field Research*, London: Sage: 13–29.

Turner, B. A. (1990) (ed.), *Organizational Symbolism*, Berlin: de Gruyter.

Van Dijk, T. A. (1977), *Text and Context*, London: Longman.

Van Dijk, T. A. (1987), *Communicating Racism*, Newbury Park: Sage.

Van Maanen, J. (1983), 'The moral fix: On the ethics of the fieldwork.' In R. M. Emerson (ed.), *Contemporary Field Research*, Prospect Heights: Waveland Press: 269–87.

Van Maanen, J. (1988), *Tales of the Field*, Chicago: University of Chicago Press.

Van Maanen, J. (2006), 'Ethnography then and now,' *Qualitative Research in Organizations and Management*, 1(1): 13–21.

Vidich, A. J. and Bensman, J. (1958), *Small Town in Mass Society*, Princeton: Princeton University Press.

Warren, C. A. B. (1988), *Gender Issues in Field Research*, Newbury Park: Sage.

Warren, C. A. B. and Rasmussen, P. (1977), 'Sex and Gender in Fieldwork Research,' *Urban Life*, 6: 359–69.

Webb, E. J., Campbell, D. T., Schwartz, R. D. and Sechrest, L. (1966), *Unobtrusive Methods*, Chicago: Rand McNally.

Wheatley, E. (1994), 'How can we engender ethnography with a feminist imagination? A rejoinder to Judith Stacey,' *Women's Studies International Forum*, 17(4): 403–16.

Whyte, W. F. (1943a), *Street Corner Society*, Chicago: Chicago University Press.

Whyte, W. F. (1943b), 'Social Organization in the Slums,' *American Sociological Review*, 8(1): 34–9.

Whyte, W. F. (1955), *Street Corner Society*, Chicago: Chicago University Press (enlarged edn).

Whyte, W. F. (1984), *Learning from the Field*, Newbury Park: Sage.

Whyte, W. F. (1993), 'Revisiting Street Corner Society,' *Sociological Forum*, 8(2): 285–98.

Wieder, D. L. (1974), *Language and Social Reality*, The Hague: Mouton.

Williams, M. (2000), 'Interpretativism and generalization,' *Sociology*, 34(2): 209–24.

Wilson, J. Q. and Kelling, G. (1982), 'Broken windows,' *The Atlantic Monthly*, 249(3): 29–39.

Wiseman, J. P. (1970), *Stations of the Lost*, Englewood Cliffs, NJ: Prentice-Hall.

Wissler, C. (1937), 'Introduction,' in R. S. Lynd and M. H. Lynd, op. cit.: 1–13.

Wolcott, H. F. (1990), *Writing up Qualitative Research*, Newbury Park: Sage.

Wolf, M. (1996), 'Afterword: musing from an old gray wolf.' In D. Wolf (ed.), *Feminist Dilemmas in Fieldwork*, Oxford: Westview Press: 215–21.

Wolfson, N. (1976), 'Speech events and natural speech. Some Implications for Sociolinguistic Methodology,' *Language in Society*, 5(2): 189–209.

Woods, J. (1972), 'Fire call: ethnography of fire fighters.' In J. Spradley (ed.), *The Cultural Experience*, Chicago: Science Research Associates: 221–39.

Woolgar, S. (1988) (ed.), *Knowledge and Reflexivity*, London: Sage.

Worth, S. and Adair, J. (1972), *Through Navajo Eyes*, Bloomington, IN: Indiana University Press.

Yin, R. K. (1984), *Case Study Research*, Thousand Oaks: Sage.

Zimmerman, D. H. and Pollner, M. (1970), 'The everyday world as a phenomenon.' In H. Pepinsky (ed.), *People and Information*, Oxford: Pergamon Press.

Index

Abelson, Robert P. 152
access 119, 131, 263
    physical 119, 120–1, 131, 132
    social 119, 121, 122, 127–8, 131, 132
accomplishment 130
account 171
accountability 264, 303
accuracy 262, 264, 266, 271, 279, 281, 287
    external 264
    internal 263, 282
actant 176–7, 187–9
action, move 6, 20, 80, 100, 103, 164, 171, 173,
    174–6, 185–7, 189, 192, 195, 197, 198, 205,
    208, 215, 228, 234, 235, 238, 239, 244, 247,
    255, 270, 320
    research 26, 307, 320, 323
Actor-Network-Theory (ANT) 176–7, 188,
    189, 238, 267, 299
Adair, John 184
adequacy (postulate of) 269
Adorno, Theodor W. 54
Africa 163
Agar, Michael H. 87, 96, 190
Agnes 155–6
Aids 89, 96
aim of research 137
Ajello, Anna M., xiv
Alasuutari, Pertti 284
Alberoni, Francesco 274
Albert, Alvarez 297
Alexander, Jeffrey C. 64
Allen, Woody 68, 167
Alpert, Richard 257
Althusser, Louis 54
amalgamated language 204, 222
American Indian 297
analogy 299, 300, 303, 304
analysis (of material) 226ff, 256
Anderson, Richard C. 73
Ang, Ien 55
anonymity 138–9
Anthony, Dick 106
anthropology 8, 9, 150
    cognitive 80
    desk 8
    vs sociology 9
applied research, clinical sociology 320,
    321, 324
Apted, Michael 124

argumentation 290
Aristotle 151
Arizona 297
Art, artist 99, 114, 241
artifact 173, 175–6, 178, 187, 188
    cognitive 175–6, 178, 188, 189
    organizational 175–6, 188
    technological 75–6, 187, 188
Ashmore, Malcolm 301
association 89, 95
    spurious 90
asymmetric relation 89, 90, 95
Atkinson, Paul 9, 15, 28, 75, 95, 128–30, 195,
    200, 202, 208, 213, 228, 231, 234, 237, 284,
    300, 315, 324
Atlas (software) 92, 252
attitude 5–6, 168, 262, 267
attribute 69, 77, 85, 93, 98, 104, 105, 160, 235,
    237, 241, 247, 256, 267
audience 262, 264, 287, 288, 299, 302, 303
    studies 54–5
Auschwitz 154
Auster, Paul 303
Austin, John Langshaw 171, 238
Australia 107, 316
Austria 9
authenticity 264, 281, 287, 293
autoethnography 25, 61–3, 66, 296
autogenic training 149
Avati, Pupi 51
axial coding 227, 234–5, 255, 256

Bachtin, Michail 133, 134, 296
Back, Les 133
Bacon, Sir Francis 60, 240
Bahr, Donald M. 297
Bailey, Kenneth D. 273
Bak, J.J. 251
Baker, Dorothy 51
Bales, Robert F. 254, 257
Ball, Mike 223
Barley, Stephen 122, 128
Beck, Bernard 278
Becker, Howard 21, 27, 37, 40, 48, 51, 99, 101,
    102, 109, 114, 190, 201, 240, 276, 278, 302
Beethoven, Ludwig van 91
behavior 5–6, 99–100, 103, 123, 126, 128, 171,
    178, 179, 191, 192, 195, 217, 218, 230, 234,
    238, 239, 241, 245, 257, 318